8/3/2015

For Lori Berenger:

One who can navigate the Erisa labyrinth can surely walk the relatively straight corridors of Dostoevsky!

Dostoevsky and the Law

Dostoevsky and the Law

Amy D. Ronner

CAROLINA ACADEMIC PRESS
Durham, North Carolina

Library of Congress Cataloging-in-Publication Data

Ronner, Amy D.
 Dostoevsky and the law / Amy D. Ronner.
   pages cm
 Includes bibliographical references and index.
 ISBN 978-1-61163-417-4 (alk. paper)
 1. Dostoyevsky, Fyodor, 1821-1881--Criticism and interpretation. 2. Dostoyevsky, Fyodor, 1821-1881--Knowledge--Law. 3. Law and literature--Rus-
sia--History--19th century. I. Title.

 PG3328.Z7L36 2015
 891.73'3--dc23

                        2014042074

                   Carolina Academic Press
                       700 Kent Street
                     Durham, NC 27701
                 Telephone (919) 489-7486
                    Fax (919) 493-5668
                    www.cap-press.com

          Printed in the United States of America

Dedicated to my husband, Michael P. Pacin, M.D., who, like Dostoevsky's Elder Zosima, embodies the "experience of active love."

All author royalties from the sale of this book are donated to the Professor Dr. Amy D. Ronner & Dr. Michael P. Pacin Therapeutic Jurisprudence Award, a scholarship for students enrolled in the Intercultural Human Rights Program at St. Thomas University School of Law.

Contents

Author's Note

Because Fyodor Dostoevsky's works have been translated from Russian to English, his name and his characters' names are spelled differently among the various translations. This Book refers to the author as "Dostoevsky," however, other acceptable spellings include "Dostoevskij" and "Dostoyevsky." These alternates are displayed in other sources referenced in this book. All variations refer to the same author. For consistency sake, this book has adopted most of the spellings contained in Joseph Frank's five-volume biography of Dostoevsky: *Dostoevsky: The Seeds of Revolt*, 1821–1849 (Princeton University Press, 1979); *Dostoevsky: The Years of Ordeal*, 1850–1859 (Princeton University Press, 1983); *Dostoevsky: The Stir of Liberation*, 1860–1865 (Princeton University Press, 1986); *Dostoevsky: The Miraculous Years*, 1865–1871 (Princeton University Press, 1995); and *Dostoevsky: The Mantle of the Prophet*, 1871–1881 (Princeton University Press, 2002).

Acknowledgments

Because so many friends, colleagues, administrators, and scholars have helped me in numerous ways, there are too many wonderful people to thank. Nevertheless, I will consider this a start.

First, I cannot emphasize enough that this book would not have seen the light of day without the influence of my father, Walter Valentine Ronner, who, born in Mogilev in what is today Belarus, introduced me to Russian classics at an early age. Special appreciation goes out to my friend and mentor, Dr. Deborah A. Martinsen, past President of the International Dostoevsky Society (2007–2013) and Adjunct Associate Professor of Russian Literature at Columbia University, who has generously granted me access to her universe of Dostoevsky studies and, many times, has dropped whatever she is doing to respond to my cry for "help." I extend another giant thank you to Professor James E. Robertson, the Editor-in-Chief of *The Criminal Law Bulletin*, Distinguished Faculty Scholar and Professor of Corrections, who has given me multiple gifts—friendship, support, and encouragement. I also extend a long-overdue thank you to Dr. Alan D. Perlis, my favorite undergraduate literature professor: he launched my Ph.D. studies, my first career as a literature professor, and forged the foundation for the teaching and interdisciplinary scholarship that I enjoy today.

I would like to recognize the late Professor Bruce J. Winick, along with Professors Michael L. Perlin, David Wexler, and David Yamata for helping me refine my scholarship over the years and for incorporating my work into their valuable courses. Law Professor Robert H. Sitkoff also deserves appreciation for acknowledging my perspective on Dostoevsky's Golyadkin and welcoming my input into his latest edition of Wills, Trusts, and Estates. I am also grateful to Lawrence C. Levine, who, from my first year law teaching, has been a lifeline and promoter. A special thank you goes out to my dear friend and colleague, Dr. Roza Pati, whose labor of love, the Intercultural Human Rights Program, makes us all better people.

In addition to Dr. Martinsen, there is also a coterie of brilliant Russian literature scholars, including the late Robert Lamont Belknap, Paul J. Contino, Irina Reyfman, Tatyana Smoliarova, William Mills Todd III, and Nancy Workman, who were willing to include a law professor in the mix and encouraged my endeavor to connect Dostoevsky's works with contemporary legal doctrines, policies, and procedures. I also thank Robin Feuer Miller, whose brilliant scholarship guided me through my many readings of multiple translations of *The Brothers Karamazov*.

I cannot emphasize enough how much this book depended on the support of other friends, family, and colleagues, including Rev. Msgr. Andrew Anderson, Rory Bahadur, Brett Barfield, Gordon Butler, John Campbell, Anna Chan, Gregory Chan, Renee Crawford, Meg Daniel, Steven and Susan Eisenberg, Lourdes Fernandez, Art Furia, Lauren Gilbert, Carson Gilmon, Marc-Tizoc Gonzalez, Alice Hector, John Hernandez, Lex Israel, John Min Kang, Gloria Kaplan, Peter T. Kelly, Jay, Justin, and Joanne Koren, Gary Kravitz, Ana Landa, Lenora Ledwon, Olga Leyva, Michael and Diane Liberman, Evelina Libhen, Beatriz A. Llorente, June Mary Makdisi, John Makdisi, Stanley Marcus, Jennifer Martin, Robert Mensel, Patricia Moore, Marcia Narine, Ira Nathenson, Amar Patel, Leonard Pertnoy, Stephen Plass, Keith Rizzardi, Mily Rodriguez-Powell, Mahalia Pugatch, Elizabeth Schwartz, Jay Silver, Barbara Singer, Nadia Soree, Todd Sullivan, Michael Vastine, Susan Weiner, Siegfriend Weissner, Mark Wolff, Robert Wolfson, Carol Zeiner, and Marc, Allison, and Landon Pacin. All of these beautiful souls, along with others (too many to enumerate), have helped propel me through a long arduous journey to completion. Also, very dear to my heart are Mitchell Kaplan and Cristina Noste of Books & Books, the very people who make life in Miami worthwhile.

Further, I am indebted to *Capital University Law Review* and *Mercer University Law Review* for publishing my articles, which I revised, expanded, and incorporated into Chapters II and III of this book. I also thank Thompson Reuters for granting me permission to incorporate into Chapter IV a revised and expanded version of my article, "Recreating Dead House: The Ouster of *Miranda* From Our Prisons," which was first published in 50 *Criminal Law Bulletin* 1 (2014).

Of course, I am deeply indebted to my talented Research Assistant, Glenys Domingo, who treated this Book as her own project, made it a top priority, and meticulously put it through a professional edit. I am also grateful to past Research Assistants, A. Starkey De Soto and Agnieszka N. Kwapisz, both of whom went beyond the call of duty to help me think, research, write, and edit. I give credit to our Law Librarian, Roy Balleste, who, like mythic Atlas, has the whole world on his shoulders and never stumbles. Specifically, Courtney Segota, our Reference and Faculty Services Librarian at my law school, deserves an accolade: she hunted down mounds of difficult-to-find interdisciplinary materials for this book, organized them, and then, as her grand finale, competently edited the entire manuscript.

No acknowledgement would ever be complete without highlighting my University President, Rev. Msgr. Franklyn Casale, who has brought St. Thomas University to new heights and consistently empowered faculty and students alike by promoting scholarship, free speech, and academic freedom. I also thank my Dean, Alfredo Garcia, and Associate Dean, Cece Dykas, for doing everything possible to assist faculty and foster scholarship. In addition, I thank my Faculty Assistant, the herculean Mariela Torres, who has been my right arm for more than two decades, along with two treasured relative newcomers, Karla Garcia and Marc Alcero who rescue me on a daily basis.

One of Dostoevsky's predominant themes is our moral responsibility to others. I am so lucky to have found a publisher—Carolina Academic Press—that actually lives by that credo and consequently, is adored by scholars and readers all over the world: I thank Keith Sipe, Linda Lacy, Scott Sipe, Tim Colton, Ryland Bowman, Beth Hall, Jefferson Moors, Roberta O'Meara, Tasha Pippin, and Charlsey Rutan—the all-star CAP team—for helping me and others self-actualize. How can there be a greater gift?

Last, but definitely not least, I once again thank my awesome husband, Michael P. Pacin, M.D., for his unconditional love and super-human patience.

Dostoevsky and the Law

Chapter One

Inexpressible Ideas: A Multifaceted Life and Legal Lens

I. Introduction

In Fyodor Mikhailovich Dostoevsky's *The Idiot*, Ippolit laments that the most important ideas are inexpressible:

> I would add that in every human idea that possesses genius or is new, or even simply in every serious human idea that is conceived in someone's head, there always remains something that cannot be conveyed to other people, even though whole volumes were written and your idea explained for thirty-five years; there will always remain something that is on no account willing to come out of your skull and will remain with you for ever; so that you will die without perhaps ever having conveyed to anyone the most important part of your idea.[1]

While as a man and writer, Dostoevsky tends to defy generalizations, there are four intertwined ones that apply. First, it can be said that, throughout his life, Dostoevsky burned with a relentless desire to convey that inexpressible "serious human idea."[2] Agony, with rare reprieve, ensued from his drive to do what

---

1. FYODOR DOSTOEVSKY, THE IDIOT 460 (David McDuff trans., Penguin Books 2004) (1868). *See also* Nariman Skakov, *Dostoevsky's Christ and Silence at the Margins of* The Idiot, 13 DOSTOEVSKY STUD. 121, 132 (2009) (explaining how Ippolit concludes that "one cannot exhaust an idea verbally—there is always something that remains hidden" and "the seeds of uncertainty and inexpressibility can be found even in Ippolit's speech").

2. DOSTOEVSKY, *supra* note 1, at 460. *But see Reminiscences of F.M. Dostoevsky by his Wife Anna Gregorevna Dostoevsky*, in S.S. KOTELIANSKY, FIODOR DOSTOEVSKY 130 (S.S. Koteliansky & J. Middleton Murray, trans., Alfred A. Knopf 1923) [hereinafter "*Reminis-*

3

he suspected could not be done. Second, Dostoevsky's fiction, blurring not only demarcations between dreams and waking states, but also boundaries between subjective and objective realities, belies his own discomfort with the indeterminacy of truth.[3] Third, Dostoevsky apotheosized suffering. It is no coincidence that in his own life and writing, there emerges a pattern in which the author or a fictive protagonist, after tasting a dollop of happiness or attaining a long-sought goal, plummets into an abyss of disappointment, pain, or despair. For Dostoevsky, however, inevitable suffering, be it self-inflicted or life-inflicted, can bring spiritual enrichment.[4] It can instill empathy, allow forgiveness of oneself and others, and inspire the epiphany that all beings are worthy of respect.[5] Fourth, Dostoevsky was preoccupied with confession in all its manifestations: while it could be abused to self-aggrandize, manipulate, or inflict harm, it could likewise induce healing, catharsis, and spiritual regeneration.[6]

Although born in nineteenth-century Russia, Dostoevsky's wisdom transcends time and place. As this book aims to show, his drive to express the inexpressible, skepticism about the existence of an objective reality, and belief in potential purification through suffering and confession feature prominently

cences"] (According to Dostoevsky's wife, "until the very end of his life Fiodor Mihailovich had not written a *single novel* with which he was satisfied himself; and the cause of this was our debts!").

3. *See generally infra* Chapter II (The Impenetrable Mental Capacity Doctrine: *The Double*) (exploring the blurred boundaries between dream and waking states, and between subjective and objective realities, along with the scholarship addressing these literary techniques).

4. *See* GEIR KJETSAA, FYODOR DOSTOYEVSKY: A WRITER'S LIFE (Siri Hustvedt & David McDuff, trans. 1985) 287 (First Ballantine Books, 1989) (discussing one of "Dostoyevsky's favorite ideas: that suffering has a purifying value for the individual").

5. *Id.* at 346 (explaining that for Dostoevsky, "[t]he capacity for suffering is a moral quality that drives man to self-understanding and gives him the chance of purification and transformation" and that it is "equally necessary as a means of curbing the self-assertion and pride that create man's rebellion against God").

6. *See generally infra* Chapter III (The Confessant Gene: *Crime and Punishment* and *The Brothers Karamazov*) (presenting the taxonomy of confessions in Dostoevsky's work and scholarly commentary on these confessions). *See also* AMY D. RONNER, LAW, LITERATURE, AND THERAPEUTIC JURISPRUDENCE 89–149 (Carolina Academic Press 2010) (analyzing how confession in *Crime and Punishment* comports with therapeutic jurisprudence and paves the way for Raskolnikov's potential spiritual regeneration); Julian W. Connolly, *Confession in* The Brothers Karamazov, in DOSTOEVSKY'S BROTHERS KARAMAZOV: ART, CREATIVITY, AND SPIRITUALITY 13, 13 (Predrag Cicovacki & Maria Granik eds. 2010) [hereinafter ART, CREATIVITY, AND SPIRITUALITY] (discussing "Dostoevsky's complex treatment of the confessional experience in *The Brothers Karamazov*, exploring the ways in which confession can be both used and abused by the novel's characters, and ultimately … determin[ing] what makes an effective confession in the world of this novel").

in his life and work. Most significantly, these defining facets are integral to Dostoevsky's keen insight into the workings of legal institutions, and to his conception of how the law, in its broadest sense, can potentially elevate or demote the human race.

This introductory chapter has five parts. Part II is a redacted account of Dostoevsky's life, which spanned from October 30, 1821, to January 28, 1881. The difficulty here stems from the fact that the author's life, one of seemingly infinite twists and turns, could be several lives rolled into one. It included abundant family history, political and romantic intrigue, conquests, defeats, roller coaster highs and lows, health obstacles, a gambling addiction, prolonged poverty, and chronic debt. Any one of these issues could easily fill tomes and, in fact, there already exist comprehensive biographies sharing copious details.[7] With the humble goal of presenting select highlights of a genius' life, this introductory biography does not attempt to enlighten experts in Slavic studies and Russian literature, many of whom already know as much about Dostoevsky's history as they do their own. It speaks instead to lawyers, along with curious lay people, who would find helpful a redacted biographical prelude to what follows: namely, an attempted journey through the timeless wisdom that Dostoevsky brings to law and humanity.

Part III has an equally ambitious goal of encapsulating what has, today, become virtually boundless. It tries to summarize some Dostoevsky scholarship in an effort to show how his work has been examined under multiple lenses. This part, containing just a sampling of commentators who interweave literary analysis with psychology, sociology, philosophy, and spirituality, also draws from Mikhail's Bakhtin's "specialized study of Dostoevsky's poetics" and "polyphonic ... artistic thinking" in an effort to articulate what it is that makes it so challenging to extract *a* meaning from a Dostoevsky text.[8]

Part IV turns to law and literature, which is as multi-faceted as Dostoevsky himself. This part suggests that reading Dostoevsky with an intensified, legal lens, one which implicates other disciplines, can be fruitful and enlightening. Such a perspective will not merely disclose the failings and salutary potential of legal institutions, but also illuminate what it truly means to live a rich, human life.

---

7. *See e.g.*, Joseph Frank, Dostoevsky: A Writer in His Time (Princeton University Press, 2010). (A 2500-page work, distilled from the five-volume *Dostoevsky*, examining the author's life and the Russian historical, cultural and ideological context); Kjetsaa, *supra* note 4 (an almost 400 page detailed portrait of Dostoevsky).

8. Mikhail Bakhtin, Problems of Dostoevsky's Poetics 3–4(Carl Emerson, trans., University of Minnesota Press, 2009). *See also* Victor Terras, Reading Dostoevsky (University of Wisconsin Press, 1998) (discussing Bakhtin's theories throughout the book).

Part V gives an overview of the book by fore-glimpsing each chapter, which build toward an overarching thesis about the potential for Dostoevsky studies to improve law practice, legal education, and justice. Even more importantly, Dostoevsky studies can enrich not just the lawyering brain, but all readers' insight into what it is that makes people tick. In fact, just learning to see the human psyche in a Dostoevskian way, which demands being open to and hearing differing, ambiguous, and conflicting voices, can add meaning to everyone's daily lives.

II. The Life

Fyodor Dostoevsky was born in Moscow on October 30, 1821. His mother, Marya Feodorovna, was a religious woman from a middle class merchant family, and had great influence on her children.[9] She taught her son to read *One Hundred and Four Old and New Testament Stories*. This, along with exposure to Nikolai Karamzin's *The History of the Russian State* and Gavriil R. Derzhavin, Vasily Zhukovsky and Aleksander S. Pushkin, helped to shape Fyodor's life and work.[10]

Fyodor's father, Mikhail Andreevich Dostoevsky, a story unto himself, also had substantial impact on his family. A complex man, he seemed destined to ignite controversy in his choice of vocation and manner of death.[11] His fam-

---

9. Frank states that "[i]t was no doubt from Marya Feodorovna that Dostoevsky first learned to feel that sympathy for the unfortunate and deprived that became so important for his work." FRANK, *supra* note 7, at 10. In his early letters, Fyodor expresses immense love and respect for his mother. *See, e.g.*, Letter from Fyodor Dostoevsky to Maria Dostoevskaya (August 23, 1833) in I DOSTOEVSKY LETTERS (1832–1859), at 16 (David Lowe and Ronald Meyer, eds., Ardis Publishers 1988) [hereinafter I LETTERS] ("Good-bye dearest Mama, I kiss your hands with respect and will remain your obedient son."); Letter from Fyodor Dostoevsky to Maria Dostoevskaya (April–May 1834), at 17, in I LETTERS ("When you left, dear Mama, I started to miss you terribly, and when I think of you now, dear Mama, I am overcome by such sadness that it's impossible to drive it away, if you only knew how much I would like to see you and I can hardly wait for that joyous moment.").

10. Frank points out that Karamzin's *History of the Russian State* was "the first work to disinter the Russian past from dusty monkish chronicles and poetic legend and to present it as a national epic appealing to a wide circle of cultivated readers," that Pushkin once remarked that Karamzin "discovered the Russian past as Columbus had discovered America," and that this was "Fyodor's bedside book, a work he read and reread continuously." FRANK, *supra* note 7, at 31.

11. Kjetsaa states: "Dr. Dostoyevsky was without a question a complicated man with conflicting personality traits. He was melancholy, taciturn, irritable, and suspicious, but he was also an enterprising and energetic man who showed a tireless concern for his family and was deeply devoted to them." KJETSAA, *supra* note 4, at 3. He notes that "[f]ew fa-

ily, originally belonging to Lithuanian nobility, came from a small village (Dostoevo, in the district of Pinsk). Due to hard times, the Dostoevskys fell into the nonmonastic clergy class, which, as Professor Joseph Frank points out, was a lowly "caste rather than a profession or a calling."[12]

It was assumed that Mikhail would follow the patriarchal priestly path, but after graduating from seminary, in defiance of his father, he left for Moscow, attended the Imperial Medical-Surgical Academy and became a physician.[13] Dr. Dostoevsky's position at Mariinsky Hospital for the Poor in Moscow's outskirts, and his dedicated service, earned him the award of the order of St. Anna, third class, and a promotion to collegiate assessor. In the Russian social system, Dr. Dostoevsky's tenacity and hard work released him from the stigmatized priestly caste, thus enabling him to ascend to the legal status of nobleman. The rank of service nobility, however, was considered beneath that of the old aristocracy to which families of other Russian writers, like Aleksander S. Pushkin, Mikhail Y. Lermontov, Nikolai Gogol, Alexander Herzen, Lev Nikolayevich Tolstoy, Ivan S. Turgenev, and Nikolai Nekrasov, belonged.[14] Fyodor's sense of being marked as inferior to the landed gentry became both blessing and curse: although stinging, it helped cultivate sensitivity to those less fortunate, which is one of the salient qualities of his writing.[15]

---

thers of writers have been so thoroughly analyzed or given such great significance as Mikhail Andreyevich Dostoyevsky, and none of them has inspired such controversy." *Id.* at 2.

12. FRANK, *supra* note 7, at 6.

13. Kjetsaa explains that Dr. Dostoevsky "left his hometown ... against his father's will" and that "[t]he break was dramatic, and he later failed in his efforts to renew relations with his family." KJETSAA, *supra* note 4, at 3. As a result, "[n]one of his children ever came to know relatives on their father's side of the family." *Id.*

14. Kjetsaa states that although the "[p]ortrayals of Dostoyevsky as a writer from the 'common people' whose origin was nearly 'proletarian' are groundless[,] ... [l]ike most nineteenth century Russian writers, he too was a nobleman." *Id.* at 7. Kjetsaa stresses "that the service nobility was of a significantly lower rank than the old landed aristocracy to which Tolstoy and Turgenev belonged," that the "[a]wareness of class distinctions was to be painful for Fyodor" and "played a role in sharpening Dostoyevsky's empathy for human suffering— not suffering that stemmed from the pain of poverty itself, but from the humiliation of being of a lower social rank than the rich and powerful in society." *Id.* at 7. *See also* FRANK, *supra* note 7, at 5 ("Of all the great Russian writers of the first part of the nineteenth century ... Dostoevsky was the only one who did not come from a family belonging to the landed gentry[,]" which "influenced the view he took of his own position ... [and gave him] a rankling uncertainty about status that helps to explain his acute understanding of the psychological scars inflicted by social inequality.").

15. *See supra* note 14.

After his wife's death in 1837, Dr. Dostoevsky retired and settled in Darovoe, where he died about two years later. Although the cause of death was officially recorded as apoplexy, many believed (and some still do believe) that Dr. Dostoevsky's peasants murdered him.[16] Several scholars even trace parts of the plot in *The Brothers Karamazov* to Dr. Dostoevsky's mysterious death.[17]

In two decades of marriage, Dr. Dostoevsky and his wife had seven surviving children, whom they sought not only to educate, but to instill with discipline and solid work ethics.[18] In 1832, visiting tutors taught Fyodor and his brother, Mikhail, at home, and from 1833, they were enrolled in boarding schools. From late 1834 to early 1837, the two brothers attended one of Moscow's finest private schools, which, as Professor Kjetsaa explains, demanded sacrifice:

> Keeping his sons in such a school was clearly beyond the doctor's means. Maintaining a single student for a year cost eight hundred rubles, roughly the doctor's annual salary at the hospital. But Mikhail Andreyevich was a proud man with ambitions. Rather than send his sons to a public school where thrashings were the order of the day, he chose to work himself to death and accept humiliating loans from ...

---

16. According to Kjetsaa, "Mikhail Andreyevich has been portrayed in the biographies of his son as a merciless tormenter of his serfs who was finally humbled by a violent death." KJETSAA, *supra* note 4, at 34. He states that "[i]t is important to note that Dr. Dostoyevsky died of natural causes, and their testimony was legally upheld in spite of considerable exertions on the part of a vindictive neighbor." *Id. See also* FRANK, *supra* note 7, at 45 ("The most important event in Dostoevsky's life during his years at the academy was the death (or the murder) of his father."). It is somewhat puzzling that Dostoevsky, whose letters tend to be expressive, says little about his father's death. *See* Letter from Fyodor Dostoevsky to Alexander and Alexandra Kumanin (January 28, 1840), at 65, in I LETTERS, *supra* note 9. In what is a rare mention of his father, Dostoevsky writes: "[u]ncle's death caused me to spill several tears in his memory. Father, Mother, Uncle, and all of that in two years!").

17. *See generally* Sigmund Freud, *Dostoevsky and Parricide*," XXI THE COMPLETE PSYCHOLOGICAL WORKS OF SIGMUND FREUD 175–194 (1961) (theorizing that Dostoevsky's father's violent demise filled him with conflicted emotions that the novelist later visits in the Karamazov murder). *But see* KJETSAA, *supra* note 4, at 29–36, 36 (explaining why "the facts contradict Freud's theory" and "[t]he absolute parallels that have been frequently drawn between Mikhail Andreyevich and Fyodor Karamazov are also dubious"); FRANK, *supra* note 7, at 45 ("The 'facts' that Freud adduces can be shown to be extremely dubious at best, and at worst simply mistakes."). *See infra* notes 123–24 and accompanying text (discussing Freudian scholarship).

18. KJETSAA, *supra* note 4, at 5 ("Mikhail and Fyodor were born a year apart; in 1822 their sister Varvara was born, and in 1825, a brother Andrei. Later there were three more surviving children born into the family: Vera, Nikolai, and Alexandra. Dostoyevsky was intimate with only his two elder siblings.")

[his wife's] family. No sacrifice was too great when it came to giving his sons a respectable education.[19]

At school, teacher Nikolai Bilevich stood out and became not only a role model for young Dostoevsky, but also the conceivable prototype for Nikolai Semyonovich, a character in *The Adolescent*.[20]

The year 1837 brought pain and change. Fyodor, who was grieving the death of his mother, suffered personally when his venerated Pushkin perished in a duel. On top of that, his and his brother's dreams of a university education and of becoming writers seemed quashed due to a decision that was made prior to their mother's death. Both parents had already planned on sending Mikhail and Fyodor to St. Petersburg's Academy of Engineers, because it was reputed to be free and would give their sons a livelihood. The boys' arrival in St. Petersburg compounded their disappointment. Due to Mikhail's poor health, the school refused to admit him, and the brothers, who had previously been inseparable, were separated. To add insult to injury, the Dostoevskys learned that the touted tuition-free vacancies were essentially bogus, and could be had only by slipping the examiners a bribe.[21]

Beginning in January 1838, Dostoevsky attended the Engineering Academy, where he, as the aspiring writer with a penchant for the humanities, had to radically shift gears and adjust to harsh discipline, military exercises, and a rigorous engineering curriculum.[22] The friendships that Dostoevsky cultivated,

---

19. *Id.* at 15.

20. *Id.* (The teacher "who played a special role … [was] Russian instructor Nikolai Bilevich," who "had been a classmate of Nikolai Gogol and was influential in exciting Dostoyevsky's admiration for this 'great teacher of all Russians.'").

21. FRANK, *supra* note 7, at 41 (describing how "Mikhail was refused entrance on grounds of 'ill health'" and "Fyodor, though passing his exam brilliantly, did not receive one of the vacancies" because "it turned out, [that they] were reserved for those students able to make 'gifts' to the examiners"). Dostoevsky tells his brother, "I've finally enrolled in the M[ain] Academy of E[ngineering]" and complains of the unfair class system:

> I recently found out that after the examination was already over the General arranged to have four new people study at public expense in addition to the candidate who … won my place. What baseness! That completely stunned me. We, who struggle for every ruble, have to pay, while others—the children of wealthy fathers—are accepted without fees.

Letter from Fyodor Dostoevsky to Mikhail Dostoevsky (February 4, 1838) in I LETTERS, *supra* note 9, at 35–36.

22. KJETSAA, *supra* note 4, at 24 (describing the strict discipline and how Dostoevsky "with his strong background in the humanities, … had to struggle with typical engineering courses such as topography, mathematics, and physics"). It is apparent from his letters that the difficulties were compounded by Dostoevsky's poverty:

> Well, brother! You complain of your poverty. There's no need to tell you that I'm

however, partially mitigated the grueling, dull regime. During this time, his close friend, Ivan Shidlovsky, poet and historian, whose passion was literature, encouraged Dostoevsky to pursue his literary aspirations.[23]

In 1843, after completing academy exams, Dostoevsky accepted a position in the St. Petersburg engineering division's drafting office, which bored him to tears. When, a year later, he learned that he might be deployed on a distant inspection mission, he, even more determined to dedicate his life to literature, obtained a discharge.[24] That very year, his first published work, a translation of Balzac's *Eugenie Grandet*, appeared, and he started writing the epistolary novel, *Poor Folk*, which would launch his career.[25]

The *Poor Folk* manuscript excited writer Dmitry Grigorovich and poet Nikolai Nekrasov so much that, after spending the night reading it, they headed to the home of the great literary critic, Vissarion Belinsky to announce, "We've a new [Nikolai] Gogol!"[26] Belinsky, initially dubious, said, "With the likes of

---

not rich either. Would you believe that on a march away from the camps I didn't have a single kopeck; on the road I fell sick from a cold (the rain poured all day, and we were out in the open) and from hunger and didn't even have half a kopeck so as to be able to moisten my throat with a swallow of tea.
Letter from Fyodor Dostoevsky to Mikhail Dostoevsky (August 9, 1838) in I LETTERS, *supra* note 9, at 40.

23. In a letter, Dostoevsky writes "Last winter I was in a rapturous state. The friendship with Shidlovsky gave me so many hours of a better life." Letter from Fyodor Dostoevsky to Mikhail Dostoevsky (January 1, 1840), in I LETTERS, *supra* note 9, at 61. *See also* KJETSAA, *supra* note 4, at 26–27 (In addition to "closest friend," Shidlovsky, there was "Ivan Berezhetsky, with whom he had frequent literary discussions; Konstantin Trutovsky, who drew his youthful portrait; Aleksei Beketov, who would become a leader of one of the 1840s radical circles, and Dmitri Grigorovich, who himself became a writer.").

24. Dostoevsky explains to his brother, "I retired because I retired, that is, I swear to you that I couldn't serve any longer" and adds, "[y]ou hate life when the best time is taken away from you for naught." Letter from Fyodor Dostoevsky to Mikhail Dostoevsky (September 30, 1844) in I LETTERS, *supra* note 9, at 97. He elaborates that "the main thing" was that "they wanted to send me off on assignment—well, tell me, please, what would I do without Petersburg? What would I be fit for?" *Id.*

25. *See infra* Chapter II (The Impenetrable Mental Capacity Doctrine: *The Double*) (discussing the jolt from the praised *Poor Folk* to the scathingly attacked *The Double*). *See also* Letter from Fyodor Dostoevsky to Mikhail Dostoevsky (March 24, 1845) in I LETTERS, *supra* note 9, at 106 ("I am seriously pleased with my novel [*Poor Folk*]. It's an austere and elegant work. There are horrible deficiencies, however. Its publication will reward me.").

26. KJETSAA, *supra* note 4, at 42. *See also* David McDuff, *Introduction*, to FYODOR DOSTOYEVSKY, POOR FOLK xi (David McDuff trans., 1988) (1846) ("'A new Gogol has appeared!' Nekrasov shouted, as he entered Belinsky's study holding the manuscript of *Poor Folk*."); *infra* Chapter II (The Impenetrable Mental Capacity Doctrine: *The Double*) (discussing how *Poor Folk* became an instant success).

you, Gogols are springing up like mushrooms."[27] Once Belinsky read the manuscript, he was immediately swayed; he could scarcely contain his enthusiasm for this "new talent ... [whose] novel reveals such secrets of life and characters in Russia as no one before him even dreamed of."[28] The *St. Petersburg Anthology*, edited by Nekrasov, published the novel and Dostoevsky, at a young age, rose to stardom.[29] St. Petersburg literary circles embraced their nouveau Gogol, who began frequenting gatherings of young, ambitious writers.

Such meteoric success, along with the Belinsky endorsement, turned out to be short-lived. Belinsky, who was already having reservations about Dostoevsky, scathingly criticized the next novel, *The Double*, by calling it "terrible nonsense" and saying that "[e]very new work of Dostoyevsky's is a further step down.... I think, dear friends, we may have hit bottom with this genius."[30] This disparagement by a cultural icon of Russian culture, along with growing "ideological differences" between Belinsky and Dostoevsky, led to a rift.[31]

---

27. KJETSAA, *supra* note 4, at 44. *See also infra* Chapter II (The Impenetrable Mental Capacity Doctrine: *The Double*) (discussing the debut of *Poor Folk*).

28. FRANK, *supra* note 7, at 76.

29. In a letter to his brother, Dostoevsky elaborates on his sudden stardom:
  I think my fame will never reach such an apogee as now. There's unbelievable admiration everywhere ... Everyone is receiving me like a miracle. I can't even open my mouth without having it repeated in all corners that Dostoev[sky] said such-and-such. Dostoev[sky] wants to do such-and-such. It would be impossible to like me more than Belinsky does.
Letter from Fyodor Dostoevsky to Mikhail Dostoevsky (November 16, 1845) in I LETTERS, *supra* note 9, at 117. *See also infra* Chapter II (The Impenetrable Mental Capacity Doctrine: *The Double*) (discussing the debut of *Poor Folk*).

30. KJETSAA, *supra* note 4, at 53. In a letter to his brother, Dostoevsky says, "[b]ut here's what vile and painful: our own people, our kind Belinsky, and everyone are displeased with me for [*The Double*]." Letter from Fyodor Dostoevsky to Mikhail Dostoevsky (April 1, 1846) in I LETTERS, *supra* note 9, at 124. *See also infra* Chapter II (The Impenetrable Mental Capacity Doctrine: *The Double*) (discussing Dostoevsky's fall from grace after the publication of *The Double*).

31. In a letter to his brother, Dostoevsky writes, "[a]s for Belinsky, he's such a weak person that even in literary opinions he keeps changing his mind" but adds, "[o]nly with him have I retained my former good relations." Letter from Fyodor Dostoevsky to Mikhail Dostoevsky (November 26, 1846) in I LETTERS, *supra* note 9, at 142. In 1871, Dostoevsky writes, "[t]he stinking little bug Belinsky ... was precisely feeble and weak in his puny little talent, and therefore cursed Russia and consciously brought her so much harm." Letter from Fyodor Dostoevsky to Nikolay Strakhov (April 23, 1871) in III DOSTOEVSKY LETTERS (1868–1871) at 352 (David Lowe, ed. & trans, Ardis Publishers, 1990) [hereinafter III LETTERS]. *See also* KJETSAA, *supra* note 4, at 53. Kjetsaa explains that by the mid-1840s, Belinsky "began to liberate himself from the Christian socialism of the utopians" and linked his ideas to "atheism" and "revolutionary socialism," which was "actively opposed to Christianity." *Id.* at 54. While Dostoevsky's "Christian socialism" had a "revolutionary message," it was very

Around this time, at a literary gathering, another smoldering tension surfaced when Turgenev's ridicule of Dostoevsky ignited, or at least prefigured, their lifelong estrangement.[32] To make matters worse, a stressed, overworked, and chain-smoking Dostoevsky experienced deteriorating health and episodes of dizziness, hallucinations, and depression. Some scholars and physicians believe that

---

different from "Belinsky's subversive atheism" and "[e]specially repugnant to [Dostoevsky] must have been Belinsky's belief that human beings are not responsible for their evil desires but are simply forced to do evil by an unjust society." *Id.* at 54–55. This lead to a "break with the Belinsky circle." *Id.* at 55. *See also* FRANK, *supra* note 7, at 94–103 (describing the Dostoevsky-Belinsky quarrel and the impact that Belinsky had on Dostoevsky's life and development).

32. Throughout most of his life, Dostoevsky had harsh words for Turgenev. *See e.g.*, letter from Fyodor Dostoevsky to Apollon Maykov (August 16, 1867), in II DOSTOEVSKY LETTERS (1860–67) at 257 (David Lowe, ed. & trans., Ardis Publishers 1989) [hereinafter II LETTERS] ("[A]lthough I had put off going to see Turgenev, I finally ventured to pay him a visit ... I'll tell you candidly: even before that I disliked the man personally ... I also dislike the aristocratically farcical embrace of this with which he starts to kiss you but offers you his cheek."); Letter from Fyodor Dostoevsky to Nikolay Strakhov (June 11, 1870) in III LETTERS, *supra* note 31, at 260 ("I read Turgenev's "The Execution of Tropman" ... but that pompous and refined piece made me indignant ... I consider Turgenev the most written out of all written–out Russian writers."); Letter from Fyodor Dostoevsky to Vladimir Meshchersky (March 1, 1874), in IV FYODOR DOSTOEVSKY COMPLETE LETTERS (1872–1877), at 124 (David A. Lowe, ed. & trans., Ardis Publishers 1992) [hereinafter IV LETTERS] ("[I]t is a very gross attack on you ... a distortion in which there may even be a design, and not just contemporary coarseness and contemporary cheap liberalism, which so many people make use of for their own profit (beginning with the swine Turgenev."); Letter from Fyodor Dostoevsky to Anna Dostoevskaya (June 6, 1874) in *id.* at 132–33 (Turgenev "bragged that he would describe 'all the reactionaries' (that is, including me). To heck with him."). *See also* KJETSAA, *supra* note 4, at 50–51 (describing how members of the Panaev circle, including Turgenev, initially "worshipped" Dostoevsky and how they began to persecute him). With respect to Turgenev, Kjetsaa explains that "[t]he final break came in the fall of 1846, when Turgenev took the ridicule too far" and "[d]uring one of the gatherings, [Turgenev] began to make fun of a man out in the provinces who went around imagining he was a genius." *Id.* at 51. *But see id.* at 212 (calling the Turgenev-Dostoevsky feud as "the most celebrated [one] in the history of Russian literature," and claiming that it began after 1867, during Dostoevsky's self-imposed exile in Europe, when "Turgenev came to see Dostoevsky at ten o'clock in the morning, well aware that he would not yet have risen, and that he would for this reason avoid meeting him"). But, "[a] quarter of a century later, Dostoyevsky took bitter revenge by depicting Turgenev as the conceited salon radical Karmazinov in *The Possessed.*" *Id.* at 51. *See also* TERRAS, *supra* note 8, at 116 (equating Karmazinov with Turgenev and also stating that "one cannot escape the impression that the figure of the Devil [in *The Brothers Karamazov*] fits the image of a man who, in one way or another, accompanied Dostoevsky through virtually all of his adult life, Ivan Turgenev") *See also infra* notes 103–108 and accompanying text. (discussing the rivalry between Dostoevsky and Turgenev at the unveiling of the Pushkin Memorial).

these were early indications of the epilepsy that would ravage Dostoevsky throughout his life.[33]

In 1847, Dostoevsky began to attend Friday-night meetings of the revolutionary and utopian socialist Mikhail Butashevich Petrashevsky. While attendees discussed literature, they also debated controversial, political, and social issues, like the emancipation of the serfs or judicial and censorship reforms. They spoke of French socialist manifestos and Dostoevsky read aloud Belinsky's banned letter, which scathingly attacked Gogol's defense of serfdom.[34]

Dostoevsky became more entrenched in perilous activities when Nikolai Speshnev, a radical member of the Petrashevsky Circle, organized a secret society, whose goal was to stir Russian revolution.[35] The members, who swore a loyalty oath, aimed to spread the seeds of discontent within government and to infiltrate those "students, dissidents, peasants, and soldiers," who were disgruntled and talking change.[36] Dostoevsky joined and, in April 1849, he, along with other members, was arrested and confined in the Peter and Paul Fortress.

---

33. KJETSAA, *supra* note 4, at 52 ("Dr. Stepan Yanovsky, Dostoyevsky's new doctor friend, later believed that these serious attacks ... were the early signs of the writer's epilepsy."). *See also* Brian R. Johnson, *Intersecting Nervous Disorders in Dostoevsky's* The Insulted and the Injured, XVI DOSTOEVSKY STUD. 73, 73 (2012) (analyzing how Dostoevsky's "early nervous condition, characterized by lightheadedness, dizziness, occasional fainting spells and aural hallucinations" and "his later epilepsy may have been related" even though Dostoevsky "claimed to have experienced them as distinct disorders"); Shirley M. Ferguson Rayport, Mark Rayport, Carolyn A. Schell, *Dostoevsky's epilepsy: A New Approach to Retrospective Diagnosis*, 22 EPILEPSY & BEHAV. 557, 557 (2011) (concluding that Dostoevsky "had temporolimbic epilepsy and that the ecstatic experience is an epileptic phenomenon"); Udaya Seneviratne, *Fyodor Dostoevsky and his* falling sickness: *A Critical Analysis of Seizure Semiology*, 18 EPILEPSY & BEHAV. 424 (2010) (analyzing the "localizing and lateralizing features" of Dostoevsky's seizures in his writings and reminiscences of his wife and friends and postulating that Dostoevsky had a partial epilepsy syndrome most probably arising from the dominant temporal lobe").

34. Frank describes "the famous session of the Petrashevsky Circle at which Dostoevsky read Belinsky's *Letter to Gogol* [,] ... the most powerful indictment against serfdom ever penned in Russia, and Dostoevsky used it effectively to reinforce their argument that serfdom was too morally intolerable to be endured a moment longer." FRANK, *supra* note 7, at 157.

35. KJETSAA, *supra* note 4, at 64 ("The goal of Spechnev's Russian Society was to lay the groundwork for political revolution."). *See also* HARRIET MURAV, RUSSIA'S LEGAL FICTIONS 29–30 (The University of Michigan Press, 1955) ("The Primary activity ... consisted in discussions—of the conditions of the peasantry, of Fourier's utopian socialism, of Belinsky's broad-ranging critique of Russian society ... [and] some possible involvement with the printing of revolutionary pamphlets.").

36. KJETSAA, *supra* note 4, at 64.

The society was one of the inspirations behind Dostoevsky's later novel, *Demons,* and Stavrogin, a main character, has been linked to Speshnev himself.[37]

During his eight months in the fortress, Dostoevsky, whose health was unstable to begin with, suffered nightmares, insomnia, hemorrhoids, constriction in the throat, and scrofula.[38] In this condition, he submitted to interrogation. The Tsar appointed a Commission of Inquiry, headed by General Ivan Nabokov (relative of the author of *Lolita*), and in the investigation, Dostoevsky refrained from snitching.[39] He did not deny involvement in the Petrashevsky group, but instead described its members as dreamers devoid of a united revolutionary goal.[40]

At age twenty-seven, Dostoevsky, "[t]he former Engineer Lieutenant," was sentenced to death before a firing squad "for [his] participation in criminal plans, for the circulation of a private letter containing rash statements against the Orthodox Church and the highest authorities, and for the attempt to dis-

---

37. *Id. See also* Richard Pevear, *Forward* in FYODOR DOSTOEVSKY, DEMONS vii– xxiii (Richard Pevear and Larissa Volokhonsky trans., 1995) (1871–72) (also known as *The Possessed* and *Devils*) (discussing Speshnev and his influence on Dostoevsky and on the character, Stavrogin); *infra* notes 170–72 and accompanying text (discussing what inspired Dostoevsky to compose *Demons*); Richard Freeborn, *The Nineteenth Century: the Age of Realism, 1855–80,* in THE CAMBRIDGE HISTORY OF RUSSIAN LITERATURE 248, 322–23(Charles A. Moser, ed., Cambridge University Press, 1992) (explaining how Dostoevsky wrote *Demons* after "he learned in late 1869 of the murder of a student named Ivanov on the orders of Nechaev" and in the novel, the "Nechaev figure, Peter Verkhovensky," and "the other members of the cell become accomplices in Shatov's murder").

38. *See* Letter from Fyodor Dostoevsky to Mikhail Dostoevsky (July 18, 1849) in I LETTERS, *supra* note 9, at 173 (Writing from the Peter-Paul Fortress, he describes "the derangement of [his] nerves, which is proceeding at a crescendo," and states, "I've begun having throat spasms, as before, my appetite is very slight, and I get little sleep, and even at that with painful dreams."); Letter from Fyodor Dostoevsky to Mikhail Dostoevsky (August 27, 1849), in *id.* at 174 ("I cannot say anything good about my health. For an entire month now I've been eating nothing but castor oil and only in that way managing to remain on this earth ... and I feel a chest pain that I never had before ... [and f]rom all this I conclude that my nerves are in disarray.").

39. KJETSAA, *supra* note 4, at 81 (discussing how "Dostoevsky "did not in any way seek to save himself by shifting blame onto his friends" and actually "tried to protect them by accepting blame for actions that may well have sent him to the scaffold").

40. *Id.* ("The circle was composed of dreamers, the writer maintained, of young people who were enchanted by the 'beauty' and 'love of mankind' presented in Fourier's 'peaceful system'" and lacked a "united revolutionary goal."). *See also* Letter from Fyodor Dostoevsky to Eduard Totleben (March 24, 1856, in I LETTERS, *supra* note 9, at 251 ("When I set out for Siberia I had, at least, one consolation, that I had conducted myself before the court honestly, I did not shift my blame onto others and even sacrificed my own interests if I saw the chance of shielding others from misfortune with my confession.").

tribute subversive works with the aid of a lithograph."[41] Officials, parading Dostoevsky and others into a public square, tethered them to execution posts before a firing squad.[42] Just before discharging their fatal shots, the soldiers received a halt command.[43] By order of Nicholas I, the Russian novelist and fellow prisoners were spared and death sentences commuted to four years of hard labor and exile in Siberia. Dostoevsky, in poor health, served his full sentence in Omsk Fortress and it is believed that while there, he experienced his first epileptic seizure.[44] In prison, he endured horrendous conditions and witnessed brutal beatings, all of which he eventually graphically depicted in his autobiographical novel, *Notes from the House of the Dead*.[45] When about two decades later, Dostoevsky was convicted of violating censorship rules, fined, and imprisoned for two days in a guardhouse, it paled in comparison to the prolonged Siberian internment that radically impacted his entire life.[46]

---

41. KJETSAA, *supra* note 4, at 87.

42. In Fyodor Dostoevsky's Letter to Mikhail Dostoevsky (December 22, 1849), in I LETTERS, *supra* note 9, at 178, he describes his near execution:

> [W]e were taken to Semyonov Square. There we were all read the death sentence, allowed to kiss the cross, had sabers broken over our heads and our pre-death attire put on (white shirts). Then three people were stood against the stakes for carrying out the execution. I was the sixth in line, people were summoned by threes, cons[equently], I was in the second row and had no more than a minute left to live. I remembered you, brother, and all of your family; at the last moment you, only you were in my mind, only then did I realize how much I love you, my dear brother.

43. *Id.* ("Finally a retreat was sounded, the ones tied to the stake were led back, and it was announced that His Imperial Majesty was granting us our lives. Then the real sentences followed.").

44. *See* Letter from Fyodor Dostoevsky to Mikhail Dostoevsky (January 30, February 22, 1854) in *id.* at 188 (writing from Omsk, he states, "Because of unstrung nerves I came down with epilepsy, but attacks occur rarely, however."). *See also* KJETSAA, *supra* note 4, at 35 ("The evidence suggests that Dostoyevsky's epilepsy first made its appearance in Siberia."); *id.* at 101 ("When he had just returned from the prison clinic, he made a retort to an order, and the Major is said to have implemented a punishment that triggered his first epileptic seizure."); Johnson, *supra* note 33, at 84 ("Dostoevsky's assertion that convulsive epilepsy first struck him while he was in prison is confirmed by virtually every source corresponding to that period."). *But see* Diane Oenning Thompson, *On the Koranic Motif in* The Idiot *and* Demons, in ASPECTS OF DOSTOEVSKII: ART, ETHICS AND FAITH 115, 116 (Robert Reid & Joe Andrew, eds. Rodopi B.V. 2012) (discussing a conversation in which Dostoevsky "told some friends about his first epileptic fit which occurred after his release from prison camp").

45. *See generally infra* Chapter IV (Prisons of Coercion: *Notes from the House of the Dead*) (focusing on prison conditions described in *Notes from the House of the Dead*).

46. According to Frank, after Dostoevsky published in *The Citizen* an article by Prince Meshchersky, which quoted the Tsar without having obtained permission, "[l]egal responsibility fell not on the author but on the editor of publication." FRANK, *supra* note 7, at 677.

In 1854, upon his release, Dostoevsky served as a private in Semipalatinsk, Eastern Kazakhstan. During this exile, Dostoevsky's friendship with Chokan Valikhanov, a young Kazakh ethnographer, and Alexander Yegorovich Wrangel, the regional prosecutor, made life tolerable for him.[47] Shortly upon his arrival, he met Alexander Isaev, a former customs officer and destitute alcoholic, and his wife Marya Dmitrievna Isaeva.[48] Initially, he pitied the sickly, twenty-nine year old woman, with her dismal marriage and a husband whose scenes scandalized both his wife and seven-year old son, Pasha.[49] Dostoevsky later fell madly in love with Mrs. Isaeva, and her husband's transfer to Kuznetsk, about six hundred kilometers from Semipalatinsk, broke Dostoevsky's heart.[50]

Consequently, Dostoevsky "was condemned to pay a fine of twenty-five rubles and spend two days in the guardhouse." *Id. See also* KJETSA, *supra* note 4, at 289 (It was "agreed that Dostoyevsky could put off serving … until it was convenient for him to do so" and he "certainly received no maltreatment" because "the jailer knew him."); IV LETTERS, *supra* note 32, at 69 n. 3 (describing how Dostoevsky served his two days 21 and 22 March 1874); Letter from Fyodor Dostoevsky to Anna Dostoevskaya (July 5, 1873) in *id.* at 76 ("Meshchersky was treating me very casually, not even expressing regret that I would be going to jail for him."); Letter from Fyodor Dostoevsky to Anna Dostoevskaya (July 10, 1873), in *id.* at 79 ("The trouble is that I have to serve my two-day term. At some point the procurator will still give me an order, write a memorandum to the police, they will come for me, and they'll arrange things so that it will be precisely a Friday or Saturday.").

47. *See generally* FRANK, *supra* note 7, at 229–231 (describing Dostoevsky's bonds with Wrangel); KJETSAA, *supra* note 7, at 112 (describing Dostoevsky's friendships during this time).

48. *See* Letter from Fyodor Dostoevsky to Mikhail Dostoevsky (January 13–18, 1856) in I LETTERS, *supra* note 9, at 225 ("I was very happy. God sent me the acquaintance with a family that I'll never forget. That's the Isaev family … [and what] attracted me … [was] his wife, Marya Dmitrievna[, who] is still a young woman, 28 years old, attractive, very well educated, very intelligent, kind, nice, graceful, with an excellent, wonderful heart.").

49. Frank states that "Isaev was another of those incorrigible and appealing Russian drunkards whom Dostoevsky had already portrayed and whom he was to immortalize in the elder Marmeladov in *Crime and Punishment*." FRANK, *supra* note 7, at 227. He adds that "[t]he Isaev family, which included a seven-year old son, Pasha, was thus living in hand-to-mouth fashion while the breadwinner nominally sought other employment" and "what little money he and his wife could scrape together was squandered by Isaev in drinking bouts with his cronies among the riffraff of the town." *Id.*

50. *See* Letter from Fyodor Dostoevsky to Mikhail Dostoevsky (December 22, 1856) in I LETTERS, *supra* note 9, at 285) (Marya's husband "received a position in … Kuznetsk … I was in despair, being separated from her."). *See also* FRANK, *supra* note 7, at 231 (When Marya's husband secured another post, "[t]he news struck Dostoevsky like a blow, and suddenly shattered the fragile world of relative contentment he had so laboriously managed to construct.")

In 1855, Dostoevsky learned that Marya's husband had died, and that the widow was alone in a strange town bereft of funds, relatives, or friends.[51] Dostoevsky, coming to her rescue with borrowed funds, sought to win her love, which turned out not to be an easy feat, partly because Marya felt that he lacked adequate resources or a future.[52] Marya also seemed to enjoy toying with her suitor's jealous proclivities and, at one point, made Dostoevsky believe that an older, wealthy competitor was courting her.[53] Oddly enough, Dostoevsky found himself wearing the skin of his own literary creation, Devushkin in *Poor Folk*, who helplessly stands by while adored Varenka leaves to wed old, rich Bykov.[54] Dostoevsky's Marya, however, shifting to apparent tenderness, told him that her gentleman suitor did not really exist, and that she had fabricated the story to test him.[55]

Shortly thereafter, a new (but real) paramour, a young school master, Nikolai Vergunov, entered the picture, and Marya proclaimed love for him. At one point, like the Dreamer in *White Nights* and Ivan Petrovich in *Humiliated and Insulted*, Dostoevsky considered sacrificing his own happiness for others.[56]

---

51. *See* Letter from Fyodor Dostoevsky to Mikhail Dostoevsky (January 13–18, 1856), in I LETTERS, *supra* note 9, at 226 (Marya "was left in alien surroundings, alone, exhausted and racked by long-term sorrow, with a seven-year-old child, and without a piece of bread. She didn't even have the means to bury her husband.").

52. *See id.* ("I have loved this woman [Marya] for a long time and I know that she can love me, too. I can't live without her, and therefore if only my circumstances change at least somewhat for the better and the positive, I'll marry her[,] … but the problem is that I have neither money nor social position."). *See also* FRANK, *supra* note 7 at 228 (discussing how Marya felt pity for Dostoevsky and saw him as a man without a future).

53. *See* Letter from Fyodor Dostoevsky to Alexander Vrangel (March 23, 1856) in I LETTERS, *supra* note 9, at 237 ("I guessed that [Marya] was hiding something from me. (Alas! I never told you this: But already during your stay here, par ma jalousie incomparable [through my incomparable jealousy] I drive her to despair and that's why she hides things from me now.) Suddenly I hear that she has given her word to marry another.").

54. *See id.* at 244 ("How could [Marya], with her heart and with her mind, spend her whole life in Kuznetsk. God knows with whom. She's in the same position as my heroine in *Poor Folk*, who marries Bykov (a self-fulfilling prophecy!)"). *See also* KJETSAA, *supra* note 4, at 118 (likening Dostoevsky at this time to "Devushkin, [who] was degraded to the position of an errand boy while his beloved made wedding plans").

55. *See* Letter from Fyodor Dostoevsky to Alexander Vrangel (April 13, 1856) in I LETTERS, *supra* note 9, at 258 (Marya "at last decided to explain everything to me: … the idea of her marriage was invented by her as a means to know and test my heart. Nevertheless this marriage had a basis.").

56. *See* Ignat Avsey, *Fyodor Dostoevsky's Life*, in FYODOR DOSTOEVSKY, HUMILIATED AND INSULTED 363, 368 (Ignat Avsey, trans. 2008) (1861) (comparing Dostoevsky to the Dreamer in *White Nights* and Ivan Petrovich in *Humiliated and Insulted*.). *See also* Letter from Fyodor Dostoevsky to Alexander Vrangel (July 14, 1856) in I LETTERS, *supra* note 9, at 262–-

Marya, however, doing her idiosyncratic about-face, again restored Dostoevsky's hope that he would triumph in the end.[57] But as soon as Dostoevsky returned to Semipalatinsk, the pendulum swung as Marya wrote that she again
preferred Vergunov.[58]

Just when Dostoevsky was feeling that all might be lost, he saw a ray of light.
All along, Dostoevsky surmised that if he improved his own station, he could
ultimately claim his paramour. He thought that with the death of Nicholas I,
along with the enthronement of Alexander II, the grudge against the Petrashevsky convicts might dissipate. Then, in October 1856, Dostoevsky was promoted to commissioned officer. When Dostoevsky, with a decent social status
and regular income, reappeared before his lover in his uniform, promising to
give her son, Pasha, a good education, Marya finally consented.[59] The two
were married on February 6, 1857.

In what seems to be a recurrent pattern in Dostoevsky's life and fiction, just
when joy ascends to an ostensible apex, there is a precipitous tragic nose dive.
After the honeymoon in Barnaul and en route to Semipalatinsk, Dostoevsky
had a sudden seizure. Frank describes the incident that was to "cast a pall on
Dostoevsky's ill-starred marriage" and devastate the new bride:[60]

> Marya Dimitrievna had never before been exposed to the unearthly
> shriek, the fainting fit, the convulsive movements of the face and limbs,
> the foaming at the mouth, the involuntary loss of urine that marked
> Dostoevsky's acute seizures; and she was terrified at discovering that
> she had unwittingly linked her fate to a husband ravaged by such an
> illness.[61]

---

63 (Marya "is now ready to marry a 24-year-old youth … with nothing, a teacher in a
provincial school … My God—my heart is breaking. I love her happiness more than my
own.").

57. Avsey, *supra* note 56, at 368 ("This fairly bowled Maria Dmitrievna over.").

58. *Id.*

59. *See* Letter from Fyodor Dostoevsky to Mikhail Dostoevsky (December 22, 1856) in
I LETTERS, *supra* note 9, at 286 ("But now, immediately following my promotion, I asked
her whether she would be my wife and honestly, frankly explained all my circumstances to
her. She consented and answered: 'Yes.'")

60. FRANK, *supra* note 7 at 240.

61. *Id.* at 241. *See also* Letter from Fyodor Dostoevsky to Mikhail Dostoevsky (March
9, 1857), in I LETTERS, *supra* note 9, at 305 ("On the journey back … a misfortune befell
me: completely unexpectedly I had an epileptic attack that scared my wife to death and
filled me with grief and despondency."); DOSTOEVSKY, *supra* note 1, at 274 ("It is well known
that fits of epilepsy, the *falling sickness*, occur instantaneously."). In *The Idiot*, there is a
graphic description of an epileptic fit:

This attack, later diagnosed as epilepsy, confirmed what Dostoevsky had only before suspected. In hindsight, he realized that he had experienced episodes in Siberia.[62] Marya, quite distraught, accused her husband of concealing his ailment, and let him know how much she regretted her choice of an old epileptic over the young, handsome teacher.[63] Such recriminations set the tone for what was to be a disappointing marriage, which took its toll on Dostoevsky's health.[64] Later on, it turned out that stepson Pasha would create stress for Dostoevsky throughout his life.[65]

In that instant the face is suddenly distorted to an extreme degree, especially the eyes. Convulsions and spasms take possession of the whole body and all the features of the face. A terrible, unimaginable howl, unlike anything else, tears from the breast; in that howl everything human seems to disappear, and it is in no way possible, or at least very difficult, for an observer to imagine and admit that it is the same person howling.

Id.

62. *See supra* notes 33 & 44 and accompanying text (discussing Dostoevsky's epilepsy).

63. *See* KJETSAA, *supra* note 4, at 125 ("Maria regretted her decision almost immediately, and she did not keep it to herself. Why hadn't she chosen the young teacher over an ageing epileptic? How could a woman with any self-respect love a jailbird, a man who spent four years in prison with thieves and assassins?"). *See* Letter from Fyodor Dostoevsky to Mikhail Dostoevsky (March 9, 1857) in I LETTERS, *supra* note 9, at 305 ("When I married I completely believed the doctors who had assured me that they're simply nervous attacks that might pass ... If I had known for certain that I had genuine falling sickness, I would not have married.").

64. *See* Letter from Fyodor Dostoevsky to Alexander Vrangel (March 31, April 14, 1865) in II LETTERS, *supra* note 32, at 151 (Marya "loved me boundlessly, I loved her without measure too, but she and I did not live happily ... [and] although she and I were absolutely miserable together (because of her strange, overly sensitive, and morbidly fantastic character)—we couldn't stop loving each other."); KJETSAA, *supra* note 4, at 125 (describing a "harrowing home life with the fickle, jealous Maria[, which] caused a swift deterioration in Dostoyevsky's health") Kjetsaa explains that "[t]he seizures came with ever greater frequency, and each time the aftermath was worse; he suffered from complete exhaustion, lasting amnesia, and deep depression." *Id. See also* FRANK, *supra* note 7, at 341–42 (describing Dostoevsky's "weariness stemming from a profound disappointment with his life" and "inner lassitude whose probable explanation is a desire to escape from the burdens of life in common with Marya Dimitrievna").

65. *See e.g.*, Letter from Fyodor Dostoevsky to Varvara Konstant (November 30, 1857), in I LETTERS, *supra* note 9, at 326 ("[T]he academy's inspector ... writes that Pasha misbehaves a lot and is doing poorly at his studies."); Letter from Fyodor Dostoevsky to Pavel Isaev (Pasha) (September 18, 1863) in II LETTERS, *supra* note 32, at 67 ("But to be an ignoramus consciously, of one's one will, to lag behind one's generation, to be lower and worse than others, and lacking an education, not to understand, therefore, what is going on around—and to sense that continually—that's what will be disgusting and awful."); Letter from Fyodor Dostoevsky to Varvara Konstant (November 10, 1863) in *id.* at 75 ("Talk

In April 1857, Dostoevsky's hereditary nobility was restored. A year later, assisted by the battalion physician's report on his epilepsy, Dostoevsky sought and ultimately obtained a military discharge. Eventually, Dostoevsky was allowed to

---

to Pasha. I think that he has used up all the money I gave him for his maintenance."); Letter from Fyodor Dostoevsky to Varvara Konstant (November 19, 1863) in *id.* at 79 ("I'm terribly worried about Pasha."); Letter from Fyodor Dostoevsky to Varvara Konstant (January 10, 1864), in *id.* at 85 (Pasha "was quite unbearable to [his mother]..is extraordinarily thoughtless, and of course, his inability to behave with the very ill."); Letter from Fyodor Dostoevsky to Pasha (January 28, 1864), in *id.* at 86 ("You're not only a bad son, with a vile, spiteful heart (you might have asked about your mother's health), but you're simply stupid."); Letter from Fyodor Dostoevsky to Pasha (January 31, 1864), in *id.* at 87 ("For someone who doesn't want to do anything there is only one road open from youth on: to be a rogue and a scoundrel. And even if you don't want to, you'll become one unwillingly."); Letter from Fyodor Dostoevsky to Pasha (June 22, 1866) in *id.* at 201 ("[D]idn't *I order you*, NO MATTER WHAT, to write me every Saturday … Can it really be that indolence has so devoured you that you can't take pen in hand? … If there are no letters…, I'll drop everything, all my affairs, and be forced to come to Petersburg, since I think you must be ill and lying there helpless."); Letter from Fyodor Dostoevsky to Pasha (May 19, 1867), in *id.* at 247 ("I hear, Pasha, that you are not behaving exactly as I would wish.… I need money myself, and I have very little of it. I won't pay any loans made by you …"); Letter from Fyodor Dostoevsky to Apollon Maykov (August 16, 1867), in *id.* at 262 ("I've received only one letter from [Pasha] this whole time. I don't think he likes me, at all. And that's really hard for me to take."); Letter from Fyodor Dostoevsky to Pasha (October 10, 1867), in *id.* at 282 ("You should know that after my marriage you have become even more dear to me … But if you didn't want to study, then at least obey me in one thing: you need not to neglect your moral development, as much as that is possible without an education."); Letter from Fyodor Dostoevsky to Apollon Maykov (December 31, 1867), in *id.* at 299 (After sending Pasha "some of the very last of [his] money," he asks, "[i]t can't be that he hates me" and elaborates, "I attribute all of this not to his heart, but to his frivolousness and inability to venture even to write a letter, since he didn't even venture to learn the multiplication table until he was twenty years old."); Letter from Fyodor Dostoevsky to Pasha (February 19, 1868), in III LETTERS, *supra* note 31, at 31 ("If you only knew, Pasha, how I have suffered over you, and most importantly, because of the fact that I can't help you at all."); Letter from Fyodor Dostoevsky to Apollon Maykov (March 2, 1868), in *id.* at 45 ("I'm terribly upset and worried because … Pasha … said arrogantly that he 'won't hear of my being in need, that I'm obligated to support him …"); Letter from Fyodor Dostoevsky to Mikhail Katkov (March 3–5, 1868) in *id.*, at 50 ("This stepson of mine … has absolutely given himself his word, since childhood, *not to do anything*, at the same time without having the slightest fortune and at the same time having the most absurd notions of life."); Letter from Fyodor Dostoevsky to Apollon Maykov (May 18, 1868), in *id.* at 77 ("Forgive me for Pasha's bothering you so. I don't understand what's going to become of you."). Letter from Fyodor Dostoevsky to Pasha (September 22, 1868), in *id.* at 97 ("Your *desperate* situation … has exhausted me with worry … because you seem to doubt my love for you. But what am I to do when I myself suffered such a serious lack of money all summer that there was no way I could send you anything."); *id.* at 98. n 8 (Lowe, editor and translator of Dostoevsky's let-

return to St. Petersburg, and a few years later, made his first trip abroad, but did so without his wife. At this time, Marya, who had tuberculosis, was quite infirm. Dostoevsky's travels to Berlin, Dresden, Wiesbaden, Baden-Baden, Cologne, Paris, London, Lucerne, Geneva, Genoa, Florence, Milan, Venice and Vienna provoked his harsh criticism of Europe, which he expressed without restraint in *Winter Notes on Summer Impressions*, first published in 1863.[66]

Dostoevsky, who had little praise for the West, nevertheless embarked again about a year later, partly because he wished to consult medical epilepsy experts and mainly because he had fallen in love with a twenty-three-year old, Apollinaria (Polina) Suslova, who awaited him in Paris.[67] Polina, the daughter of a

---

ters, notes that "Dostoevsky learned to his horror upon his return to St. Petersburg [that Pasha] raised money for himself by selling off Dostoevsky's library."); *Reminiscences, supra* note 2, at 115 (Dostoevsky's wife describes the painful loss of the library and states, "[w]hen I expressed regret at the loss ... [Pasha] turned round on me and declared that we ourselves were to blame for everything" because they hadn't sent Pasha "money punctually."); Letter from Fyodor Dostoevsky to Apollon Maykov (August 14, 1869), in III LETTERS, *supra* note 31, at 175 ("I fret and worry, thinking and wondering about [Pasha]."); Letter from Fyodor Dostoevsky to Apollon Maykov (February 12, 1870), in *id.* at 231 ("I'm really quite persuaded that such a dreamy head as Pasha's is capable of imagining for itself current speculations on the stock market."); Letter from Fyodor Dostoevsky to Pasha (January 6, 1871), in *id.*, at 303 ("I had already heard a long time ago ... that you were getting married.... [and] was also distressed at the fact that you hadn't notified me: that meant, I thought that you had given me up entirely and burned your bridges, and I felt sad about that."); Letter from Fyodor Dostoevsky to Pasha (December 11, 1874), in IV LETTERS, *supra* note 32, at 184 ("I kept you, raised you, taught you, and even now have been endeavoring on your behalf ... Meanwhile you, so prickly, even regarding me and my family, who have always endeavored on your behalf."); Letter from Fyodor Dostoevsky to Pasha (January 7, 1876), in *id.* at 268–69 ("I'm sending you the last of my money ... I have not abandoned you to this day, but you're now close to 30 years old, and I'm not to blame for the circumstances of your life."); Letter from Fyodor Dostoevsky to Pasha (August 22, 1878), in V DOSTOEVSKY LETTERS (1878–81), at 56 (David Lowe, ed. & trans., Ardis Publishers, 1991) [hereinafter V LETTERS] ("The favor was not at all a large one, but you decided to dodge it. You could have realized, however, that I have done you no small number of favors.") Apparently, Pasha was a problem even when Dostoevsky was on his death bed. *See* KJETSAA, *supra* note 4, at 372 ("There was great consternation when Pasha turned up and demanded that 'father' should write a will ... His deathbed was painful enough as it was.").

66. *See* KJETSAA, *supra* note 4, at 143 ("One would think that Dostoyevsky would have gotten something positive out of this trip [abroad], but no, he found simply what he sought: his *Winter Notes on Summer Impressions*, published in the first issue of *Time* in 1863, is truly the most damning account of the West ever written by a Russian.")

67. *See* Letter from Fyodor Dostoevsky to Ivan Turgenev (June 17, 1863), in II LETTERS, *supra* note 32, at 50 ("I am asking to be allowed to go abroad ... I am very ill with falling sickness, which keeps intensifying and drives me even to despair ... We don't have

peasant who had bought his freedom from serfdom and managed an estate of Count Sheremetev, was a young Russian feminist, described as a "hot-blooded beauty with great feline eyes and a proud head held high and framed by thick red braids."[68] Initially, Polina, glorifying Dostoevsky into the poster child of her social causes, became quite infatuated with him. Later, however, dissatisfaction set in, and their liaison became turbulent.[69]

During the Polina era, Dostoevsky pursued another, but more destructive, love affair—this one with gambling—which would mutate into an uncontrollable affliction that would consume and nearly destroy him.[70] It was during this period of feverish travel with Polina that an insolvent Dostoevsky, driven by unrequited lust for roulette, likely conceived of the idea for *The*

---

any specialists."). In a letter, written while Dostoevsky was in Paris, he speaks of Polina as a "certain person." Letter from Fyodor Dostoevsky to Nikolay Dostoevsky (August 16, 1863), in *id.* at 54.

68. KJETSAA, *supra* note 4, at 152. In his letter to his brother, Dostoevsky refers to Polina as "the person with whom I am traveling." Letter from Fyodor Dostoevsky to Mikhail Dostoevsky (September 8, 1863), in II LETTERS, *supra* note 32, at 62. *See also id.* at 63 ("In Baden I saw Turgenev and Turgenev did not see [Polina]. I hid her."). After his wife's death, there was another woman, Anna Vasilievna Korvin-Krukovskaya, who entered Dostoevsky's life. *See id.* at 140 n. 1 (Lowe discusses how after Dostoevsky "fell in love with Korvin-Krukoskaya and proposed to her[, s]he accepted, but later backed out of the engagement.").

69. *See* FRANK, *supra* note 7, at 385–86 ("Nothing reliable is known about the intimate details of their relationship, but there is ample evidence that the Dostoevsky-Suslova liaison did not go smoothly after the first excitement of possession and novelty had worn off."). In a letter to Polina's sister, who was Russia's first woman doctor, Dostoevsky writes:

> Apollinaria is a sick egoist. The egoism and vanity in her are colossal. She demands *everything* from people, every perfection, does not forgive even a single imperfection in deference to other good traits; she, however, spares herself even the slightest responsibilities to people. She still stings me with the fact that I was not worthy of her love, complains and reproaches me continually, but meets me herself in 1863 in Paris with the sentence "You are a little late in arriving," that is, that she had fallen in love with another, when two weeks before that she had written me ardently that she loved me.

Letter from Fyodor Dostoevsky to Nadezhda Suslova (April 19, 1865) in II LETTERS, *supra* note 32, at 157. *See also infra* note 178 (describing the expert testimony of Polina's sister in the Kronenberg trial).

70. *See e.g.*, Letter from Fyodor Dostoevsky to Varvara Konstant (August 20, 1863) in II LETTERS, *supra* note 32, at 57–58 ("Please don't think that I am bragging from joy that I didn't lose when I say that I know the secret of how not to lose but to win [at gambling] ... it is terribly stupid and simple and consists of restraining oneself at every moment, no matter at what phase of the game, and of not losing one's head."); Letter from Fyodor Dostoevsky to Nikolay Strakhov (September 18, 1863) in *id.* at 70 (discussing his plans to write *The Gambler*, a story about a "Russian living abroad," in which "all his life juices, energies, violence, boldness have gone *into roulette*"). *See also infra* note 85 and accompanying text

Gambler.[71] Dostoevsky and Polina eventually parted, but for a time kept in touch through correspondence.[72] Dostoevsky's obsession with gambling, however, did not just curtsy and make its exit.

In 1863, the news of his dying wife severed Dostoevsky from Bad Homburg's gaming tables and beckoned him home. The couple settled in Moscow, where a doctor was caring for Marya on her death bed.[73] During this time, Dostoevsky dutifully attended to his wife, who was more irritable and moody each day, and her condition was reminiscent of both Marmeladov's wife in *Crime and Punishment* and Ippolit in *The Idiot*.[74] When in 1864 Marya died, Dostoevsky, who grieved deeply, was freed from his first marriage.[75] About three months later, the death of beloved brother Mikhail delivered an excruciating blow.[76] Compounding this, Dostoevsky, whose family blamed him for

---

71. *See* KJETSAA, *supra* note 4, at 161 ("During his restless travels with Polina, ... Dostoevsky had the idea for *The Gambler*[, in which he] describes not only his experience of the casino's hell, but also his destructive relationship with Polina.")

72. *See* Letter from Fyodor Dostoevsky to Apollinaria Suslova (April 23, 1867), in II LETTERS, *supra* note 32, at 227 ("You must not know anything about me, dear, or at least you didn't know anything when you sent your letter? I got married in February of this year."). Kjetsaa points out that, "Polina's importance for Dostoyevsky may be seen in nearly a dozen female characters that inhabit his work—from Polina in *The Gambler* to Grushenka and Katerina Ivanovna in *The Brothers Karamazov*." KJETSAA, *supra* note 4, at 163.

73. In a letter, Dostoevsky explains that he is moving to Moscow, that his wife's "health is very bad" and "[s]he has been terribly ill for two months." Letter from Fyodor Dostoevsky to Varvara Konstant (November 10, 1863), in II LETTERS, *supra* note 32, at 75.

74. *See* Avsey, *supra* note 56, at 369–70 (stating that Marya's "suffering and moodiness are reflected in the description of Marmeladov's wife in *Crime and Punishment* and of Ippolit in *The Idiot*"). *See also* Letter from Fyodor Dostoevsky to Varvara Konstant (January 10, 1864) in II LETTERS, *supra* note 32, at 85 ("Marya ... has become irritable to the highest degree because of her illness" and "has death on her mind constantly: she grieves and is reduced to despair.").

75. In a letter, Dostoevsky speaks of his "miserable" marriage, but adds:

> When she died—though I was tormented, seeing (all year) her dying, though I appreciated and was painfully aware of what I was burying with her, I could not at all imagine how painful and empty my life would become when she was strewn with earth. And it's been a year now, and the feeling is the same, it is not diminishing.

Letter from Fyodor Dostoevsky to Alexander Vrangel (March 13, April 14, 1865) in II LETTERS, *supra* note 32, at 151–52.

76. *See* Letter from Fyodor Dostoevsky to Andrey Dostoevsky (July 29, 1864) in *id.* at 127 (Speaking of his brother's death, he writes, "[h]ow much I lost with him—I won't tell you. That man loved me more than anything else on earth ... Ahead are a cold, lonely old age and my falling sickness.").

the huge debt that his brother left behind, assumed the burden of paying creditors and caring for his brother's family.[77]

After Dostoevsky's release from Siberia, his life had been complicated, thorny,
and erratic: it entailed obsessive love leading to a dismal marriage, deteriorating health, and repeated debilitating seizures. In spite of this upheaval, but
prior to the 1864 deaths, Dostoevsky had somehow managed to write. In 1859,
Dostoevsky published *Uncle's Dream* and *The Village of Stepanchikovo*, both
of which met with a lukewarm reception. Between 1860 and 1862, *Notes From
the House of the Dead* came out in segments.[78] During 1861, the journal *Time*
also serially published *Humiliated and Insulted* and, when in 1864, the Dostoevsky brothers founded the journal, *Epoch*, it featured *Notes from Underground*.

In 1865, Dostoevsky found himself in dire financial straits, stalked by creditors, and fearful of landing in debtors' prison. Such desperation was what
drove him to sell a new work to Fyodor Stellovsky, a publisher with a bad reputation.[79] In fact, the Stellovsky contract hyperbolically epitomizes the legal
concept of unconscionability. Dostoevsky agreed to accept three thousand
rubles for the edition, which was a miniscule sum (even back then) for such a
popular author.[80] More menacing was the contractual clause providing that if

---

77. Only a few months after Mikhail's death, Apollon Grigoryev died. He was a contributing
editor of *Epoch*, a journal founded by Dostoevsky and his brother, Mikhail, and this exacerbated the stress. *See* KJETSAA, *supra* note 4, at 173. Kjetsaa explains that during this time
"Dostoyevsky did not write a single line: his time was entirely taken up with editorial work,
proofreading and dealing with contributors and the censor." *Id.* He also "had to worry about
his alcoholic brother Nikolai, and his dissipated stepson Pasha." *Id.*

78. Starting in 1860, the introduction and first four chapters of *Notes from the House of
the Dead* were published in a daily newspaper, *The Russian World*. *See* Avsey, *supra* note 56,
at 370. The journal, *Time*, which Dostoevsky founded with his brother, picked up the novel
and re-published a revised version of the initial chapters, and the concluding Part II appeared in 1862. *Id.*

79. *See* Letter from Fyodor Dostoevsky to Anna Korvin-Krukovskaya (June 17, 1866),
in II LETTERS, *supra* note 32, at 200 ("I was in such bad financial circumstances that I was
forced to sell the copyright to everything I had written earlier, all at once, to a speculator,
Stellovsky, a rather bad person."). *See also* FRANK, *supra* note 7, at 457 (calling Stellovsky
"ill famed for driving hard bargains"); KJETSAA, *supra* note 4, at 178 (calling Stellovsky a
"crude speculator"); Avsey, *supra* note 56, at 370 (saying that Stellovsky was "by all accounts
a ruthless and unprincipled money-grubber").

80. *See* Letter from Fyodor Dostoevsky to Ivan Turgenev (August 3/15, 1865) in II LET-
TERS, *supra* note 32, at 165 ("Stellovsky bought my works (the right to publish them in two
columns) for three thousand, of which a part is in promissory notes."). *See also id.* at 164
(Lowe, the editor and translator of Dostoevsky's letters, calls this "the most notorious contract in Russian literary history."). Avsey points out that "[o]ver half of this money was already spoken for; it was needed for the discharge of promissory notes, the irony being that

Dostoevsky failed to submit a new novel before November 1 of the following year, Stellovsky would have the right to publish the author's works free of charge for nine years. Obviously Stellovsky had every incentive to thwart Dostoevsky's fulfillment of his obligations. Moreover, the conniving Stellovsky had done his due diligence: he had information on the extent of the debt, knew about the epileptic attacks that tended to derail the writer's work schedule, and assumed that Dostoevsky, who had committed himself to writing *Crime and Punishment*, could not simultaneously complete two novels.[81] In short, Stellovsky had planted a proverbial land mine under Dostoevsky's writing table.

As the Stellovsky deadline neared, the whole thing nearly exploded.[82] By the end of September 1866, Dostoevsky was still finishing the masterpiece, *Crime and Punishment*, and had not even begun penning the contractual novel. When he complained to writer friends that he could not finish a two-hundred page manuscript in a month, they offered to use Dostoevsky's plot and in a team effort, help him finish the book. Because Dostoevsky objected to signing off on work written by others, he rejected the offer. His friend, writer Alexander Milyukov, came up with the strategy of hiring a secretary.

This collaboration, which would change the course of his life, began when a bright, twenty-year old stenographer, Anna Grigoryevna Snitkina, diffused the situation.[83] Although Dostoevsky had some initial reservations about stenographers, he, accepting Anna's assistance, started writing *The Gambler* in early October. In nearly miraculous time, they completed it on October 30, right on the cusp of the deadline.[84] Unbeknownst to Dostoevsky, however, Stellovsky had in his arsenal a default ploy for sabotaging *The Gambler*'s timely

---

most of these—unbeknown to Dostoevsky—were already in Stellovsky's hands." Avsey, *supra* note 56, at 370–71.

81. Avsey, *supra* note 56, at 371.

82. *See* Letter from Fyodor Dostoevsky to Alexander Milyukov (July 10–15, 1866), in II LETTERS, *supra* note 32, at 208 ("I haven't *gotten down to work* on the novel for Stellovsky … Stellovsky worries me to the point of torture; I even dream of him.").

83. Dostoevsky writes, "I am now hiring a stenographer, and although, as before, I look over what I've dictated three times and redo it, nonetheless the stenography shortens the work nearly by half." Letter from Fyodor Dostoevsky to Nikolay Lyubimov (November 2, 1866), in II LETTERS, *supra* note 32, at 211. He explains that "[o]nly by that means was I able to finish, in *one* month, ten signatures for Stellovsky; otherwise I wouldn't have written even five." *Id.*

84. *See* Letter from Fyodor Dostoevsky to Apollinaria Suslova (April 25, 1867), in *id.* at 227 (describing his "stenographer, Anna Grigorievna Snitkina, … [as] a young and rather attractive girl, … with an extraordinarily kind and clear character," and explaining that the "work went wonderfully well" and "[t]he novel *The Gambler* … was finished … in twenty-four days").

delivery. Stellovsky had arranged to be absent from his office on delivery day with no staff members willing to accept the manuscript. Late in the evening, prior to the expiration of the midnight deadline, Dostoevsky obtained a receipt for the package from a district police officer, which was legally sufficient.[85] Not only had Dostoevsky, with Anna's support, foiled Stellovsky's plot, but they had managed to construct a fine piece of literature from the ground up in a mere twenty-six days.

In February 1867, Dostoevsky married Anna, who was twenty-five years his junior, and two months later, they went abroad.[86] Although they initially planned to be away just a few months, this self-imposed exile lasted more than four years. During this time, Anna, who took charge of business management and practical affairs, proved to be worth her weight in gold. Her efforts might have freed her husband to focus on writing without distraction.[87]

What undermined Anna's frugality, business acumen, and resolve to be a positive influence was her husband's gambling, which flared up with intensity in Europe.[88] Although the couple was poor and drowning in debt, Dostoevsky

---

85. According to Frank, when Dostoevsky tried to deliver the manuscript to Stellovsky's home, he "was told that [he]had left for the provinces, nor would the manager of his publishing firm accept it." FRANK, *supra* note 7, at 516–17. The problem was that "[b]y this time it was too late for a notary, and the police officer of the district would not be returning to his office until ten o'clock in the evening." *Id.* at 517. Dostoevsky, however, "just managed to meet his deadline two hours before its expiration." *Id.*

86. Frank describes Anna Grigoryevna Snitkina as a "reserved and attractive young lady" who came from a "comfortable family of mixed Ukranian and Swedish origin," was fluent in German, and had taken a course in stenography. *Id.* at 510–11. Anna had to drop out of secondary school to care for her father, who had become ill, and "exhibited a sense of duty and capacity for self-subordination that was to mark her conduct as Dostoevsky's spouse." *Id.* In a letter to his fiancé, Dostoevsky writes, "I kiss you countless times over … Entirely *yours*, faithful, most faithful, and unfailing. And I believe and trust in you, as my whole future." Letter from Fyodor Dostoevsky to Anna Snitkina (December 29, 1866), in II LETTERS, *supra* note 32, at 218–19.

87. Kjetsaa points out that some consider Dostoevsky's marriage to Anna "as the most important in Russian literary history" and that "[o]ver the years her persevering endurance and pragmatism enabled her to cope with the problems of everyday life in such a way that he was able to devote himself exclusively to his literary work." KJETSAA, *supra* note 4, at 200.

88. *See, e.g.*, Letter from Fyodor Dostoevsky to Anna Dostoevskaya (May 6, 1867) in II LETTERS, *supra* note 32, at 231–32 ("I could have won 300, because it was already in my hands but I took a risk and lost it … if one is prudent, that is, if one is as though made of marble, cold, and inhumanely cautious, then definitely, *without any doubt*, one can win *as much as one wishes*."); Letter from Fyodor Dostoevsky to Anna Dostoevskaya (May 9, 1867), in *id.* at 238 ("We'll leave for Switzerland and I'll get down to work quickly … perhaps this is

would dash off to the casino, lose his last kopeck, and pawn the remnants of their possessions, including their wedding rings, his winter coat, and his wife's earrings, broach, lace shawl and spare frock.[89] Intermittently, falling to his knees, he would weep, beg his Anna's forgiveness, promise to stop, and then, grabbing whatever he could grab, make another mad dash for the tables.[90] After learning that Anna was pregnant, Dostoevsky, still unable to rein in his

---

even all for the best: I'll be rid of that cursed thought, the monomania, about gambling."); Letter from Fyodor Dostoevsky to Anna Dostoevsky (May 10, 1867), in *id.* at 239 ("I ought to have stopped and left … so as to calm my excited nerves (moreover, I have the observation (a most accurate one) that I can't be calm and cool at gambling for *more than a half hour at a time*)."); Letter from Fyodor Dostoevsky to Anna Dostoevskaya (May 24, 1967), in *id.* at 243 ("Anya, dear, my friend, my wife, forgive me, don't call me a scoundrel! I have committed a crime, I have lost everything that you sent, everything, down to the last kreuzer … gambling is hateful to me.") ; Fyodor Dostoevsky to Anna Dostoevskaya (September 24, 1867), in *id.* at 269 ("Anya, dear, I'm worse than a beast! Last night … I had winnings of 1300 francs, clear. Today—not a kopeck. Everything! I lost everything!"); Letter from Fyodor Dostoevsky to Anna Dostoevskaya (November 5, 1867), in *id.* at 290 ("Oh, darling, you shouldn't even allow me to get at the roulette wheel. As soon as I touch it, my heart stops, and my arms and legs tremble and go cold."); Letter from Fyodor Dostoevsky to Anna Dostoevskaya (March 23, 1868), in III LETTERS, *supra* note 31, at 60 ("My dear angel … I lost everything as soon as I arrived, in a half hour I had lost everything."); Letter from Fyodor Dostoevsky to Anna Dostoevskaya (April 16, 1871), in *id.* at 339–40 ("My priceless one, my eternal friend, my heavenly angel, you realize, of course, that I lost everything, the whole 30 thayers that you sent me … I'm not a scoundrel, just a passionate gambler.").

89. *See* Letter from Fyodor Dostoevsky to Apollon Maykov (August 16, 1867), in II LETTERS, *supra* note 32, at 256 ("I began losing the *last* of my money … I started pawning my clothing. Anna Grigorievna pawned *everything* of hers, her last things …"); Letter from Fyodor Dostoevsky to Anna Dostoevskaya (November 6, 1867), in *id.* at 291 ("I pawned both the ring and the winter coat and lost everything."); Letter from Fyodor Dostoevsky to Apollon Maykov (March 2, 1868), in III LETTERS, *supra* note 31, at 47 ("[E]verything, up to the last rag, mine and my wife's has been pawned."); Letter from Fyodor Dostoevsky to Apollon Maykov (May 18, 1868), in *id.* at 76 ("I myself have *almost* nothing, and … I even pawned my clothes and my wife's."); Letter from Fyodor Dostoevsky to Nikolay Strakhov (February 26, 1869), in *id.* at 140 ("[T]he last of our linen has even been pawned now."). *See also* FRANK, *supra* note 7, at 541 ("Dostoevsky himself was astonished at Anna's extraordinary tolerance of his failings, even when this meant pawning not only their wedding rings but the earrings and brooch he had given her as a present and, as a last resort, Dostoevsky's overcoat and Anna's lace shawl and spare frock.").

90. Kjetsaa explains that "when everything had been pawned, a small win would follow, or a small remittance from Russia would allow them to redeem one or two of the pawned items[, b]ut soon everything was lost again, and once more the way led to the pawnbroker." KJETSAA, *supra* note 4, at 212. "Soon Anna could no longer show her face on the street, as both her dress and her shoes were worn though." *Id. See also supra* notes 88–89 (letters in which Dostoevsky describes his own compulsive gambling and his losses).

destructive urge, became even more determined to try his luck in the casino to score the big win.[91] In March 1868, their first child, Sonya was born, but even that bliss was shortlived.[92] Sonya's death from pneumonia only three months later plunged him into agony and despair.[93]

In spite of the gambling, with its irresistible, vicious cycle, comprised of excruciating guilt and remorse, the couple's incessant travels from one foreign resort to another, and the redundant epileptic fits, Dostoevsky finished *The Idiot* in 1869. Dostoevsky, who had hoped that *The Idiot* would relieve the burden of their burgeoning debt, realized that the novel, not a financial success, would probably fail to obtain a decent fee for book-form release.[94] When in September 1869 his daughter, Lyubov, was born, Dostoevsky, with another mouth to feed, contended with mounting financial pressure.[95]

---

91. In a letter to his wife, Dostoevsky writes, "in a half hour I had lost everything. Forgive me, Anya, I have poisoned your life! And in addition, I have Sonya." Letter from Fyodor Dostoevsky to Anna Dostoevskaya (March 23, 1868), in III LETTERS, *supra* note 31, at 60.

92. In a letter Dostoevsky writes, "[t]he child is only just a month old, but she already even has absolutely my facial expression, my whole face, including the wrinkles on the brow—she lies there and looks as though she's writing a novel!" Letter from Fyodor Dostoevsky to Apollon Maykov (March 21–22, 1868), in *id.* at 53.

93. *See* Letter from Fyodor Dostoevsky to Pavel Isaev (Pasha) (June 9, 2868), in *id.* at 80 ("God has struck me a blow ... I'm so depressed and sick at heart that it would be better to die."); Letter from Fyodor Dostoevsky to Apollon Maykov (June 22, 1868), in *id.* at 81–82 ("[T]he further along the time goes, the more painful the recollection and more vividly the image of my late Sonya presents itself to me. There are moments that are unbearable."). *See also* KJETSAA, *supra* note 4, at 219 ("The period that followed [the death] was almost unbearable. The couple wept, and the neighbors would beat on the walls in an attempt to make them stop.").

94. *See* Letter from Fyodor Dostoevsky to Nikolay Strakhov (February 26, 1869), in III LETTERS, *supra* note 31, at 139 ("I sense that compared to *Crime and Punishment* the effect of *The Idiot* on the public is weaker."); Letter from Fyodor Dostoevsky to Vera and Sofya Ivanova (May 7, 1870), in *id.* at 254 ("The novel [*The Idiot*] turned out to be unsatisfactory."). *But see* Letter from Fyodor Dostoevsky to Sofya Ivanova (March 8, 1869), in *id.* at 143 ("[A]lthough many criticize *the Idiot* and although there are many flaws in it, everyone is reading it with great interest (that is, those people who are reading it).").

95. In a letter, Dostoevsky writes: "[A] daughter was born to me, LYUBOV. Everything went superbly, and the baby is big, healthy, and a beauty." Letter from Fyodor Dostoevsky to Apollon Maykov (September 17, 1869), in *id.* at 185. About a month later, Dostoevsky writes: "How can I write when I'm hungry, when I've pawned my pants in order to raise two talers for a telegram ... But after all, she is nursing a baby. What if she *herself* goes to pawn her last warm wool skirt!" Letter from Fyodor Dostoevsky to Apollon Maykov (October 16, 1869), in *id.* at 193.

Year 1871 spelled change. When Anna became pregnant with their third child, Dostoevsky finally did what he had repeatedly vowed, but failed to do, for years: he actually stopped gambling. One night, he declared himself cured and never again touched a roulette table. Among the speculators over what might have prompted this precipitous conversion, there is Frank, who attributes it to Dostoevsky's "superstitious" nature, his anti-Semitism, and "suscep-tib[ility] to being influenced by any intimations of the dictates of a higher will."[96] According to Frank, after Dostoevsky's gambling loss in Wiesbaden, he meandered through dark and unfamiliar streets in quest of a Russian priest to hear his confession. When Dostoevsky landed at what he mistook for a Russian church, he was traumatized to learn that it was a Jewish synagogue, which for him, was the proverbial omen of disaster.[97] Frank elaborates: "It could be that Dostoevsky took his error to indicate, by a signal from on high, that his gambling mania was bringing him into a degrading proximity with those people traditionally linked with amassing of filthy lucre."[98]

When the Dostoevskys returned to Russia in July of that year, there were positive events: part of *Demons* was already published and their son, Fyodor,

---

96. FRANK, *supra* note 7, at 613–14.

97. This is borne out in Dostoevsky's letter to his wife, in which he writes:

I lost everything … and … I immediately ran to see a priest…. I thought on the way, running to see him, in the dark, down unfamiliar streets, … that I'd talk to him not as with a private person, but as at confession. But I got lost in town, and when I reached the church that I'd taken for a Russian one, I was told at a shop that it wasn't a Russian one, but a Jewish one. It was as though I'd had cold water poured on me, I came running home.

Letter from Fyodor Dostoevsky to Anna Dostoevskaya (April 16, 1871), in *id.* at 341. Dostoevsky adds, "Anya, I lie at your feet and kiss them, and I know that you have every right to despise me, and therefore to think: 'He's going to gamble again.'" *Id.* Then he exclaims, "What can I swear by to you that I *won't*." *Id.*

98. FRANK, *supra* note 7, at 614 ("Perhaps, whenever he was tempted to gamble in the future, this (for him) demeaning and chilling recollection continued to recur and acted as a barrier."). There is evidence that Dostoevsky always associated gambling with Jews, who were one of multiple ethnic groups that Dostoevsky abhorred. *See e.g.*, Letter from Fyodor Dostoevsky to Anna Dostoevskaya (May 6, 1867), in II LETTERS, *supra* note 32, at 232. ("There is a Jew here … [who] … has been playing for several days now, with horrible, *inhuman* composure and calculation (he was pointed out to me), and the bank is already beginning to fear him."). *See also infra* note 160 (discussing Dostoevsky's anti-Semitism). David Lowe, editor and translator of Dostoevsky's letters, states that the "episode" of wandering to the synagogue might not have "cured him, but as "[s]cholars have pointed out, … Dostoevsky simply had no further opportunity to gamble, because all of the casinos in Germany were soon closed by official decree." III LETTERS, *supra* note 31, at 342 n. 5.

was born.[99] The Dostoevskys' emergence from exile, however, was not altogether festive, because a hoard of creditors for debts incurred prior to their departure came out of the woodwork and stalked the couple. But as Kjetsaa describes it, Anna, who had evolved into "an imposing woman with the ability to fight for her family," did damage control:[100]

> The siege continued—several times Dostoyevsky was made the subject of legal proceedings. His creditors were planning to have him put in a debtors' prison in the hope that he would be bailed out by the Literary Fund. It was at this point that Anna took up the fight. First, she managed to secure for herself the publication rights to her husband's works. Then she began to negotiate with the creditors to repay the debts in reasonable stages.[101]

In spite of all of the time spent negotiating with creditors and struggling to make ends meet, Dostoevsky renewed his creative energy by reuniting with friends, like Apollon Maikov and Nikolay Strakhov, and solidified the bond with Vsevolod Solovyev, who would encourage the writer's development. The later years were prolific: *Demons* appeared in 1871–72, and *A Writer's Diary*, which began in 1876, and later resumed for single issues. *The Adolescent* was published in 1875 and five years later, *The Brothers Karamazov* would take the world by storm. Unfortunately, during this time, the Dostoevskys mourned the death of their fourth child, Alyosha, who, born in August 1875, perished before reaching the age of three.[102]

On June 8, 1880, at the unveiling of the Pushkin Memorial in Moscow, Dostoevsky delivered one of the most famous speeches in Russian history. When Tolstoy declined to attend the event, organized by the Society of the Friends of Russian letters, it meant that two longstanding rivals—Dostoevsky and Turgenev—were the attending stars.[103] Initially, it appeared that Turgenev, the aristocrat,

---

99. Letter from Fyodor Dostoevsky to Sofya Ivanova (July 18, 1871) in III LETTERS, *supra* note 31, at 365 ("God gave me a son Fyodor (who at this moment is being swaddled, and he is yelling with a strong healthy cry).").

100. KJETSAA, *supra* note 4, at 266.

101. *Id. See also Reminiscences, supra* note 2, at 136–37 (Dostoevsky's wife explains: "[a]t first I allowed the creditors to carry on negotiations with Fiodor," but the "results of those negotiations were disappointing" and that "without telling him, I decided ... to take all this annoying business on myself alone.").

102. In a letter to Pasha, Dostoevsky writes: "Our Alyosha died yesterday, from a sudden fit of epilepsy, which he had never had before." Letter from Fyodor Dostoevsky to Pavel Isaev (May 16, 1878) in V LETTERS, *supra* note 65, at 43.

103. With respect to Tolstoy, Frank explains that "Turgenev had been assigned the delicate, unenviable task of journeying to Yasnaya Polyana to persuade Tostoy to attend the Pushkin celebration, even though Tolstoy by this time had renounced literature for reasons

who, presented with an honorary doctorate for his "talented mastery of Pushkin's language," and described as "first among the delegates," was garnering the lion's share of popularity.[104]

The tides turned, however, at the first session of the Pushkin event, when Turgenev's speech failed to mesmerize the audience.[105] Although Turgenev praised Pushkin, he declined to condemn the radicals' criticism of the poet and give the author of *Eugene Onegin* the title of national and world poet, equal to William Shakespeare, Molière (Jean-Baptiste Poquelin), and Johann Wolfgang von Goethe.[106] He instead declared: "for the moment, we shall leave this open."[107] Dostoevsky, reacting, wrote his wife, Anna, that Turgenev had actually "denigrated Pushkin by refusing him the title of national poet."[108]

---

comparable to those of the radical critics who had denounced Pushkin in the 1860s." FRANK, *supra* note 7, at 817. *See also* KJETSAA, *supra* note 4, at 356 ("Tolstoy was one of the few who refused to attend: a celebration of this type was in his view a great sin, the more so because he believed the people were completely indifferent to this aristocratic poet."). At the celebration, writer Dmitri Grigorovich was assigned the task of keeping the "two rivals" (Dostoevsky and Turgenev) apart. *Id.* at 358. When he "came into the room together with Turgenev, Dostoevsky turned demonstratively away, and looked out of the window." *Id.* When "Grigorovich said, nervously, 'Come over here—I want to show you a fine statute,' Turgenev pointed to Dostoyevsky. 'Well, if it looks anything like him, please count me out.'" *Id.*

104. KJETSAA, *supra* note 4, at 358, 359. In a letter, Dostoevsky writes; "The professors ... are paying court to Turgenev, who is absolutely turning into a personal enemy of mine." Letter from Fyodor Dostoevsky to Konstantin Pobedonostsev (May 19, 1880), in V LETTERS, *supra* note 65, at 200. *See also* Letter from Fyodor Dostoevsky to Anna Dostoevskaya (June 2–3, 1880), in *id.* at 224 ("[T]here was a gathering at Turgenev's of almost all the participants (I was excluded!) ... [T]hey simply left me out ... [T]his is Turgenev and Kovalevsky's doing.").

105. FRANK, *supra* note 7, at 823–24 (explaining that Turgenev "tried to unite a eulogy of Pushkin with an apologia for his rejection by the radical critics of the 1860s, and ... had also expressed his own opposition, as a liberal Westernizer, to the Slavophil and Populist idolization of 'the people'" and that "[a]ll of these opinions were hardly in accord with the overheated emotional temperature of the moment, and he was well aware of his failure to stir his audience"). *See also* Letter from Fyodor Dostoevsky to Anna Dostoevskaya (June 7, 1880) in V LETTERS, *supra* note 65, at 233 ("Turgenev ... denigrated Pushkin, denying him the title of national poet.").

106. FRANK, *supra* note 7, at 822 (Turgenev defined national poet as "imparting to the values of one's own culture, a national significance, thus attaining a level of universality that transcends mere class or regional boundaries" and said that "[s]uch poets unquestionably represent their people, but they have so absorbed its values that they raise those to the universal level of the ideal.").

107. *Id.*

108. *Id.* at 823.

In contrast, no synopsis of Dostoevsky's speech, which was delivered eloquently the next day, can truly do it justice. As Kjetsaa puts it, the "hall grew silent" immediately and the audience knew that "[t]his was going to be something heavy, something Karamazovian, which no one would be able to tear himself away from."[109] Dostoevsky lauded Pushkin as "prophetic"—the national writer, who not only showed the striving of the Russian national character, but also revealed the universality and commonality of humanity.[110] He proclaimed that Pushkin marked the beginning of Russian self-consciousness and presented the archetypal Russian citizen as a wanderer and sufferer in his own land. The speech climaxed with an electrifying exhortation for all to settle their conflicts without weapons or violence, to unify, and to embrace the power of brotherly love.[111] Dostoevsky himself describes the ensuing rapture:

---

109. KJETSAA, *supra* note 4, at 359. *See generally* FYODOR DOSTOEVSKY, II A WRITER'S DIARY (1877–1881) 1271–1280 (Kenneth Lantz, trans., Northwestern University Press, 1994) (describing the points that he wanted to make about Pushkin's "significance for Russia," which includes "his purely Russian heart," the fact that he is "the first … who gave us artistic types of Russian beauty," his "capacity to respond to the entire world and to assume completely the form of the genius of other nations in a reincarnation that is almost total," along with his "altogether Russian [capacity]," which he "shares … with our entire people."). *See also id* at 1281–1295 ("Pushkin (A Sketch) Delivered on June 8 at the Meeting of the Society of Lovers of Russian Literature").

110. KJETSAA, *supra* note 4, at 359. *See also* FRANK, *supra* note 7, at 829 (summarizing Dostoevsky's speech) ("No other poet or writer in world literature has this capacity to enter into and reproduce the spirit of other cultures to the same degree because no other people except the Russian possess such universal empathy."); DOSTOYEVSKY, *supra* note 109, at 1295 ("[W]e can now point to Pushkin and to the universality and panhumannness of his genius. He could accommodate the geniuses of other nations within his soul as if they were his own … Had Pushkin lived longer, perhaps there would be fewer misunderstandings and disputes among us than we see now.")

111. Dostoevsky said:

I am certain, we (I mean not we, of course, but Russian people to come) will realize to the very last man that to become a genuine Russian will mean specifically … to indicate that the solution to Europe's anguish is to be found in the panhuman and all-unifying Russian soul, to enfold all our brethren within it with brotherly love, and at last, perhaps, to utter the ultimate word of great, general harmony, ultimate brotherly accord of all tribes through the law of Christ's Gospel!

DOSTOYEVSKY, *supra* note 109, at 1294. *See also* KJETSAA, *supra* note 4, at 360 ("By the end of the speech Pushkin had become a symbol of the realization of Dostoyevsky's vision of Russia's future."). *See also* Paul J. Contino, *Incarnational Realism and the Case for Casuistry: Dimitry Karamazov's Escape*, in ART, CREATIVITY, AND SPIRITUALITY, *supra* note 6, at 132 ("In [Dostoevsky's] 1880 speech in praise of Pushkin, he affirms what he held to be exemplary in the poet's work: its transformational capacity.")

When I spoke at the end, however, of the *universal unity* of people, the hall was as though in hysteria. When I concluded—I won't tell you about the roar, the outcry of rapture: strangers among the audience wept, sobbed, embraced each other and *swore to one another to be better, not to hate one another from now on, but instead to love one another.* The meeting's order was violated: everyone rushed to the platform to see me: ... they all hugged me and kissed me ... All of them, literally all of them wept from delight. The calls continued for half an hour ... "Prophet, prophet!" people in the crowd shouted. Turgenev, for whom I put in a good word in my speech, rushed to embrace me with tears ... Students came running in. One of them, in tears fell to the floor before me in hysteria and lost consciousness.[112]

That night, Dostoevsky placed a huge laurel wreath at the foot of the Pushkin Memorial.

After returning home, Dostoevsky finished most of the *Brothers Karamazov* and worked on his *Writer's Diary* while his health deteriorated and he suffered redundant epileptic episodes.[113] The writer, unsettled by surrounding political controversies and financial worries, had his first hemorrhage in January 1881. His plans to embark on more writing projects, including a sequel to *Brothers Karamazov*, were accompanied by premonitions of death. Later that

---

112. Letter from Fyodor Dostoevsky to Anna Dostoevskaya (June 8, 1880), in V Letters, *supra* note 65, at 236–37. Frank describes the audience's reaction:
> The hall seemed to hold its breath, as if expecting something more ... The entire auditorium began to stir. You could hear the shrieks, "You solved it! You solved it!" a storm of applause, some sort of rumbling, stamping, feminine screeches. I do not think that the walls of the Hall of the Moscow Nobility either before or since had ever resounded with such a tempest of ecstasy.

Frank, *supra* note 7, at 831 (quoting D.A. Lyubimov, a young student and son of Dostoevsky's editor). Frank says that "[t]he effect of this speech on the audience was absolutely overwhelming, and the emotions it unleashed may be compared with the hysterical effusions typical of religious revival meetings." *Id. See also* Kjetsaa, *supra* note 4, at 361 ("Hysterical ladies had to be guided out of the hall; a young man managed to press Dostoevsky's hand before passing out" and "[t]here was no end to the ovations and embraces.").

113. *See* Letter from Fyodor Dostoevsky to Vladimir Kachenovsky (October 16, 1880), in V Letters, *supra* note 65 at 280 ("I'm a quite unwell person ... with two incurable diseases that depress me very much and cost me very dearly: epilepsy and ... emphysema—so that I know myself that my days are numbered ... I am obliged to work constantly, without rest."); Letter from Fyodor Dostoevsky to Alexander Saveliev (November 29, 1880), in *id.* at 295 ("I've been terribly unwell because of *my emphysema*: I don't have enough breath, and then a stomach disorder is starting, quite serious, also from the emphysema,...[there is] a lack of breath.").

January, a vein burst, filling Dostoevsky's lungs with blood and then another hemorrhage occurred.[114] Shortly thereafter, Dostoevsky died from what his death certificate said was a "pulmonary hemorrhage."[115]

When the news hit, a nation mourned. University classes were cancelled, Russian newspapers printed obituaries, praising and honoring the great writer, and throngs gathered for the memorial services. When Dostoevsky was laid to rest near his favorite childhood writers, Karamzin and Zhukovsky, there were impressive speeches.[116] Here, his close friend, Vladimir Solovyev, stressed that Dostoevsky "believed in the infinite strength of the human soul, the strength that triumphs over all outer forces and all inner defeats...."[117]

III. Critical Perspectives

While scholars have examined Dostoevsky from nearly every conceivable angle, most literary criticism tends to fall into five intersecting, multi-dimensional categories.

First, there is the lens of psychology, which some scholars, like Professor Deborah A. Martinsen, combine with exacting literary analysis.[118] Martinsen delves into the branch of psychology dealing with shame, and as a starting point, shows how Dostoevsky "uses the dynamics of shame as a narrative strategy, collapsing the intersubjective distance between characters and readers."[119] Focusing mainly on Dostoevsky's liars, scandals, and the "narrative dynamic" of *The Idiot, Demons,* and *The Brothers Karamazov,* Martinsen explores "shame's paradox—its ability to both isolate and relate."[120] She explains that in Dosto-

---

114. *See* Letter from Fyodor Dostoevsky to Yelizaveta Geyden (January 28, 1881), in *id.* at 310 (unfinished draft dictated to Anna Dostoevskaya) ("[A]n artery in his lungs burst and finally flooded his lungs ... After the first attack another one followed, in the evening, with a great loss of blood and choking ... his confession was heard and he took communion.").

115. KJETSAA, *supra* note 4, at 373.

116. *See supra* note 10 and accompanying text (discussing Dostoevsky's early reading).

117. KJETSAA, *supra* note 4, at 381–82.

118. DEBORAH A. MARTINSEN, SURPRISED BY SHAME: DOSTOEVSKY'S LIARS AND NARRATIVE EXPOSURE (Ohio State University Press, 2003). *See also* Deborah A. Martinsen, *Introduction*, in NOTES FROM UNDERGROUND, THE DOUBLE, AND OTHER STORIES xiii (Barnes & Noble Books, 2003).

119. MARTINSEN, *supra* note 118 at xiii.

120. *Id.* at xiii, xvi.

evsky, "shame makes us self-conscious of how we differ from others [and] at the same time ... makes us feel our common post-lapsarian heritage."[121] With respect to Rodion Raskolnikov, who is one of the most complex, enigmatic, and haunting characters in all of world literature, Martinsen suggests that Dostoevsky, by "gradually revealing the psychology behind a shame-driven crime, ... evokes a dual response, making readers complicit with Raskolnikov, yet arousing our ethical qualms."[122]

Martinsen's psychological lens eclectically includes ethical philosophy, anthropology, sociology, and literary interpretation, which fits an author like Dostoevsky, who himself studied everything he could get his hands on. There are others, however, who perform pure psychoanalysis to probe the author's psyche or put characters on the analytic couch. Sigmund Freud, in a study that has been criticized and refuted, diagnoses Dostoevsky with an oedipal complex, opining that the epilepsy and fascination with patricide had their roots in cognitive dissonance over Dr. Dostoevsky's death.[123] According to Freud, Dostoevsky's desire for and relief over his father's demise triggered his initial epileptic seizure and infected him with festering guilt pangs that would culminate in the fictive Karamazov murder.[124]

---

121. *Id.* at xvi.

122. *Id.* at 12.

123. Freud states that "[i]n addition to the hate which seeks to get rid of the father as a rival, a measure of tenderness for him is also habitually present" and "[t]he two attitudes of mind combine to produce identification with the father; the boy wants to be in his father's place because he admires him and wants to be like him, and also because he wants to put him out of the way." Freud, *supra* note 17, at 183. Scholars have criticized and rebutted Freud's theories. *See supra* note 17; SUSAN FUSSO, DISCOVERING SEXUALITY IN DOSTOEVSKY xiii (Northwestern University Press 2006) ("In his magisterial five-volume biography of Dostoevsky, Joseph Frank has shown in impressive detail that Freud's psychoanalytic edifice is built on a shaky foundation of erroneous biographical 'facts.'"). *See also supra* notes 33 & 44 (commentary on the causes and beginning of Dostoevsky's epileptic seizures).

124. Freud, *supra* note 17, at 186. Freud elaborates that "[i]nfantile reactions from the Oedipus complex ... may disappear if reality gives them no further nourishment ... [b]ut the father's character remained the same, or rather, it deteriorated with the years, and thus Dostoevsky's hatred for his father and his death-wish against that wicked father were maintained." *Id.* Because "it is a dangerous thing if reality fulfills such repressed wishes," as occurred with Dostoevsky, his "attacks ... assumed an epileptic character" and thus "signified an identification with his father as punishment, but they had become terrible, like his father's frightful death itself." *Id.* Scholars have criticized and rebutted Freud's theories. *See supra* note 17, 33 &44 (addressing those who refute Freud's theories and ideas about Dostoevsky's epilepsy). *See also supra* FUSSO, note 123, at xiii ("[I]n a 1928 essay[, Freud] ... attributes to Dostoevsky a variety of psychological disorders, including masochism, sadism, hysteria,

Other analysts, borrowing Freudian psychology, blame Raskolnikov's mother complex for the murder of the cadaverous pawnbroker, Alyona Ivanovna. For example, Louis Breger attributes Raskolnikov's crime to his "overwhelming ambivalence" toward his mother, which has both "sadistic and masochistic components" and poses a dilemma whereby "[h]e can attack the maternal figure or submit to her."[125] Similarly, Kathleen Donnellan Garber "surmise[s] that Raskolnikov's oral needs as an infant were not satisfied," that he is "unable to distinguish himself as separate from his mother," and that he exhibits "behavior replete with manifestations of infantile dependence."[126] Others add family members to the causal indictment, or, as Psychiatry Professor Jeffery C. Hutzler puts it, "the inevitable march of powerful family influences force[ed] Raskolnikov into survival tactics which result in his crime, punishment, and the resolution of his fearfully pathologic family conflict."[127] Raskolnikov is not the only patient on the therapist's couch. Assorted psychological theories have been pinned on Dostoevsky and his characters,[128] and as developed in the next chapter, Golyadkin, "hero" of *The Double*, is a most baffling specimen, one who evades diagnostic consensus.[129]

Second, there is the socioeconomic lens, which hones in on Dostoevsky's portrayal of poverty and oppressive inequality. Some, like Dr. Atkin, even posit that *Crime and Punishment* is all about "social determinants" and that it is the

---

a desire to kill his father which is then transferred to the tsar, and a compulsion to masturbate which is expressed as addictive gambling.")

125. LOUIS BREGER, DOSTOEVSKY: THE AUTHOR AS PSYCHOANALYST 23 (New York University Press,1989). Breger has pointed out that *Crime and Punishment* is replete with mothers, ones like the landlady, the "bad" mother, the "source of food, shelter, and comfort, … whose care is bound up with anger, fear and guilt" and the landlady's maid, the "good" mother, who "attends to [Raskolnikov's] needs in a simple and straightforward manner." *Id.* *See also* David Kiremidjian, *Crime and Punishment: Matricide and the Woman Question*, 33 AM. IMAGO 403 (1976) (analyzing Raskolnikov's infantile dependencies and his matricidal impulses).

126. Kathleen Donnellan Garber, *A Psychological Analysis of a Dostoyevsky Character: Raskolnikov's Struggle for Survival*, 14 PERSPECTIVES IN PSYCHIATRIC CARE 16–17 (1976).

127. Jeffrey C. Hutzler, *Family Pathology in Crime and Punishment*, 38 AM. J. OF PSYCHOANALYSIS 335, 335 (1978). He suggests that the "concept of family pathology explains Raskolnikov's odd symptoms (diagnosis), his motivation for the murders he committed (dynamic) and the resolution of his conflict." *Id.*

128. *See e.g.* BREGER, *supra* note 125. *But see* TERRAS, *supra* note 8, at 13 (discussing how "some [Dostoevsky] critics found his psychologism excessive … and it was suggested that Dostoevsky's morbidly self-conscious and self-lacerating characters were unrepresentative of Russian society, but were, rather, projections of the author's own diseased mind.")

129. *See generally infra* Chapter II (The Impenetrable Mental Capacity Doctrine: *The Double*) (analyzing *The Double* and the mental capacity doctrine).

wretched poverty-stricken state that co-conspires with Raskolnikov to crush the old moneylender's head with an axe.[130] Atkin, calling Raskolnikov the "type of Russian intellectual who was able to observe the superficial social contradictions, but saw no way out in the fog of Westernism, Slavophilism, Nihilism, Liberalism and other 'isms' of the disrupted intelligentsia," concludes that, "[j]ust as the causation of criminal behavior rests both in society and in the individual, so must responsibility be shared by the two."[131] While Dostoevsky scowled at those who blamed criminality on the environment, he did concern himself with the social climate and the tribulations of those ill off.[132] Raskolnikov, like other Dostoevsky characters (some totally innocent of crime), is downtrodden, penurious, clothed in rags, and resides in a suffocating box.

In addition to predecessor Nikolai Gogol, who fostered compassion for the underdog, several other factors abetted Dostoevsky's concern with the unfortunate, one of which was his own precarious ancestry.[133] As discussed above, unlike other Russian greats, Dostoevsky could not boast of first class membership in the landed gentry.[134] Insecurity over his own societal niche helped sensitize him to others, who were humiliated, scarred by poverty, or emblazoned with badges of inferiority.[135] Dostoevsky's time in the Siberian hard-labor camp, in which he was forced to suffer alongside peasant-convicts, also kindled the epiphany that all souls, regardless of rank, deserve dignity and respect.[136] Professor Nancy Ruttenberg, pointing out that "the [project for Dostoevsky's democracy] occupied him for the duration of his career," says that "*Notes from the House of the Dead* establishes the ground rules [for] the discovery of the outwardly coarse and brutal peasants' spiritual preeminence and central role in the unfolding of Russia's redemptive mission and glorious destiny."[137]

---

130. I. Atkin, *Raskolnikov: The Study of a Criminal*, 5 J. OF CRIMINAL PSYCHOPATHOLOGY 255 (1943)

131. *Id.* at 255–56, 262, 278–79.

132. *See also* DOSTOEVSKY, *supra* note 1, at 393 ("Not long ago everyone was talking and writing about that dreadful murder of six people by that ... young man and about the strange speech of the defence counsel, in which it was said that because of the criminal's impoverished state it must have been *natural* for him to kill those six people.").

133. *See supra* notes 14 & 15 and accompanying text (discussing class status and its impact on Dostoevsky).

134. *See supra* notes 14 & 15 and accompanying text (discussing class status and its impact on Dostoevsky).

135. *See supra* notes 14 & 15 and accompanying text (discussing class status and its impact on Dostoevsky).

136. *See infra* Chapter IV (Prisons of Coercion: *Notes from the House of the Dead*) (focusing on Dostoevsky's experience of and realizations in the Siberian prison).

137. NANCY RUTTENBURG, DOSTOEVSKY'S DEMOCRACY 59 (Princeton University Press,

It was not simply Omsk prison that moved Dostoevsky to share his vision of the commonality of, and bonds between, all beings. His personal, physical, and psychological pain, loss of loved ones, the stress of indebtedness, and the chronic sting of living hand-to-mouth helped to rouse his emotional intelligence and empathy.[138] Dostoevsky's readers do not just read about, but actually *live* the heart-wrenching epistolary exchange between poor Devushkin and Varenka in *Poor Folk*; mourn the battered life of the pawnbroker's wife, who, clutching her icon, leaps to her death from the window in *A Gentle Creature*; recoil when Golyadkin emits his parting shriek in *The Double*; crave solace for child-heroine Netochka's hardships in the unfinished novel, *Netochka Nezvanova*; dream of curing the terminally ill, epileptic girl Nelly in *Humiliated and Insulted*; desire prison reform after feeling the fiery lashings of Siberian convicts in *Notes From the House of the Dead*; want to defend the kind prostitute, Liza, whom the underground man ravishes, sermonizes, and humiliates in *Notes from the Underground*; hope to bestow healing and charity on the pauperized Marmeladovs in *Crime and Punishment*; wish to derail Christ-like Prince Myshkin's tragic regression to idiocy and retreat into the bosom of the sanatorium in *The Idiot*; help halt the ruthless terrorism and senseless violence in *Demons*; shelter the victimized children and women depicted in Dostoevsky's *A Writer's Diary*; and partner with Alyosha while he sits bedside in the stifling room where little Ilyusha lay dying in *The Brothers Karamazov*.

Third, there is the philosophical lens, and *The Brothers Karamzov* is amenable to this interdisciplinary tool. The compendium of essays in *Dostoevsky's Brothers Karamazov: Art, Creativity, and Spirituality*, "cross[ing] the often too rigid lines between philosophy and literature,"[139] substantiates Professor Victor Terras's thesis that Dostoevsky's books are "about ideas as much

2008). *See also infra* Chapter IV (Prisons of Coercion: *Notes from the House of the Dead*) (focusing on Dostoevsky's experience of and realizations in the Siberian prison).

138. Kjetsaa discusses the "poverty theme," along with another "to which Dostoevsky returned again and again in the course of his career: man's perpetual battle for self-respect," and how self-respect connects with compassion and empathy. KJETSAA, *supra* note 4, at 46. "Without self-respect a man cannot be truly human; without it, his life goes to pieces" and "[m]an is a being who may easily be degraded, but to degrade him is wrong." *Id. See also* TERRAS, *supra* note 8, at 13 ("Dostoevsky had a deep understanding of humans under conditions of great stress caused by want, suffering, frustration, rejection, and despair. He understood the psychology of poverty, humiliation, resentment, jealousy, cynicism, and cruelty better than most.") .

139. Predag Cicovacki and Maria Granik, *Introduction*, in ART, CREATIVITY AND SPIRITUALITY, *supra* note 6, at 9. *See also* JAMES P. SCANLAN, DOSTOEVSKY THE THINKER (Cornell University Press 2002).

as about people."[140] Scholars have enlisted a wide range of philosophers, including Plato,[141] Aristotle,[142] Thomas Hobbes,[143] Rene Descartes,[144] John Locke,[145] Baron Gottfried Wilhelm Leibniz,[146] Immanuel Kant,[147] Georg Wilhelm Friedrich Hegel,[148] Soren Aabye Kierkegaard,[149] Frederick Wilhelm Ni-

---

140. TERRAS, *supra* note 8, at 9.

141. *See e.g.*, Predag Cicovacki, *Dostoevsky's Uncommon World View* in ART, CREATIVITY AND SPIRITUALITY, supra note 6, at 191 (discussing how "Plato and Aristotle rightly insist that wonder at the complexity, beauty, and order of the world is the source of all philosophizing" and stating that Dostoevsky is among those who "can appreciate the immediate and aesthetic aspects of their experience, even if that means leaving the phenomena unexplained, or declaring some of them unexplainable"). *But see* SCANLAN, *supra* note 139, at 92 ("Dostoevsky decisively rejects the Platonic contention that to know the good is to do it.").

142. *See e.g.*, Cicovacki, *supra* note 141, at 191. *See also* SCANLAN, *supra* note 139, at 173 (Dostoevsky "appears to have been influenced by Aristotle's negative appraisal of democracy as meaning rule by the poor in their own interest.").

143. *See e.g.*, SCANLAN, *supra* note 139, at 166 ("Dostoevsky's parable makes novel use of a conceptual devices popularized by Hobbes, Locke, and Rousseau before him: he posits a 'state of nature' or original condition in which people live together in the absence of political relations.").

144. *See e.g., id.* at 20 (explaining that a Dostoevsky notebook entry "is reminiscent of Descartes's 'Meditations,' wherein the French philosopher was attempting to find some proposition that could not be doubted, so as to have an indisputable foundation for a structure of knowledge").

145. *See e.g., id.* at 166 (discussing how Dostoevsky "makes novel use of a conceptual device popularized by Hobbes, Locke, and Rousseau" by "posit[ing] a 'state of nature' or original condition in which people live together in the absence of political relations").

146. *See e.g., id.* at 51 (applying "Leibniz's memorable phrase, 'the best of all possible worlds,' to Ivan Karamazov's problem with the presence of evil in the world").

147. *See e.g.*, Ruben Apressyan, *The Practices of Mercy* in ART, CREATIVITY, AND SPIRITUALITY, *supra* note 6, at 118 (suggesting that "Dostoevsky presented a solution contrary to the one proposed by Kant: love, or as Dostoevsky put it, the heart, is the metaphysical basis of morality, which is impossible without merciful love and compassion"). *See also* SCANLAN, *supra* note 139, at 21 (examining Dostoevsky's notebook reflections on his wife's death and finding "remarkable parallels ... between Dostoevsky's reasoning ... and Immanuel Kant's case for the immortality of the soul").

148. *See e.g.*, SCANLAN, *supra* note 139, at 165 (pointing out that Dostoevsky suggests "something like the 'cunning of reason' that is so critical an element in the Hegelian dialectic: a force opposed to the goal is an essential element in working toward it").

149. *See e.g. id.* at 5 ("To the existentialists Dostoevsky resembled no one so much as Kierkegaard, and they ascribed something like the Danish philosopher's consummate irrationalism to the Russian thinker."). *See also* FRANK, *supra* note 7, at 221 ("Like Dostoevsky, and even more rigorously, Kierkegaard decided to take his stand with the irrationality of faith against reason and to push the opposition between the two to the point of paradox.").

etzsche,[150] and Martin Heidegger,[151] in an effort to shed light on Dostoevsky as thinker.

Those engaged in this genre tend to acquiesce to Professor James P. Scanlan's proposition that Dostoevsky's philosophy is inextricable from his life's quest to solve the "puzzle" of humanity.[152] As Scanlan explains, "[l]ike that of most Russian philosophers, … [Dostoevsky's philosophy] is decidedly anthropocentric" or "prompted not by abstract cosmological and epistemological concerns but by an obsession with humanity."[153] He elaborates: "Whatever subject [Dostoevsky] took up—religion, art, the state, history, morality—he was interested above all in its human significance and specifically in what clues he could find in it to the question of what it means to be human."[154] For Dostoevsky, what it means to be human (or a moral human) converges with Professor Ruben Apressyan's "*agape*[,] defined as compassionate, benevolent, careful, loving attitude toward others," which is the core of *The Brothers Karamazov* and his other fiction, in which dialogue plus narrative reveal how individuals perceive and treat others.[155]

The New Testament's image of Christ, along with the ideal of compassion and brotherly love, permeates Dostoevsky's understanding of what it is to be a free moral agent. In fact, the philosophical lens is more effective when combined with the fourth lens, that of theophany.[156] Professor Predag Cicovacki,

---

150. *See e.g.*, Atkin, *supra* note 130, at 271 (suggesting that we follow the "fuller development of Raskolnikov's ideas by Nietzsche[,] who also envisages a society which is divided into two distinct classes, an aristocratic ruling caste (the 'free spirits') and an inferior slave class" and that Raskolnikov's theory is thus seen as a foreshadowing of the ideology of a fascist society"); Lyudmila Parts, *Christianity As Active Pity in* Crime and Punishment, 13 DOSTOEVSKY STUD. 61, 61 (2009) (discussing how "Dostoevsky builds an argument against such detractors of pity as Kant and Nietzsche"). Parts explains that Dostoevsky "argues against Kantian distrust of pity and in fact preempts Nietzsche's future claim that pity is the most harmful of all Christian virtues …" *Id. But see* FRANK, *supra* note 7, at 327 n. 6 (describing how "Nietzsche read *The Insulted and Injured* with great appreciation" and how the "formidable Nietzsche surrendered completely to Dostoevsky's efforts to pluck the heartstrings of his readers").

151. *See e.g.*, Ulrich Schmid, *Heidegger and Dostoevsky: Philosophy and Politics* 15 DOSTOEVSKY STUD. 37, 37 (2011) (examining how "Heidegger, in his existentialist thinking, develops key concepts of Dostoevsky's narrative philosophy").

152. SCANLAN, *supra* note 139, at 9.

153. *Id.*

154. *Id.*

155. Apressyan, *supra* note 147, at 116.

156. Scanlan, examining the "conception of human beings as free moral agents that Dostoevsky advanced against the Rational Egoists[,]" explains that "[a]lthough [Dostoevsky] viewed individuals as complex, rational-irrational personalities endowed with the ineradicable but demanding faculty of free choice and with an inherent need for self-expression, he also saw them as moral creatures whose standards of both personal conduct

suggesting that philosophy takes a back seat to faith, explains how Dostoevsky's Christianity is not about the "mere acceptance of religious dogmas, nor the mere observation of church rituals, but a way of life":[157]

> Christianity, Dostoevsky believes, comes closer than philosophy to il-luminating for us what that way of life is: it comes closer because re-ligion offers us concrete images and parables of Jesus' life, not only abstract and theoretical constructs. Searching for wisdom and imi-tating Jesus do not necessitate belonging to any school, just as they do not require belonging to any church.[158]

In his fiction and *A Writer's Diary*, Dostoevsky pays homage to Christ as role model, and posits imitation of the Savior, along with acceptance of suf-fering, as a path to purity, peace, and redemption.[159] Individuals, like *Crime and Punishment*'s Sonya, *The Idiot*'s Prince Myshkin, and radiant souls Alyosha Karamazov and Father Zosima in *The Brothers Karamazov*, exemplify the true Christian life. Among those scholars who read *The Brothers Karamazov* in this vein, Professor Paul J. Contino believes that *Karamazov* particularly can help readers "become better people" through its persuasion "that a saintly Chris-tian life [is] both real and possible for them."[160]

---

and social relationships were provided by the New Testament image of Jesus Christ." SCAN-LAN, *supra* note 139, at 11. *See also* 13 DOSTOEVSKY STUD. (2009) (special issue devoted to Dostoevsky and Christianity).

157. Cicovacki, *supra* note 141, at 197.

158. *Id.*

159. Diane Oenning Thompson, *Islamic Motifs: Poetic Transformations of Historical Events*, in ART, CREATIVITY, AND SPIRITUALITY, *supra* note 6, at 101 (Dostoevsky "believed that over the ages the Russian people, as opposed to many of the Europeanized Russian in-telligentsia, had preserved the true image of Christ, the true meaning of Christianity and was thus destined to be a beacon of faith to Russia, the West, and perhaps all humanity.") Thompson points out that in *A Writer's Diary*, Dostoevsky expresses his "anxious concern for Russian youth, that it direct its energies and idealism to Christian values rather than the views of the radicals." *Id.* at 102. *See also* Katherine Jane Briggs, *Dostoevsky, Women, and the Gospel: Mothers and Daughters in the Later Novels*, 13 DOSTOEVSKY STUD. 109, 114 (2009) ("Dostoevsky's Christian faith is constantly expressed, both implicitly and explic-itly, through his journalistic writings, letters and novels.").

160. Contino, *supra* note 111, at 132. *See also* Parts, *supra* note 150, at 61 ("Dostoevsky presents pity and/or compassion as the most important Christian value, one above the other Christian virtues and human emotions for which scientific and political theories have no place."). It is, of course, hard to reconcile Dostoevsky's spiritual views with his anti-Semitism. *See, e.g.*, DOSTOEVSKY, *supra* note 109, at 901–925 (defending his position on the Jews and repeatedly referring to them as "Yids"); Letter from Fyodor Dostoevsky to Sofya Ivanova

Fifth, there is the poetic lens, in which literary scholars define stylistic, lex-ical, and narrative techniques in Dostoevsky's prose. This endeavor, especially when it comes to Dostoevsky, fuses with the exegesis of psychological, social, philosophical, and religious motifs. In fact, Walter Pater, nineteenth century art critic, and Mikhail Bakhtin, twentieth century literary theorist, can lend per-spective. Although Pater is not commenting on Dostoevsky, he is nevertheless relevant because he knighted music as the "ideally consummate art," exalted the oneness of import and medium, and felt that "[a]ll art constantly aspires toward the condition of music."[161] Pater knew that "while in all other kinds of

---

(July 18, 1871) in III LETTERS, *supra* note 31, at 365 (complaining of the "rotten Jewish landlords"); Letter from Fyodor Dostoevsky to Nikolay Grishchenko (February 28, 1878) in V LETTERS, *supra* note 65, at 13 ("the Yids are spreading with horrifying rapidity. And after all, the Yid[s] … are the same thing as a plot against Russians!"); Letter from Fyodor Dostoevsky to Nikolay Dostoevsky (January 1, 1879), in *id.* at 71 ("As for myself, I'm cough-ing like a Yid."); Letter from Fyodor Dostoevsky to Olga Novikova (March 28, 1879), in *id.* at 77 ("How disgusting that the Kutaisi Yids were acquitted."); Letter from Fyodor Dosto-evsky to Anna Dostoevskaya (July 28, 1879), in *id.* at 114–15("[T]he door right next to mine, live two rich Yids … [who] poison my life for me … [and] talk all day and night … and all of that with the most foul Yiddish intonation."); Letter from Fyodor Dostoevsky to Anna Dostoevskaya (July 30, 1879), in *id.*at 119 ("The … adventure was with my Yid neigh-bors … [and] I in fact yelled *when getting into bed:* 'Oh, these damned Yids!'… [and] the Yids had called [the landlady] in and announced to her that they were greatly offended by my calling them *Yids*."); Letter from Fyodor Dostoevsky to Anna Dostoevskaya (August 4, 1879) in *id.* at 124 ("I'm alone, there isn't a single family face. On the contrary it's all such vile Yid mugs."); Letter from Fyodor Dostoevsky to Konstantin Pobedonostev (August 9, 1879), in *id.* at 133 ("[I]t's literally half Yids … [and] in my view Germany, at least Berlin, is be-coming terribly Judaized."); Letter from Fyodor Dostoevsky to Anna Dostoevskaya (August 16, 1879), in *id.* at 144 ("[N]ever in Russia have there been such unscrupulous merchants as there are now in Germany. They're all Yids, the Yids have taken over everything, and they swindle boundlessly."). *See also supra* note 96–98 and accompanying text (describing how his anti-Semitism might have compelled him to stop gambling); ELENA M. KATZ, NEI-THER NOR WITH WITHOUT THEM, THEM: THE RUSSIAN WRITER AND THE JEW IN THE AGE OF REALISM 120 (Syracuse University Press, 2008) (explaining how Dostoevsky "would transform and use Gogolian tropes of the petty Jew to define him as the potent enemy of the Russian people"); GARY ROSENSHIELD, THE RIDICULOUS JEW: THE EXPLOITATION AND TRANSFORMATION OF A STEREOTYPE IN GOGOL, TURGENEV, AND DOSTOEVSKY (Stanford University Press, 2008) (discussing how Dostoevsky stereotyped the Jew as comic, ridicu-lous, obsessed with money, and in league with the devil). *But see* Letter from Fyodor Dos-toevsky to Arkady Kovner (February 14, 1877), in IV LETTERS, *supra* note 32, at 353 ("I'm not at all an enemy of the Jews and never have been one … In all my 50 years of life I've seen that Jews, good and wicked, will refuse to sit down at a table with Russians, while a Russ-ian won't disdain to sit down them. Just who hates whom?").

161. Walter Pater, *The School of Giorgione*, in THE RENAISSANCE 153, 156 (William E. Buckler ed., 1986) (explaining that although poetry, music, and painting are each collected

art it is possible to distinguish the matter from the form, and the understanding can always make this distinction, yet it is the constant effort of art to obliterate it."[162] Dostoevsky's compositions, perhaps more uniquely than those of any narrative artist, attain the musical aspiration by discouraging the excision of meaning from modes of expression. That is, Dostoevsky's style seems to work as if by magic, and articulating what it is that makes it so is like trying to get figs from thistles. Nevertheless, Bakhtin created an idiom for elucidating the Dostoevsky phenomenon.

Drawing from the lexicon of music, Bakhtin calls Dostoevsky "the creator of the polyphonic novel," or a "fundamentally new novelistic genre," whereby his work refuses to "fit any of the preconceived frameworks or historico-literary schemes that we usually apply to various species of the European novel."[163] Bakhtin describes how polyphony enables Dostoevsky to orchestrate a fugue of at times dueling voices performing dialogue and debate:

> A plurality of *independent and unmerged voices and consciousnesses, a genuine polyphony of fully valid voices is in fact the chief characteristic of Dostoevsky's novels.* What unfolds in his works is not a multitude of characters and fates in a single objective world, illuminated by a single authorial consciousness; rather a *plurality of consciousnesses, with equal rights and each with its own world,* combine but are not merged in the unity of the event.[164]

It is this "plurality of *independent and unmerged voices*" that makes Dostoevsky's text treacherously cabalistic for some readers, who are forced to roll up their sleeves and toil to extract message or meaning.[165] Such a "new type of

---

under general category of "art," each form addresses different senses and is peculiar to its own form, like music).

162. *Id.* (stating that all art forms must be measured against music because only music achieves perfect merger of form and matter).

163. BAKHTIN, *supra* note 8, at 7.

164. *Id.* at 6–7 (emphasis in original). *See also* TERRAS, *supra* note 8, at 10 ("Bakhtin showed that Dostoevsky's text creates a polyphonic concert of living voices, one of which is the narrator's (which itself may well be dialogic!), rather than a homophonic narrative dominated by the narrator's voice.") Terras explains that Dostoevsky "will write elegantly only when the voice in question demands it … [and i]f one disregards the 'polyphony' argument, Dostoevsky's highly uneven narrative style, often distinctly colloquial, often journalistic, sometimes chatty, then again lyrical, solemn, or pathetic, places his work with the *roman-feuilleton* and may be legitimately seen as an aesthetic flaw." *Id.*

165. BAKHTIN, *supra* note 8, at 6. *See also* KJETSAA, *supra* note 4, at 335 (discussing Bakhtin's "polyphony" and stating that Dostoevsky "disagreed with the notion that everything in a work of art must be easily comprehended and pleasantly obvious at whatever

artistic thinking," encompassing differing points of view and the *"plurality of consciousnesses,"* lets Dostoevsky induce disquieting uncertainty, and frees him to be the very doubter that he was.[166] As a psychologist, critic of social injustice, and philosopher, Dostoevsky wrestled with paradox, irresolution, and ambiguity. For him, Christianity was likewise a challenge, and as it was for Ivan Karamazov, theodicy chronically bullies faith. Consequently, the novels' scores, replicating life itself, proffer opinion plus dissent, and there are contradictory takes on events, parlayed from multifarious angles.[167] The tenacious dialectic, transcending the mere act of reading, equals an experience analogous to a narrative (even at times combative) Socratic methodology. It so submerges us in the text that we, ceasing to be mere readers, become more like participants in a fugue of divergent ideas, which implicitly invites us to adopt one—or instead just use one, or all, to formulate our own.[168]

IV. The Legal Lens

The legal lens is not a sixth, distinct one, but partners with all others by embracing psychology, socioeconomics, philosophy, and spirituality. Because Dostoevsky is foremost an artist, the legal perspective also necessitates lens five of literary analysis and close attention to technique. Although Dostoevsky was not a lawyer and lacked formal legal training, he was fascinated with the workings of legal institutions, justice and, most notably, the human psyche, especially that of individuals accused of or guilty of crime.

---

price ... [:] 'Let the readers do some of the work themselves,' he would say, defending his right to produce books that were difficult and intricate").

166. Bakhtin, *supra* note 8, at 3, 6. *See also* Kjetsaa, *supra* note 4, at 335 ("One frequent difficulty in arriving at clear, unambiguous conclusions is due to the fact that Dostoyevsky was from many points of view himself a doubter" and even "his Christianity was far from conflict-free."). *See also* Gary Saul Morson, *Sideshadowing and Tempics*, 29 New Literary History 599, 601 (1998) (coining the term "sideshadowing" to apply to Dostoevsky's technique, which "conveys the sense that actual events might just as well not have happened" and that "what exists need not have existed").

167. *Cf.* Morson, *supra* note 166, at 602 (Dostoevsky's "sideshadowing ... permit[s] us to catch a glimpse of unrealized by realizable possibilities, ... [and] demonstrates that our tendency to trace straight lines of causality (usually leading to ourselves at the present moment) oversimplifies events, which always allow for many possible stories.").

168. Kjetsaa, *supra* note 4, at 335 ("Dostoevsky offers no conclusive answers to the questions he poses in his didactic writings, partly because he could not give conclusive answers and partly because he thought it up to his readers to draw their own conclusions.").

Dostoevsky wrote *Demons, A Writer's Diary, The Brothers Karamazov,* and *Crime and Punishment* after the passage of Russian legal reforms in 1864, which installed trial by jury in many criminal cases, the adversarial process, a professional bar, and justices of the peace.[169] The reforms also replaced secret proceedings with open court sessions, ones the public could attend and follow in daily newspaper accounts. These developments had a profound effect on Dostoevsky's work, including *Demons,* which was based on the publicized trial of Sergey Nechaev.[170] Nechaev, a protégé of notorious revolutionary Mikhail Bakunin and leader of the terrorist group, People's Justice, was convicted of ordering the murder of student Ivanov.[171] In *Demons,* with its nihilistic Nikolai Stavrogin and power-crazed Pyotr Stepanovich Verkhovensky, Dostoevsky drew from the case to depict rampant violence used as a political tool, along with a conspiracy, putatively directed from abroad, to demolish the Russian order.[172]

---

169. Gary Rosenshield, Western Law, Russian Justice: Dostoevsky, The Jury Trial, and The Law 20 (University of Wisconsin Press, 2005) ("As a result of the 1864 reforms, jury trials were opened to the public (*'glasnost'*) [and t]he judicial system attained autonomy."). Rosenshield explains that "[j]uries became most representative of all Russian institutions, with jurors recruited from all sectors of the population" and that "[a]n independent judiciary became well established ... and more lawyers became trained and rose to distinction." *Id. See also* Louise McReynolds, Murder Most Russian: True Crime and Punishment in Late Imperial Russia 29–32 (Cornell University Press 2013) (discussing reforms in the Russian legal system); Murav, *supra* note 35, at 55 ("The legal reform ... initiated by the government of Alexander II transformed the trial from a secret written proceeding based on the 'inquisitorial' principle into an open, public, oral proceeding organized to a far greater degree by the adversarial principle.").

170. *See* Frank, *supra* note 7, at 601–602 (discussing the newspaper reports on Nechaev and how "[t]he 'Nechaev affair'—the murder by a secret revolutionary group led by Sergey Nechaev of a student named Ivan Ivanov—had seized Dostoevsky's imagination[,]" and climaxed in Nechaev's appearance in *Demons*). *See also* Letter from Fyodor Dostoevsky to Mikhail Katkov (October 8, 1870), in III Letters, *supra* note 31, at 274–75 ("One of a number of the major events in my story will be the well-known murder of Ivanov in Moscow by Nechaev.").

171. *See generally* Frank, *supra* note 7, at 601–615 (discussing Nechaev and how he worked his way into Dostoevsky's writings); Kjetsaa, *supra* note 4, at 250 (describing the Nechaev incident).

172. *See* Letter from Fyodor Dostoevsky to Mikhail Katkov (October 8, 1870), in III Letters, *supra* note 31, at 275 ("My Pyotr Verkhovensky may not resemble Nechaev at all; but I think that in my stunned mind there has been created by imagination the person, the type that corresponds to that villainy."); *id.* ("This other character (Nikolay Stavrogin) is also a gloomy character, also a villain. But I think that this character is a tragic one ..."). *See also supra* note 37 and accompanying text (discussing what inspired *Demons*).

In *A Writer's Diary*, a mélange of fiction, journalism, and autobiography, Dostoevsky engrossed himself in jury trials and sporadically carped at legal outcomes.[173] Sometimes, new defense strategies, such as temporary insanity, and the then-fashionable treatment of hostile socioeconomic forces as the guilty culprits, annoyed the *Diary*'s author.[174] Dostoevsky also denounced some courtroom histrionics and the exploitation of rhetoric whereby deft lawyers could, by waxing poetic, effectively recast victims into perpetrators (or vice versa).[175]

One *Diary* highlight is the critique of renowned attorney Vladimir Spasovich, who represented Stanislav Kronenberg, accused of child abuse.[176] When Kronenberg, who maltreated his daughter and kept her locked in a room, discovered that the seven-year old had stolen her stepmother's prune, he beat her for a quarter of an hour with a rod, comprised of nine rowan switches, and only halted when he himself nearly collapsed from exhaustion.[177] Spasovich, however, managed to convince the jury that Kronenberg, who had graciously accepted paternity of the child, was pure as driven snow, and that the little girl,

---

173. *See generally* FRANK, *supra* note 7, at 723–59 (discussing the launch of *A Writer's Diary*). Frank explains that the *Diary* "was an adventurous gamble that marked a new stage in his astonishing career" and that it enabled Dostoevsky to "reach[] out to a much larger and diversified reading public, to whom he spoke eloquently and passionately about matters that were uppermost in the minds of all literate Russians." *Id.* at 723. He points out that "[m]uch attention is paid in the *Diary* to criminal trials, which he always regarded as an indispensable barometer of the moral climate of the times." *Id.*

174. *See* Harriet Murav, *Dostoevsky and the Law*, in TEACHING LAW AND LITERATURE 316 (Austin Sarat, Cathrine O. Frank, Matthew Anderson, eds. 2011) (discussing Dostoevsky's fascination with the law, as expressed in the *Diary*).

175. *Id.* ("Dostoevsky is particularly upset by excesses of courtroom oratory, whereby a talented attorney could change the entire emphasis of a case, even representing a victim as a perpetrator."). *See also* MURAV, *supra* note 35, at 126 (noting that Dostoevsky was "dismayed by what he saw as the high numbers of acquittals").

176. FYODOR DOSTOEVSKY, A WRITER'S DIARY 356–384 (Kenneth Lantz, trans. 1994) (1873–1876) (attacking Spasovich and his tactics). *See also* MCREYNOLDS, *supra* note 169, at 38 ("Spasovich is among the best-known prerevolutionary jurists ... [who] enrolled in the law faculty at St. Petersburg University in 1845[, and q]uickly ascendant, he defended two dissertations, the first in maritime law and the second on property relations in Poland, ... [and was] recommended ... for a faculty position in criminal law.") *See generally infra* Chapter III (The Confessant Gene: *Crime and Punishment* and *The Brothers Karamazov*) (discussing how in *The Brothers Karmazov* Mitya's defense counsel is based on Spasovich).

177. DOSTOEVSKY, *supra* note 176, at 356 ("[A] father had whipped his child, a girl of seven, with excessive cruelty" and "[a] stranger ... could not stand the screams of the tortured girl who, for a quarter of an hour (according to the charge), had cried out, 'Papa! Papa!' while being beaten with switches" which "turned out not to be switches but *Spitzruten*—that is, proper sticks—absolutely unthinkable to be applied to someone of seven.").

a thief and liar, was evil incarnate.[178] Spasovich also swayed the jury to see such corporal punishment, which broke no bones, as a deserved, rightful exercise of paternal authority.

Dostoevsky, after sharing his own memory of the swollen, shredded backs of adult Siberian prisoners, flogged with rods like Kronenberg's, rebukes Spasovich's manipulation of language and jury to legitimate the infliction of pain on a child:[179]

> Do you know what it means to abuse a child? Their hearts are full of innocent, almost unconscious love, and blows such as these cause a grievous shock and tears that God sees and will count. For their reason is never capable of grasping their full guilt. Have you seen or heard of little children who were tormented, or of orphans, say, who were raised among wicked strangers? Have you seen a child cowering in a corner trying to hide, and weeping there, wringing his hands (yes, wringing his hands—I've seen it myself) and *beating his chest with his tiny fist*, not knowing himself what he is doing, not clearly un-

---

178. *Id.* at 365 (Spasovich "even repudiated the child and her tender years; he destroyed any pity for the child among his audience and tore it from their hearts by its very roots."). Dostoevsky accuses Spasovich of "telling us about some girl, perverse and corrupt, caught stealing more than once, with a secret vice in her soul, and he seems to forget entirely (and we do as well) that the case concerns an infant who is only seven, and that same *flogging* that lasted a quarter of an hour with those nine 'spitzrutens' of rowan wood would probably have been ten times easier for an adult and even for a fourteen-year-old than it was for this poor, tiny creature!" *Id.* at 376. Fusso explains that Spasovich "resorts to the strategy of dwelling on Mariia Kronenberg's own deficiencies," and several witnesses spoke of "a more mysterious defect," called "'evil propensities and habits' that she acquired from the peasants in Switzerland" while the father testified that "'the little child had vices about which he did not wish to speak." Fusso, *supra* note 123, at 89. At the trial, Nadezhada Prokof'evna Suslova, the first woman doctor in Russia, testified and was the only witness who described the "child's 'secret vice' explicitly without euphemisms." *Id.* Suslova said that "'the girl had bad habits which had a great effect on her health, namely: she engaged in onanism.'" *Id.* at 91. Incidentally, expert witness Suslova is the sister of Polina, with whom Dostoevsky had "a passionate but painful affair." *Id.* at 89. *See also supra* notes 67–72 and accompanying text (discussing Dostoevsky's "Polina era").

179. DOSTOEVSKY, *supra* note 176, at 374 ("I will inform Mr. Spasovich that in the prisoners' wards of the hospital in Siberia I happened to see the backs of prisoners who had just been administered … blows with 'spitzrutens'… and some backs had swollen up nearly two inches (literally) and imagine how little flesh there is on the back … [and] they were precisely this dark-purple color with a few scratches that seeped blood."). *See also infra* Chapter IV (Prisons of Coercion; *Notes from the House of the Dead*) (describing the beatings in *Notes from the House of the Dead*).

derstanding his own guilt or why he is being tormented but sensing all too well that he is not loved?[180]

In another *Diary* entry, one seemingly at variance with his decrial of the Kronenberg child-abuse acquittal,[181] Dostoevsky pursues a point, also raised in *Notes from the House of the Dead*, in which he asserts that because each individual is unique and every crime *sui generis*, uniform penalties are inherently unfair. Dostoevsky, role-playing as lawyer for Ekaterina Kornilova, a pregnant woman convicted of pushing her small stepdaughter out of a window, actually helped secure her eventual acquittal. In the case, the child survived unscathed and Kornilova, who instantly confessed to police, said that she sought revenge on a husband, who made her feel inferior to his first wife and barred her from visiting her family.[182]

---

180. Dostoevsky, *supra* note 176, at 380. *See also* McReynolds, *supra* note 169, at 41 ("Beginning with the premise that a seven-year-old is by virtue of her age an innocent, Dostoevsky was appalled to read Spasovich portraying her as a lying, thieving, masturbating wretch who required corporal punishment."); Rosenshield, *supra* note 169, at 40 ("[W]hat reader would not be shocked upon realizing that this tiny seven-year-old child (*mladenets*) was tortured with instruments similar to those used on hardened criminals and that the perpetrator of the torture was acquitted because no crime had been committed.").

181. Dostoevsky also supported an acquittal for Vera Zasulich, who was indicted for attempting to assassinate the military governor of St. Petersburg. *See generally* Frank, *supra* note 7, at 763–65 (giving account of the trial of Vera Zasulich, which Dostoevsky "felt ... revealed the deep fissures splitting Russian society apart, and which surely filled him with gloomy forebodings"); Kjetsaa, *supra* note 4, at 310–311 (describing how Dostoevsky "horrified his conservative friends by coming out in favor of [Vera Zasulich's] acquittal"). *See* Rosenshield, *supra* note 169, at 25 ("The Zasulich affair probably gave Dostoevsky the idea of incorporating the jury trial in *The Brothers Karamazov*, using it as a means of filtering all his ideas about art, justice, good and evil, salvation, Russia and the West.").

182. Dostoevsky, *supra* note 176, at 642. In a letter, Dostoevsky writes about his visit to Kornilova in the hospital, where she had given birth five days before:

I asked how she had done it. In a cordial, sincere voice she answered: "I don't know myself. It's as though there was someone else's will in me." ... She added to me with sincere expression, that her *"husband comes and cries about her,"* that is showing me: See what a good person he is. She started crying bitterly when recalling the prison police officer's testimony that from the very beginning of her marriage she had hated both her husband and her stepdaughter: "It's not true. I could never have said that. Toward the end it got bitterly hard for me with my husband, I cried all the time, and he kept railing against me, and on the morning when the crime occurred he had beaten me."

Letter from Fyodor Dostoevsky to Konstantin Maslyannikov (November 5, 1876), in IV Letters, *supra* note 32, at 339. *See also* Letter from Fyodor Dostoevsky to Konstantin Maslyannikov (November 21, 1876), in *id.* at 342 ("I have been to see Kornilova again and ... I came away with the same impression ... only perhaps intensified ... I need to

Dostoevsky, strategizing her defense, supplies alternate narratives, one in which Kornilova, pregnant, exhausted, saddled with arduous household duties, and detesting her overbearing husband, reacted impulsively when she "lifted the girl's legs from behind and sent her tumbling out into space."[183] Here Dostoevsky unsteadies his audience's faith in the ability of legal proceedings or juries to reach right results, and in so doing, more broadly intimates that any quest for one unassailable truth is feckless.

With respect to Kornilova, Dostoevsky alternatively suggests that it is within the realm of possibility that people can be both conscious of and unaccountable for their actions.[184] He felt that there was something strange about what Kornilova did, and that a fresh look might prompt reprieve. In her support, Dostoevsky proffers that the pregnant woman might have been suffering from a form of temporary insanity. Although the examining physician concluded that Kornilova acted "consciously," and thus, legal incompetence could not be established, Dostoevsky raises the specter of things that might be done consciously, but without legal culpability.[185] He recounts a childhood tale about a Moscow lady who developed a "passion for stealing" whenever she became pregnant and added: "It is well known that a woman at the time of pregnancy is very often subject to certain strange influences and impressions," which sometimes take on "extraordinary, abnormal, almost absurd forms."[186] If Kornilova had not been pregnant, she might have just fantasized about defenestration, without actually doing it.[187] For Dostoevsky, a jury factoring pregnancy into the calculus might, and should, lean toward mercy. As it turned out, Dostoevsky's plea on Kornilova's behalf led to an appeal, retrial, and an eventual acquittal.[188]

---

arrange things with her lawyer … you are the whole hope, because the Senate … will not decide in her favor."); ROSENSHIELD, *supra* note 169, at 29 (explaining how the "Kornilova case differed radically from the Kronenberg case" because "Dostoevsky became personally involved with the defendant and her cause").

183. DOSTOEVSKY, *supra* note 176, at 642.

184. *Id.* at 644 ("Even medicine surely recognizes that someone can commit an act quite consciously but yet not be fully responsible for committing it.").

185. *Id. See* MURAV, *supra* note 35, at 126–27 ("Dostoevsky's arguments on Kornilova's behalf are based on the plea of temporary insanity, a defense strategy that he will otherwise hold suspect—in the *Diary*, in *Crime and Punishment*, and in the *Brothers Karamazov*.").

186. DOSTOEVSKY, *supra* note 176, at 643–44.

187. *Id.* at 645 (If not pregnant, she might "have sinned in mind but not in deed[, b]ut now, pregnant, *she carried it out.*"). *See* ROSENSHIELD, *supra* note 169, at 71 ("To justify his call for acquittal by reason of what might be called 'pre-partum depression,' Dostoevsky briefly outlines Kornilova's situation at home and her actions directly after the crime.").

188. See Murav, *supra* note 174, at 319 (The case ended in an acquittal after appeal,

The Brothers Karamazov, similar to the *A Writer's Diary*, evokes humbling incertitude about crime, guilt, and justice. Attorney Spasovich, a *Diary* personality, resurfaces in *The Brothers Karamazov* as Mitya's defense counsel, whose final emphasis is that Fyodor Karamazov is a non-father, neglectful of his own sons.[189] Here, as in the *Diary*, Dostoevsky jabs at a legal system that exiles itself from concerns with ascertaining truth. The "famous" Fetyukovich, whose "talent was known everywhere," convinced of his own client's guilt, asserts that when the victim is a father in name only, patricide is not patricide.[190] The "vain" prosecutor, Ippolit Kirillovich, who believed "his talents were not properly appreciated ... and even dreamed of [using the case to] resurrect[...] his flagging career," harbors novelist aspirations.[191] Ivan's guilt over his deathwish for his father and the sense that he tacitly participated in the murder, triggers his mental breakdown in the very courtroom he views as a flawed, even diabolical, venue.

Dostoevsky's rendition of that "fatal day" in the Karamazov case, "publicized all over Russia," in which "all the tickets were snapped up," corroborates Ivan's perspective.[192] Ladies, some of whom "appeared in the gallery of the courtroom extremely dressed up," with "[h]ysterical, greedy, almost morbid curiosity ... on their faces," were rooting for acquittal while "the entire male contingent, as opposed to the ladies, was aroused against the defendant."[193] Along with celebrity Fetyukovich, and supposed psychologist Ippolit Kirillovich, there presides a "rather vain" judge, who, although "educated and humane," is chiefly

---

and "[a]s ... research has shown, the writer's plea for mercy on Kornilova's behalf led to an appeal[,] ... [t]he grounds for [which] ... were based on a legal formality; the same individual had testified both in the capacity of witness and expert."). *See generally* IV LETTERS, *supra* note 32, at 342 n. 2 (The editor notes that "the Senate decided in favor of Kornilova, that approved the appeal for cassation" and "[s]ubsequently, the court reexamined Kornilova's case and acquitted her on the grounds that the case was committed in a state of temporary insanity."). Kjetsaa points out that the "case was reopened and ended in the woman's full acquittal" although "the presiding judge warned members of the jury against allowing themselves to be influenced by 'certain talented authors.'" KJETSAA, *supra* note 4, at 329. Later, Dostoevsky learned in a letter from Kornilova's husband that his wife had died suddenly and "[t]he suspicion of suicide must have given him an unpleasant time." *Id.*

189. KJETSAA, *supra* note 4, at 324 (describing Spasovich as "one of the prototypes of Mitya's defense attorney in *Karamazov*"); Murav, *supra* note 174, at 319 ("Dmitry Karamazov's defense attorney is based on Spasovich.").

190. FYODOR DOSTOEVSKY, BROTHERS KARAMAZOV 658 (Richard Pevear and Larissa Volokhonsky, trans. 1990) (1879–80).

191. *Id.*

192. *Id.* at 656.

193. *Id.* at 657.

concerned with being "a progressive man."[194] The jury, consisting of four "officials, two merchants, and six local peasants and tradesman," incite questions of whether "the fatal decision in such a subtle, complex, and psychological case is to be turned over to a bunch of officials, and even to peasants," and "[w]hat can such people possibly grasp of such a case?"[195]

Dostoevsky *sub silentio* answers both questions respectively with a "no" and "nothing." For Dostoevsky, the infirmity is not the composition of the jury, which includes different castes, even peasants. For him, the impasse is that no jury, no judge, no lawyers, and no readers can or do get a "grasp of such a case," or of any case.[196] Professor Robert Belknap points out that when Dostoevsky was writing *Brothers*, "he distrusted judges, prosecutors, and eloquent lawyers," and that "the long trial … reflects the intensity of his disillusionment with the way the jury system seemed to be shifting from the adversarial pursuit of truth and justice to an amoral contest in rhetorical persuasiveness."[197] Professor Harriet Murav, who similarly remarks that "Dmitry's trial leads neither to a restoration of order nor to the discovery of the truth," adds:[198]

> Knowledge of the events that have transpired becomes uncertain. The narrator confesses that he may not have reported the most important aspects of Dmitry's trial to the readers. Neither the prosecution nor the defense can tell Dmitry's story accurately, and both have been influenced by Smerdyakov, whose own involvement with the murder remains hidden. The defense argues that the prosecutor has been overcome by the need to exercise the psychological gifts for which he is already famous in order to create a "novel" about Dmitry.[199]

Mitya's trial goes beyond reflecting "disillusionment" with the legal system[200] or demonstrating how "[a] lawyer's skill in constructing an aesthetically pleas-

---

194. *Id.* at 658. *See* ROSENSHIELD, *supra* note 169, at 81 ("[I]n *The Brothers Karamazov* Dostoevsky excoriate[es] almost every aspect of court proceedings, including attorneys, witnesses, the public and the press" and "the whole procedure suffers irreparably from the absence of collective spirit (*sobornost'*)" whereby "[e]very participant has his or her own agenda, siding with or against Dmitry for the wrong reasons.").

195. DOSTOEVSKY, *supra* note 190, at 659–660.

196. *Id.* at 660 ("Nevertheless their faces made a certain strangely imposing and almost threatening impression: they were stern and frowning.").

197. Robert Belknap, *The Trial of Mitya Karamazov* in ART, CREATIVITY, AND SPIRITUALITY, *supra* note 6, at 91.

198. Murav, *supra* note 174, at 317.

199. *Id.*

200. Belknap, *supra* note 197, at 91.

ing story may cause a jury to depart from the truth."[201] The trial (and the novel as *gestalt*) bombards readers with a panoply of messy things that are betwixt and between. Even wrongfully convicted Mitya is a paradox, not so unlike his brother, Ivan, who is the guilty, yet guiltless, agent of patricide. In making such a nimbus of contradiction and doubt hover over all of the trial's players—the accused, witnesses, jury, judge, prosecutor, and defense counsel—Dostoevsky broaches the question of whether any mechanism which is concocted and implemented by mortals can ever render right answers, find absolute truth, or effectuate justice.

In contrast to the attenuated Mitya trial, Rodion Raskolnikov's in *Crime and Punishment* is svelte, telling us little more than the fact that Porfiry Petrovich kept his leniency promise and that the perpetrator put himself through living hell for something that really had nothing to do with money. That is, it comes out that Raskolnikov failed to "remember the details of any of the goods he had stolen" and was "even mistaken as to their number."[202] Also, he had never once even tried to peek into the purloined purse, and when he essentially abandoned it, "the largest denominations had suffered serious water damage."[203] Unlike the protracted trials, discussed and presented in *A Writer's Diary* and *The Brothers Karamazov*, the *Crime and Punishment* blip serves to metathetically carry the protagonist from conviction to "gradual rebirth" in Siberia.[204] This is because the novel's topic is not courts, proceedings, justice, or crime. Rather, as developed further in Chapter III, *Crime and Punishment* is a psychological portrait of someone who, although a unique human being, is also a species of offender, the kind that craves confession, suffering, acceptance of responsibility, and spiritual transformation.[205]

Crime and Punishment, with its disturbing protagonist, whose murder is ostensibly nihilistic and inexplicable, has tantalized legal scholars, who have stared at it from every conceivable angle. For a long time, scholars, obsessed with motive, have pointed to all sorts of personal, psychological, monetary, and

---

201. Murav, *supra* note 174, at 317.

202. FYODOR DOSTOYEVSKY, CRIME AND PUNISHMENT 638 (David McDuff ed., Penguin Books 2003) (1866)

203. *Id. See also* RONNER, *supra* note 6, at 119–121 (refuting the putative monetary motive that is sometimes assigned to impoverished Raskolnikov).

204. DOSTOYEVSKY, *supra* note 202, at 656.

205. *See* RONNER, *supra* note 6, at 89–146 (arguing that *Crime and Punishment* is "not just an exposé of the subliminal forces that propel a criminal to accept responsibility for a heinous act[,] ... [but also] a testimonial to confession as a celebrated event, as the prime catalyst for deep moral, spiritual, and psychological regeneration.").

philosophical demons at play within Raskolnikov.[206] Others, like Professor William Burnham, are more concerned with the backdrop of the legal system. He, relying on Russian legal history, considers the evidentiary rules in place at the time of *Crime and Punishment* and traces the strategy of Porfiry Petrovich, the examining magistrate, to Russia's stringent requirements for admissible confessions.[207] On the other hand, attorney Vera Bergelson tries to contemporize the novel by conducting a "hypothetical retrial" of Rodion Raskolnikov under the legal and moral principles reflected in the Model Penal Code.[208]

Studies, like those of Burnham and Bergelson, are, of course, instructive and intriguing, but they do not tap into the real core of *Crime and Punishment*—namely, confession, which has long troubled the United States Supreme Court and criminal justice experts.[209] Although the novel entails a brutal murder of two women, its real focus is not on the crime itself, but on its aftermath, on Raskolnikov's psychological anguish, and on what eventually preempts all else— the murderer's need, or rather compulsion, to come clean. As Chapter III posits, *Crime and Punishment* can shed light on today's criminal investigations, along with the defense bar's reflex to "treat confession as a Pandora box that should remain hermetically sealed at all costs."[210] In this respect, several legal commentators, including myself, have suggested that this "great Russian novel is a

---

206. *Id.* at 108–109 (discussing "[h]istorians, literary scholars, philosophers, psychiatrists, and psychologists [who] have exhaustively feasted on Raskolnikov, trying to understand his motives for violently murdering the old moneylender."); *id.* at 117–22 (discussing and refuting the various theories about Raskolnikov's motives for the crime). *See also supra* notes 122, 125–27 and accompanying text (discussing the psychological and socioeconomic theories with respect to Raskolnikov and his crime).

207. William Burnham, *The Legal Context and Contributions of Dostoyevsky's* Crime and Punishment, 100 MICH. L. REV. 1227 (2002)

208. Vera Bergelson, *Crimes and Defenses of Rodion Raskolnikov*, 85 KY. L.J. 919, 921 (1996–97).

209. *See generally* RONNER, *supra* note 6, at 89–148 (exploring confession in *Crime and Punishment*); Robert F. Cochran, *Crime, Confession, and the Counselor-At-Law: Lessons from Dostoyevsky*, 35 HOUS. L. REV. 327, 365–66 (1968) ("Though Dostoevsky's characters emphasize the psychological and rational effects of confession, some of his characters [like those in *Crime and Punishment*] recognize eternal implications."); Paul J. Contino, *Zosima, Mikhail, and Prosaic Confessional Dialogue in Dostoevsky's* Brothers Karamazov, 27.1 STUD. IN THE NOVEL 63, 63 (1995) (showing how Dostoevsky's "confessors," including Sonya Marmeladov in *Crime and Punishment*, "assist others when they are most violently fractured and self-destructive").

210. RONNER, *supra* note 6, at 53. *See also* Cochran, *supra* note 209, at 331. ("[T]he common practice of lawyers is to rush to the police station or corporate office and tell the client not to talk to anyone about the offense," and "many lawyers tell their clients that they do not want to know whether the client committed the crime.").

veritable testimonial to confession as a potentially celebrated event, as the prime catalyst for deep moral, spiritual and psychological regeneration."[211]

Also, as explored in Chapter III, mainly in connection with *The Brothers Karamazov*, Dostoevsky questions whether confession can and should even play a role in a jurisprudence, constructed and implemented by mortals. Dostoevsky here and elsewhere, funnels out, beyond what is literally *law* material, beyond the circumference of crimes and investigations, to panoramically scan the variegated shapes, causes, and aftermaths of confession.

The law lens, of course, naturally seduces readers to zero in on the blatantly legal events in books, like *Demons, A Writer's Diary, The Brothers Karamazov*, and *Crime and Punishment*, in hopes of extracting gnomic sound bites about offenders, crimes, trials, and punishment. While such a pursuit can be fun and fruitful, Dostoevsky knows that the law resists that kind of confinement. Rather, Dostoevsky sees the law for what it is—timeless, protean, and ubiquitously presiding over all facets of life. Also, according to him, the law is anthropocentric and inevitably raises a range of human questions.[212] Good practitioners, scholars, and judges, who ineluctably shut their laptops and leave libraries, offices, or chambers to consort with flesh and blood people, do not disagree. Counsel, judges, and even clients and juries, the very modules of the legal landscape, implicitly propel the law into other dimensions, like psychology, socioeconomics, philosophy, and theophany. Judges, who are not merely purging dockets and awaiting pensions, or lawyers, at least ones not living to just deposit retainers, churn files, and perfunctorily march off to combat, have to recurrently pause to appreciate the omnipresent mystery of "what it means to be human."[213]

Dostoevsky believed that an individual's comportment, along with his or her treatment of others, can be either ligature to or rupture with the self, human race, and God.[214] As *A Writer's Diary* admonishes, language is power: legal advocacy, poetics, rhetoric and stylistic strategy can serve any master, be it good or evil.[215] Through the medium of language, with all its frustrating

---

211. RONNER, *supra* note 6, at 92. *See also* Cochran, *supra* note 209.

212. *See* SCANLAN, *supra* note 139, at 9. *See also supra* notes 152–60 and accompanying text (discussing Dostoevsky's anthropocentric philosophy and spirituality).

213. SCANLAN, *supra* note 139, at 9. *See also supra* notes 152–60 and accompanying text (discussing Dostoevsky's anthropocentric philosophy and spirituality).

214. *See supra* notes 156–60 and accompanying text (discussing Dostoevsky's spirituality and understanding of what it means to be a Christian).

215. *See supra* notes 175–80 and accompanying text (examining Dostoevsky's examples in *A Writer's Diary* of how lawyers can manipulate language and poetic techniques).

limitations, lawyers, lay people, and writers strive to express "inexpressible ideas."[216]

V. The Organization of The Book

This book does not just examine Dostoevsky's offenders, crimes, investigations, trials, and punishments. Instead the next four chapters aspire to illuminate how law, in its broadest sense, operates in Dostoevsky's writings.

Chapter II cordons the concept of testamentary capacity, along with the psychiatric definitions of "bizarre" and "non-bizarre" delusions, to Dostoevsky's thesis in *The Double*, one of Dostoevsky's early, but lesser known, novels.[217] In *The Double*, civil servant Golyadkin suddenly meets his identical twin, who ostensibly wreaks havoc on his life. From day one, this novel generated controversy, not just over its meaning, but also over whether Golyadkin is mentally ill or sane. This chapter explores Dostoevsky's technique of obfuscation and retraction, in conjunction with his implicit proposition that, in many instances, lawyers (or mere mortals) are incapable of discerning a line between reality and insane delusion.

Chapter III, focusing mainly on *Crime and Punishment* and *The Brothers Karamazov*, juxtaposes Dostoevsky's work with confession jurisprudence. It aims to depict what has been the United States Supreme Court's fixation with external factors and its perennial struggle to implement safeguards and rules to precipitate a free, voluntary, and true confession. In contrast to the Supreme Court, Dostoevsky is *the* confession expert: in all of his books, characters spill their guts, divulge secrets, and even take credit for things they did not do. While some of these confessants have no contact with official interrogators or external coercive forces, their confessions are nevertheless neither free nor voluntary, and, at times, they are completely fabricated. After analyzing a sampling of the novels' confessants, this chapter closes with Dostoevsky's perspective on one of the thorniest criminal procedure issues.

Chapter IV, shifting from investigatory issues to post-conviction, turns to Dostoevsky's autobiographical novel, *Notes From the House of the Dead*, and anatomizes the prison environment that conspires to strip Siberian inmates of

---

216. DOSTOEVSKY, *supra* note 1, (Dostoevsky's belief, articulated by Ippolit of *The Idiot* that our most important ideas are inexpressible).

217. AM. PSYCHIATRIC ASS'N, DIAGNOSTIC AND STATISTICAL MANUAL OF MENTAL DISORDERS: DSM-V-TM 87(5th ed. 2013) (Defining "bizarre" and "non-bizarre" delusions) [hereinafter "DSM"].

their free will and human dignity. The chapter, shifting from nineteenth-century Russia to America today, returns to the topic of confessions to revisit the rise and fall of free will and human dignity under the seminal Due Process Clause and *Miranda* cases.[218] It tracks not just the progressive dismemberment of *Miranda*, but dissects the reasoning in more recent Supreme Court confession decisions, like *Maryland v. Shatzer*[219] and *Howes v. Fields*,[220] which act as such a detriment in the lives of prison inmates. In this regard, the chapter aims to show not only how such trends in the law condone, and even encourage, tactics that resemble the dehumanization that once presided over Dostoevsky's notorious torture chamber, but also how they impact all people—even those living outside prison walls.

Chapter V, the Conclusion, winding back to Chapter I, returns to the four intertwined generalizations about Dostoevsky's life and work. It hopes to show how Dostoevsky's lifelong efforts to express that "inexpressible idea" can advance our own insights into the law, including mental capacity doctrines, confessions, and prisons.[221] Beyond that, it will suggest that Dostoevsky did express that "inexpressible idea" by answering the overarching question of what it means to be human and live morally in a world comprised of imperfect legal constructs.[222]

---

218. Miranda v. Arizona, 384 U.S. 436 (1966).
219. 130 S. Ct. 1213 (2010).
220. 132 S. Ct. 1181 (2012).
221. DOSTOEVSKY, *supra* note 1.
222. *Id.*

Chapter Two

The Impenetrable Mental Capacity Doctrine: *The Double*

I. Introduction

In Fyodor Dostoevsky's novel, *The Double*, Mr. Golyadkin, a civil servant, meets his identical twin:

> Sitting on *his* bed, also wearing a hat and coat, smiling slightly, puckering up his eyes and tipping him a friendly nod, was the stranger. Mr. Golyadkin wanted to scream, but could not—wanted to make some form of protest, but lacked the power. His hair stood on end, and he collapsed senseless with horror on the spot. And small wonder. He had fully recognized his friend of the night. It was none other than himself—Mr. Golyadkin ... Another Mr. Golyadkin, but exactly the same as him ... It was, in short, his double ...[1]

The Double, a product of the twenty-four year old Russian genius and only his second published work,[2] was published during Dostoevsky's pre-Siberian period, a time when Dostoevsky was shaping his own "personal and literary identity."[3] Although the author himself was never quite satisfied with *The Dou-*

---

1. FYODOR DOSTOEVSKY, THE DOUBLE (George Bird trans., 1958) (1846), *reprinted in* GREAT SHORT WORKS OF FYODOR DOSTOEVSKY, 44 (1st Perennial Classics ed. 2004). This chapter refers to the main character in *The Double* as "Golyadkin," while others translate his name as "Goljadkin." Both are acceptable and refer to the same character. This chapter is a substantially revised and expanded version of an article, originally published in *Capital University Law Review*, 40 Cap. U. L. Rev. 195 (2012).

2. Ronald Hingley, *Introduction* to GREAT SHORT WORKS OF FYODOR DOSTOEVSKY, at ix (1st Perennial Classics ed. 2004).

3. *See* Richard Rosenthal, M.D., *Dostoevsky's Experiment with Projective Mechanisms And The Theft of Identity in* The Double, in 31 RUSSIAN LITERATURE AND PSYCHOANALYSIS 59, 59 (Daniel Rancour-Laferriere ed., 1989).

ble [4]—one of the great, but lesser known, Russian novels—it dispatches a time-less message that not only speaks to today's lawyers, judges, and legal scholars, but also could motivate us to re-think legal concepts of mental capacity.

While Siberia was a turning point in Dostoevsky's career, the brilliance of his fiction, along with his psychological insights, was evident before his imprisonment.[5] What we see in his later novels, particularly *Crime and Punishment, The House of the Dead, Demons,* and *Brothers Karamozov,* is an evolved perspective, not just on the law and the workings of the justice system, but also on the human psyche, which was not limited to just individuals accused of crime.[6] Even before Siberia, Dostoevsky, who himself had suicidal tendencies and suffered from nervous attacks, seizures, and hallucinations, acquired expertise in mental illness and instability.[7] Psychological nuggets of wisdom

---

4. Dimitri Chizhevsky, *The Theme of the Double in Dostoevsky,* in DOSTOEVKSY: A COLLECTION OF CRITICAL ESSAYS 112 (1965) (discussing Dostoevsky's disappointment with the story's form); JOHN JONES, DOSTOEVSKY 83, 83–84 (Oxford University Press,1983) (discussing the author's feelings of failure about the story); David Gasperetti, The Double: *Dostoevskij's Self-Effacing Narrative* 33 THE SLAVIC & E. EUR. J. 217, 217–218 (1989) (analyzing Dostoevsky's "grave doubts" about the novel); Lonny Roy Harrison, *Duality and the Problem of Moral Self-Awareness in Dostoevsky's* Dvoinik (The Double), 188–89 (unpublished Ph.D. thesis, University of Toronto) (on file with this book's author) (explaining that some of Dostoevsky's discontent with the novel and desire to rework it was due to the critics' unflattering assessments). *See also infra* III. B (*The Double*: the Critics) (describing the reaction on the part of his contemporaries to *The Double*).

5. *See* William Burnham, *The Legal Context and Contributions of Dostoyevsky's* Crime and Punishment, 100 MICH. L. REV.1227, 1228 (2002) (discussing the significance of the Siberian experience in Dostoevsky's career); JOSEPH FRANK, DOSTOEVSKY: THE MIRACULOUS YEARS, 1865–1871, 3 (1995) (describing the period following exile as "the most remarkable in Dostoevsky's career...."). *See also infra* Chapter IV (Prisons of Coercion: *Notes from the House of the Dead*) (discussing *Notes From the House of the Dead*).

6. *See* David McDuff, *Translator's Introduction,* FYODOR DOSTOYEVSKY, THE HOUSE OF THE DEAD 7 (David McDuff trans., Penguin Books 2003) (1861) (also called *Notes From the House of the Dead*) (noting that while in prison, Dostoevsky wrote to his brother Mikhail, "I had got to know something of the convict population back in Tobolsk; here in Omsk I was to live for four years in close proximity to it. These men were coarse, irritable and malicious.") Burnham, *supra* note 5, at 1228–29 ("[T]he experience in Siberia threw Dostoevsky together for several years with a wide variety of ordinary and political offenders. This experience undoubtedly informed him well and piqued his curiosity about the nature of both crime and its punishment."). *See also infra* Chapter IV (Prisons of Coercion: *Notes from the House of the Dead*) (discussing *Notes From the House of the Dead*).

7. *See generally* Letter from Fyodor Dostoevsky to Stepan Yanovsky (November 1–2, 1867) in II DOSTOEVSKY LETTERS, 1860–67, at 289 (David Lowe, ed. & trans. Ardis Publishers, 1989) [hereinafter II LETTERS] ("My memory has grown completely dim ... I don't recognize people anymore; I forget what I read the day before. I'm afraid of going mad or

surface in the *The Double*, which, as discussed below, is an important but sadly underrated novel.

The Double is an uncomfortable story, not just because it forces readers to experience the kind of living hell that most hope to avoid, but also because its thesis is something people prefer to block. Despite the many debates over the enigmatic *The Double*, commentators and scholars tend to concede that with respect to the protagonist, Golyadkin, they are never quite sure what is really happening and what is mere hallucination.[8] This poses one big question: Does Golyadkin really have a double?[9] Masterfully conjuring uncertainty, Dostoevsky leaves readers with an unsated hunger for the answer.

---

falling into idiocy."). *See also* JONES, *supra* note 4, at 107 (discussing Dostoevsky's suicidal impulses and how he "showed signs of being really ill" and stating that "the main reason why experts still argue about the origins of his epilepsy is that his own letters … and accounts of him by others, are strewn with references to nervous attacks spasms, seizures, fits, faintings, hallucinations."); Brian R. Johnson, *Intersecting Nervous Disorders in Dostoevksy's* The Insulted and the Injured, 16 DOSTOEVSKY STUD. 73, 73 (2012) (discussing Dostoevsky's nervous disorder, "characterized by lightheadedness, dizziness, occasional fainting spells and aural hallucinations" and how this condition surfaces in his fiction.) Lawrence Kohlberg, *Psychological Analysis and Literary Form: A Study of the Doubles in Dostoevsky*, 92 DAEDALUS 345, 354 (1963) (discussing potential effects of Dostoevsky's severe epilepsy).

   8. *See e.g.*, Julian W. Connolly, *The Ethical Implications of Narrative Point of View in Dostoevsky's* The Double, XVII DOSTOEVSKY STUD. 99, 107 (2013 (explaining how "[m]any critics have found the overall presentation of Golyadkin's story to be disorienting or confusing" because "it is not clear whether Goliadkin is entirely imagining the existence of his double"); Gasperetti, *supra* note 4, at 225 ("*The Double* completely upsets normal reading strategies … [E]ach turn of the page leaves [the reader] more and more confused as to what, if anything, has really taken place"); Rosenthal, *supra* note 3, at 78 (discussing the confusion in *The Double* as to "what is real and what is not."); Nikolaj S. Trubeckoj, *The Style of "Poor Folk" and "The Double"* 7 AM. SLAVIC & E. EUR. REV. 150, 163 (1948) ("Real happenings and hallucinations are so mixed that one can no longer separate the two, cannot tell what really happened or what took place in the sick mind of [Goljadkin].").

   9. There are scholars that suggest that the Double exists partially or solely in Golyadkin's consciousness. *See, e.g.*, JONES, *supra* note 4, at 82–83 ("As the novel proceeds and 'our hero' and the Double sometimes become Messrs Golyadkin Senior and Junior respectively, Dostoevsky can be felt nudging us towards the conclusion that the two are also one and that the pinching and prodding register the pains of consciousness."); Chizhevsky, *supra* note 4, at 115 (describing the Double as a "delusion" that "entered Golyadkin's soul."); Gasperetti, *supra* note 4, at 222 (suggesting the possibility that the Double, along with everything else in the novel is all a dream or the result of Golyadkin's "feverish imagination."); Kohlberg, *supra* note 6, at 350 ("[Dostoevsky] intended … [the Double] to be a hallucination representing the assertive, shameless impulses which first 'propelled' Golyadkin I into his patron's ballroom…."). Others believe that the Double is objectively real. *See e.g.*, Harrison, *supra* note 4, at 121 ("The authenticity of the double is never called into

While *The Double* appears to have nothing to do with the law and has not caught the attention of legal scholars, this chapter suggests what could irritate staunch traditionalists—namely, that the law school curriculum should embrace Dostoevsky's novel. It is this chapter's narrow thesis that *The Double* debunks, or at least sheds doubt, on traditional mental capacity and insane delusion doctrines. On the broadest level, this chapter, partitioned into four parts, explores Dostoevsky's proposition that in many instances, lawyers (or mere mortals) are incapable of determining unsound mind and insane delusions. In fact, Dostoevsky questions whether an objective reality even exists.

Although the mental capacity concept arises in diverse areas of the law, Part II of this chapter focuses mainly on wills and trusts, partly because it is manageable and purports to have a sacrosanct policy favoring testamentary freedom.[10] Under that policy, aiming to protect individuals' ability to control the disposition of their property upon death, courts are commanded not to impose their

---

question. All secondary characters acknowledge the presence of both Golyadkins.");Hingley, *supra* note 2, at ix ("[T]he second Golyakdin … is treated entirely as a matter of course in the office where both Golyadkins work; no one is inclined to regard this [as] astonishing and impossible."). *But see* Deborah A. Martinsen, *Introduction*, in NOTES FROM UNDERGROUND, THE DOUBLE AND OTHER STORIES xiii, xix (Barnes and Noble Books, 2003) ("Dostoevsky … signals his literary mastery by creating a narrative ambiguity around Golyadkin Junior's objective existence: All … could be happening in Golyadkin's head [a]nd yet, Golyadkin's double does seem to have an objective existence, since other people see and interact with him.").

10. *See generally* Jane B. Baron, *Empathy, Subjectivity, and Testamentary Capacity*, 24 SAN DIEGO L. REV. 1043, 1043 (1987) ("The law of wills … is premised on the importance of effectuating a person's wishes as to the disposition of his or her property after death. Courts may not judge the wisdom of those wishes because the testator's ends are personal and individual to him or her alone."); Susanna I. Blumenthal, *The Deviance of the Will: Policing the Bounds of Testamentary Freedom in Nineteenth Century America*, 119 HARV. L. REV. 959, 966–76 (2006) (discussing the history of testamentary freedom from the Roman Republic to the present); Bradley E.S. Fogel, *The Completely Insane Law of Partial Insanity: The Impact of Monomania on Testamentary Capacity*, 42 REAL PROP. PROB. & TR.J. 67, 72 (2007) ("Testamentary freedom—the ability of a decedent to control the disposition of his property at death—is a fundamental tenet of American Law."); Ashbel G. Gulliver & Catherine J. Tilson, *Classification of Gratuitous Transfers*, 51 YALE L.J. 1, 2 (1941) ("One fundamental proposition is that, under a legal system recognizing the individualistic institution of private property and granting to the owner the power to determine his successors in ownership, the general philosophy of the courts should favor giving effect to an intentional exercise of that power."); John H. Langbein, *Substantial Compliance with the Wills Act*, 88 HARV. L. REV. 489, 491 (1975) ("The first principle of the law of wills is freedom of testation."); Melanie B. Leslie, *The Myth of Testamentary Freedom*, 38 ARIZ. L. REV. 235, 235 (1996) ("Courts and scholars often treat freedom of testation as if it were a fundamental tenet of [the] liberal legal tradition.").

morals, biases, or preconceptions on estate plans.[11] They are told to respect the testator's judgment and refrain from either re-doing a will or trust or supplanting it with one of their own.[12]

Despite the stronghold of testamentary freedom, courts have, in some cases, limited or eradicated a decedent's ability to direct the disposition of property upon death.[13] One instance is where contestants successfully argue lack of mental capacity or "insane delusion" or "monomania" to invalidate wills that either omit them entirely or slight them as beneficiaries.[14] While some commentators snipe at the doctrines and the way courts have construed them, the mental capacity rule endures and remains indelibly ingrained in our law.[15]

---

11. *See* Baron, *supra* note 10, at 1043 ("Courts may not judge the wisdom of those [testamentary] wishes.").

12. *Id.*(noting "the importance of effectuating a person's wishes").

13. As in most things, there are limitations on testamentary freedom: for example, elective share statutes prohibit testators from disinheriting their spouses and under certain circumstances, pretermission statutes bar testators from disinheriting children. *See* JESSE DUKEMINIER & ROBERT H. SITKOFF, WILLS, TRUSTS, AND ESTATES (9th ed. 2013) at 511–77. *See also* Baron, *supra* note 10, at 1046 (discussing the "obvious and important limitations on the freedom granted the testator" which are "regulatory in purpose and effect" and "are designed not to effectuate private intent, but to defeat it in furtherance of explicitly identified social goals").

14. *See generally* DUKEMINIER & SITKOFF, *supra* note 13, at 274–83 (exploring the insane delusion doctrine). Wills can also be challenged on the basis of lack of mental capacity, *id.* at 266–74; undue influence, *id.* at 283–13; duress, *id.* at 313–17; and fraud, *id.* at 317–20. *See also* Baron, *supra* note 10, at 1055–56 (discussing the sound mind and insane delusion doctrines); Blumenthal, *supra* note 10 (discussing "monomania"); Fogel, *supra* note 10, at 102–11 (criticizing the doctrine of monomania or insane delusion, which permits a court to invalidate a will). *But see infra* notes 23–25 and accompanying text (discussing attempts to harmonize mental capacity and insane delusion doctrines with testamentary freedom). Wills may be challenged on other grounds, including failure to satisfy state statutory requirements. *See* DUKEMINIER & SITKOFF, *supra* note 13, at 147–263 (exploring wills, formalities, and forms); Lawrence A. Frolik, *The Biological Roots of the Undue Influence Doctrine: What's Love Got to Do With It?*, 57 U. PITT. L. REV. 841, 847 (1966) ("Most fundamentally, a will can be challenged as being invalid because it does not meet the statutory technical requirements.").

15. Several scholars have pointed out flaws in decisions based on the insane delusion doctrine and other challenges lodged in will contests. *See, e.g.,* Pamela Champine, *Expertise and Instinct in the Assessment of Testamentary Capacity*, 51 VILL. L. REV. 25, 49 (2006) (discussing how some courts "identify whether the testator had the capability of exercising the requisite judgment to make a will ... [by] examin[ing] the content of the will that the testator's judgment produced," which is "associated with the policy of protecting the testator's family rather than fairness per se, because it is the closest family members who most typically will benefit from a successful will contest"); Fogel, *supra* note 10, at 70–71 (argu-

Although in wills law, sound mind and insane delusion are legal constructs, this chapter, borrowing from contemporary psychiatric definitions of "bizarre" and "non-bizarre," connects the science with Dostoevsky's thesis in *The Double*.[16]

Part III, shifting from law to Dostoevsky, summarizes the story in *The Double* and the debate over the meaning of the novel and whether Golyadkin is mentally ill or sane. This part suggests that the controversy belies the fact that in *The Double* readers cannot distinguish between what is real and what is hallucination. Dostoevsky intentionally keeps readers in limbo, leaving them to wonder if anything at all really happens to his Golyadkin. Dostoevsky thus compels his readers to surrender to what he suggests is an exercise in futility: the quest to find a precise boundary between the objective and subjective spheres.

Part III, linking Dostoevsky's thesis to the traditional mental capacity doctrines, suggests that Golyadkin, as do many testators, would baffle fact finders if his psyche were under the will-contest microscope. Moreover, it seeks to show that the uncertainty in *The Double* mirrors the disquieting dubiousness of will-contests, particularly in litigation in which individuals are alleged to have "non-bizarre" delusions.

Part IV concludes by revisiting the one (or two) Golyadkin(s), who not only disclose(s) the most deleterious effect of current capacity law, but also invite(s) us to consider whether it is even worthwhile to believe that there is *a* truth.

II. Testamentary Freedom and the Mental Capacity Doctrine

Our legal system, founded on the individualistic institution of private property, empowers property owners to determine their successors in ownership.[17]

---

ing that the "standards for monomania ... provide fact-finders—both judges and juries—with significant leeway to express their biases" and that "[g]enerally, these biases run in favor of traditional dispositive schemes, such as leaving property only to close family and treating all children equally"); Milton D. Green, *Proof of Mental Incompetency and the Unexpressed Major Premise*, 53 Yale L. J. 271, 278–79 (1944) (discussing cases in which courts validated wills even when testators lacked mental capacity because the courts approved of the wills and found their contents to be reasonable); Melanie B. Leslie, *supra* note 10 (pointing out that will contest doctrines can end up defeating testamentary freedom when estate plans do not adhere to what courts feel is the normative disposition).

16. *See infra* Part II. B. (defining "bizarre" and "non-bizarre").

17. *See* Baron *supra* note 10, at 1043; Blumenthal, *supra* note 10, at 975; *infra* notes 23–32 and accompanying text (discussing the theory and policies underlying testamentary freedom). *See also* Hodel v. Irving, 481 U.S. 704 (1987) (holding that the abolition of the

At least in theory, testamentary freedom is sacrosanct: courts are told to give effect to the intent of decedents who dispose of property by will or will substitute.[18] Courts are commanded not to impose their morals, biases, or preconceptions on estate plans.[19] Instead, courts are ordered to honor the testator's judgment and refrain from either re-writing an estate plan or substituting it with their own.[20]

Despite such deification of freedom of testation, often denominated the "fundamental tenet of our liberal legal tradition," the system has limited a decedent's ability to direct the disposition of property upon death.[21] Contestants can avail themselves of lack of mental capacity or "insane delusion" to invalidate wills that either omit them entirely or diminish their shares as beneficiaries.[22] The law, straining to harmonize the mental capacity requirement with testamentary freedom, implies that when an unsound or delusional mind affects an estate plan, the will or trust does not reflect, and in fact frustrates, true intent.[23] Thus, in the name of testamentary freedom, courts find and then implement what should have been that true intent if the testator had not been mentally infirm or deluded.[24] Too often such a rationalization is disin-

---

right to pass property upon death can be a taking within the meaning of the Just Compensation Clause).

18. *See* Baron *supra* note 10, at 1043.

19. *Id.* at 1049; Leslie, *supra* note 10, at 235.

20. *See* Baron, *supra* note 10, at 1057.

21. Leslie, *supra* note 10, at 235.

22. Frolik, *supra* note 14, at 848–49.

23. *See generally* Baron, *supra* note 10, at 1048 (discussing how the mental capacity doctrine "can be understood [as] guarantee[ing] that the testator is capable of forming the intent which the law is designed to protect," and how that "perspective illustrates the individualism of wills law ... [which] ensures that the wishes appearing in the will 'truly' are the testator's own"); Frolik, *supra* note 14, at 849–50 ("[C]ourts are justified in disallowing a will that reflects a serious misappreciation of reality since the delusion has caused an outcome that is inconsistent with the testator's true intent (that is, what would have been the intent but for the insane delusion).").

24. Fogel, *supra* note 10, at 75 n.45 ("Of course, if the testator did not have capacity when he executed the will, it is unclear whether the purported will is an accurate statement of the testator's testamentary intent," arguably allowing a court to reject a will "out of respect for testamentary freedom"). *But see id.* at 74–75 ("To some extent, the requirement of testamentary capacity inherently conflicts with respect for testamentary freedom" and "[w]hen a court rejects a will, the court is failing to implement the testator's desires as expressed in the purported will."); Leslie, *supra* note 10, at 236, 268, 288 (questioning whether courts truly value testamentary freedom and showing how courts tend to manipulate doctrines to ensure that estates fit their normative values).

genuous and the court is just shredding the will to replace it with one of its own.[25]

Other policies sustain mental capacity doctrine. The sound-mind rule serves to protect the family: when relatives or children bestow resources, love, and comfort on a declining testator, the law impliedly reciprocates with remuneration.[26] Further, the mental capacity rule aims to grant testators peace of mind that their wishes will be honored if they try to undo their will or trust after their mental condition deteriorates.[27] The testamentary capacity doctrine recognizes that the elderly, especially the senile or incompetent, can be vulnerable to unscrupulous people, who seek to exploit or unduly influence them.[28]

Although the reasons behind the rule that will-makers be of sound mind and free of insane delusions are salutary, another goal, that of promoting public perception of the law as legitimate, is quite significant.[29] There is an aspiration that our legal institutions, including those governing succession of property, will be seen as sensible.[30] People want to believe that courts are adept

---

25. *See infra* Part II.B.2.a (discussing how courts can be motivated by bias to invalidate wills).

26. *See* Baron, *supra* note 10, at 1050 (discussing how some individuals have suggested "that the mental capacity requirement has little to do with effectuating individuals' choices but instead is designed to protect the testator's family from disinheritance"); Champine, *supra* note 15, at 44 (discussing the "norm of reciprocity" theory based on "implicit understandings between testators and beneficiaries involving reciprocal exchanges [that] should be enforced" and explaining that this norm "looks to the testator's interactions with individuals rather than the familial relationship per se to define fairness"); Milton D. Green, *Public Policies Underlying the Law of Mental Incompetency*, 38 MICH. L. REV. 1189, 1218 (1940) ("The argument that mental soundness as a prerequisite to testamentary capacity is bottomed upon the policy of the law to protect the family...."); Leslie, *supra* note 10, at 246 (discussing the "unspoken presumption that a testator would always want to benefit family members as opposed to others...."); Amy D. Ronner, *Homophobia: In the Closet and in the Coffin*, 21 LAW & INEQ. 65, 72 (2003) (explaining that "if the named beneficiaries are spouses, children, or other [traditional] family members, courts typically refrain from entangling themselves in the decedent's motives or morals" and are less inclined to invalidate the wills).

27. DUKEMINIER & SITKOFF, *supra* note 13, at 265 (describing the law "governing will contests" as "attempts to balance the risk of giving effect to an involuntary act of testation with the risk of denying effect to a voluntary one.").

28. *Id.* at 265–66 ("If courts are too reluctant to set aside a will, the unscrupulous will find profit in subverting vulnerable testators.").

29. *See generally* Amy D. Ronner, *When Courts Let Insane Delusions Pass the Rational Basis Test: The Newest Challenge to Florida's Exclusion of Homosexuals from Adoption*, 21 U. FLA. J.L. & PUB. POL'Y 1, 21 (2010) ("There is the hope that our legal institutions, including those governing succession of property, will be seen as legitimate and rational.").

30. *Id.* ("We need to trust probate and surrogate courts to perform such a task competently and have enough moxie to say, 'No this is wholly irrational.'").

at rooting out things that simply do not and cannot have any basis in reality.[31] Stated another way, people want to believe first that there is an indestructible boundary between what is real and what is not, and second that human beings can easily locate it.[32] Dostoevsky, by the way, is not convinced that either part of that aspiration can be realized.[33]

While the same policies minister to both mental capacity and insane delusion theories and in practice, contestants frequently lodge them together, courts treat them as two distinct attacks.[34] If Dostoevsky were alive today, he would likely advocate a fusion of the two theories and give will contestants additional hurdles to overcome before they can brand someone sick with insane delusions.[35]

A. Lack of General Mental Capacity

The rule requiring a testator to be of sound mind in order to make a will has been in existence for about five centuries.[36] In deference to testamentary

---

31. *See* Grant H. Morris & Ansar Haroun, *"God Told Me to Kill"Religion or Delusion?*, 38 SAN DIEGO L. REV. 973, 1012 (2001) ("The Law presumes that everyone experiences the same reality. This presumption is only overcome by total cognitive impairment.... [T]he court examines the defendant's subjective reality when it decides whether the defendant suffered from a mental disorder.").

32. *Id.*

33. *See e.g.*, DOSTOEVSKY, *supra* note 1, at 171 (narrating a scene in which Golyadkin's response to the inexplicable appearance of used dishware, serviette, and silverware is an exclamation, "[a]nything is possible").

34. *See, e.g.*, Breeden v. Stone (*In re* Estate of Breeden), 992 P.2d 1167 (Colo. 2000) (delineating and defining distinct tests for capacity and insane delusion). *See also* DUKEMINER & SITKOFF, *supra* note 13, at 274–75 ("A person may satisfy the test for testamentary capacity but nonetheless be suffering from an *insane delusion* that causes the entire will or a particular disposition to fail for lack of capacity."); Fogel, *supra* note 10, at 67–68 (addressing whether "a delusion about a specific subject [can] obviate testamentary capacity even though the testator is, in all other respects, sane.").

35. *See infra* Part III. D (proposing a modification of our mental capacity law that would be consistent with Dostoevsky's perspective).

36. *See generally* Eunice L. Ross and Thomas J. Reed, *The Common Law Development of Testamentary Capacity in England*, in WILL CONTESTS §2:6 (2d ed. 1999) ("The first attempt to make a judicial synthesis and to develop a doctrinal test for testamentary capacity occurs in 1601 in *Pawlet, Marquess of Winchester's Case*"). In *Pawlet*, when the Marquess of Winchester's will gave most of his property to illegitimate children, the legitimate son sued, arguing that his father was not sane when he executed his will. *Id.* Attorney General, Lord Coke argued that courts should first decide whether a testator is mentally competent to make a will and the court agreed, announcing the rule:

freedom, the mental-capacity test is designed to be lenient:[37]

> [T]he testator or donor must be capable of knowing and understanding in a general way [1] the nature and extent of his or her property, [2] the natural objects of his or her bounty, and [3] the disposition that he or she is making of that property, and must also be capable of [4] relating these elements to one another and forming an orderly desire regarding the disposition of the property.[38]

The individual with sound mind does not have to be particularly bright, accurate, or unmistaken.[39] Imperfect people with all sorts of quirks can pass the test.[40] A seminal case, *In re Wright's Estate*,[41] proclaimed that wills should not be invalidated simply because the testator is eccentric, nonconforming, or outlandish, and helped cement that legal cliché in place.[42]

In *Wright*, the often drunk testator lived in a shack packed with dirt and junk, picked up trash and hid it in his house, falsely bragged of owning lots of homes, insisted on buying furniture that was not for sale, offered someone kerosene-soaked fish to eat, sporadically pretended to be dead, and failed to ac-

---

by law it is not sufficient that the testator be of memory when he makes his will, to answer familiar and usual questions, but he ought to have a disposing memory so that he is able to make a disposition of his lands with understanding and reason; and that is such a memory which the law calls sane and perfect memory. *Id.* (quoting *Pawlet, Marquess of Winchester's Case*, (1601) 77 Eng. Rep. 287 (K.B.) 288). The modern test for testamentary capacity derives from two later English cases, *Greenwood v. Greenwood*, (1790) 163 Eng. Rep. 930 (K.B.) and *Harwood v. Baker*, (1840) 13 Eng. Rep. 117 (P.C.); it is sometimes called the *Greenwood-Baker* rule. Thomas J. Reed, *Breaking Wills in Indiana*, 14 IND. L. REV. 865, 867 (1981). In *Greenwood*, Lord Kenyon charged the jury, requiring the testator to understand (1) what he possessed, and (2) what were the natural objects of his bounty, while the court in *Baker* later added the third prong—that the testator must be capable of forming an intelligent distribution plan.

37. *See* Fogel, *supra* note 10, at 79 ("Courts have frequently stated that an individual may execute a valid will even though his capacity is significantly impaired.")

38. RESTATEMENT (THIRD) OF PROPERTY: WILLS AND OTHER DONATIVE TRANSFERS § 8.1(b) (2003).

39. *See* DUKEMINIER& SITKOFF, *supra* note 13, at 266 (explaining how "the requirements for mental capacity are minimal.").

40. *E.g.* Hindmarch v. Angell (*In re* Wright's Estate), 60 P.2d 434, 436 (Cal. 1936) (describing the testator's eccentricities).

41. 60 P.2d 434 (Cal. 1936).

42. *Id.* at 438; *accord Breeden*, 992 P.2d at 1168 (adhering to the basic dictate of the *Wright* court, the court upheld the holographic will of a testator whom the court found to be delusional).

knowledge his own granddaughter in the street.[43] He "picked up paper flowers from garbage cans ... and pinned them on rose bushes in his yard and took the witness to look at his roses."[44]

The Supreme Court of California said that Wright was sufficiently sound and found "no evidence that he did not appreciate his relations and obligations to others, or that he was not mindful of the property, which he possessed."[45] It stressed that "[t]estamentary capacity cannot be destroyed by showing a few isolated acts, foibles, idiosyncrasies, moral or mental irregularities or departures from the normal unless they directly bear upon and have influenced the testamentary act."[46] As addressed below, the case law is woefully inconsistent and courts invalidate wills of testators much less outlandish than Mr. Wright and deem testators to be insanely deluded.[47]

B. Insane Delusion

An insane delusion can also nullify an estate plan.[48] The theory is that a testator may have adequate general mental capacity, but nevertheless suffer from a delusion or monomania, which confines itself to and affects one or several aspects of a person's life.[49] Such cases involve testators who, allegedly without basis, believe family members are possessed by the devil or trying to kill them,[50]

---

43. *Wright*, 60 P.2d at 436–47. One witness said that Wright "often chased the children out of his yard and turned the hose on them and that children in the neighborhood were afraid of Mr. Wright." *Id*. at 436.

44. *Id*. at 436. Further, Wright "went away with a blanket wrapped around him and was gone several days and made no explanation as to where he went ... [and] took from his daughter's house a radio which the witness said he had given to his daughter and granddaughter without making any explanation as to why he did so." *Id*.

45. *Id*. at 438.

46. *Id*.

47. *See infra* Part II. B and accompanying notes (discussing cases in which wills have been invalidated when it is not crystal clear that the testator was insanely deluded or whether the supposed delusions caused the disposition.).

48. DUKEMINIER & SITKOFF, *supra* note 13, at 274–75.

49. Blumenthal, *supra* note 10 at 979.

50. *See, e.g.,* Zielinski v. Moczulski (*In re* Estate of Zielinski), 623 N.Y.S.2d 653, 655 (App.Div. 1995) (testator believed that her son and already dead husband were harming her); M.I. Marshall & Ilsley Trust Co. of Ariz. v. McCannon (*In re* Killen), 937 P.2d 1369, 1370 (Ariz. Ct. App. 1996) (testator believed that nieces and nephews were harming her). *Cf.* Dew v. Clark (*Dew III*) (1826) 162 Eng. Rep. 410 (K.B) 421 (testator called his daughter names, like "the special property of Satan").

spouses are cheating,[51] their children are fathered by someone else,[52] they have a wife and children when they do not,[53] or FBI or DEA agents are monitoring their lives.[54] Courts have held that insanely delusional testators cannot execute valid wills if the wills are the product of the delusion.[55] But what is an insane delusion?

Although delusion is a legal construct, psychiatry can assist.[56] For a long time, mental health experts have tried to define delusional thought, which has been considered the core of insanity.[57] The Diagnostic and Statistical Manual

---

51. *See, e.g.,* Benjamin v. Woodring, 303 A.2d 779, 783 (Md. Ct. App. 1973) (husband believed that wife was unfaithful and accused her of going to bars and picking up men); *In re* Kaven's Estate, 272 N.W. 696, 697 (Mich. 1937) (testator believed that her husband was having extramarital affairs): *In re* Honigman's Will, 168 N.E.2d 676, 677–78 (N.Y. 1960) (testator believed that his elderly wife was unfaithful, was hiding male suitors "in the cellar … in various closets, and under the bed"); Joslin v. Henry (*In re Estate of Joslin*), 89 N.W.2d 822, 823 (Wisc. 1958) (woman believed that husband was squandering money on other women and carrying on an adulterous affair with a neighbor).

52. *See, e.g.,* Davis v. Davis, 170 P. 208, 210 (Colo. 1918) (father believed, without a rational basis, that his son was not his son).

53. *See, e.g.,* Athey v. Rask (*In re Estate of Rask*), 214 N.W. 2d 525, 529 (N.D. 1974) (testator, who was never married, believed that he had a wife and child, and left his estate to his adoptive niece, whom he was convinced was his daughter.)

54. *See, e.g.,* Petitioners-Appellants' Opening Brief at 5, in Estate of Breeden v. Stone (*In re* Estate of Breeden), 992 P.2d 1167 (Colo. 2000) (No. 98SC570) (arguing that an example of the testator's delusional beliefs was his conviction that everyone was an FBI or DEA agent, that they were watching him, and that the FBI was working in partnership with the Public Service to tunnel into his house when new sewer lines were being installed).

55. To invalidate a will on this basis, contestants must prove that the testator suffered from an insane delusion and that the will or part of the will was a product of the insane delusion. *See* Fogel, *supra* note 10, at 86. The contestant must also show that the will or part of the will contested was a product of the insane delusion. *Id.* at 96. A majority of courts will not invalidate a will unless the insane delusion materially affected or influenced the will's provisions. DUKEMINIER & SITKOFF, *supra* note 13, at 282; *accord* Breeden, 992 P.2d at 1174, 1176 (noting that although the testator suffered from insane delusions, they did not materially affect or influence the disposition of property in the will). The minority view, however, is that a will is invalid if the testator's insane delusion "might have … caused or affected" the disposition. *In re* Honigman's Will, 168 N.E.2d at 679 (quoting Am. Seaman's Friend Soc. v. Hopper, 33 N.Y. 619, 625 (N.Y. 1865)). *See also* Fogel, *supra* note 10, at 95–96 (explaining that the "affected standard in *Honigman* was a "much easier standard to meet than the standard required by most courts—including other New York courts—that the will be a product of the delusion").

56. *See generally* DUKEMINIER & SITKOFF, *supra* note 13, at 275 ("Insane delusion is a legal, not a psychiatric concept.").

57. *See* Grant H. Morris & Ansar Haroun, *supra* note 31, at 1019 (2001) ("[D]elusional thought has been considered the very essence of insanity.… [P]sychiatrists today define

of Mental Disorders (DSM), published by the American Psychiatric Association,[58] and, at times, called "the psychiatric profession's diagnostic Bible,"[59] gives a definition that heeds today's legal formula: "A false belief based on incorrect inference about external reality that is firmly sustained despite what almost everyone else believes and despite what constitutes incontrovertible and obvious proof or evidence to the contrary."[60] Unlike a mistake, an insane delusion cannot be corrected by presenting, or even bombarding, the afflicted with evidence that their beliefs are false.[61]

Under the DSM, there are two categories of insane delusions: the non-bizarre and the bizarre.[62] Both categories entail the kind of facts that exist in will contests. The non-bizarre encompasses situations that occur in real life, such as "the belief that one is under surveillance by the police, despite a lack of convincing evidence."[63] The bizarre, on the other hand, goes beyond the pale: they

---

delusion in much the same way they defined delusion in the mid-nineteenth century."). *Compare* Rex v. Hadfield (1800) 27 Howell's St. Tr. 1281, 1313 (K.B.) (noting that after defendant entered a theatre and fired a shot at King George III, Hadfield's barrister, Thomas Erskine, won an acquittal and argued that in madness, "reason is not driven from her seat, but distraction sits down upon it along with her, holds her, trembling upon it, and frightens her from her propriety") with Norman J. Finkel, Insanity on Trial, 14–15 (1988) (describing how Hadfield had delusions and believed it was his mission to kill the King to pave the way for the second coming of Christ); J.C. Oleson, *Is Tyler Durden Insane?* 83 N.D. L. Rev. 579, 601 n. 144 (2007) (discussing insane delusion test, Hadfield's trial, and comparing Hadfield's "fascinating delusions" to those of Unabomber Theodore Kaczynski, "who believed that his actions were necessary to save humanity from the evils of modernity").

58. Am. Psychiatric Ass'n, Diagnostic And Statistical Manual of Mental Disorders: DSM-5-TM (5th ed. Text rev. 2013) [hereinafter DSM].

59. Morris & Haroun, *supra* note 31, at 1023 n. 298. Morris & Haroun also explain that another definitive work used by psychiatrists (but not generally in the United States) is the World Health Organization's *International Classification of Diseases*, which discusses and uses the term "delusion," but does not define what a "delusion" is. *Id.* at 1022.

60. DSM, *supra* note 58, at 819. According to the DSM, a delusion is not a belief "ordinarily accepted by other members of the person's culture or subculture...." *Id.*; *see also* Morris & Haroun, *supra* note 31, at 1025–26.

61. *See* Dukeminier & Sitkoff, *supra* note 13, at 275 ("An insane delusion—which bears on testamentary capacity—is one to which the testator adheres against all evidence and reason to the contrary" and "[t]he law ... draws a distinction between an insane delusion and a mistake," which is "susceptible to correction if the testator is told the truth."). DSM, *supra* note 58, at 87 (defining delusion as "fixed beliefs that are not amenable to change in light of conflicting evidence.").

62. DSM, *supra* note 58, at 87. *See also id.* at 90 (describing types of delusions, including erotomaniac, grandiose, jealous, persecutory, and somatic delusions). Morris & Haroun, *supra* note 31, at 1026 (listing thought broadcasting and thought insertion also).

63. DSM, *supra* note 58, at 87.

are "clearly implausible, not understandable to same-culture peers and do not derive from ordinary life experiences."[64] For example, "a bizarrely delusional individual might believe that an outside force has removed his or her internal organs and replaced them with someone else's organs without leaving any wounds or scars."[65] When it is demonstrated to them that there are no wounds or scars and that what they believe is totally implausible, they nevertheless cling like a winkle to their falsehoods.[66]

1. The Bizarre

The facts in *Estate of Zielinski v. Moczulski* [67] mirror the DSM example of "bizarre."[68] In *Zielinski*, Cecilia Zielinski left everything to her sister, Barbara, and Barbara's husband.[69] When Cecilia excluded her only son, grandchildren, and great-grandchildren, the omitted beneficiaries opposed probate on insane delusion grounds.[70]

---

64. *Id.*

65. *Id. See also id.* ("Delusions that express a loss of control over mind or body are generally considered to be bizarre; these include the belief that one's thoughts have been removed by some outside force (*thought withdrawal*), that alien thoughts have been put into one's mind (*thought insertion*), or that one's body or actions have been acted on or manipulated by some outside force (*delusions of control*)."); Morris & Haroun, *supra* note 31, at 1031 (quoting the definition of bizarre delusion from the third edition DSM as "[a] false belief whose content is patently absurd and has no possible basis in fact").

66. *See* Baron, *supra* note 10, at 1055 ("A large number of the definitions ... state that an insane delusion exists where there is no evidence to support the testator's belief."); Fogel, *supra* note 10, at 68 (giving an example of an insane delusion as the testator who believed she was the Holy Ghost). Despite the fantastic nature of the previous examples, a majority of courts find that "a delusion is insane even if there is some factual basis for it.... [but] a rational person in the testator's situation could not have drawn the conclusion reached by the testator." *See* DUKEMINIER & SITKOFF, *supra* note 13 at 275 ("In most states, if there is any evidence to support the testator's delusion, the delusion is not insane.").

67. *In re* Estate of Zielinski, 623 N.Y.S.2d 653 (N.Y. App. Div. 1995).

68. *See supra* notes 64–66 and accompanying text (defining "bizarre" delusions).

69. Zielinski, 623 N.Y.S.2d at 654.

70. In *Zielinski*, Cecilia Zelinski was admitted to the hospital and diagnosed with colon cancer. *Id.* While there, Cecilia's sister, Barbara, and Barbara's husband visited daily. *Id.* In the hospital, and in Barbara's presence, Cecilia executed her will, which provided for the distribution of her residuary estate in equal shares to Barbara and Barbara's husband. *Id.* As it turned out, Cecilia's assets were considerable: she had a house and about 200 savings bonds, which she had purchased over a 20-year period and were payable to either a grandchild or great-grand child. *Id.* As the court noted, "[n]o bonds were issued in the name of proponent, proponent's husband or any of decedent's other siblings." *Id.* On the day that Cecilia executed her will, she also signed a power of attorney in favor of her sister, Barbara.

The *Zielinski* contestants had heavy artillery: the consulting hospital psychiatrist said that Cecilia was diagnosed on the date of her admission with a delusional disorder relating to her son.[71] Cecilia believed that her son, along with her husband, plotted to and did inject her in the buttocks.[72] The psychiatrist "opined that patients with this disorder could be competent in some respects and delusional with respect to others."[73] According to another psychiatrist, Cecilia thought that "her husband [who was already dead] broke her legs" and that her son "was getting instructions from a 'device' that turned the world inside out."[74]

According to other witnesses, Cecilia thought that her son was inserting balloons into her stomach, that her husband ran over her legs and replaced them with a stranger's legs, that her son injected her with chemicals, and that her husband, son, and doctors were ganging up on her.[75] She also felt that her husband and doctors had shoved her eyes way back into her head.[76] In an abundance of caution, Cecilia regularly spit into a jar to preserve evidence of these horrors.[77] In fact, at the trial, it was revealed that twenty-five to thirty one-gallon jars, supposedly full of saliva, were stashed in Cecilia's closet.[78]

Id. Barbara, acting pursuant to the power of attorney, redeemed as many of the savings bonds as she could and deposited the proceeds in a bank account in Cecilia's name. *Id.* When Cecilia died, Barbara and her husband became entitled to the proceeds because they were the beneficiaries under the will. *Id.* After a nonjury trial, the court denied probate and directed Barbara to pay the named beneficiaries the amounts they would have received had the bonds not been redeemed. *Id.* On appeal, the court affirmed the finding of self-dealing and found "sufficient credible evidence to support the conclusion ... that [Barbara], in redeeming the savings bonds at issue, intended to make a gift to herself and in so doing breached her fiduciary duty to decedent." *Id.* at 656.

71. *Id.* at 655.

72. *Id.*

73. *Id.*

74. *Id.* Attending nurses also testified confirming "the delusional statements regarding [Cecilia's] son" and "[t]wo additional psychiatrists, one proffered by proponent and the other by the challengers, confirmed such diagnosis after their review of the medical records." *Id.* Significantly, they bolstered the finding of causation by testifying that "such delusions may have directly affected decedent's decision to exclude Zielinski from the will." *Id.*

75. *Id.*

76. *Id.*

77. *Id.*

78. *Id.* The son's wife "testified that when she met [Cecilia]..., [Cecilia] told her about her legs being substituted and the balloons" and "confirmed prior testimony about the 'devices' and the spitting into a jar." *Id.* Significantly, all "witnesses ... testified that there was no basis for such statements and that there existed a good relationship between ... [Cecilia and her son]." *Id.*

Proponent Barbara lost in the trial court and on appeal.[79] The appellate court noted that the contestants bore the difficult burden of showing "that [Cecilia's] mind was affected by an insane delusion regarding her son."[80] Nevertheless, the appellate court concluded that Cecilia was suffering from an insane delusion, which directly caused her to exclude her son.[81] The court felt that "[e]ven if it could be said that decedent had general testamentary capacity, she could, at the same time, have an insane delusion which controlled her testamentary act, thus rendering it invalid."[82]

There are other cases in the *Zielinski* genre in which people are inextricably wedded to sheer impossibility: for example, there is the testator who met a headless wolf while taking a stroll.[83] In another case, the testator believed that he had personally toured other planets, made friends there, and learned that, postdeath, he would run a stone quarry on Saturn.[84] In still another case, the testator fought with the devil, visited both heaven and hell, spoke with devils, imps, demons and angels, saw "the devil making candy out of plow points," heard the devil "playing a tune on the fiddle," and met "the devil's horse, which was so big it had one foot in St. Louis and the other in California."[85] The common thread in these *Zielinski*-type cases is an individual's unshakable faith in something that normatively people agree cannot occur. Most people (including *The Double*'s author) are not likely to pick a bone with the assessments in the bizarre cases.

---

79. *Id.* at 656.
80. *Id.* at 654–55.
81. *Id.* at 655.
82. *Id.* at 656.
83. Masters v. Haywood (*In re* Haywood's Estate), 240 P.2d 1028, 1032 (Cal. Ct. App. 1952). In *Haywood*, the evidence demonstrated that, "[d]uring the psychiatric examination, the testator [said] ... that ... while he was walking on a road, a headless animal resembling a wolf appeared and then suddenly disappeared." *Id.* Because this delusion or "hallucination was not related to the will in any way," the court affirmed a finding of mental competency. *Id.* at 1034.
84. *McReynolds v. Smith*, 86 N.E. 1009, 1011 (Ind. 1909). The *McReynolds* court found that the evidence established insane delusion, and that the will was "at least in some measure, the result of such delusion," elaborating:

> [T]he testator believed that he was in direct and active communication with the spirit world; that he had ... personally visited the planets, formed an acquaintance with their inhabitants, and had had it revealed to him that he should, after death, go to the planet Saturn and conduct a stone quarry, and furthermore, that he had been instructed from the spirit world by revelation, how he should make his will.

Id. at 1012.
85. Gulf Oil Corp. v. Walker, 288 S.W.2d 173, 179 (Tex. Civ. App. 1956).

2. The Non-Bizarre

Most will contests are not that extreme and tend to fall into the non-bizarre category.[86] Non-bizarre testators do not adhere to total implausibility.[87] Instead, what they perceive *is* possible, but the events may not actually be happening.[88] Here, what decision-makers must decide is whether the testators had a reasonable basis for their beliefs or perceptions. Dostoevsky, a psyche virtuoso, would likely chuckle and proclaim the task here to be as futile as fetching water in a sieve.

The extant case law supports Dostoevsky. The only consistency in the non-bizarre decisions is inconsistency, which commentators tend to pin on two culprits. Some critics detect a proclivity on the part of judges and juries to invalidate estate plans when they dislike either a testator or the chosen beneficiaries.[89] Other legal analysts blame the conflicting results on the particular jurisdiction's approach to the burden of proof.[90] The decisions in will contests based on lack of general mental capacity are just as inconsistent, with results just as questionable, when they do not involve individuals with bizarre delusions.[91] However, when a testator is suffering from bizarre delu-

---

86. *See supra* notes 64–66 and accompanying text (the DSM definition of "non-bizarre").

87. *E.g.,* Benjamin v. Woodring, 303 A.2d 779, 783 (Md. Ct. App. 1973) (noting that the husband believed that his wife was unfaithful, and accused her of going to bars and picking up men).

88. *Id.*

89. *See, e.g., In re* Strittmater's Estate, 53 A.2d 205 (N.J. 1947) (invalidating will where testator overtly chose not to pick her family as primary beneficiaries); Sanford v. Freeman (*In re* Estate of Watlack), 945 P.2d 1154 (Wash. Ct. App. 1997) (invalidating will where nephews and nieces who never visited or went to decedent's funeral inherited in lieu of decedent's own children, who cared for their father in his declining years).

90. *See* Dukeminier & Sitkoff, *supra* note 13, at 282 (discussing the differing standards for establishing causation in insane delusion cases).

91. *Compare In re* Estate of Washburn, 690 A.2d 1024, 1026–27 (N.H. 1997) (upholding the probate court's finding that the testatrix lacked testamentary capacity where she suffered from "some degree of Alzheimer's" and "lay witnesses indicated confusion, forgetfulness, and a lack of competency") *with* Wilson v. Lane, 614 S.E.2d 88, 88–89 (2005) (disagreeing with jury and instead agreeing with the trial judge that testatrix had sufficient testamentary capacity even though she was "was in some form of the early to middle stages of dementia of the Alzheimer's type," had "called the fire department to report a non-existent fire," exhibited "an irrational fear of flooding in her house," had "trouble dressing and bathing herself," had a "guardianship petition filed on her behalf only a few months before the will execution," and a physician's letter stated that she "suffered from senile dementia"). The court upheld the validity of the will in *Wilson,* where there is more evidence of incompetency than in *Washburn,* where the court invalidated the will. Here, too, we could blame the ostensible inconsistency on the evidentiary burdens in each case. Dukeminier & Sitkoff,

sions, society and the courts tend to be more at peace with the resultant will invalidation.[92]

a. Blame It on Bias

There are non-bizarre cases in which decision-makers invalidate wills because they dislike the testators or their chosen beneficiaries. According to Professor Melanie B. Leslie, these cases extinguish testamentary freedom:

> [C]ourts impose upon testators a duty to provide for those to whom the court views as having a superior moral claim to the testator's assets, usually a financially dependent spouse or persons related by blood to the testator. Wills that fail to provide for those individuals typically are upheld only if the will's proponent can convince the fact finder that the testator's deviation from normative values is morally justifiable. This unspoken rule, seeping quietly but fervently from the case law, directly conflicts with the oft-repeated axiom that testamentary freedom is the polestar of wills.[93]

When courts prefer wills reflecting "prevailing normative views," they can issue unpredictable and disingenuous decisions.[94] Ironically, *Dew v. Clark*,[95] the very

---

supra note 13, at 274 (explaining how putting the ultimate burden of proof (or, more specifically, the burden of persuasion) on the proponent to show testamentary capacity, as in *Washburn*, is the minority rule while majority rule, as in *Wilson* … is that once the proponent adduces *prima facie* evidence of due execution, the party contesting the will on the grounds of lack of capacity has the burden.). It is possible to say that decision-maker bias is at work here as well. In *Washburn*, the testatrix executed three wills, eventually leaving just about everything to her caretaker in lieu of her family members. *Washburn*, 690 A.2d 1026. In *Wilson*, the testatrix left her property equally to seventeen beneficiaries, only one of which was a "non-relative" care taker. *Wilson*, 614 S.E.2d at 88–89. It is thus possible that, unlike the *Washburn* court, which might have sensed undue influence and felt that the distribution was not normative, the *Wilson* court was comfortable because almost all of the beneficiaries were blood relatives.

92. *See, e.g., Gulf Oil Corp. supra* note 85, 179–80 (Tex. Civ. App. 1956) (a case involving bizarre delusions, where the testator believed, among other things, that he was in combat with the devil, had visited both heaven and hell, and "talked with the devil, imps, demons, and angels, …" and in which the court said that "the evidence [went] beyond a mere showing that [testator] … had insane delusions, and show[ed] evidence of an unsound mind generally.")

93. Leslie, *supra* note 10, at 236.

94. *Id.*

95. Dew v. Clark, (1826) Eng. Rep. 410 (K.B.). *Dew* involved three distinct cases with the same litigants and same will, each decided by the Prerogative Court. Fogel, *supra* note

decision that originated the insane delusion doctrine, is itself at least assailable and possibly wrong.[96]

The 1826 *Dew* case focused on Doctor Ely Stott, a vile man, who virtually disinherited his only child, Charlotte.[97] After Stott left the bulk of his estate to nephews, Charlotte contested the will on the novel theory of insane delusion.[98] In *Dew*, Charlotte described her dreadful life with her father. Charlotte described how her father, from her infancy, had exhibited an "insane aversion to [her]," called her names like "fiend," "a very devil," and the "special property of Satan," and flogged her "on the most trivial occasions."[99] Once, Stott locked her in an asylum for a night so that she could spend it with an insane female patient.[100] The contestants' corroborators portrayed Charlotte as an "unexceptional character," while they contrasted her with Stott, a "deranged … monster."[101] Charlotte did not assail her father's general testamentary capacity; instead, she argued that Stott's insanity solely fixated on her.[102]

The proponents tried to rebut Charlotte's case with a different narrative.[103] They did not dispute the fact that the testator was reprehensible, but argued that the will was rational and consistent with Stott's rigid Calvinism and vision of "human nature" as "total[ly] and absolute[ly] deprav[ed.]"[104] As they argued, Stott was a man of "irritable and violent temper; of great pride and con-

---

10, at 83 n. 95. The first allowed Charlotte to admit proof regarding her father's insane delusion. *See* Dew v. Clark (Dew I), (1822) 162 Eng. Rep. 98 (K.B.) 98. The second *Dew* also involved evidentiary issues. Dew v. Clark (Dew II), (1824) 162 Eng. Rep. 233 (K.B.) 233. The third *Dew* invalidated the will. *See* Dew v. Clark (Dew III) (1826) 162 Eng. Rep. 410 (K.B). *See also* Fogel, *supra* note 10, at 83 n.95 (calling the decision *Dew* III) 455.

96. Professor Fogel states that *Dew* III is "generally cited as the first monomania case." Fogel, *supra* note 10, at 83 n.95; *accord* ISAAC RAY, A TREATISE ON THE MEDICAL JURISPRUDENCE OF INSANITY 181–83 (Winfred Overholser ed.,1962) (discussing *Dew* as the early recognition of "partial mania.").

97. *Dew III*, 162 Eng. Rep. at 454.

98. *Id.* at 411–12, 414.

99. *Id.* at 427, 433. *See also* RAY, *supra* note 96, at 182 ("Repeatedly, and on the most trivial occasions, he struck her with his clenched fists, cut her flesh with a horsewhip, tore out her hair, and once aimed at her a blow with some weapon which made a dent in a mahogany table and which might have killed her, had she not avoided it.").

100. Dew II, 162 Eng. Rep. at 235.

101. Dew III, 162 Eng. Rep. at 425, 428.

102. *Dew I*, 162 Eng. Rep. at 100 ("[S]he can only prove it by making out a case … that the deceased was insane as to her, notwithstanding his general sanity.").

103. *Dew III*, 162 Eng. Rep. at 421.

104. *Id.* at 420.

ceit; very precise in all his domestic and other arrangements; very impatient of contradiction; and embued [sic] with high notions of parental authority."[105] The proponents, painting Charlotte as "disobedient" and "very perverse, sullen, and idle," implied that her father's treatment of her was justified, or at least comprehensible.[106] Pounding the pulpit of testamentary freedom, they asserted that insanity did not affect the estate plan, and should not divest Stott of the right to choose his beneficiaries.[107]

Sir John Nicholl, the decision's author, saw it as a "perfectly novel case" and pointed to "delusion" as "the true test … of the absence or presence of insanity."[108] He elaborated:

> Wherever the patient once conceives something extravagant to exist, which still has no existence whatever but in his own heated imagination; and whatever, at the same time, having once so conceived, he is incapable of being … permanently […] reasoned out [of] that conception; such a person is said to be under a delusion, in a peculiar, half-technical, sense of the term.[109]

Sir Nicholl, concluding that Charlotte had established not only insane delusion but also requisite causation, opined that Stott's will was "the direct unqualified offspring of that morbid delusion."[110] While Sir Nicholl admitted that there was some factual basis for Stott's hatred of his daughter, he made a point of praising Charlotte and vilifying the testator.[111] Sir Nicholl, noting that a jury would likely be sympathetic with Charlotte,[112] "protested" (and perhaps too much) that emotion did not drive his opinion.[113]

---

105. *Id.*

106. *Id.* at 425.

107. *See id.* at 434 (arguing that testamentary decision was instead a result of Charlotte's choice of a husband).

108. *Id.* at 412, 414.

109. *Id.*

110. *Id.* at 456.

111. *Id.* at 444.

112. *Dew II*, 162 Eng. Rep. at 236–37 ("It [was] said that the plaintiff was naturally anxious to submit her case … to a jury, that with such a case she had a much better prospect of succeeding with a jury through the medium of their feelings than of obtaining the sentence of a court…. The Court … avow[ed] that it participate[d] to some extent in the feeling with which a British jury may be supposed to have looked at [the] case….").

113. *Dew III*, 162 Eng. Rep. at 456 ("The [c]ourt has only again to protest that its feelings in this case have been suffered to bias in its judgment."). *See also* Fogel, *supra* note 10, at 84–85 (discussing the court's protestations that sympathy did not "cloud its judgment.").

The *Dew* case inaugurated not only the doctrine, but also the nimbus of uncertainty that today still hovers over the non-bizarre landscape. Although most readers would likely dislike Stott and, of course, censure child abuse, it is not a given that such disapproval warrants will-nullification. Stated otherwise, as bad as Stott was, he might retain the right to disinherit a child he happened to detest. Was Stott really sick with an aversion to Charlotte, or was his dead hand desperately contriving to flog a "disobedient" and "perverse, sullen, and idle" daughter?[114] It is at least conceivable that Sir Nicholl, understandably appalled by Stott and desirous of rescuing Charlotte, tweaked the estate plan to benefit one whom *he* designated the natural object of the testator's bounty.[115]

Another classic case, *In re Strittmater's Estate*,[116] displays bias, which even more pronounced than that in *Dew*, corroborates Professor Leslie's thesis that courts reject estate plans that deviate from "prevailing normative views."[117] In *Strittmater*, the New Jersey Court of Errors and Appeals (now the Supreme Court of New Jersey) declined to probate the will of Louisa Strittmater, who left her property to the National Woman's Party (hereinafter, "The Party").[118] Louisa, who never married, lived with her parents until their death.[119] Although she had a "normal childhood" and loved her parents, she seemed to despise them after their death: she called her father "a corrupt, vicious, and unintelligible savage, a typical specimen of the majority of his sex" and wrote, "[b]last his wormstinking carcass and his whole damn breed."[120] Louisa, who apparently detested her mother as well, denominated her the "[m]oronic she-devil."[121]

At trial, it was shown that Louisa once smashed a clock, killed a kitten, and used foul language.[122] The only medical expert, Dr. Smalley, Louisa's general practitioner, who was not a psychiatrist, said that Louisa "suffered from paranoia of the Bleuler type of split personality."[123] Although the court "regret[ted]

---

114. Dew III, 162 Eng. Rep. at 425.

115. *See, e.g.,* Fogel, *supra* note 10, at 70–71 (discussing how the doctrine allows for "significant leeway" for courts to invalidate wills that do not comport with their own notions of family or to give property to those whom the courts designate the natural objects of the testators' bounty).

116. 53 A.2d 205 (N.J. 1947).

117. Leslie, *supra* note 10, at 236.

118. *Strittmater, supra* note 116 at 205–06.

119. *Id.* at 205.

120. *Id.*

121. *Id.*

122. *Id.*

123. *Id.*

not having had the benefit of an analysis of the data by a specialist in diseases of the brain," it nevertheless rubber-stamped Smalley's opinion.[124]

What apparently irritated the court was Louisa's chosen beneficiary,[125]— the Party, a feminist organization.[126] When Louisa was about twenty-nine years old, she joined the Party's local branch, and for several years before her death, volunteered in its New York office.[127] During this period, Louisa discussed leaving her estate to the Party.[128] At trial, it was shown that she had "entirely reasonable and normal" relations with both her lawyer and her bank.[129]

When Louisa died, she left everything to the Party, and "some cousins of whom she saw very little during the last few years of her life" challenged the will on an insane delusion theory.[130] Although the will was initially admitted to probate, the intermediate court, reversing, sided with the cousins.[131] In affirming the decision not to probate the will, New Jersey's highest court said that "the proofs demonstrated 'incontrovertably [sic] her morbid aversion to men' and feminism to a neurotic extreme."[132] The court felt that Louisa, who "regarded men as a class with an insane hatred[,] … looked forward to the day when women would bear children without the aid of men, and all males would be put to death at birth."[133] The court concluded that Louisa's "paranoic condition, especially her insane delusions about the male, […] led her to leave her estate to the … Party."[134]

Under a contemporary lens, we likely see Louisa's chosen beneficiary as the "natural [object] of … her bounty."[135] Louisa devoted almost two decades of her life to the Party and gave it her labor. For Louisa, the Party became a sur-

---

124. *Id.*

125. *See id.* at 206 (dismissing the long-lasting nature of Louisa's dedication to the beneficiary, the National Woman's Party).

126. The National Woman's Party was founded in 1916 by Alice Paul, who drafted the Equal Rights Amendment in 1921 and fought to have sex discrimination added to the protections of Title VII in the 1964 Civil Rights Act. Jo Freeman, *How "Sex" Got Into Title VII: Persistent Opportunism as a Maker of Public Policy*, 9 LAW & INEQ. 163, 165 (1991).

127. *Strittmater, supra* note 116, at 205.

128. *Id.*

129. *Id.*

130. *Id.*

131. *Id.*

132. *Id.*

133. *Id.*

134. *Id.* at 296.

135. RESTATEMENT (THIRD) OF PROP: WILLS AND OTHER DONATIVE TRANSFERS §8.1 (b) (2003).

rogate family, one to whom she chose to transmit her property.[136] The court, disliking the Party and damning what it viewed as man-hatred,[137] did not feel (in the words of Professor Leslie) that Louisa's "deviation from normative values [was] morally justifiable."[138] While it is, at least, conceivable that a court today might see things differently and probate both the *Strittmater* and *Dew* wills, there are more recent analogues in which contestants prevail not because the testator is genuinely deluded, but because of the mindset or bias of a particular jury or judge.[139]

b. Blame It on Burdens of Proof

In addition to bias, differing burdens of proof are also to blame for incon-

---

136. *Cf.* Alexander M. Meiklejohn, *Contractual and Donative Capacity*, 39 Case W. Res. L. Rev. 307, 325–26 (1988–89) (citing E. Erickson, Identity and the Life Cycle 54, app., Worksheet, col. B (1980)) (providing the theoretical implications of the mental capacity doctrine for contracts and gifts, and explaining that "[t]he circle widens in childhood to include first parental persons, then 'basic family,' then neighbors, teachers, and other school children." It "later encompasses peer groups and then expands further to take in those with whom the young adult cooperates and competes in the world of work.").

137. *Strittmater, supra* note 116, at 205.

138. Leslie, *supra* note 10, at 236. *See, e.g.,* Holland v. Traylor (*In re Will of Moses*), 227 So.2d 829, 831–32, 838 (Miss. 1969) (affirming the invalidation of the will of fifty-seven year old Fannie Taylor Moses on the ground of undue influence when she left her property to her lover, a lawyer, who was fifteen years younger, but had no involvement in the preparation or execution of the will). *See also* Amy D. Ronner, Homophobia and the Law 161–92 (American Psychological Assoc., 2005) (discussing discrimination against sexual minorities in wills and trusts law and cases in which courts have deprived the surviving partner in a same-sex relationship of his or her inheritance).

139. *See, e.g.,* Sanford v. Freeman (*In re Estate of Watlack*), 945 P.2d 1154 (Wash. Ct. App. 1997). In that case, the will disinherited the children and left everything to collateral relatives. *Id.* at 1155. The jury found, and the appellate court agreed, that the testator, who thought that his daughter was plotting to steal his money, suffered from an insane delusion, which caused the testamentary disposition. *Id.* at 1155–56. In *Watlack*, the testator's will gave reasons for the disinheritance and the evidence showed, moreover, that there was quite a bit of truth to these statements. *Id.* Watlack had already given his car to his daughter and said that after he was divorced, "maintained only sporadic contact with his two children." *Id.* at 1155. The court, brushing facts aside, said that the father's pretexts were not real. *Id.* at 1157. In the *Watlack*-like cases, courts stretch to find insane delusion when they do not approve of the disposition or when they want to protect family members. *See* Baron, *supra* note 10, at 1049 ("Courts repeatedly criticize juries' tendencies to strike down, on mental competency grounds, wills of which they disapprove. If the wishes set forth in the will are deemed to be the testator's own, they may not be judged by others.").

sistencies in the case-law.[140] For example, divergent causation tests might account for the ostensible irreconcilability of *In re Honigman's Will*,[141] in which a sharply divided court denied probate, and *Breeden v. Stone*,[142] where a court granted probate after an arguably more viable challenge.[143]

In *Honigman*, Frank and Florence had a childless, but "congenial and harmonious," marriage for about four decades.[144] They partnered in business and amassed a "substantial fortune."[145] Sometime before his death, however, Frank believed that his wife was unfaithful and ranted about it to "friends and strangers alike ... using obscene and abusive language."[146] For Frank, one villain was Mr. Krauss, a mutual friend, whom Frank believed was having a tawdry affair with his wife.[147] He also claimed that his wife was:

> misbehaving herself in a most unseemly fashion, by hiding male callers in the cellar of her home, in various closets, and under the bed; ... hauling men from the street up to her second-story bedroom by use of bed sheets; ... making contacts over the household telephone; and ... passing a clandestine note through the fence on her brother's property.[148]

When Frank died, he left his wife, Florence, the minimum amount necessary to satisfy her elective share, and gave the rest to siblings.[149]

---

140. *See generally* Dukeminier & Sitkoff, *supra* note 13, at 274 (discussing the evidentiary burdens with respect to testamentary capacity), and 282–83 (discussing the different standards for proving causation in insane delusion contests).

141. 168 N.E.2d 676 (N.Y. 1960).

142. (*In re* Estate of Breeden), 992 P.2d 1167 (Colo. 2000).

143. *See generally* Dukeminer & Sitkoff, *supra* note 13, at 282–83 (suggesting that the "outcome in [In re *Honigman's Will*, 168 N.E.2d 676 (N.Y. 1960)] [would] have been different if the court applied the [*Breeden*] ... test for causation").

144. *Honigman*, *supra* note 141, at 677.

145. *Id.*

146. *Id.*

147. *Id.* at 678.

148. *Id.*

149. *Id.* at 676–77 ("Just one month before his death, [Honigman] gave $5,000 to each of three named grandnieces, and cut off his wife with a life use of her minimum statutory share plus $2,500, with direction to pay the principal upon her death to his surviving brothers and sisters and to the descendants of any predeceased brother or sister, per stirpes. The remaining one half of his estate was bequeathed in equal shares to his surviving brothers and sisters and to the descendants of any predeceased brother or sister, per stirpes, some of whom resided in Germany.").

After Florence argued insane delusion, the will proponents tried to prove that there was a reasonable basis for Frank's belief: they had an anniversary card from Krauss, which bore "a printed message of congratulation in sweetly sentimental phraseology … addressed to the wife alone and not received on the anniversary date."[150] For Frank, this confirmed his suspicions.[151] Evidence existed that whenever the phone rang, Florence would dash to grab it.[152] For Frank, this supposed incident, fueling his notion that Florence was cavorting with Krauss, prompted him to forbid his wife to answer the phone.[153] There was also an episode in which Florence asked her husband, as he was walking out the door, when she could expect him home.[154] Frank, again enraged, "secreted himself at a vantage point in a nearby park and watched his home."[155] Lo and behold, there was Krauss entering his home![156] This story emerged in a statement that Frank had allegedly made to one witness, but Florence testified that this never happened.[157]

The jury found that Frank was "suffering from an unwarranted and insane delusion that his wife was unfaithful to him, thereby affecting the disposition made in his will."[158] The surrogate denied probate, and the court of appeals ultimately approved the jury's decision.[159] The court of appeals, opining that the jury "had the right to disregard the proponents' proof, or to go so far as to hold that such trivia afforded even additional grounds for decedent's irrational and unwarranted belief," found that Florence had met the burden of proving incapacity.[160]

The *Honigman* proponents' best argument was lack of causation: they contended that, even if Frank had an insane delusion, there were sound alternative reasons for his disposition.[161] After all, Florence was independently wealthy, and the chosen beneficiaries, Frank's brothers and sisters, were poor and needed

---

150. *Id.* at 677–78.
151. *Id.* at 678.
152. *Id.*
153. *Id.*
154. *Id.*
155. *Id.*
156. *Id.*
157. *Id.*
158. *Id.* at 677.
159. *Id.* The appellate division reversed the surrogate court, but the court of appeals reversed that ruling, upholding the jury's decision.
160. *Id.* at 678.
161. *Id.* at 679.

the gift.[162] In rejecting this argument, the court applied a minority causation test that a will is bad when "its 'dispository provisions were or *might have been caused* or affected by the delusion.'"[163] The *Honigman* court essentially assumed causation and shifted the burden to the proponents of proving that Frank's will did not ensue from delusion.[164]

The *Honigman* holding is debatable. Its tortuous procedural path—with the surrogate denying probate,[165] an appellate division reversing,[166] and a court of appeals reversing once again[167] (but with three dissenters)—leads to destination doubt. The court of appeals framed the legal issue as "not whether Mrs. Honigman was unfaithful, but whether Mr. Honigman had any reasonable basis for believing that she was."[168] In spite of that technically legal instruction, fact finders (and even professional case readers) cannot resist tasting the juicy non-issue of whether Florence was actually having that affair or whether, in Sir Nicholl's words, it was "the direct unqualified offspring of … morbid delusion."[169] Case readers cannot help but wonder whether Krauss clandestinely slipped Florence that sugary note, whether Florence jumped up each time the phone rang, hoping to intercept her paramour's call, and whether Florence and Krauss had that tryst as Frank spied from the shrubbery.

Although some of Frank's indictments are more plausible than others, few of his envisioned episodes are impossible. The proponents' presentations included things that can and do happen, and might actually have been happening, in the Honigman marriage. Of course, the *Honigman* decision could also intersect with the judicial bias cases. That is, the *Honigman* court, *sub silentio*, conceivably likened its task to equitable distribution. As such, the court did what it felt was normatively fair by bestowing an amount equal to an intestate share on a spouse who, for almost forty years, co-partnered in the home

---

162. *Id.*

163. *Id.* (quoting Am. Seaman's Friend Soc'y v. Hopper, 33 N.Y. 619, 625 (N.Y. 1865)). Judge Fuld, authoring the dissenting opinion in which two other Judges joined, said: "I share the Appellate Division's view that other and sound reasons, quite apart from the alleged decision, existed for the disposition made by the testator. Indeed, he himself had declared that his wife had enough money and he wanted to take care of his brothers and sisters living in Europe." *Id.* at 680.

164. *Id.* at 678.

165. *Id.* at 677.

166. *Id.*

167. *Id.*

168. *Id.* at 678.

169. Dew III, 162 Eng.Rep. at 456. *See also supra* Part II. B.2.a. (discussing Sir. Nicholl's decision in *Dew*).

and in business.[170] Legal training, however, inclines us to chiefly attribute the *Honigman* result to the application of a minority causation test.[171]

Breeden v. Stone[172] is another delusion case, but in contrast to *Honigman*, it is one in which the court upheld the will.[173] The rich testator, Spicer Breeden, shot himself two days after his hit-and-run accident that killed the other car's driver.[174] Breeden left behind a holographic will excluding family members and igniting a contest.[175] The probate court found that the decedent had used cocaine and alcohol proximate to the time of his death.[176] Based on the testimony of Breeden's friends, the court found "that decedent's moods were alternatively euphoric, fearful, and depressed, and that he was excessively worried about threats against himself and his dog from government agents, friends, and others."[177] His siblings presented abundant evidence of Breeden's allegedly delusional state.[178] On one occasion, Breeden was "so delusional as a result of cocaine and alcohol" that he called his friend, Chelwick, to come to the house because he "was covered with bugs" and felt that he needed to go to the emergency room.[179] Chelwick responded by rubbing Benedryl on Breeden's body to calm him down.[180] A month later, the delusions escalated:

> [Breeden] thought that people were watching him, following him and that everyone was a FBI agent or DEA agent. [Breeden] received a VCR rewinder as a gift which he promptly stomped, destroyed and threw away because he thought that Chelwick had planted a listening device in it. [Breeden was also]…convinced that the FBI was working in conjunction with Public Service to tunnel into his house when new sewer lines were being installed in his neighborhood, that people could monitor his

---

170. *See* Ronner, *supra* note 26, at 72 (2003) (discussing the judicial predilection to favor spouses and traditional families in will contests).

171. *See* Dukeminier & Sitkoff, *supra* note 13, at 282–83 (suggesting that the court's approach to causation explains why the *Honigman* case came out the way it did).

172. *Breeden, supra* note 142.

173. *Id.* at 1168.

174. *Id.*

175. *Id.* His will stated, "I want everything I have to go to Sydney Stone—'houses,' 'jewalry' [sic], stocks[,] bonds, cloths [sic]. P.S. I was *Not* Driving the vehical-[sic]." *Id.* Breeden printed, "SPICER H. BREEDEN" at the bottom and signed below his printed name. *Id.*

176. *Id.* at 1169.

177. *Id.*

178. *Id.*

179. *See* Petitioners-Appellants' Opening Brief at 5, in Breeden v. Stone (*In re* Estate of Breeden), 992 P.2d 1167 (Colo. 2000) (No. 98 SC 570), 1999 WL 33748234 at *5.

180. *Id.*

behavior through his television set so he climbed up on the roof and destroyed the antenna, that the cable company could monitor him through the cable wires so he cancelled his cable service, that the FBI could use information against him so he shredded bills, cards and letters, that he had individuals search his house for listening devices, and that he had friends drive by his house to ensure that he was not being "watched."[181]

Breeden also thought that a friend was the Unabomber and had put a bomb in his house, that his father had planted drugs in his Porsche, and that another friend had swiped his car keys to copy and use against him.[182] Breeden "spread[...] corn flakes in the hall outside his bedroom to 'crunch' if someone sought to accost him when he slept," and he frequently changed the locks to his house to make sure that no one had access.[183] In his last months, Breeden thought that his father, his sister, and friends were "spying on him, planting drugs, bombs, or listening devices in his house or cars, or otherwise threatening his life or freedom."[184] Once when Chelwick visited, Breeden exploded, hurled his drink at her, and held her hostage at gunpoint.[185]

Despite the showing of such aberrant behavior, the *Breeden* contestants lost.[186] In affirming probate, the Supreme Court of Colorado found that Breeden met the sound mind test, and that, although he did have insane delusions, they "did not materially affect or influence the disposition made in the holographic will."[187] The court, employing the majority causation test, noted that, in the probate court, there had been testimony that Breeden was alienated from family members and had little contact with them.[188] Breeden also once said that he thought his father was "irresponsible with money," that he "disliked his sister's husband, and that his relationship with his brother was distant."[189] Further, Breeden had not included his brother or sister in an earlier will.[190] Consequently, the court approved the most threadbare holograph—an undated,

---

181. *Id.* (citations omitted).

182. *Id.* at 6.

183. *Id.*

184. *Id.*

185. *Id.* at 7.

186. *Breeden, supra* note 142, at 1176.

187. *Id.* at 1174.

188. *Id.*

189. *Id.*

190. *Id.*

scribbled note, omitting not just the word "will" but also any reference to death—and said that the delusions were not causal.[191]

Like most non-bizarre cases, *Breeden* is debatable. Although the alleged delusions in *Breeden* might seem more severe than those of Ely Stott, Louisa Strittmater, and Frank Honigman, Breeden's will is nevertheless honored. This occurs even though the will is scrappy and the court found Breeden delusional.[192] Incidentally, the *Breeden* court's finding of delusion is also not impervious to refutation. Although some of Breeden's beliefs are pretty peculiar (to say the least), most were things that could have happened. People can and do experience the sensation of bugs crawling on their skin, and bed bugs, which can precipitate this, are not uncommon.[193] People can and do spy and even acquire listening devices.[194] In fact, at least one of Breeden's horrors turned out to be true: his close friend, Michael Crow, was an FBI informer.[195] Moreover, a rational person in Breeden's shoes could feel that folks are out to get him. It is not difficult to fathom that some affluent people, with Breedenesque lifestyles, replete with a fleet of elite cars, a stash of recreational drugs, and a flair for hosting wild parties, might be encircled by false friends and flatterers, who, while using them, secretly wish them ill. Although Breeden was eccentric, and perhaps even a bit "touched," not all would agree that he fit the legal definition of being insanely deluded.

The *Breeden* court's conclusion that the disposition was not the product of insane delusions is just as debatable. In *Honigman*, the contestant won despite countervailing proof that the insane delusion did not affect the will.[196] In *Bree-*

---

191. *Id.* at 1176. *See also* Dukeminier & Sitkoff, *supra* note 13, at 282 (asking whether the holograph in *Breeden*, "which does not contain the word 'will,' does not mention death and is not dated ... [s]hould ... have been admitted to probate as a holographic will.").

192. *Breeden*, 992 P.2d at 1174.

193. *See* Donald G. McNeil, Jr., *They Crawl, They Bite, They Baffle Scientists*, N.Y. Times, Aug. 31, 2010, at D1 (discussing delusions formed by people who have come into contact with bed bugs).

194. *See* Elaine Sciolino, *Europe Union Finds Bugging of Offices of 5 Nations*, N.Y. Times. Mar. 20, at A9 (discussing the discovery of listening devices at a European Union headquarters building).

195. *See* Respondent's Answer Brief at 22 n.8, in Breeden v. Stone (*In re* Estate of Breeden), 992 P.2d 1167 (Colo. 2000) (No. 98 SC 570), 1999 WL 33748234 at *5. In that filing, the proponents of Spicer Breeden's holographic will argued that Breeden's delusions were not so bizarre, nothing that "[m]edia reports since Spicer Breeden's death have confirmed, however, that Michael Crow was indeed a government informant at all times when the Breedens allege that Spricer's 'insane delusions' about Michael Crow occurred." *Id.*

196. *Honigman*, *supra* note 141, at 679.

den, however, the contestants lost despite more convincing evidence of a causal nexus between Breeden's delusions and his will.[197] That is, quite a few of Breeden's putative delusions were directed at his family, the very people excluded from the will.[198] Breeden thought that his father had planted drugs and that family members spied on him, and hid drugs, bombs, or listening devises in his house and cars.[199] Even without resorting to the less demanding *Honigman* approach to causation, the *Breeden* court could have credibly found that Breeden's delusions induced him to disinherit family. In the non-bizarre cases, the decision makers reach inconsistent and dubious results. Readers can be just as uncomfortable with these cases as they are with Dostoevsky's protagonist, Golyadkin.

III. Dostoevsky's *The Double* Debunks Our Mental Capacity and Insane Delusion Doctrines

Golyadkin could be a typical testator in a mental capacity contest. In *The Double*, Dostoevsky makes us, the readers, into effectual fact-finders, charged with the task of deciding whether his "hero" is mentally ill or insanely deluded.[200] Readers, however, are preordained to shake their heads, admit defeat, and concede inability to reach a unanimous verdict.

A. The Putative Story

For those who have not read *The Double*, what follows is a plot summary, preceded by an apology: namely, all or some of the events might not have happened.[201] In short, there might be no plot at all.

Golyadkin is a "minor civil servant," with two "love" interests—one past, one present.[202] In the present, Klara Olsufevna, the daughter of a high official, appears unattainable.[203] She seems to prefer and even be engaged to someone

---

197. *Breeden, supra* note 142, at 1174.

198. *Id.*

199. *Id.*

200. Dostoevsky repeatedly calls Golyadkin "our hero." DOSTOEVSKY, *supra* note 1, at 30, 31, 57, 81, 90, 116,144.

201. *See* Gasperetti, *supra* note 4, at 225–26 ("Despite repeated textual assurances that the story unfolds over the course of four days, day four looks suspiciously like day one.")

202. DOSTOEVSKY, *supra* note 1, at 3, 17, 26.

203. *Id.* at 36–37

else, Vladimir Semyonovich, the nephew of Golyadkin's superior, who has been promoted (probably through nepotism) to the rank of Collegiate Assessor.[204] In the murk of Golyadkin's past, there is a German lady, Karolina Ivanovna.[205] What is not clear, but only hinted at, is that Golyadkin had been Karolina's tenant.[206] It seems that, after promising to marry her, Golyadkin absconded and remained in her debt.[207] This scandal, which might have been known to Klara and her father, could be one of the factors disqualifying Golyadkin as Klara's potential suitor.[208]

The story, spanning a mere four days, opens with Golyadkin waking up in a dingy room, one prefiguring a Raskolnikov chamber.[209] That morning, Golyadkin hires a carriage, visits his physician, Dr. Rutenspitz, and complains, "I have enemies, I have deadly enemies who have sworn to ruin

---

204. *Id.* at 28, 188. *See* Richard Peace, *The Nineteenth Century:1840–55*, in THE CAMBRIDGE HISTORY OF RUSSIAN LITERATURE 189, 222 (Charles A Moser, ed., Cambridge University Press 1992) [hereinafter THE CAMBRIDGE HISTORY] (Comparing Golyadkin's mental problems to those "which appear to unhinge Poprishchin in [Gogol's] 'The Diary of a Madman,': defeat in both career expectations and love"). *See also* Martinsen, *supra* note 9, at xix ("A midlevel clerk with ambition, Golyadkin lacks imagination and aspires to be like his superiors in all ways. He wants higher rank and social standing, more power, more money, a better address.").

205. DOSTOEVSKY, *supra* note 1, at 17.

206. *Id.* at 89.

207. *Id.*

208. *Id.* at 119.

209. *Id.* at 3. (describing the room as "messy green walls..., begrimed with soot and dust, ... [a] mahogany chest of drawers, ... imitation mahogany chairs, ... red painted table, ... reddish oil cloth covered ottoman patterned with sickly green flowers, and lastly the clothing he had hastily discarded the night before and thrown in a heap onto the ottoman."). In *Crime and Punishment*, Raskolnikov's room is "a tiny little cell, about six paces long, and it presented a most pitiful aspect with its grimy, yellow wallpaper that was everywhere coming off the walls; it was so low-ceilinged that to a person of even slightly above-average height it felt claustrophobic as though one might bang one's head against the plaster at any moment." FYODOR DOSTOEVSKY, CRIME AND PUNISHMENT 35 (David McDuff trans., Penguin Books 2003) (1886) (1866). *See also* AMY D. RONNER, LAW, LITERATURE, AND THERAPEUTIC JURISPRUDENCE at 111 (2010) ("This hovel, in fact takes on a life (or rather death) of its own: Dostoevsky reminds us repeatedly of the tomb's stifling wretchedness and we see that it is something that Raskolnikov detests and yet clings to for refuge."); Gary Saul Morson, *Axes to Grind: A Russian Literature Scholar Reflects on the Interiors of Crime and Punishment*, INTERIORS, May 1999, at 142 (asserting that the "awful room" equals Raskolnikov's "sordid state of mind" and that "[i]n Dostoevsky, dirty yellow is the color of mental illness, and lying on the couch feeds Raskolnikov's nervous, irritable condition and his mad dreams ...").

me...."[210] Rutenspitz tells him not only to take his medicine, but also to get out more, "[g]o to theatres, go to a club, and don't be afraid of an occasional glass."[211]

After leaving Rutenspitz, Golyadkin decides to attend Klara's birthday party and "shops" for the event at the arcade.[212] Darting from store to store, he fondles all sorts of expensive merchandise while promising various shop keepers that he will return later or send for the coveted item.[213] Golyadkin ends up with a pair of gloves and a bottle of perfume, costing just one and a half roubles.[214]

Klara's party is a big bash and anyone of importance will attend.[215] It is a formal ball, hosted by Klara's father, who is Golyadkin's former patron.[216] Although Golyadkin has not been invited, he arrives in formal attire, with a rented carriage, two horses, and livery for his servant, Petrushka.[217] The footman who opens the door, however, tells Golyadkin that he is not welcome.[218] After a bout of indecision, Golyadkin enters, marches up to Klara, and brazenly insists on dancing with her.[219] When Klara screams, others rush to extricate her, and Golyadkin is ignominiously ejected into the "chill blast" of the street.[220]

After the scandal, Golyadkin's evening goes from bad to worse. As he wanders in anguish and even considers suicide, he has this "uneasy feeling that someone is stalking him."[221] When he gets a better look, he sees someone "dressed and muffled exactly like [him] from head to foot ... scuttling along ... with the same short rapid step."[222] When Golyadkin corners this "late-night companion" and tries to initiate conversation, the stranger initially rebuffs him, but later ends up in Golyadkin's flat "sitting on his bed."[223]

The plot is interrupted and jumps to Golyadkin waking up in the morning.[224] The Double is gone.[225] Despite his "strong presentiment of something

---

210. DOSTOEVSKY *supra* note 1, at 14.
211. *Id.* at 11.
212. *Id.* at 18–19.
213. *Id.* at 19
214. *Id.* at 20.
215. *Id.* at 26–27.
216. *Id.* at 26.
217. *Id.* at 5–6, 23
218. *Id.* at 23.
219. *Id.* at 31–33, 35
220. *Id.* at 35.
221. *Id.* at 39–41.
222. *Id.* at 41.
223. *Id.* at 42–44.
224. *Id.* at 44.
225. *Id.* at 44–45

being not quite right," Golyadkin nevertheless dons his "uniform jacket" and goes to work.[226] At work, he sees that there is a new clerk, who happens to be his Double from the night before.[227] As it turns out, the Double's name is also Golyadkin.[228] At the end of the work day, the Double introduces himself to Golyadkin and gets invited for dinner.[229]

Petrushka admits both master and guest, helps them off with their coats, and serves them a meal.[230] Golyadkin, who had been quite fearful and suspicious of the Double, is now "moved" and "genuinely touched" by his guest's sob story.[231] Golyadkin "[f]orgetting his recent misgivings," becomes drunk, confesses his darkest secrets to the Double, and lets him sleep over.[232] The next morning, the Double is gone and Golyadkin regrets his loose-lipped disclosures of the night before.[233]

When Golyadkin goes to work the next day, he meets the Double in the antechamber, but now things have changed, including the Double.[234] The Double is no longer the modest, grateful guest of the night before, but has become icy and indifferent.[235] Not only does the Double snub Golyadkin, but he bustles about the office like an arrogant, ruthless careerist.[236] The Double plays devious tricks on Golyadkin and recruits colleagues to witness the "perfidious[...] abuse."[237]

The next day, Golyadkin awakens, "stark frozen with horror," and heads off to the office, but decides not to enter.[238] Instead, Golyadkin, cornering a colleague outside, learns that he is going to lose his job and that another official occupies his desk.[239] It is almost dark when Golyadkin ventures into his of-

---

226. *Id.* at 46.
227. *Id.* at 47–49. Dostoevsky at times refers to Golyadkin as "Senior," "Golyadkin I," and "elder Golyadkin," among other names. He also refers to the Double as "Junior," Golyadkin II," and "new Golyadkin." This may be an effort to nudge the readers toward the conclusion that the two are also one. However, to eliminate confusion in this analysis, the author refers only to Golyadkin and the Double. Other quoted material may reference other names to be applied accordingly.
228. *Id.* at 50.
229. *Id.* at 55–56.
230. *Id.* at 56–59.
231. *Id.* at 59.
232. *Id.* at 59, 61–62.
233. *Id.* at 64–65.
234. *Id.* at 66.
235. *Id.* at 66–67.
236. *Id.*
237. *Id.* at 70, 72–73.
238. *Id.* at 95, 97.
239. *Id.* at 97, 100.

fice.[240] When he approaches his co-workers, he is "unpleasantly struck by a certain iciness, abruptness," and the Double, now the popular fixture, again "treacherously insult[s]" and humiliates Golyadkin.[241]

While wandering about later, Golyadkin discovers a love letter from Klara Olsufevna in his pocket.[242] In her letter, Klara begs Golyadkin to "save" her and meet her at her house so that they can elope.[243] Golyadkin obeys by hiring a carriage and going to Klara's house, where another party is in full swing.[244] When Klara fails to appear, Golyadkin waits outside under the "soothingly protective shadow of the wood stack."[245] Suddenly, house curtains are drawn back and Golyadkin, who is noticed, is led inside.[246] While the Double, who is in attendance, gives Golyadkin a "treacherous friend smile" and a "quick mischievous wink to all around," others stare at Golyadkin with curiosity, kindness, and compassion.[247] The guests are all expecting someone, who is supposedly en route.[248] That man happens to be Doctor Rutenspitz, who arrives, guides Golyadkin by the hand, puts him in a closed carriage, and whisks him off to an insane asylum.[249] Golyadkin "[gives] a scream and clutche[s] his head."[250]

B. The Critics

The Double has ignited debate, and Golyadkin's mental condition is one of the biggest question marks. What many critics ask is whether the Double is objectively real.[251] While some say "yes" and others "no," the lack of consensus belies the quandary: the indeterminacy of truth.[252]

Some literary critics, seeking to place The Double in a temporal context, try to explain why the novel was not well-received at first, and some even view it

---

240. *Id.* at 103.
241. *Id.* at 104–105.
242. *Id.* at 118.
243. *Id.*
244. *Id.* at 126, 131–33.
245. *Id.* at 137.
246. *Id.* at 137–39.
247. *Id.* at 142.
248. *Id.* at 141.
249. *Id.* at 142–43.
250. *Id.* at 144.
251. *See supra* note 9 (discussing the scholarly debate over the existence of the Double).
252. *See supra* note 9 and accompanying text (discussing the scholarly debate over the existence of the Double).

as a setback in Dostoevsky's early career.[253] In 1845, Dostoevsky made his debut with *Poor Folk*, an epistolary novel, featuring Devushkin, a poor government clerk, and Varenka, a younger woman and an impoverished orphan.[254] Although Devushkin and Varenka are neighbors, they speak to each other in letters through which readers share their pasts, melancholy lives, unrequited yearnings, and dire poverty.[255]

This first novel, rooted in the naturalistic tradition of the 1840s, instantly became a hit, with critics deifying its young author as a nouveau Nikolai V. Gogol.[256] Before Gogol, the fictional underdog had been stereotyped as a buffoon, subject of ridicule, or object of charity.[257] Gogol, however, broke new ground with *The Overcoat* by portraying such poor souls as human beings,

---

253. *See e.g.*, Jones, *supra* note 4, at 48 (speaking of the pre-Siberia period, he states that while "*Poor People* [had] relative success—critics loved it, the general public enjoyed it moderately— ... [,] *The Double's* discipline was stricter, and it failed."); Chizhevsky, *supra* note 4, at 112 ("The first version of the theme, *The Double* (1846) received rather unfavorable criticism, and until recently was considered an unoriginal work ..."); Gasperetti, *supra* note 4, at 217–18 (explaining that "[a]t least part of the reason for the negative critical reception accorded *The Double* can be attributed to the author himself ... [who] expressed grave doubts about the form ..."); Rosenthal, *supra* note 3, at 60 ("The story was deeply disturbing to Dostoevsky's contemporaries, and both public and critics rejected it."); Trubeckoj, *supra* note 8, at 161 (explaining how the stories, which "immediately followed [*Poor Folk*] caused some disappointment.").

254. Fyodor Dostoevsky, Poor Folk (David McDuff trans., 1988) (1846) in Poor Folk And Other Stories 1–129 (Penguin Classics 1988) (1846). *See also* Trubeckoj, *supra* note 8, at 150 (discussing how Dostoevsky "made his debut with *Poor Folk*, a novel in letters."); *supra* Chapter I (Inexpressible Ideas: A Multifaceted Life and Legal Lens), II (The Life) (discussing Dostoevsky's pre-Siberian work).

255. *See* Trubeckoj, *supra* note 8, at 150–51.

256. David McDuff, *Introduction*, to Poor Folk And Other Stories at xi (Penguin Classics 1988) ("'A new Gogol has appeared!' Nekrasov shouted, as he entered Belinsky's study holding the manuscript of *Poor Folk*."); Harrison, *supra* note 4, at 4 (Dostoevsky "appropriate[s] ... motifs and stylist mannerisms of Nikolai Gogol, for which Dostoevksy was even accused of plagiarism"), 77 (a "new Gogol"); Victor Terras, *Problems of Human Existence in the Works of Young Dostoevsky*, 23 Slavic Rev. 79, 80 (1964) ("*Poor Folk* is explicitly an echo of, and a reply to Gogol's *Overcoat*."); Trubeckoj, *supra* note 8, at 158 (explaining how Devushkin in *Poor Folk* "correspond[s] to ... [the] Gogolian depiction of a small government clerk"). *But see* Jones, *supra* note 4, at 31 ("[M]uch has been made of *Poor People's* debt to Gogol's story, *The Overcoat*. This is a different kettle of fish. People are fond of quoting [Dostoevksy] as saying 'We have all come out of Gogol's *Overcoat*'. He probably didn't [say that].").

257. *See generally* David Magarshack, *Introduction*, to Nicolai V. Gogol, The Overcoat and Other Tales of Good and Evil 8 (W.W. Norton & Co. 157) ("With ['The Overcoat,'] Gogol began a new chapter in Russian literature in which the underdog and so-

worthy of dignity in their own right.[258] With the publication of *Poor Folk,* the critics, especially renowned Visarion Belinsky, felt that it tipped its hat to the Gogolian conception of literature as capturing society and disclosing social ills.[259] *Poor Folk* thus installed Dostoevsky—at the tender age of twenty-four— as hero, master, head of a literary school.[260]

After *Poor Folk* "giveth," *The Double* "taketh away," and thus, in artistic peripeteia, *The Double* catapulted to failure.[261] Many readers turned their thumbs down, and Belinsky, in his 1846 review, felt it was boring and redundant.[262] Although initially deflated, a more mature Dostoevsky conceded that he himself had qualms about *The Double.*[263] Approximately thirty years later, in *Diary of a Writer,* Dostoevsky said:

---

cial misfit is treated not as a nuisance or a figure of fun, or an object of charity, but as a human being who has as much right to happiness as anyone else.").

258. Trubeckoj, *supra* note 8, at 159–60 ("The lowly clerk was canonized by the naturalistic school as the hero of its short stories. But he was characterized purely externally as a comic figure. Gogol's 'Cloak' discovered a new side to this figure, one that aroused pity. As a poor human being, socially neglected but pitiable, he appeared in a new light.")

259. *See* McDuff, *supra* note 256, at xi (describing Belinsky's enthusiasm over *Poor Folk*). *See also supra* Chapter I (Inexpressible Ideas: A Multifaceted Life and Legal Lens), II (The Life) (discussing Dostoevsky's pre-Siberian work).

260. *See generally* Harrison, *supra* note 4, at 77–78 (describing *Poor Folk* as a "resounding success with readers and critics, who saw the author as the new herald of Natural School social realism."). *But see id.* at 78 (explaining that "the praise of [*Poor Folk*] was not unmitigated."). *See also* McDuff, *supra* note 256, at xiv ("When *Poor Folk* was finally published in the *St. Petersburg Almanac* for January 1846, its reception by the critics was far less positive than might have been expected after the furor of interest and publicity that had been whipped up by Belinsky's sudden enthusiasm.").

261. *See, e.g.,* Chizhevsky, *supra* note 4, at 112 (discussing the "unfavorable criticism" of *The Double* and how it was considered "an unoriginal work, influenced either by Gogol's *Overcoat* or his *Nose.*"). *See also supra* note 253 and accompanying text (noting the critics that viewed *The Double* as a setback).

262. Jones, *supra* note 4, at 48 (pointing out that readers were "puzzled or bored"); Gasperetti, *supra* note 4, at 217 at 217 ("In a February 1846 review of *The Double* for *Notes of the Fatherland,* Visarion Belinskij criticized the redundancy of Dostoevskij's tangled web of dreams, impostors, and mirror images. While expressing admiration for individual incidents in the novel, he declared that … [it] … wearies and bores."). *But see* Peace, *supra* note 204, at 223 (explaining that *The Double* is "a penetrating and serious account of a mental breakdown, much too far ahead of its time for Dostoevsky's contemporaries, who scarcely understood it").

263. *See* Gasperetti, *supra* note 4, at 218. In his letters, Dostoevsky mentions Golyadkin, is initially hopeful about the success of *The Double,* and later, bewails its poor reception. *See, e.g.,* Letter from Fyodor Dostoevsky to Mikhail Dostoevsky (September 1845), in I DOSTOEVSKY LETTERS, at 112 (David Lowe and Ronald Meyer, eds. & trans., Ardis Pub-

This tale of mine did not turn out well at all, but the idea behind it was clear and logical, and I never expressed anything in my writing more serious than this idea. But I did not succeed at all with the form of the tale.... [S]ome fifteen years later, I revised it thoroughly..., but then, too, I came to the conclusion that the thing was a total failure; and if I now were to take up the idea and elaborate it once more, I would choose an entirely different form.[264]

---

lishers, 1988) [hereinafter I Letters] ("What's going to happen, what's going to happen in the future? I'm really a Golyadkin now ... Golyadkin has profited from my spleen."); Letter from Fyodor Dostoevsky to Mikhail Dostoevsky (October 8, 1845), in *id.* at 113 ("*Golyadkin* is standing quite firm in character. A horrible scoundrel, he's unapproachable; refuses to move ahead at all, claiming that after all, he's not yet ready."); Letter from Fyodor Dostoevsky to Mikhail Dostoevsky (November 16 1845), in *id.* at 118 ("Golyadkin is turning out superbly; that will be my chef d'oeuvre."); Letter from Fyodor Dostoevsky to Mikhail Dostoevsky (February 1, 1846), in *id.*, at 122 ("Golyadkin is coming out today.... I was incredibly successful with Golyadkin ... You'll like it even better than *Dead Souls* [Gogol].""). Later, Dostoevsky felt that his "fame has reached its apogee," that he "failed to meet expectations," and "ruined a thing that could have been a great work." Letter from Fyodor Dostoevsky to Mikhail Dostoevsky (April 1, 1846), in *id.* at 124–25. He also said that "Golyadkin ha[d] become "repulsive" to him, and explained: "along with brilliant pages there is foul stuff, trash, it's nauseating, one doesn't want to read it." *Id.* at 125. He further elaborated on the criticism of his Golyadkin:

> [E]veryone in the general clamor, i.e., *our people* and the entire public have found Golyadkin so boring and flaccid, so drawn out that it's impossible to read it. But what's most comical of all is that everyone is angry at me for long-windedness and every last person is reading me in a frenzy.... Some of the readers yell that this is quite impossible, that it's stupid both to write and to print such things.

Id. See also Letter from Fyodor Dostoevsky to Mikhail Dostoevsky (January–February 1847), in *id.* at 150 ("I hear on the sly (and from many people) such rumors about Golyadkin that it's simply horrible). *But see id.* ("Some say right out that the work is a *wonder* and hasn't been understood."). Dostoevsky planned to revise *The Double*, but the revised version was not published until 1866. In a Letter from Fyodor Dostoevsky to Mikhail Dostoevsky (October 1, 1859), he states: "[b]elieve me, brother, that this revision, ... will be the equivalent of a *new novel*. They will finally see what *The Double* is!" *Id.* at 380.

264. Fyodor Dostoevsky, II A Writer's Diary (1877–1881) at 1184 (November 1877) (Kenneth Lantz, trans. Northwestern University Press, 1994). *See also* Jones, *supra* note 4, at 83–84 (discussing Dostoevsky's dissatisfaction with the novel and the entry in his *Diary*). Dostoevsky, dissatisfied with the novel, tried to revise it, and produced another version in 1866. *Id.* at 60–65 (discussing differences between the 1846 and 1866 versions); Harrison, *supra* note 4, at 195–211 (analyzing the projected revisions to *The Double*). The 1866 version was subtitled *A Petersburg Poem* and Dostoevsky "removed the summarizing sentences at the beginning of each chapter," but "[i]n the final accounting, few changes were made to the text itself." *Id.* at 202–203.

Later critics, also flummoxed by the novel's "form" and trying to get a handle on that "serious" idea, fall into four overlapping groups. First, there are scholars, like Professor Victor Terras, who see *The Double* as "a psychological experiment concerning some problem of human existence."[265] For Terras, the main character in *Poor Folk* is "cast in the role of a sentimental lover," while the "thoroughly prosaic, 'ordinary,' trivial Golyadkin in *The Double* develops a Doppelganger complex," which flouts romantic conventions.[266] Terras sees the "Doppelganger complex" as Dostoevksy's portrayal of "[h]uman existence [which is] … a loud and ugly dissonance between what man is trying to be and what he is."[267] Taking this a step further, *The Double* subsumes another, but broader, unresolved "dissonance"—one between subjective and objective "facts."[268]

Second, other scholars see *The Double* as commentary on literature, or more precisely, as a jab at the votaries of naturalism. According to Professor David Gasperetti, early critics, like Belinsky, missed the boat when they "failed to see … that there indeed is a method to the madness in *The Double*" and that the novel "succeeds quite well if [viewed] as a challenge to the literary competence demanded of those who read the fiction of the Natural School."[269] Dostoevsky was not just a writer, but also a voracious reader, well versed in world literature.[270] Gasperetti suggests that, in *The Double*, Dostoevsky exploited and parodied naturalist devices to intentionally agitate readers and dare them to reassess their own literary values.[271] While this analysis is sensible, it too could be more

---

265. Terras, *supra* note 256, at 80.

266. *Id.* at 79. Terras states: "[W]here the struggle between truly 'romantic' Doppelgangers would reflect a struggle between heaven and hell, the struggle between the two Goliadkins is only a wretched intrigue, carried on by two underlings for nothing more than a snug little job. What difference does it make, which of the two—or if either—occupies a desk at the 'department'… ?" *Id.* at 84. *See also* Harrison, *supra*, note 4, at 18–32 (discussing the "Doppelganger Motif").

267. Terras, *supra* note 256, at 90. *See also* Leon Burnett, *Effacement and Enigma in the Making of* The Meek Girl," in ASPECTS OF DOSTOEVSKII: ART, ETHICS AND FAITH 149, 150 (Robert Reid & Joe Andrew, eds., Rodopi B.V., 2012) (speaking of Dostoevsky's use of the "*Doppelganger* … [and how p]sychologically, the act of doubling is an effacement of the individual self").

268. *See* DOSTOEVSKY, *supra* note 1, at 44–45 (describing how Golyadkin questions whether the appearance of his Doppelganger was a "delirious fancy" or objectively real).

269. Gasperetti, *supra* note 4, at 217.

270. *Id.*

271. *Id.* ("Confronted with a set of literary conventions that seem to be as empty as [Goljadkin] himself, readers are forced to re-evaluate their allegiance to the fiction of the Natural School.").

elastic: that is, Dostoevsky sought to provoke readers to not just question *literary* "allegiances," but also to mistrust their allegiance to an objective reality.

Third, some scholars foist Golyadkin's distraught psyche under a microscope.[272] They disagree not only on the name tag to pin on Golyadkin's inner demons, but also on the degree of blame to impute to the oppressive social order of the day.[273] Some Dostoevsky scholars suggest that *The Double* depicts middle-class socio-economic striving, which inevitably pulverizes human consciousness.[274] For Nikolaj S. Trubeckoj, Golyadkin's flaw is "ambition"—his burning "to get ahead in his career, climb higher, be more than he actually is"—which collides with his inferiority complex.[275] Lonny Roy Harrison, labeling Golyadkin's stress as "moral self-awareness," says that "the protagonist's will to succeed in the civil bureaucratic order of nineteenth-century Petersburg is incompatible with his implicit need to find moral rectitude."[276] Harrison further claims that Golyadkin's "[e]go-driven motivations provide contrapuntal tensions to exacerbate his experience of inner division."[277] These analyses, parsing the tension between inner desires and the social order, are illuminating and interesting. What they fail to do, however, is locate a fence between the inner and outer, between Golyadkin's illusions and actual occur-

---

272. *See, e.g.*, Jones, *supra* note 4, at 70 (calling *The Double* "a study in selfhood" and stating that "[t]he affair of Golyadkin […] and [the Double] … can be transposed into the language of self-identity and self-alienation"); Kohlberg, *supra* note 7, at 350 (analyzing how *The Double* "offers a compelling picture of psychopathology"); Rosenthal, *supra* note 3, at 59 ("*The Double* is about an individual's failure to develop and maintain his own sense of himself."); Trubeckoj, *supra* note 8, at 162 (Golyadkin's "whole state of mind is that of a diseased person" and "[h]is illness develops further, and soon he suffers from hallucinations.").

273. *Compare, e.g.*, Harrison, *supra* note 4, at ii (calling the problem "moral self-awareness" and ascribing its source to the pressures of nineteenth century social and work politics) *with* Kohlberg, *supra* note 7, at 350 (describing the problem as one of persecution, or dualism, personal to the author).

274. *See infra* notes 275–76 and accompanying text. *See also* Martinsen, *supra* note 9, at xix–xx (calling Golyadkin "a midlevel clerk with ambition" and explaining how "[h]e paradoxically yet tragically chooses Russia's corrupt bureaucrats as his ideals").

275. Trubeckoj, *supra* note 8, at 162.

276. Harrison, *supra* note 4, at ii (Abstract). Temira Pachmuss calls the combatants "the spiritual" and "animal" facets of human nature. Temira Pachmuss, *The Theme of Vanity in Dostoevskij's Works*, 7 THE SLAVIC AND E. EUR. J. 142, 142 (Summer 1963). For her, *The Double* reflects "[a] main concern in Dostoevsky's fiction … [with] the moral decay of the individual which springs from the neglect of his spiritual being." *Id.* She concludes that Golyadkin's ensuing insanity is a result of all his neglect of "all interests other than the gratification of his ambitious ego." *Id.* at 144.

277. Harrison, *supra* note 4, at ii.

rences. In short, these critics do not do what Dostoevsky tells us is impossible.

Fourth, there are critics who, branding Golyadkin "insane," either track his descent into madness or psychoanalyze him.[278] In an early article, Otto Rank, a Freud disciple, saw *The Double* as a "classic portrayal of a paranoid state."[279] Decades later, Doctor Lawrence Kohlberg, dissenting from Rank and the "popular-psychiatry" concept of "split personality," diagnosed Golyadkin with "autoscopic syndrome."[280] Kohlberg illustrates the syndrome by recounting his study of an autoscopic patient, Mrs. A., who communes with her duplicate:

> [S]he had been visited almost daily by her "astral body," as she called it, mostly at dusk when she was alone. Of the double she says, "In a detached intellectual way I am fully aware that my double is only a hallucination. Yet I see it; I hear it; I feel it with my senses. Emotionally I feel it as a living part of myself. It is me split and divided."[281]

Kohlberg links Golyadkin's double to those envisioned by "autoscopic patients," which he, in turn, ties to autoscopic episodes sometimes experienced by individuals with the "severe epilepsy of the sort known to have affected Dostoevsky."[282]

Unlike Kohlberg, who finds biographical support for his diagnosis, Doctor Richard Rosenthal, confining himself to the four corners of the novel, turns to Freudian and post-Freudian psychology.[283] For Rosenthal, projection is the novel's central metaphor, which he defines as a mechanism by which "unacceptable aspects of the self are disavowed and attributed to some person or group or some other part of the external world."[284] Rosenthal delves into Golyadkin's narcissistic nightmare, "in which his every step produces yet another Golyadkin until there is a multitude of doubles mocking and displacing him," which is a "descriptive-representational dream of ego disruption and fragmentation."[285]

---

278. *See infra* notes 279–85 and accompanying text.

279. Kohlberg, *supra* note 7, at 350. *See also* OTTO RANK, THE DOUBLE: A PSYCHOANALYTIC STUDY 27 (Harry Tucker, Jr. trans., University of North Carolina Press, 1971) ("The novel describes the onset of mental illness in a person who is not aware of it, since he is unable to recognize the symptoms in himself, and who paranoiacally views all his painful experiences as the pursuits of his enemies.").

280. Kohlberg, *supra* note 7, at 352–53.

281. *Id.* at 354.

282. *Id.*

283. Rosenthal, *supra* note 3, at 59–61.

284. *Id.* at 61 ("It's not I who is ambitious, angry, unfaithful, etc. it is *he*.").

285. *Id.* at 65. Rosenthal also sees *The Double* as a "story of intrusiveness and usurpation [that] can also be taken up from an oedipal point of view." *Id.* at 73. He notes that

These perspectives on *The Double*, rooted in psychiatry and Freud, are seductive, but leave much unsaid. Yes, Golyadkin could be mad, paranoid, schizophrenic, bipolar, or split. Yes, he could suffer from autoscopic syndrome, be projecting, or jousting with oedipal rivals, who menace his paternal fiefdom.[286] On the other hand, Dostoevsky lets his readers know that little to nothing is clear-cut and that mental anguish defies nomenclature. The author purposely leaves open the most horrific prospect of all—namely, that nothing at all is wrong with Golyadkin. In short, through the literary techniques of intentional obfuscation and retraction, Dostoevsky introduces a character, who is the unremarkable Homo sapiens, doubling as sane-insane.

C. Indeterminate Reality

Although some critics see *The Double* as an individual's progressive descent into madness, a close read reveals stasis, or a Golyadkin who does *not* change: he is the same Golyadkin before he meets his Double, when he meets his Double, and after he meets his Double. In trifurcated phases, Dostoevsky compels readers to endure (not just read about) stagnation and agonizing uncertainty in a world lacking demarcation between reality and hallucination.

1. Pre-*Double*

When we first meet Yakov Petrovich Golyadkin, "a minor civil servant," the author uses the devices of intentional obfuscation and redundant retraction, which persist throughout the novel.[287] Dostoevsky muddles facts, and when something appears to happen, he instantly takes it back, leaving readers to wonder if it, or anything, happened at all.[288]

When his "hero" first opens his eyes, he is "like a man as yet uncertain whether he is aware or still asleep, whether all at present going on about him

---

while the oedipal myth entails a "child's precocious intrusion into parental territory," it houses a subset of "retaliatory fantasies, one of which is of a younger sibling coming along and usurping the child's place with the beloved parent." *Id.* According to Rosenthal, Golyadkin's former benefactor is one of Golyadkin's "symbolic fathers," and Klara, along with Semyonovich, the soon to be son-in-law, become symbolic sibling "rivals" in the "psycho-drama." *Id.* After the symbolic father's rejection, Golyadkin tries to reconstruct the lost relationship with the Double, who, becoming his persecutor, "lives on as an object of terror" and mutates into the "ultimate rival," accelerating Senior's disintegration. *Id.* at 74–75.

286. *See supra* notes 280–85 and accompanying text.

287. DOSTOEVSKY, *supra* note 1, at 3.

288. *See id.*

is reality or a continuation of his disordered dreams."[289] The first clue is that the awake and dream states swirl together, thus eroding the assumption that these are separate domains. *The Double*, however, goes even further than that by obliterating any line between the inner life of the mind and objects of the outside world.

Dostoevsky presciently used and collapsed a poetic device later called the "objective correlative."[290] According to T.S. Eliot, "[t]he only way of expressing emotion in the form of art is by finding an 'objective correlative' [or] a set of objects, a situation, a chain of events, which shall be the formula of that particular emotion."[291] Golyadkin's room in the tenement house in St. Petersburg is an "objective correlative" where furnishings and even daylight comprise "the formula [for his] *particular* emotion."[292] Golyadkin's things come alive as they "look[...] back at him familiarly," and "the foul murky, grey autumnal day peer[s] in at him through the dirty panes in such a sour, ill-humoured way."[293] Dostoevsky anthropomorphizes the context, which reflects Golyadkin's reluctance to leave "recently-ended slumber" and his premonition that "something untoward had happened."[294] Typically, though, "objective correlatives" are rooted in the premise that inanimate things out there *do* exist and, for this reason, can stand for something separate, but inner, like emotions or moods.[295] *The Double*, however, chisels away at the underlying premise. That is, exterior and interior, no longer distinct components in a poetic equation, become inextricably conjoined for Golyadkin.

Golyadkin experiences radical mood swings. On day one, Golyadkin embarks in a "sky-blue carriage," in mirth, emitting a "gleeful outburst" of laughter, which "immediately" morphs into "a most unpleasant sensation."[296] Although this shift may seem inexplicable, it could be explained as a stroke of bad luck. At the time, Golyadkin is engaged in a charade, in which he is all gussied up, with new boots, "an almost new pair of trousers, a shirt front with little bronze buttons, [...] a waistcoat brightly adorned with nice little flowers [... and] a speckled silk cravat."[297] He has hired a ritzy carriage "em-

---

289. *Id.*
290. *See* T.S. Eliot, *Hamlet* 48 (1919), *reprinted in* Selected Prose of T.S. Eliot 45, 48 (Frank Kermode ed., Harcourt Brace 1975) (first using the term).
291. *Id.*
292. *Id.*
293. Dostoevsky, *supra* note 1, at 3.
294. *Id.*
295. *Cf.* Eliot, *supra* note 290, at 48 (defining objective correlative).
296. Dostoevsky, *supra* note 1, at 6–7.
297. *Id.* at 6.

blazoned with some sort of coat of arms" and plays his fantasy role as the re-spected gentleman, the sort of man he envies and would like to be.[298] But in the throes of this "high," an incident whacks him, reminding him of his own limitations.[299]

The incident is traumatic because Golyadkin aches with chronic, unre-quited ambition. He, like others, is obsessed with excelling and rising above his station, but his inability to realize this goal stymies him.[300] While Golyad-kin desperately wants to be confident, assertive, popular, glib, and slick, he is shackled to his own nature, which is shy, modest, cautious, irresolute, fear-ful, and embarrassed.[301] As Trubeckoj puts it, this is the "cleavage [that] leads to a constant inner struggle, a struggle against his inferiority complex," which is "the strongest motivating force in his life."[302] Golyadkin can only attain his lofty aspirations through costumes, props, hired coaches, and make believe.[303]

Golyadkin's spirits plummet on day one, when he is caught red-handed in his masquerade. Two work colleagues and Andrey Filippovich, his department head, spot the underling in his highfalutin garb and hired coach.[304] Golyadkin, who is "suddenly petrified," turns red "up to the ears," gropes for a response, and then, tipping his hat to Andrey Filippovich, says, "It really isn't me, it *isn't* me, and that's all there is to it."[305]

Golyadkin's utterance is both a literal-figurative double entendre and key to the novel. On one level, it conveys to Audrey Filippovich that the uppity specimen in the carriage is a sham and not the person he is. On another level, it suggests that no one is who they are. More broadly, it intimates to readers that the novel provides no tangible reality, and that what readers think they see or know, they might not see or know. Right after his words, the narrator even suggests that there were no words because Golyadkin regrets the fact that he did *not* "respond" or did *not* speak to his department chief.[306] There may have been talk, or there may have been silence. If we are to truly enter the world of

---

298. *Id.*

299. *Id.* at 7 (Golyadkin encounters two colleagues who call out to him in a "very un-becoming" and "[u]ncouth" fashion just as Golyadkin's superior passes in his own coach).

300. Trubeckoj, *supra* note 8, at 161–62.

301. *Id.*

302. *Id.* at 162.

303. *Id.*

304. Dostoevsky, *supra* note 1, at 7.

305. *Id.* at 7–8.

306. *Id.* at 8.

The Double (and Dostoevsky deserves that), we must cede to the unrelenting tension of equal, coexisting, antipodal "realities."

After the chance encounter with Fillipovich, Golyadkin, "for his own peace of mind" visits Doctor Rutenspitz, his "confessor."[307] In this meeting, Golyadkin, the embodiment of contradiction, rebuts himself at every turn.[308] Golyadkin (whose Russian name means "naked") aims to bare his soul to the doctor, but cloaks himself in fictive frocks.[309] The very Golyadkin who has just been frolicking as gentry defines himself as "straight and open" and states, "[t]he only time I put on a mask is when I go to a masquerade."[310] In self-contradiction, Golyadkin tells Rutenspitz that he both does and does not wear masks.

The session proceeds as one protracted oxymoron: Golyadkin informs Rutenspitz that he is "just like anyone else," but in a nanosecond, professes, "I am not as other people."[311] Readers look to Rutenspitz for objectivity, clarification, an anchor to reality, or at least a preliminary diagnosis. But here, too, Dostoevsky intentionally disappoints. Rutenspitz does not appear beset by Golyadkin, and dismissively prescribes medicine, an occasional drink, and fun with friends.[312] Rutenspitz, also apparently vexed, shoots his patient a "searching inquisitorial gaze," says, "[y]ou seem to have wandered a little off the subject," and "unpleasantly grimace[s] [...] as if preoccupied with a presentiment of some sort."[313] Then, after Golyadkin erupts, "quite unexpectedly[...] burst[ing] into tears," with his head "bobbing ... up and down, beating his breast with one hand and clutching at the lapel of Rutenspitz' coat," the "amazed" doctor tries to pacify him.[314]

---

307. *Id.*

308. *Id.* at 8–9.

309. Jones, *supra* note 4, at 49 ("The novel's verbal and formal economy is stated in its first sentence through its hero's name, Mr. Golyadkin, Mr. Naked (*goli*). But the Russian word also suggests destitution ..."); Martinsen, *supra* note 9, at xiv ("Golyadkin's name means 'naked' or 'insignificant,' expressing the character's dual sense of being exposed and invisible.").

310. Dostoevsky, *supra* note 1, at 13.

311. *Id.* at 10–11.

312. *Id.* at 110–11, 15. *Cf.* Letter from Fyodor Dostoevsky to Mikhail Dostoevsky (January–February 1847), in I Letters, *supra* note 263, at 148 ("[T]he dissonance and disequilibrium that society present to us are terrible. *The external* must be balanced with *the internal*. Otherwise, with the absence of external phenomena, the internal will gain too dangerous an influence. Nerves and fantasy will occupy too much space in a being.").

313. Dostoevsky, *supra* note 1, at 10, 12.

314. *Id.* at 14.

Just when readers think that Doctor Rutenspitz has put it in writing that Golyadkin is mentally ill, Dostoevsky erases it as easily as chalk on a blackboard. The outburst subsides as suddenly as it began, and Golyadkin bows politely, leaves the doctor's home smiling, and decides that he is "the happiest of mortals."[315] Once again, readers wonder if anything happened. The author, not content to leave it at that, goes further: he retracts the retraction, because when Rutenspitz is seen next, he is at his window "gazing rather curiously at our hero," possibly speculating that Golyadkin is either mad or en route to a breakdown.[316]

Obfuscation and retraction also operate in Golyadkin's shopping spree. Golyadkin, who is not wealthy, somehow has a "pleasant sum" of "[s]even hundred and fifty roubles in notes"—but that too changes.[317] While in Nevsky Prospect, Golyadkin gets smaller denominations from a money changer.[318] Although he loses value on the transaction, "[he] acquir[es] nevertheless a great number of small notes to swell his pocket-book, which evidently afford[s] him the keenest satisfaction."[319] Professor Jones observes: "The standpoint from which there is now more money in that wallet may not strike the rest of us as rational, but it happens to be Mr. Golyadkin's, and *he* is pleased, and presumably *his* money is worth the pleasure it gives *him*."[320] As Jones concludes, "[h]owever irrational, his standpoint has its rationale."[321] What Golyadkin does here (lose money) may not be economically sound, but it is defensible as Golyadkin's fair price for his pageant, in which the "poor" clerk struts about with an impressively engorged wallet. Jones notes that "the objective sense of money and money's worth is being undermined," and thus, readers must accept the antinomy that the "hero" is both poorer and richer at once.[322] Also, for Golyadkin, shopping is about posturing. Running from shop to shop, pretending to be "a man with his hands full and a terrible amount to get through," he settles on

---

315. *Id.* at 18.

316. *Id.*

317. *Id.* at 4.

318. *Id.* at 19.

319. *Id.*

320. JONES, *supra* note 3, at 49.

321. *Id.*

322. *Id.* Jones states: "As the book proceeds and Mr. Golyadkin begins seeing and hearing and touching things that are unapparent to other people, one recalls the seven hundred and fifty roubles.... [Dostoevsky] is relying on his reader to keep the question alive, and to return to it with the thought that the money may not exist outside Mr. Golyadkin's fancy." *Id.*

random expensive items.[323] After this frenetic splurge, Golyadkin has little to show for it, and it is as if the shopping spree had never occurred.[324]

Lunch proceeds in a similar vein. Golyadkin, now hungry, dines at a fine restaurant, where he poses at an empty table with a newspaper.[325] Then, when it dawns on him that "it is was not proper to just sit there, [...] he order[s] a chocolate drink that he d[oes] not particularly want."[326] In another retraction by the author, Golyadkin eats, but neglects to eat.[327] While "lunching," Golyadkin bumps into his two office colleagues.[328] Feeling embarrassed, partly because he is putting on airs, Golyadkin delivers a diatribe, which echoes what he might have earlier said: "You all know me, gentlemen, but up to now you have only known one side of me [...] [u]p to the present you have not really known me, gentlemen."[329] Reminiscent of his words to Filippovich, "it really isn't me, it *isn't* me," Golyadkin implies that what one sees, they might not see.[330] Here, Dostoevsky, developing that "serious" idea, intimates not only that we might not know his hero, but that we might never really know anyone.

Before the Double appears, the climax is Klara's birthday party. When Golyadkin crashes this "brilliant ball," the narrator's voice intercedes: "Let us rather return to Mr. Golyadkin, the true hero of my veracious tale [...] [whose] present position ... [is] curious to say the least."[331] Equivocation follows: "[Golyadkin] also was there, ladies and gentleman—not *at* the ball, that is, but very nearly."[332] Here the author casts doubt on whether Golyadkin is present or "nearly" present or whether there even exists a party at which he, or anyone, can be present. After it appears that Golyadkin is hiding for "nearly three hours on a cold dark landing," Dostoevsky, through his narrator, notes that "to explain exactly what had been happening to him is difficult."[333] The author asks his readers to accept inexplicability along with dense fog.

---

323. DOSTOEVSKY, *supra* note 1, at 19–20. He apparently orders a "complete tea and dinner service for one thousand five hundred roubles, together with a fantastically-shaped cigar-case and a complete shaving outfit in silver for a similar sum," plus "furniture for six rooms, and admire[s] an intricately designed ladies' dressing-table in the latest style." *Id.*

324. *Id.* at 20.

325. *Id.*

326. *Id.*

327. *Id.*

328. *Id.*

329. *Id.* at 20–21.

330. *Id.* at 8, 20–21.

331. *Id.* 26–27, 30.

332. *Id.* at 30.

333. *Id.* at 30–31.

Once Golyadkin enters the ball-room, retraction propels and freezes the narrative. We learn that Golyadkin "[sees] one or two other people [...] [o]r rather—he [does not]."[334] When he clumsily jostles various guests, he, "noticing none of this, or, more accurately, *noticing* it," looks at no one, but finds "himself face to face" with Klara.[335] Almost every sentence has in its wake an equal and opposite jolt of erasure. When Golyadkin makes an ass of himself, he blurts out, "It's nothing, nothing, gentleman," which could also translate into nothing having happened.[336]

In fact, the whole party may be ersatz: a man with a proud head of hair could really be "wearing a wig," which, if ripped off, could expose a head as bare as "a billiard ball."[337] After the servant tries to cajole Golyadkin into leaving on his own accord by telling him that someone needs to talk to him, Golyadkin says, "No ... [y]ou are mistaken, quite mistaken."[338] "Mistaken" becomes the mantra, which Golyadkin chants as "unpardonably mistaken."[339] Through this, Dostoevsky suggests that life is one big illusory ball, in which "unpardonably mistaken" people feign a chuckle and a waltz.[340]

2. Meeting the Double

Some scholars, like Trubeckoj, feel that Golyadkin only "thinks that he meets his double," because Golyadkin is "insane."[341] For Trubeckoj, Golyadkin is hallucinating: "[t]he cleavage existing in his inner self materializes," and the "whole tragedy really takes place in [Golyadkin's] consciousness."[342] Although there is textual corroboration for his view, there is equal proof of the opposite—the Double's authenticity.[343]

After Klara's party, Dostoevsky hints at an impending suicide: the weather is "driving [Golyadkin] ... out of his mind" while he seeks to "annihilate completely, to return to dust and cease to be."[344] Sensing that "someone had just been standing right there beside him," Golyadkin asks, "[w]hat's wrong with

---

334. *Id.* at 32.
335. *Id.*
336. *Id.* at 33.
337. *Id.* at 34.
338. *Id.* at 36.
339. *Id.*
340. *Id.* at 36–37.
341. Turbeckoj, *supra* note 8, at 162.
342. *Id.*
343. *See supra* note 9 (scholarly debate on the authenticity of the Double).
344. DOSTOEVSKY, *supra* note 1, at 39.

me ... [h]ave I gone mad or something?"[345] As soon as the author builds a case for insanity, he recants, because as he first appears, the Double is not a madman's vision. He is plainly "illuminated by a nearby lantern," and when Golyadkin tries to initiate conversation, he interacts like flesh and blood.[346] That evening, when the Double heads for Golyadkin's home, concrete details, like the ringing of a bell and an "iron bolt grat[ing] back" establish that a corporeal form is crossing the gate around the building.[347]

Then, just when readers start to believe that the Double is genuine, Dostoevsky changes course. Although it is a near Herculean task to navigate up Golyadkin's dark staircase without "breaking a leg," readers witness the Double "darting lightly up the stairs, encountering no difficulties, and showing perfect knowledge of the ground."[348] The Double, who did the impossible, might be nothing but a phantom. Dostoevsky, however, deflates that theory instantly when the Double sits squarely on Golyadkin's bed, as real as real can be.[349]

The next morning, skepticism presides. The narrator refers to "the almost impossible adventures of the whole incredibly strange night," which "was all so peculiar, incomprehensible and absurd, it all seemed so impossible even, that really one could hardly credit it."[350] Golyadkin thinks that "the whole thing ... [was] a delirious fancy, a momentary derangement of the imagination or a clouding of the mind;" but then, in a retractile flash, he feels that "[t]he reality of last night's walk and to some extent of what had occurred during that walk, was, moreover, confirmed ..."[351] It appears that Petrushka, Golyadkin's servant, might have also seen the visitor, because something is gnawing at him: "squint[ing]" around the flat, he seems "even more sullen and uncommunicative than usual."[352] It is just as probable, however, that Petrushka's upset is due to the fact that he has noticed abnormal behavior, and senses his master's impending mental degeneration.

As Golyadkin learns that the Double is the new hire in his office, Dostoevsky strings together beads of refutation. Golyadkin takes one look at his twin and thinks, "[t]he reality of the thing sp[eaks] for itself," and then decides that

345. *Id.* at 40– 41.
346. *Id.* at 42.
347. *Id.* at 44.
348. *Id.*
349. *Id.*
350. *Id.* at 45
351. *Id.*
352. *Id.*

he is dreaming.[353] Significantly, the Double is both "different" from and "identical" to Golyadkin, which causes him "to doubt his own existence."[354] Here what readers yearn for is an objective lens, and Dostoevsky responds by teasing us with a mixed messenger, Anton Antonovich.

He tells Golyadkin that the new man's name is also Golyadkin and admits that he detects a mere "family resemblance."[355] What this implies is that the Double and Golyadkin are not identical, but just a tad similar. Wondering "[h]ow *could* anyone speak of a family resemblance when here was a mirror image[...]," a dissatisfied Golyadkin presses his friend to reconsider.[356] Only when pushed, Anton Antonovich changes his mind: "Yes. Quite right. Really, the resemblance is amazing, and you're perfectly correct—you could be taken for one another ... Do you know, it's a wonderful—it's a fantastic likeness, as they sometimes say. He's you exactly."[357] The implication here is that the Double and Golyadkin are veritable clones. Which of the conflicting impressions is accurate? Dostoevsky leaves that, like everything else, unresolved.

At the end of the work day, the Double, wearing the same outfit as Golyadkin, follows him home.[358] Golyadkin, believing it to be an "illusion" but deciding that "[i]t is no illusion," admits that "he had no idea what was happening to him" and "could not trust his own senses."[359] When they arrive at Golyadkin's home, the two clerks sound the same and even share the same Christian name—"Yakov Petrovich."[360] Because of such coincidences, some scholars, like Mikhail M. Bakhtin, describe the evening as an inner dialogue where "[t]he [D]ouble speaks in Golyadkin's own words, bringing with him no new words or tones," and echoes "the cringing and self-effacing Golyadkin."[361] Professor Terras similarly sees solipsism in the "unspeakable horror about that scene in which Goliadkin thinks he is entertaining a visitor (the other Goliadkin) and is entertaining

---

353. *Id.* at 48.

354. *Id.* at 48–49.

355. *Id.* at 50.

356. *Id.*

357. *Id.* at 51.

358. *Id.* at 55.

359. *Id.* at 55–56

360. *Id.* at 57.

361. Mikhail M. Bakhtin, Problems of Dostoevsky's Poetics 215–16 (Caryl Emerson trans., University of Minnesota Press 1984). Bahktin essentially hears three voices: one, Golyadkin's original, "uncertain" and "timid" voice; two, the voice that Golyadkin addresses to himself, which is "confident and calmly self-satisfied;" and three, the voice "which does not recognize Golyadkin and yet is not depicted as actually existing outside Golyadkin ..." *Id.* at 213, 217.

himself!"[362] These are tenable theories and Dostoevsky wants us to consider them, but his very technique discourages readers from taking refuge in them.

Rather, the author has us yearn for a neutral party to give at least a hint about whether Golyadkin is talking to a guest or to himself. Unfortunately, the only available witness is the unreliable drunkard Petrushka. When both get home, Golyadkin searches Petrushka's face for a reaction, but poker-faced Petrushka treats the duplicates as humdrum: he "show[s] no surprise," helps both men with their coats, and asks casually whether he should bring "dinner for two."[363] Conterminously, a distraught Petrushka is initially "in the doorway, his eyes fixed on the opposite corner of the room to that in which his master and the guest were sitting," and later, insubordinately refuses to go to bed. [364] Readers cannot tell whether Petrushka sees dual diners, or his boss chirping away at an invisible pal.

3. Post-*Double*

In stage three, the Double becomes more evasive, and there are letters that seem to materialize and then vanish. In this way, Dostoevsky unveils his subject—naked incertitude.

When Golyadkin awakens to "find not only the guest but also the bed on which he had slept gone," readers suspect that the evening was a dream, or a figment of Golyadkin's imagination.[365] The rebuttal to that suspicion is Petrushka, who confuses the Double with Golyadkin and informs his master that "his master … [is] not at home."[366] When Golyadkin rebukes, "*I'm* your master, Petrushka, you fool," the servant, backing off, "announce[s] that *the other* had left about an hour and a half ago...."[367] When readers feel momentarily secure in assuming that Golyadkin had harbored a guest, Dostoevsky injects doubt in the form of spooked Petrushka's "offensive" look and surly tone.[368]

At the office, the Double, radically different from the humble, self-deprecating house guest, embodies what Golyadkin had said to the clerks earlier in the restaurant—"[U]p to now you have only known one side of me."[369] Office Double, now cold, unfriendly, "official and business-like," snubs Golyadkin,

362. Terras, *supra* note 256, at 85.
363. DOSTOEVSKY, *supra* note 1, at 56–57.
364. *Id.* at 57, 63.
365. *Id.* at 64.
366. *Id.* at 64–65.
367. *Id.*
368. *Id.*
369. *Id.* at 21.

which makes his "flesh creep."[370] Golyadkin says to Antonovich, "I'm merely developing the theme, putting forward the idea that people who wear masks are no longer uncommon and that it's difficult nowadays to recognize the man underneath."[371] Golyadkin's comment doubles as Dostoevsky's gnome about the masked, indiscernible quality of all beings and of life itself.

The author's voice intercedes again after boss Filippovich asks Golyadkin for documents.[372] The Double, cunningly duping Golyadkin into believing that there is a blemish on the paper, offers to extract it for him with a penknife "out of friendship and pure goodness of heart."[373] Instead, the Double snatches the documents, delivers them to the boss, and takes credit for Golyadkin's work.[374] Golyadkin reflects:

> Anything as black as this [is] really quite inconceivable. It's nonsense. It can't happen. It's probably been some sort of an illusion—either something different happened from what actually did—or it was me who went, and somehow I took myself for someone else. To put it briefly, the whole thing is impossible.[375]

This thought encapsulates the theme. Dostoevsky conveys that events equal "inconceivable nonsense," that what happens might not happen or could be "different ... from what actually did" happen, and that certainty doubles as illusion.[376] Going even further, Dostoevsky implodes the paradox, because as soon as Golyadkin "decide[s] that the whole thing was impossible," the Double arrives "with papers in both hands and under both arms" to affirm the conjecture that what happened might have happened.[377]

Uncertainty intensifies as the Double exploits his popularity to torment Golyadkin. Golyadkin yearns to revisit the warm "friendship" and "cordial relationship of the night before."[378] Lonely, he pines not just for an ouster of solitude, but also for a ratification of his reality.[379] His hunger, however, is left unsated as the Double's skittishness increases, so much so that he personifies

---

370. *Id.* at 66–67.
371. *Id.* at 68.
372. *Id.* at 69.
373. *Id.* at 69–70.
374. *Id.* at 70.
375. *Id.* at 71.
376. *Id.*
377. *Id.*
378. *Id.* at 74–75.
379. *Id.* at 76–77.

evasive reality. For example, when the Double tricks Golyadkin into paying for ten fish pasties at the restaurant, the cagey Double "look[s] as though he might at the least provocation disappear into the next room and slip out by a back way, foiling all attempts at pursuit."[380] Each time Golyadkin manages to grab and seize the Double, the Double, as slippery and protean as truth itself, squirms free to defeat capture.[381]

Another scene dashes all hopes of certitude or clarification. Trying to mingle with "icy" colleagues, Golyadkin spies the popular Double, who is "[g]ay, smiling, full of beans as ever, nimble-footed, nimble-tongued" as he "frolick[s], toadie[s], gambol[s], and guffaw[s]."[382] The Double, working the room like a seasoned politician, turns to shake Golyadkin's hand, "tearfully grasp[ing] it ... in the firmest and friendliest manner."[383] For a nanosecond, this looks like that coveted change of heart, a gesture of inclusion. When the Double "brazenly, callously ... snatch[es] his hand away," the other shoe drops:

> Not satisfied with that, ... [the Double] shook ... [Golyadkin's hand] as if it had been contaminated. Even worse, he spat, and made a most offensive gesture! And worst of all, taking out his handkerchief, he wiped each finger that had momentarily rested in the hand of Golyadkin []. All the while he looked about him deliberately, in his usual blackguardly way, so that all should see what he was doing, and looked everyone in the face in an obvious attempt to convey to them most unpleasant things about Golyadkin.[384]

This scene presents a multi-faceted quandary. Did their friendship and bonding ever happen? Did the handshake or the retracted handshake even occur?

Elusiveness builds when Golyadkin tries to placate the Double in a coffee shop. Initially, the Double greets Golyadkin as a "dear good friend," shooting him a winning smile.[385] Instantly, doing his characteristic about-face, the Double taunts Golyadkin with allusions to his past, resumes his "former heinous trick of pinching—regardless of his resistance and subdued cries—the indignant Mr. Golyadkin's cheek," and replays that devastating retracted handshake.[386] Just

---

380. *Id.* at 81.

381. *See id.* at 66 (When Golyadkin "seiz[es] [the Double] by the hand," the Double darts away.).

382. *Id.* at 104.

383. *Id.* at 105.

384. *Id.*

385. *Id.* at 112.

386. *Id.* at 113, 115.

when it seems that Golyadkin managed to get him to sit still, the Double bolts, sticks Golyadkin with the bill, and slips away.[387]

Flighty malice continues after the Golyadkins appear to leave the café. Golyadkin frantically chases his Double and successfully "clamber[s] onto the carriage, while [the Double] did his utmost to fight him off."[388] At one point, Golyadkin, by "gripping the moth-eaten fur collar of … [the Double's] over-coat," has the Double cornered.[389] But once again losing hold, Golyadkin is hurled "from the carriage like a sack of potatoes."[390] The Double, like fugitive reality, redundantly eschews capture.

In the novel, letters similarly materialize and vanish, leaving readers to wonder if they ever existed.[391] In a letter, Golyadkin begs the Double to "restor[e] the status quo ante," but when Golyadkin orders Petrushka to de-liver it, the servant laughs and then denies laughing.[392] Later, when Petrushka returns and his master inquires about the letter, Petrushka insists that such a letter did not exist.[393] Readers cannot be sure of that, however, because the Dou-ble mentions the letter while berating Golyadkin in the coffee shop.[394] Oc-cluding truth, Dostoevsky also sheds doubt on the letter's recipient. Specifically, when Golyadkin asks his servant to divulge the Double's address, Petrushka provides Golyadkin's own address.[395] Golyadkin replies, "[t]hat's me you're talking about. There's another Golyadkin, and I mean *him*, you twister."[396] At the moment readers are on the brink of concluding that the servant does not believe in the existence of the Double, Petrushka informs his master that he is quitting so that he can work for "nice people" because "[n]ice people

---

387. *Id.* 115–16.

388. *Id.* at 116.

389. *Id.* at 116–17.

390. *Id.* at 117. *See* Martinsen, *supra* note 9, at xiv (Golyadkin's "first name comes from the biblical twin Jacob, the younger son who cunningly cheats his brother Esau out of his birthright" and "[f]ittingly … Golyadkin Junior uses his social cunning to usurp his elder's position.").

391. *See* Gasperetti, *supra* note 4, at 223 ("As disconcerted as readers must be by the spatial and temporal black holes that cut up *The Double*, they become even more confused when forced to deal with the five letters that appear in rapid succession near the end of the novel. One by one each of the letters either cannot be found at a crucial moment or disap-pears altogether.").

392. DOSTOEVSKY, *supra* note 1, at 82–83.

393. *Id.* at 86.

394. *Id.* at 115.

395. *Id.* at 87.

396. *Id.*

don't live falsely and don't have doubles."[397] According to Petrushka, the Double does and does not have authenticity.

Another apparitional letter suddenly appears.[398] Golyadkin, at first "[d]read[ing] that it might prove an illusion or figment of his imagination," later decides it is "no illusion, no figment of the imagination."[399] This letter, from colleague Vakhrameyev, condemns Golyadkin's behavior, calls him a "moral menace," and severs ties with him.[400] Pushing Golyadkin's paranoiac buttons, the letter engenders "hideous visions" and nightmares.[401] When Golyadkin awakens, he discovers that the letter is gone, which makes the readers doubt that it had ever arrived.[402]

Still another letter comes and goes.[403] When a porter delivers it to Golyadkin, he shoves it in a pocket.[404] Later, Golyadkin seats himself at an inn table and extracts what turns out to be Klara's elopement letter.[405] Klara begs Golyadkin to rescue her from her enemies, and tells him: "Await me in your carriage outside Olsufy Ivanovich's windows at nine exactly. We are having another ball."[406] While several critics agree that Klara's letter is climactic, and that Klara herself did not write it, they disagree over the author's identity.[407] Because, as Jones points out, "[t]he letter is a novelettish farrago which suggests the escapist reading of half-educated clerks like Mr. Golyadkin and Mr. Devushkin," it could have been the Double's or some other clerk's nasty prank.[408] Also, because Golyadkin habitually talks to himself and the letter replicates his erratic tone, "our hero" could have composed it himself. Another possibility is that the letter, along with the elopement plot, is totally imagined.[409]

---

397. *Id.* at 88.

398. *Id.* at 89.

399. *Id.*

400. *Id.* at 89–90.

401. *Id.* at 93–95.

402. *Id.* at 96.

403. *Id.* at 109, 133.

404. *Id.* at 109.

405. *Id.* at 118.

406. *Id.*

407. *See, e.g,* JONES, *supra* note 4, at 88 ("[I]n *The Double* Mr. Golyadkin has to mount his own Double Act, which is why the elopement letter is both the novel's climax and its central inspiration, embracing the nowhere of the hut on the shore and the nobody of Sir Golyadkin to the rescue.").

408. *Id.* at 54.

409. *See* Gasperetti, *supra* note 4, at 226 (suggesting that "[d]ay four for Golyadkin is actually day one for everybody else," and that "much of the story, including Klara's letter, is imagined.").

Dostoevsky ensures that nothing about the Klara letter makes sense. When Golyadkin "drag[s] out the letter[,]" he is "dazed and incapable of thought or action" and "unable to read it."[410] When Golyadkin later gropes in his pocket, "to his amazement[,] the letter [is] not there."[411] It, like everything else, disintegrates. The events linked to the letter are just as mind-boggling. If the secret rendezvous is Klara's connivance, it is illogical to select the time and venue of a formal ball with so many guests present.[412] Also, the fact that nothing appears to go according to plan might be indicative of no plan. That is, Golyadkin waits while Klara fails to show.[413]

Significantly, when Golyadkin reads the Klara letter, Dostoevsky accelerates the obfuscation and retraction, so much so that the narration becomes feverish. At the inn, Golyadkin does not appear to order food, yet on his table appear "plates ... [,] a dirty serviette, and a recently-discarded knife, fork and spoon."[414] Golyadkin asks himself, "Who's been eating here? ... Could it have been me?"[415] When he asks the waiter, "What do I owe you, old chap?" the whole place bursts into laughter.[416] Golyadkin and the reader are unsure whether our hero actually ate or whether, tragicomically, he offered to pick up someone else's tab. As Golyadkin admonishes, "[a]nything is possible."[417]

In the muddle, Golyadkin, thrusting his hand into his pocket, extracts a vial, possibly the one prescribed by Doctor Rutenspitz, which inexplicably makes him "shudder[] and almost scream[] with terror."[418] The vial, like just about everything else, "slip[s] from his grasp" and smashes to the floor.[419] Professor Gasperetti asserts that this scene supports his theory that "[d]ay four for [Golyadkin] *is* actually day one for everybody else" and that all events in the interstices are imagined.[420] Dostoevsky says "maybe" in lieu of a committal to "yes." The vial, a metaphor for shattered reality, correlates with the author's

410. DOSTOEVSKY, *supra* note 1, at 123.

411. *Id.* at 133.

412. *See* Gasperetti, *supra* note 4, at 226 ("[w]hy choose a time when so many people are present to foil their elopement?").

413. DOSTOEVSKY, *supra* note 1, at 137.

414. *Id.* at 119.

415. *Id.*

416. *Id.*

417. *Id.*

418. *Id.* at 120.

419. *Id.*

420. Gasperetti, *supra* note 4, at 225–26 ("No time has elapsed ... [t]he credibility of Klara's declaration of love, the appearance of the double, and even [Golyadkin's] blunder at the party is shattered just as completely as the vial of medicine that bursts on the floor.").

postulate that truth (temporal and spatial) is nothing but a cluster of shards on an eating house floor.

When Golyadkin is later led into Klara's party, he drifts into a haze: "To say that he went is not, however, strictly accurate, for he had little idea what was happening to him."[421] When the Rutenspitz of day one arrives, he reminds his patient that he is "an old friend," and Golyadkin confirms, "I have complete faith in Dr. Rutenspitz."[422] Seconds later, the reader—leery about the doctor whose "eyes [are] burning with evil and infernal glee," and who, out of the blue, is speaking with a German accent—wonders if he is Doctor Rutenspitz.[423] Golyadkin expresses his (and the reader's) thoughts: "This wasn't [Doctor] Rutenspitz! Who was it? Or was it him? It was! Not the earlier [Doctor] Rutenspitz, but another, a terrible [Doctor] Rutenspitz!"[424] Even Doctor Rutenspitz may have a double.

D. Does the Double Truly Exist?

If Golyadkin were a testator in a will contest, charged with having insane delusions, how might the court rule? In most states, a delusion is not insane if there is any factual basis for it.[425] Under such a test, Golyadkin could walk away with either a clean bill of health or an insanity diagnosis.

In the hypothetical *in re Golyadkin*, readers of this chapter (the fact-finders) could understandably balk at the assigned task because a chunk of the puzzle is missing—the will itself   and thus, they could object on the basis that ignorance of the chosen disposition is, for them, fatally disabling. If that is what is keeping the fact-finders from opining on Golyadkin's mental state, it substantiates a main gripe by the critics about the capacity doctrine: these are the ones who blame the woeful inconsistency of the cases on bias or the tendency of decision-makers to perform the task backwards.[426] Rather than deciding *the* issue, whether the testator has the requisite sound-mind, they side-step it by preliminarily (and often clandestinely) fixating on the will con-

---

421. DOSTOEVSKY, *supra* note 1, at 139.

422. *Id.* at 143.

423. *Id.* at 144. *See also* JONES, *supra* note 4, at 103 ("[I]n his first meeting with Mr. Golyadkin ... he spoke rather colourless but correct Russian. Whereas now ... he speaks the broken Russian of a member of the Petersburg German Colony: 'You vill official quarters haf, with firewood and *Licht* and service, the vich you deserf not.'").

424. DOSTOEVSKY, *supra* note 1, at 144. *See also* JONES, *supra* note 4, at 104 (exploring the possibility that "the second Dr. Rutenspitz is a different man").

425. *See generally* DUKEMINIER & SITKOFF, *supra* note 13, at 275.

426. *See, e.g.,* Champine, *supra* note 15, at 49.

tents.[427] Then, only *after* doing that, they predicate their testamentary capacity finding on whether the will itself coddles their hearts or comports with normative values.[428]

The Golyadkin matter at hand, however, is a will contest *sans* will. Such a scenario forces the readers—us—to relinquish this impulse, and enables fact-finders to isolate and confront the real issue of whether Golyadkin is insanely deluded. If the fact-finders resist and are reluctant to play along, what holds them back is a different something. This is the veritable impasse, the one the fact-finders deny, sugarcoat, or repressively inter in the unconscious vault. It is the one that *The Double* shoves right in the readers' faces.

If Golyadkin even has delusions, they, at best, fit into the non-bizarre category. Not one of his beliefs is "clearly implausible," but rather, all of them embrace "situations that [can] occur in real life."[429] In making his hero's life so drably prosaic, Dostoevsky has taken great pains to tell us that his "minor clerk," who appears to visit a doctor, shop, dine, go to work, and crash a party, is not some freakish anomaly.[430] Unlike Cecilia Zielinski, he does not think that people are getting orders from a machine that turns the world inside out, sticking balloons in his belly, pushing his eyes back into his head, or breaking his legs and replacing them with someone else's legs.[431] Unlike the testator in *McReynolds v. Smith*,[432] he is not touring other planets, befriending aliens, and planning a stone quarry franchise on Saturn.[433] Moreover, unlike the situation in *Gulf Oil Co. v. Walker*,[434] the devil is neither giving Golyadkin a concert on his fiddle nor flaunting a gigantic horse that straddles two states.[435]

---

427. *Id.*

428. *See supra* Part II.B.2 (discussing the bias and inconsistency in the non-bizarre delusion cases).

429. *See supra* notes 62–66 and accompanying text (discussing the DSM definitions of bizarre and non-bizarre).

430. Dostoevsky, *supra* note 1, at 3 (noting that Golyadkin is "so insignificant a character as to be certain of commanding no great attention at first glance").

431. Zielinski v. Moculski (*In re* Estate of Zielinski), 623 N.Y.S.2d 653 (N.Y. App. Div. 1995). *See also supra* Part II.B.1 (discussing the *Zielinski* case in greater depth).

432. 86 N.E. 1009 (Ind. 1909).

433. *Id.* at 1012. The *McReynolds* court found that the evidence established insane delusion and that the will was, "at least in some measure, the result of such delusion," where the testator believed, among other things, that he "had personally visited the planets, formed an acquaintance with their inhabitants," and learned that "after death, [he would] go to planet Saturn to conduct a stone quarry ..." *Id.*

434. 288 S.W.2d 173 (Tex. Civ. App. 1956).

435. *Id.* at 179. The testator saw "the devil's horse, which was so big it had one foot in St. Louis and the other in California." *Id.*

The most aberrant event in Golyadkin's life is his encounter with the Double, and even that is not "clearly implausible."[436] In real life, such a thing transpires more than one might expect. Accounts of identical twins separated at birth who suddenly meet for the first time are plentiful.[437] Cognizant of such encounters, Dostoevsky even has his character Anton Antonovich address the phenomenon.[438] Anton Antonovich, referring to the "generosity of Mother Nature," speculates that both Golyadkins might come "from the same parts," and says: "[D]on't you worry. *It's a thing that does happen.* Do you know, I must tell you this, the very same thing occurred to an aunt of mine on my mother's side. She saw her own spitting image before she died...."[439]

In *The Double*, Dostoevsky supplies, at least, a "reasonable basis" for the belief that the Double is genuine.[440] With respect to this issue (the one that sows the most discord), some scholars, such as Harrison, feel that "[t]he authenticity of the double is never called into question," and that "[a]ll secondary characters acknowledge the presence of both Golyadkins and ... do not

---

436. *See supra* notes 64–66 and accompanying text (defining bizarre delusions).

437. *See, e.g.,* Thomas Catan, *Spanish Twins Separated at Birth By Mistake Are United By Chance,* THE TIMES (May 28, 2008), http://www.timesonline.co.uk/tol/news/world/europe/article4016045.ece (May 28, 2008) (detailing a story of twins, mistakenly separated at birth, who suddenly meet after a shop keeper is "taken aback by the unfriendly manner of the woman who she thought was her friend...."); Rebecca Leung, *Twist of Fate,* CBS NEWS (Feb. 11, 2009, 8:24 PM), http://www.cbsnews.com/stories/2003/11/04/48hours/main581771.shtml (June 18, 2004) (detailing a story of a woman who, for twenty years, did not know that she had a twin sister until they met in a fast food parking lot); Becky Sheaves, *The Twins Brought Up On Either Side of the Iron Curtain..But Who Lived Identical Lives,* MAIL ONLINE (Dec. 20, 2007, 10:54 PM), http://www.dailymail.co.uk/femail/article-503775 (Dec. 20, 2007) (describing identical twins who met after the fall of the Berlin Wall); Elizabeth Wolf, *Dual Lives of Twins Separated at Birth,* N.Y. POST (Sept. 23, 2007, 5:00 AM), http://www.ny-post.com/f/print/regional/item_4AFadAQePr4GNZdswlhPzM (detailing a story of twins, separated at birth, adopted by different families, and made the subjects of a secret mental illness study who, thirty-five years later met in a café). *See also* Rosenthal, *supra* note 3, at 59 (describing a news story about a man who strangled his twin brother because he was impersonating him). Rosenthal opines that this story, published 130 years after *The Double,* "would have probably pleased [Dostoevsky], who avidly read the papers of his day for things to write about ..." *Id.*

438. *See supra* notes 355–57 and accompanying text (discussing the dialogue between Golyadkin and Anton Antonovich in the office).

439. DOSTOEVSKY, *supra* note 1, at 51 (emphasis added).

440. *See In re* Honigman's Will, 158 N.E.2d 676, 678 (N.Y. 1960) (The court emphasized that the issue was "not whether Mrs. Honigman was unfaithful, but whether Mr. Honigman had a reasonable basis for believing that she was."). *See also supra* II.B.2.b (discussing the *Honigman* case in greater depth).

think it incredible that the original Golyadkin should have a perfect double."[441] While equally compelling opponents insist that the Double is imaginary, a mere hallucination or projection, Martinsen hits the nail on the head by accepting that there is a "narrative ambiguity around [the Double's] objective existence."[442]

The problem is that each of the novel's impartial witnesses gives conflicting testimony. Petrushka, for example, takes two coats and serves two meals.[443] He confuses Golyadkin with the Double and quits because "[n]ice people ... don't have doubles."[444] In contrast, however, Petrushka, corroborating the hypothetical contestants' contention that the Double is imagined, considers the task of taking Golyadkin's letter to the Double to be a joke, and claims that both Golyadkins have the same address.[445] Witness Antonovich also speaks to both sides by detecting a slight "family resemblance" between the two, but then anointing them veritable clones.[446] The very reason we cannot confidently convict or acquit the author's hero is that an objective truth is simply non-existent.

Reader discomfort throughout *The Double* replicates the reaction legal commentators have to the mental capacity and delusion cases, especially those that fall into the non-bizarre fact class. As discussed above, unanimous ratification of the reasoning and result in cases such as *Dew, Strittmater, Honigman,* and *Breeden* is lacking.[447] Not all case readers are wholeheartedly convinced that Ely Stott, who detested his daughter; pioneer Louisa Strittmater, who cham-

---

441. Harrison, *supra* note 4, at 121–22. *See also supra* note 9 and accompanying text (discussing the scholarly debate over the existence of the Double.).

442. Martinsen, *supra* note 9, at xix. *See also id.* (Discussing the "ambiguity" and likening the narrative to Henry James "The Turn of the Screw," Martinsen states that "Golyadkin's double does seem to have an objective existence since other people see and interact with him."). For those commentators who see the Double as a figment of the imagination or a projection of Golyadkin's anxieties, see, for example, Chizhevsky, *supra* note 4, at 115 (asserting that the Double is "conditioned psychologically" and "rises from the depths of Golyadkin's soul."). *See also supra* notes 8 and 9 and accompanying text (discussing the confusion and debate over the authenticity of the Double).

443. DOSTOEVSKY, *supra* note 1, at 56–57, 63 (describing Petrushka's conflicting reactions to the Double).

444. *Id.* at 88.

445. *Id.* at 83, 86–88. *See also supra* Part III.C.3 of this chapter (discussing the vanishing letters).

446. DOSTOEVSKY, *supra* note 1, at 50–51. Similarly, when Golyadkin, in the restaurant, treats himself to just one "fish pasty," he is charged for eleven. *Id.* at 80. It turns out that the Double ate the other ten fish pasties, but the waiter thought it was Golyadkin himself. *Id.* This, of course, suggests that if this happened and if there is a double, they do indeed look alike.

447. *See supra* Part II.B.2 of this chapter (discussing the non-bizarre delusion cases).

pioned feminism; Frank Honigman, who dreaded cuckoldry; and Spicer Bree-den, who was mortified by spying eyes; are insanely delusional.[448] In seeking the source of their discontent, legal commentators like to blame the dubious results on differing evidentiary burdens or on judges or juries, who let their own biases and prejudices affect their decisions.[449] By implying that such excuses are vacuous, *The Double* exposes the true source of our vexation.

The Double dispatches the bitter dictum that, when it comes to the realm of the non-bizarre, which encompasses most of life, the lawyers or proverbial reasonable men and women are capable neither of defining delusion nor of finding that a delusion caused, or might have caused, a disposition. The legal profession has brainwashed itself into believing that lawyers can do what Dos-toevsky knew (and was big enough to admit) is not humanly possible. The reason our cases, along with our inept stabs at justifying them, ring false is that the lawyers are the ones who are not just deluded, but bizarrely deluded. This is unfortunate, because one salutary goal behind the sound-mind re-quirement is to promote the perception of law as legitimate.[450] The hope is that legal institutions, including those governing succession of property, will be seen as rational and fairly predictable.[451] Specifically, practitioners would like to be able to sit down with clients and help them navigate through choices by giving them not just the pros and cons of venturing forth, but also tenta-tive forecasts of closure. When a potential contestant or proponent walks through the law office door, it is the non-bizarre case that inevitably hobbles the profession, obstructs counseling, and undermines legitimacy.

Professor Bradley E.S. Fogel actually offers a palatable solution, proposing that we jettison the insane delusion doctrine altogether and retain only the tra-ditional mental capacity test.[452] Fogel thinks that, even absent a distinct insane delusion or monomania doctrine, extreme cases, like *Zielinski*, would still re-sult in will invalidation.[453] He aptly points out that in cases with testators, like Cecilia, who falsely believe that those "closest to [them]" are trying to hurt them in "bizarre ways," there will likely be a sufficient showing of their inabil-

---

448. *See supra* Part II.B.2 of this chapter (discussing the uncertainty in the non-bizarre cases).

449. *See supra* Part II.B.2 of this chapter (discussing the bias and the putative effect of different evidentiary burdens).

450. *See supra* notes 26–32 and accompanying text (discussing the policies behind the mental capacity doctrine).

451. *See supra* notes 26–32 and accompanying text (discussing the policies behind the mental capacity doctrine).

452. Fogel, *supra* note 10, at 108–09.

453. *Id.*

ity to know the natural objects of their bounty.[454] In support of Fogel, it is worth reiterating that the delusional Cecilias of the world relentlessly cling to what we normatively deem impossible.

Because there is a discernible link between a truly unsound mind and bizarre delusions, Fogel's solution probably does not go far enough.[455] Incorporating DSM science into the mental capacity inquiry could better safeguard testamentary freedom. Fogel is correct that the legal system should jettison insane delusion as a distinct basis for will invalidation and, instead, install the sound-mind-test as sole dictator. Going further, it should also engraft onto the old *Greenwood-Baker* test an added mandate that a mentally incompetent testator must also suffer from what the DSM defines as bizarre delusions.[456] In doing so, the law would at least honestly stipulate to our mortal limitations and concede that the *Stott-Strittmater-Honigman-Breeden* (and now we add Golyadkin) non-bizarre group of testators tends to throw a wrench in the works.[457]

This friendly amendment would, of course, continue to minister to the policies behind the testamentary capacity doctrine.[458] As revised, the doctrine would still aim to ensure that a will express true intent, protect the family, grant a modicum of peace of mind, and help shield targets from exploitation and undue influence.[459] Additionally, by ousting the inconsistent, unpredictable, and disingenuous culprit—non-bizarre delusions—the updated test would also more effectively help foster the perception of law as legitimate and essentially rational.[460]

---

454. *Id.* at 109 ("In *Zielinski*, testator's paranoia seems to have prevented the testator from appreciating her relationship with her son or understanding her obligations to him.").

455. *Id.* at 108 (suggesting that some delusions can be so "clearly implausible" and "not understandable" that they can only originate in an unsound mind). *See, e.g.,* Gulf Oil Corp. v. Walker, 288 S.W.2d 173 (Tex. Civ. App. 1956) (dealing with a testator who had bizarre delusions and the court held that the evidence sustained the finding that the decedent lacked testamentary capacity).

456. *See supra* note 36 (discussing the *Greenwood-Baker* test and its origins); *supra* notes 37–46 and accompanying text (discussing the sound-mind rule and how it is designed to be lenient); *supra* note 57 and accompanying text (describing the core of insanity as delusion).

457. *See generally* Part II.B.2 of this chapter (discussing the non-bizarre cases).

458. *See supra* notes 26–32 and accompanying text (discussing the policies underlying the testamentary capacity requirement).

459. *See supra* notes 26–32 and accompanying text (discussing the policies underlying the testamentary capacity requirement).

460. *See supra* notes 29–32 and accompanying text (discussing the goal of legitimacy behind the testamentary capacity rule).

IV. Conclusion: Golyadkin's Human "Shriek"

When a decedent's will is the product of a bizarre delusion, its resultant invalidation is not particularly earthshaking, and oftentimes, most people acquiesce to the decision.[461] For non-bizarrely deluded decedents, the fact-finding task is formidable and the fact-finders (and at times the courts themselves) cringe at decisions that effectually obliterate an estate plan.[462] The general testamentary capacity cases are rife with the same defects—inconsistency and dubious results—when the contests focus on individuals without bizarre delusions.[463] For too long, this area of the law has spawned controversy and discontent.[464]

From the instant Dostoevsky created *The Double*, it similarly ignited controversy, discontent, and even outrage.[465] Part of this is attributable to the author's use of devices such as intentional obfuscation and retraction, along with his creation of a world in which the readers cannot be sure what is really happening and what is hallucinatory. It is not just the uncertainty that has rattled readers for more than a hundred and fifty years, though. Russian literature scholars have struggled to explain exactly what it is about this pre-Siberian masterpiece that makes so many readers' skin crawl.

Professor Julian W. Connolly attributes the jarring negativity in *The Double* to the fact that "the *narrator* treats his main character so disdainfully," and broaches the question: "how can the *reader* have any sympathy for him?"[466] Professor Gasperetti answers by conceding that "this experience of reader discomfort and alienation ... lies at the heart of [Dostoevsky's] self-effacing discourse" and emphasizing that, "[i]f *The Double* is successful at no other level, it certainly invites readers to see themselves in [Golyadkin]."[467] For Dostoevsky, Golyadkin's mental condition is not *sui generis*, but a state of affairs with which he himself could identify. He, like Golyadkin, frequently found his own "nerves ... in

---

461. *See supra* Part II.B.1(discussing the bizarre cases).

462. *See supra* Part II.B.2 (discussing the non-bizarre cases).

463. *See supra* note 91 and accompanying text (giving an example of inconsistency with respect to the general mental capacity decisions).

464. *See supra* Part II.B.2(giving examples of questionable non-bizarre cases).

465. *See supra* notes 8–9 and accompanying text (discussing scholarly response to and dispute over *The Double*); *supra* Part III.B (discussing the critics' reactions to *The Double*).

466. Connolly, *supra* note 8, at 108.

467. Gasperetti, *supra* note 4, at 231. *See also* Elliott D. Mossman, *Dostoevskij's Early Works: The More than Rational Distortion*, 10 Slavic And E. Eur. J. 268, 272 (1966) (explaining that the novel, which "is a split vision [where] [the readers] see both the external and the internal at the same time ... unsettles [the readers] because [they] can never be quite sure which is which").

disarray," and admitted to "having long, hideous dreams ... [where] the floor keeps seeming to sway beneath [him], and [he] sit[s] in [his] room as though in a ship cabin."[468] At one point, Dostoevsky confessed: "My memory has grown completely dim (completely!). I don't recognize people anymore; I forget what I read the day before. I'm afraid of going mad or falling into idiocy. My imagination is overflowing, working in a disorderly way; at night I have nightmares."[469]

In his day, some of his reviewers criticized Dostoevsky for his focus on supposedly deranged or unbalanced individuals.[470] In *The Double* and, later, in *The Adolescent*, Dostoevsky delved into a phenomenon that fascinated him, one he called "the split," "duality," or "the double."[471] In *The Adolescent*, Andrei Petrovich Versilov finds himself in "the double" predicament:

> You know, it seems to me as if I'm divided in two ... Truly, mentally divided in two, and I'm terribly afraid of that. Just as if your double were standing next to you; you yourself are intelligent and reasonable, but that one absolutely wants to do something senseless next to you.[472]

---

468. Letter from Fyodor Dostoevsky to Mikhail Dostoevsky (August 27, 1849), in I LETTERS, *supra* note 263, at 174.

469. Letter from Fyodor Dostoevsky to Stepan Yanovsky (November 1867), in III DOSTOEVSKY LETTERS, at 289 (David Lowe, ed. and trans., Ardis Publishers 1989) [hereinafter III LETTERS]. With respect to his poor mental state, Dostoevsky often blamed his epileptic attacks. *See e.g. id.* ("O my friend Stepan Dmitrievich, this epilepsy will end up carrying me off!").

470. *See, e.g.,* Letter from Fyodor Dostoevsky to Yelena Shtakenshneyder (June 15, 1879), in V DOSTOEVSKY LETTERS, at 94 & 95 n. 6 (David Lowe, ed. and trans., Ardis Publishers 1991) [hereinafter V LETTERS] (responding to Evgeny Markov's criticism in " 'A Novelistic Psychiatrist,' in the May and June 1879 issues of *Russian Speech*, which criticized Dostoevsky for his interest in unbalanced protagonists").

471. FYODOR DOSTOEVSKY, THE ADOLESCENT 506–512, 552 (Richard Pevear and Larissa Volokhonsky, trans. 2004) (1875) (addressing the "split" or "the double") *See also infra* notes 475–77 and accompanying text (discussing "duality").

472. DOSTOEVSKY, *supra* note 471, at 506–507. *See also id.* at 509 ("But the 'double' was also undoubtedly next to him; of that there was no doubt at all ..."); *id.* at 511 (" 'But the double, the double!' I exclaimed. 'He really has lost his mind!' "); *id.* at 512 ("How could I not stay—what of the double? Hadn't he smashed an icon before my eyes?"); *id.* at 533 ("I just had a dream; in comes an old man with a beard and with an icon, an icon that's split in two, and he suddenly says, 'That's how your life will be split!' "); *id.* at 546 (" 'And Versilov will do her in! ... It's the double!' "); *id.* at 552 ("[T]hat scene at mama's, that split icon, though it undoubtedly occurred under the influence of a real double ..."). *See also infra* note 473 and accompanying text.

In that same novel, the narrator says that "[a] double, at least according to a certain medical book by a certain expert, [...] is none other than the first step in a serious mental derangement, which may lead to a rather bad end."[473] Golyadkin and Andrei Petrovich Versilov, although conceivably split or doubling, are not the crazed or mad *others*, who are so radically different from the rest of the human species and from their author. Dostoevsky understood that, while "the double" can be a "step" that "*may* lead" to disaster, it does not always do so.[474] In a letter that Dostoevsky penned to his friend Yekaterina Yunge, an artist and memoirist who had confided that she suffered from chronic "duality," he empathically and candidly expressed his views:

> [Duality is] ... the most ordinary trait of people, who are not entirely ordinary, however. A trait peculiar to human nature in general, but far, far from occurring in every human nature in such force as with you. That's precisely why you are so kindred to me, because that *split* in you is exactly the way it is in me and has been all my life.[475]

Dostoevsky felt that, in his own case, the "ordinary trait"—that of duality—is "a great torment, but at the same time a great delight too."[476] He told Yunge it was a "powerful consciousness, need for self-evaluation, and the presence in your nature of the need for moral obligation toward yourself and toward humanity."[477] In essence, doubling can be normative, part and parcel of the creative process, a connection between internal and external realms, and that sacrosanct conduit between the self and the human race.

It is not surprising that psychiatrist Rosenthal, coming to a similar realization, aligns Golyadkin with all of postlapsarian humanity:

> To some extent we all struggle against deep urges to yield up our identities, to erase separations and differences, and to get others to think and feel and act for us; sometimes, like Golyadkin, we try to clothe our-

---

473. DOSTOEVSKY, *supra* note 471, at 552.

474. *Id.*

475. Letter from Fyodor Dostoevsky to Yekaterina Yunge (April 11, 1880), in V LETTERS, *supra* note 470, at 189.

476. *Id.* In that same letter, Dostoevsky asks, "do you believe in Christ and in His promises?" and advises: "[i]f you believe (or very much want to believe), then give yourself over to Him completely, and the torments from that split will be greatly assuaged, and you will receive an emotional answer." *Id.* at 190.

477. *Id.* at 189. He adds, "[t]hat's what the split means. If you were less developed in intellect, if yours were limited, you would be less conscience-stricken and there wouldn't be that split." *Id.* at 189–90.

selves in an omnipotent other self, a self we could have been or secretly believe we someday still will be, a self who is free of the painful awareness of just those limitations which define our boundaries and make us who we are.[478]

The "all" and "everybody" in Golyadkin becomes apparent in the novel right before Rutenspitz carts our "hero" off to the asylum: he stands there, scanning the attendees at the party, and sees "[a] whole procession of identical Golyadkins ... bursting loudly in at every door."[479] The implication here is that everyone is or might be Golyadkin: Dostoevsky compels his readers to see not some peculiar anomaly, but rather, just a parade of everyday selves. The novel urges readers to examine doubly both Golyadkin's "struggle against deep urges" and their own, and to endure that all-too familiar "painful awareness" of their own "limitations."[480] Like it or not, readers tend to meld with Golyadkin as his fate becomes their own.

This chapter began with Golyadkin meeting his double—when he "wanted to scream, but could not."[481] In the end, Golyadkin succeeds at emitting that blood-curdling shriek while being whisked away.[482] Rutenspitz's "stern and dreadful ... sentence" does not merely exile Golyadkin from society, but also strips him of the power to make his own choices, obliterates his autonomy, and shatters his human dignity.[483] To make matters worse, the readers entertain the disturbing prospect of a wrongful conviction. Even Golyadkin's own concession, that "[he] had felt this coming on for a long time," does not fully persuade readers that banishment is kind or appropriate.[484] The same rings true of results in litigation that divest individuals of freedom without solid proof that their take on reality is bizarre, or even implausible.

---

478. Rosenthal, *supra* note 3, at 83. *See also* Martinsen, *supra* note 9, at xx ("Golyadkin's dilemma plays out in the gap between his actual and ideal selves: He resolutely refuses to recognize that he does not fit into the world he longs to join.").

479. DOSTOEVSKY, *supra* note 1, at 142.

480. Rosenthal, *supra* note 3, at 83.

481. DOSTOEVSKY, *supra* note 1, at 44.

482. *Id.* at 144.

483. *Id.*

484. *Id.*

Chapter Three

The Confessant Gene: *Crime and Punishment* and *The Brothers Karamazov*

I. Introduction

In *Crime and Punishment*, Luzhin, Dunya's fiancé, scheming to frame Sonya for theft, presents witnesses and pulls stolen banknotes from her pocket:

> From the second pocket, however, a piece of paper suddenly leapt out and, describing a parabola in the air, fell at Luzhin's feet. Everyone saw it; many exclaimed out loud. Pyotr Petrovich stooped down, retrieved it with two fingers from the floor, raised it for all to see and unfolded it. It was a hundred-rouble banknote, folded in eight. Pyotr Petrovich moved his arm around, showing the note to everyone.[1]

In spite of what looks like irrefutable evidence against her, Sonya does not confess. In Dostoevsky's novels, such silence is a near anomaly as characters, even the innocent, have a propensity to self-incriminate.[2] As J.M. Coetzee puts

---

1. FYODOR DOSTOYEVSKY, CRIME AND PUNISHMENT 473 (David McDuff ed., Penguin Books 2003) (1866). This chapter is a substantially revised and expanded adaptation of Amy D. Ronner, *Mitya Karamazov Gives the Supreme Court an Onion: The Role of Confessions*, published in 66 MERCER L. REV. (2014).

2. In Dostoevsky's *Notes From the House of the Dead* [hereinafter *Dead House*], there is one man who is accused and convicted of murdering his father so that he can "get his hands on his inheritance." FYODOR DOSTOEVSKY, THE HOUSE OF THE DEAD 37 (David McDuff, Penguin Books, trans. 2003) (1861). After he served ten years of penal servitude, "the true perpetrators of the crime had apparently been found and had confessed." *Id.* at 302–03. The falsely convicted one, "stripped of his nobility and government service rank," had never

it, in Dostoevsky's writings, "confession itself, with all its attendant psychological, moral, epistemological and finally metaphysical problems, moves to the
center of the stage."[3] In fact, Dostoevsky implies that the whole human race is
blessed and cursed with a confessant gene. In three parts, this chapter, focusing on that blessing-curse, discusses the novelist's posthumous contribution
to criminal justice.

---

made a confession. *Id.* at 37. *See generally infra* Chapter IV(Prisons of Coercion: *Notes from
the House of the Dead*) (describing the conditions and inmates in *Dead House*).

3. J.M. Coetzee, *Confession and Double Thoughts: Tolstoy, Rousseau, Dostoevsky*, 37 Comp.
Lit. 193, 215 (1985). Coetzee explains that "it may be fruitful to treat confession in the
major novels as, on the one hand, a form of masochism or a vice that Dostoevsky finds
typical of the age, or on the other as one of the generic forms yoked together to make up
the Dostoevskian novel." *Id.* at 215-15. *See also* Mikhail Bakhtin, Problems of Dostoevsky's Poetics 227 (Carl Emerson trans. University of Minnesota Press, 2009) (discussing
Dostoevsky's *Notes From Underground* as a "confessional *Ich-Erzahlung*" in which there is "extreme and acute dialogization" and "literally not a single monologically firm, undissociated
word"); Peter Brooks, Troubling Confessions 32 (University of Chicago Press, 2001)
(describing "the self-abasing and self-aggrandizing confessional speeches of Dostoevsky's
Karamazov, or Raskolnikov, or his Underground Man"); Deborah A. Martinsen, Surprised by Shame 92 (Ohio State University Press 2003) (stating that "Dostoevsky's experiments in confession not only manifest his lifelong polemic with Rousseau, they also express
his lifelong interest in narrative form" and that "[b]oth lying and confession are rhetorics
of identity" or "vehicles for self-presentation"); Julian W. Connolly, *Confession in* Brothers
Karamazov, in Dostoevsky's Brothers Karamazov: Art, Creativity, and Spirituality 13, 13 (Predrag Cicovacki & Maria Granik eds. 2010) [hereinafter Art, Creativity,
and Spirituality] (discussing "Dostoevsky's complex treatment of the confessional experience in *The Brothers Karamazov*, exploring the ways in which confession can be both used
and abused by the novel's characters, and ultimately ... determin[ing] what makes an effective confession in the world of this novel"); Paul J. Contino, *Zosima, Mikhail, And Prosaic Confessional Dialogue in Dostoevsky's* Brothers Karamazov, in 27.1 Stud. In The Novel
63 (1995) (explaining how "[i]n each of [Dostoevsky's] major novels, [his] confessors —
Sonia Mameladov in *Crime and Punishment*, Prince Myshkin in *The Idiot*, Father Tikhon
in *The Possessed*, Alyosha Karamazov and Father Zosima — assist others when they are most
violently fractured and self-destructive" and "[t]he splintered selves of these confessants is
often due to their overweening concern about the way they are being perceived by others");
Vladimir K. Kantor, *Confession and Theodicy in Dostoevsky's Oeuvre (the Reception of St.
Augustine)*, 50 Russ. Stud. in Phil. 10 (Winter 2011–12) (analyzing how Dostoevsky developed "[t]wo classical problems of Christian philosophy — theodicy and confessional —
into a new literary-philosophical system unprecedented in nineteenth-century European
Culture"); Robin Feuer Miller, *Dostoevsky and Rousseau: The Morality of Confession Recon-
sidered*, in Dostoevsky: New Perspectives 82 (Robert L. Jackson, Prentice-Hall, 1984)
(explaining how "[c]onfessions may seek to provoke, titillate or lie; the narrator may expose,
disguise, justify, or lacerate himself. But rarely does the confession consist of a simple re-
pentant declaration of wrongdoing or moral weakness").

Part II summarizes seminal United States Supreme Court confession cases. The United States Supreme Court has a longstanding love-hate relationship with confessions: while it believes that such evidence can valuably assist the truth finding process, it has at times questioned its reliability and mistrusted the coercive methods used for extraction. The Court's express goal under the Due Process Clause and in *Miranda* is to ensure that confessions are the product of a free and rational choice.[4] Although Sixth Amendment law explicitly aims to protect the integrity of the adversarial process, policies of freedom and rationality also (but more subtly) undergird its reasoning.[5] When it comes to confessions, the Supreme Court's *modus operandi* entails fixating on externalities, formulating safeguards, and regulating conduct. Its focus tends to be on things peripheral to the confessant; typically relevant factors include the conduct of state actors, coercive techniques, or deliberate elicitation tactics.[6]

When it comes to confession, Dostoevsky's perspective is worlds apart from that of the U.S. Supreme Court, and Part III hones in on the differences. While the law's focus is on external forces, Dostoevsky essentially relegates them to the realm of the irrelevant—or at least, sees them as only a small part of the problem. In his fiction, confession, an elusive phenomenon of infinite variety, pertains solely to the individual soul and psyche. For him, confession, by its very nature, is detached from free will and rationality: that is, there exists in all Homo sapiens an inner coercive drive to divulge a slew of true or false secrets. Dostoevsky, moreover, pokes holes in the notion that confessions can and should play a role in criminal prosecutions. For him, confession can minister to only one process: it is an incipient step in an individual's spiritual evolution, and interrogators, judges, or juries simply have no business meddling in that ineffability.[7]

Any attempt to analyze all confessants in Dostoevsky's fiction is a virtual impossibility, and would require coverage in a multi-volume treatise, one pos-

---

4. *See infra* II. A. 1 &2 (discussing the Supreme Court's perspective on confessions under the Due Process Clause and *Miranda v. Arizona*, 484 U.S. 436 (1966)).

5. *See infra* II.A. 3 (discussing the Supreme Court perspective on confessions under the Sixth Amendment).

6. *See generally infra* II. A. (summarizing the Supreme Court's perspective on confessions and its efforts to prevent coercive tactics and deliberate elicitation and to implement remedies and safeguards).

7. *See e.g., infra* notes 144–55, 392–401 and accompanying text (Raskolnikov's confession as first step toward spiritual rebirth); notes 456–59 and accompanying text (Mikhail's genuine confession in *The Brothers Karamazov*, which issues outside of the confines of the courthouse); and notes 491–99 and accompanying text (Mitya's dream in the wake of his confession in *The Brothers Karamazov*).

sibly rivaling Joseph Frank's unredacted biography.[8] This chapter inevitably settles for just a sampling of Dostoevsky's self-incriminators, who are compelled to admit to deeds they did or did not do. Individuals like Rodion Raskolnikov[9] and Ivan Fyodorovich ("Ivan") and Dmitri Fyodorovich ("Mitya"), two of the Karamazov brothers,[10] are all kindred spirits, who tropistically lean toward unburdening their crime, shame, or spiritual crisis, all of which would inexorably emerge without any poking or prodding on the part of legal agents.

Part IV, the Conclusion, returning to this chapter's origin, takes a closer look at the rarity—Sonya with her disinclination to self-incriminate.[11] It will end with conjecture of what Dostoevsky (and Sonya herself) might impart to the United States Supreme Court and legal scholars, who have long struggled to make sense out of the senseless confession phenomenon.

II. Confession Jurisprudence

According to the United States Supreme Court and some legal scholars, a predominant law enforcement objective is to obtain a free and reliable confession to introduce into evidence in a criminal prosecution. For at least a century, an ever-evasive goal is to isolate what causes individuals to admit to things they did or did not do. The Supreme Court has proffered answers, but none of them would likely impress Dostoevsky.

A. United States Supreme Court

In its longstanding effort to discover the causes of a coerced and involuntary confession, the United States Supreme Court tends to indict external forces,

---

8. JOSEPH FRANK, DOSTOEVSKY: A WRITER IN HIS TIME (Princeton University Press, 2010) (a 2500-page work, distilled from the five volume biography, which examines the author's life and the Russian historical, cultural and ideological context). *See generally* ROBIN FEUER MILLER, THE *BROTHERS KARAMAZOV*: WORLDS OF THE NOVEL 30 (Twayne Publishers 1992) ("[V]irtually every work of fiction Dostoevsky wrote contains some grain of his fascination with the act of confession.")

9. DOSTOEVSKY, *supra* note 1 (the protagonist in *Crime and Punishment*).

10. FYODOR DOSTOEVSKY, BROTHERS KARAMAZOV (Richard Pevear and Larissa Volokhonsky, trans. 1990) (1879–80). Ivan and Mitya are half-brothers, while Alexei Fyodorovich ("Alyosha") is Ivan's brother and Mitya's half-brother. The father of all three men is Fyodor Pavlovich Karamazov ("Fyodor"), who, according to rumor, is also the father of an illegitimate son, Pavel Fyodorovich Smerdyakov.

11. *See infra* notes 145–49 and accompanying text (Sonya's intuitive wisdom); note 500 and accompanying text (Sonya's refusal to confess).

mostly consisting of law enforcement tactics. This focus is understandable in criminal procedure, which typically involves an imbalance of power in the combat between the state, with its enormous resources, and a vulnerable, relatively powerless accused. The psychological wrangling between police and suspects in the interrogation room is not just the hackneyed drama of news and media, but often the fact pattern in actual due process, *Miranda*, and Sixth Amendment confession cases.

1. Due Process: Totality of the Circumstances

The Supreme Court initially relied on the Due Process Clause to ban the use of confessions extracted by physical torture and, later, more expansively prohibited psychological coercion.[12] While the next chapter deals with the policies behind due process decisions (and behind *Miranda* as well), here the discussion confines itself primarily to doctrinal tests. In the due process context, the suspect's idiosyncrasies are, of course, relevant, but police conduct and the interrogation environment dominate the analysis. The due process trilogy, *Ashcraft v. Tennessee*,[13] *Spano v. New York*,[14] and *Colorado v. Connelly*,[15] illustrates the Supreme Court's preoccupation with the effect of interrogators' coercive tactics on an accused.

In *Ashcraft*,[16] the defendant, charged with having hired a man to murder his wife, was convicted as an accessory before the fact. Ashcraft argued that his alleged confession, "extorted" from him, violated due process and, based

---

12. *See* U.S. Const. amend.V ("nor shall any person … be deprived of life, liberty, or property, without due process of law"). In *Brown v. Mississippi*, 297 U.S. 56 (1936), police officers whipped the defendants and one was even strung up in a mock lynching and repeatedly choked. *See also* Wakat v. Harlib, 253 F.2d 59, 61–62 (7th Cir. 1958) (noting that the defendant was beaten by police, had multiple bruises and broken bones, and spent months in the hospital); People v. Matlock, 336 P.2d 505, 511–12 (Cal. 1959) (finding that the defendant was interrogated under sleep deprivation tactics and put on an icy board when he became sleepy); Bruner v. People, 156 P.2d 111, 120 (Colo. 1945) (the defendant was not allowed to eat for fifteen hours, deprived of the use of the toilet, and held over two months); Kier v. State, 132 A.2d 494, 496 (Md. 1957) (defendant was strapped naked to a chair and police indicated that they would take skin and hair from his body); People v. Portelli, 205 N.E. 857, 858 (N.Y. 1965) (suspect was beaten and tortured until he gave an incriminating confession). *See generally* Steven Penney, *Theories of Confession Admissibility: A Historical View* 25 Am. J. Crim. L. 309, 333 (1998) (discussing the *Brown* line of cases and judicial responses to such police interrogation).

13. 322 U.S. 143 (1944).

14. 360 U.S. 315 (1959).

15. 479 U.S. 157 (1986).

16. Ashcraft, 322 U.S. 143.

on the totality of circumstances, the Court agreed.[17] Police officers kept Ashcraft in custody for thirty-six hours without sleep or rest. Relays of experienced investigators and lawyers questioned him practically without respite from Saturday evening until Monday morning. The record reflected that the reason the officers worked in shifts was because they, exhausted, needed breaks.

Similar facts existed in *Spano*,[18] which involved the post-indictment confession and first-degree murder conviction of a 25-year-old Italian immigrant. While the Court noted that Spano had limited education and was "emotionally unstable and maladjusted," what mattered most were the tricks of the experienced officers and prosecutors who had spearheaded the investigation.[19] Questioning did not occur during regular business hours, but began in the early evening and ended about eight hours later. Interrogators, persisting despite Spano's repeated refusals to answer on the advice of his attorney, ignored his requests to contact retained counsel.[20]

On the *Spano* menu was deception: the interrogators instructed Bruno, Spano's buddy who was a "fledgling police officer," to falsely inform Spano that his "telephone call had caused him trouble, that his job was in jeopardy, and that loss of his job would be disastrous to his three children, wife, and unborn child."[21] Spano ostensibly buckled under such pressure and lies. The Court, considering "all the facts in their post-indictment setting," found that the "official pressure, fatigue, and sympathy falsely aroused" were the demons that overcame Spano's free will and made him talk.[22]

Connelly,[23] a post-*Miranda* decision, is on a different footing, and would have most intrigued Dostoevsky.[24] The case cements in place what the *Ashcraft* and *Spano* decisions posit: namely, that what causes an involuntary and unconstitutional confession is coercive conduct on the part of state actors. Unlike the situations in *Ashcraft* and *Spano*, in *Connelly*, it was the defendant

17. *Id.* at 145.

18. Spano, 360 U.S. 315.

19. *Id.* at 322 n.3.

20. In *Spano*, Justice Stewart (joined by Justices Douglas and Brennan) relied on *Powell v. Alabama*, 287 U.S. 45 (1932), invoked Sixth amendment concerns, and opined that the absence of counsel alone rendered the confession inadmissible. 360 U.S. at 327 (Stewart, J. concurring). *See also infra* II.A. 3 (discussing confessions in the context of the Sixth Amendment right to counsel).

21. Spano, 360 U.S. at 317, 319.

22. *Id.* at 323.

23. Connelly, 479 U.S. 157.

24. *See infra* notes 452–57 and accompanying text (juxtaposing *Connelly* with Ivan and Mikhail's confessions).

himself, "without any prompting," who courted police contact.[25] Connelly just walked up to an officer, blurted out that he had murdered someone, and said that he wanted to discuss it. When the officer read him his *Miranda* rights, Connelly stated that he understood them, but still needed to talk about the murder. After a detective reiterated the warnings, Connelly said that he had travelled a long way to come clean and then, while in police headquarters, gave details.

The next day, however, after Connelly became disoriented during a public defender interview, he was sent for a hospital evaluation. Connelly told the psychiatrist that he was listening to the "voice of God" when he confessed.[26] In the suppression hearing, the psychiatrist testified that Connelly suffered from a psychosis with auditory hallucinations, which impaired his ability to make free and rational choices.[27]

The Supreme Court, at odds with the Colorado courts, concluded that there was no constitutional issue because no third party (state agent) was making Connelly confess. The Court found a lack of coercive or causal police activity, which is the "necessary predicate to the finding that a confession is not 'voluntary.' "[28] Justice Rehnquist, the opinion's author, interpreted "the cases over the 50 years since *Brown v. Mississippi* [as focusing] upon the crucial element of police overreaching," and said that, while the defendant's mental state can be a "significant factor in the 'voluntariness' calculus," it is not controlling.[29] The Court said that Connelly's "perception of coercion flowing from the 'voice of God,' however important or significant such a perception may be in other disciplines, is a matter to which the United States Constitution does not speak."[30]

---

25. Connelly, 479 U.S. at 160.

26. *Id.* at 161.

27. On the basis of the psychiatrist's testimony, the trial court found that Connelly's initial statements and custodial confession were involuntary. *Id.* at 162. That court relied on the decisions in *Townsend v. Sain*, 372 U.S. 293 (1963) and *Culombe v. Connecticut*, 367 U.S. 568 (1961) and held that a confession is admissible only if it is a product of the defendant's rational intellect and "free will." *Id.* The trial court suppressed the incriminating statements, even though the police had not done anything improper or coercive. Also, the court believed that Connelly's mental illness vitiated his putative waiver of the right to counsel and privilege against self-incrimination. The Colorado Supreme Court affirmed that decision in *People v. Connelly*, 702 P.2d 722 (1985).

28. Connelly, 479 U.S. at 167.

29. *Id.* at 163–67 (discussing *Brown v. Mississippi*, 297 U.S. 278 (1936)).

30. *Id.* at 170–71. The Court found that the Colorado Supreme Court had also erred by finding the waiver of *Miranda* rights to be invalid. The Court faulted the state court for "importing into this area of constitutional law notions of 'free will' that have no place there," and said that, while "*Miranda* protects defendants against government coercion leading

Dostoevsky, however, intrigued by that very "matter to which the ... Constitution does not speak," finds "importance" and "significance" in the "perception of coercion" by those whispers or howls emanating from deep within the psychic trenches.[31] Further, Dostoevsky would likely concur with the *Connelly* dissenters, especially with their inkling that Connelly's statements were unreliable, and also with their view that they should not have been introduced into evidence.[32]

2. *Miranda*: Coercion

Once again, the next chapter addresses what was once sacrosanct and is now essentially ignored: namely, the policies behind the landmark decision in *Miranda v. Arizona*.[33] Here, the focus is primarily on the *Miranda* doctrine itself and factors that, according to the Supreme Court, can either coerce or help stave off unconstitutional self-incrimination. While the Court's progressive obliteration of *Miranda* and revitalization of the older due process approach is also considered in more depth in the next chapter, it suffices to

---

them to surrender rights protected by the Fifth Amendment[,] it goes no further than that." *Id.* at 169–70.

31. *Id.* at 170–71. *See also infra* III (discussing Dostoevsky's confessant gene).

32. In his dissent, Justice Brennan pointed out that "the use of a mentally ill person's involuntary confession is antithetical to the notion of fundamental fairness embodied in the Due Process Clause," and asserted that "[m]inimum standards of due process should require that the trial court find substantial indicia of reliability, on the basis of evidence extrinsic to the confession itself." 479 U.S. 174, 183. *See also infra* notes 452–56 and accompanying text (discussing the *Connelly* dissent in the context of Ivan's breakdown on the witness stand).

33. 384 U.S. 436 (1966). In *Miranda*, the Court said that the decision "in no way creates a constitutional straitjacket" and "encourage[d] Congress and the States to search for effective ways of protecting [individual] rights." *Id.* at 467. Post-*Miranda*, Congress enacted a statute replacing it with the totality-of-the-circumstances approach of the due process era. 18 U.S.C. § 3501. *See* Dickerson v. United States, 530 U.S. 428, 435 (2000). In *Dickerson*, the Supreme Court deemed *Miranda* a constitutional decision, declined to overrule it, and invalidated the statute. 530 U.S. 435. In spite of *Dickerson*, the Supreme Court has nullified *Miranda*. *See id.* at 437 (admitting that the court has "created several exceptions to *Miranda's* warnings requirement and [has] repeatedly referred to the *Miranda* warnings as 'prophylactic'... and 'not themselves rights protected by the Constitution'") (citing New York v. Quarles, 467 U.S. 649, 653 (1984) and Michigan v. Tucker, 417 U.S. 433, 444 (1974). *See also* Dickerson, 530 U.S. at 438 n.2 (listing other cases in which the Court has diminished *Miranda's* Constitutional status); Yale Kamisar, *Miranda's Reprieve*, 92 A.B.A. J. 48, 51 (2006) ("[T]he Supreme court has now made it clear that what it reaffirmed in *Dickerson* was not the *Miranda* doctrine as it burst onto the scene in 1966, but rather *Miranda* with all its post-Warren court exceptions frozen in time.").

note here that under decisions in *Miranda*'s wake, police conduct and the details of the interrogation environment have (in theory) become more relevant and determinative.[34]

In *Miranda*, Chief Justice Warren, the decision's author, reasoned that rules were necessary to protect a suspect's Fifth Amendment right to remain silent from the inherently coercive pressures of custodial interrogation.[35] The Court saw that the consolidated cases before it all "share[d] salient features—incommunicado interrogation of individuals in a police-dominated atmosphere, resulting in self-incriminating statements without full warnings of constitutional rights."[36] From there, the Court reviewed intimidation techniques, beginning with physical brutality, as in the New York incident in which "police [had] brutally beat, kicked and placed lighted cigarette butts on the back of a potential witness under interrogation for the purpose of securing a statement incriminating a third party."[37]

The Court, recognizing that the coerciveness inherent in custody can be mental as well as physical, worried about privacy imposing a "gap" in our awareness of what actually happens in the interrogation chamber.[38] Consequently, a substantial portion of the *Miranda* opinion is devoted to exposing tactics that police manuals taught, which were designed to undermine the suspect's right to remain silent.[39] Popular practices included (and still include)

---

34. *See supra* note 33 (describing how the Supreme Court has butchered *Miranda*). *See also infra* notes 81–87 and accompanying text (discussing how the Supreme Court has created a plethora of *Miranda* loopholes and has repeatedly stated that, in order for a confession to be suppressed, it must have been extracted in violation of the Due Process Clause). *See generally infra* Chapter IV (Prisons of Coercion: *Notes from the House of the Dead*) (discussing the inapplicability of *Miranda* to prisoners' confessions).

35. *See* U.S. CONST. amend. V ("nor shall any person ... be compelled in any criminal case to be a witness against himself ...").

36. Miranda, 384 U.S. at 445.

37. *Id.* at 446 (discussing *People v. Portelli*, 15 N.Y.2d 235 (1965)). *See also supra* note 12 (giving examples of other cases involving physical torture).

38. Miranda, 384 U.S. at 448.

39. *See generally* FRED E. INBAU & JOHN E. REID, CRIMINAL INTERROGATION AND CONFESSIONS (1962). *See also* Miranda v. Arizona, 384 U.S. 436, 449 (1966) (discussing the methods described in the manuals by Inbau and Reid as "reflect[ing] their experiences and ... the most effective psychological stratagems to employ during interrogation"); BROOKS, *supra* note 3, at 13 (discussing the police interrogation manuals by Fred E. Inbau, John E. Reid, and Charles E. Ohara, "works which at the time of *Miranda* had attained a circulation of over forty-four thousand copies (and in their revised editions continue to be widely used)" and stating that "[t]he tactics preached by these manuals are as chilling as one might imagine"); Yale Kamisar, *Fred E. Inbau: "The Importance of Being Guilty"* 68 J. CRIM. L. & CRIMINOLOGY 182, 183 (1977) ("Inbau taught criminal procedure and its constitutional

placing suspects in isolation and unfamiliar surroundings, exhibiting an air of confidence in their guilt, minimizing the gravity of the offense, and interrogating relentlessly to overwhelm them.[40] The manuals also urged playing the "Mutt and Jeff" charade, where one officer acts friendly and the other hostile, putting suspects in fraudulent lineups where they are identified as the perpetrators, telling them that silence indicates that they have something to hide, and advising them to go it alone to spare themselves and their family the cost of representation.[41]

The *Miranda* Court acknowledged that such overbearing tactics could produce a confession that is not "involuntary" within the precise meaning of the due process clause.[42] Nonetheless, the Court found such "techniques" to be "menacing" and rife with "potentiality for compulsion."[43] The Court felt that, even without use of such methods, the "very fact" of custodial interrogation "exacts a heavy toll on individual liberty and trades on the weakness" of suspects.[44] The Court believed that absent "safeguards" to dispel inherent compulsion, no confession "can truly be the product" of a suspect's "free choice."[45]

The Court set forth a bright-line rule that a confession given during custodial interrogation is inadmissible unless suspects, after receiving specific warnings describing their rights, provide a "waiver ... made voluntarily, knowingly

---

dimensions—all the while he yearned for, and fought for, the day when criminal procedure would have no (or at least very few) constitutional dimensions."); Douglas Starr, *The Interview: Do Police Interrogation Techniques Produce False Confessions?*, THE NEW YORKER, December 9, 2013, 42, 44 (describing how "a postdoctoral fellow in psychology, named Saul Kassin" read the *Miranda* decision, found "that it repeatedly cites the Reid Technique manual as the most authoritative source on American interrogation techniques" and, after becoming "a leading expert on false confessions ... believes that the Reid Technique is inherently coercive").

40. *See supra* Starr, note 39, at 42 (explaining how the "standard Reid Technique manual, first published in 1962 and now in its fifth edition," is still used in training today). *See also infra* notes 75–87 and accompanying text (discussing how interrogators still employ the very tactics that mandated the *Miranda* safeguards, and now, since there are so many loopholes, they can make those into new coercive tactics as well). *See generally infra* Chapter IV (Prisons of Coercion: *Notes from the House of the Dead*) (discussing in greater depth the abundant *Miranda* loopholes).

41. Miranda, 384 U.S. at 452 (describing "Mutt, the relentless investigator," and Jeff, the "kindhearted man, ... [who] disapproves of Mutt and his tactics[,] ... [but] can't hold Mutt off for very long.").

42. *Id.* at 457.

43. *Id.*

44. *Id.* at 455.

45. *Id.* at 458.

and intelligently."[46] Moreover, a police officer must cease questioning whenever suspects invoke the right to silence or the right to counsel, even if waivers precede those invocations. In short, the *Miranda* mandate derives from the assumption that outside forces can and do undermine the will to remain silent, along with the hope that the imposition of a conduct code on state actors can help ensure that a confession is the result of the suspect's free will. As elaborated below, for Dostoevsky, all of this is a pipe dream. For him, confessions, which, by their very nature, are *in*voluntary, *ir*rational, and not infrequently *un*reliable, impugn the underpinnings and stated goal of *Miranda*.

3. Sixth Amendment: Deliberate Elicitation

The Sixth Amendment right to assistance of counsel is an independent restraint on governmental efforts to get self-incriminating evidence.[47] The doctrine emerged before *Miranda* when, in *Massiah v. United States*, the Supreme Court held that the Sixth Amendment required exclusion from trial of the statements that an already indicted defendant made to a government agent.[48]

While *Miranda*'s objective is to block or mitigate undesirable effects of pressure imposed on suspects during custodial interrogation, what belies *Massiah* and other cases of that ilk is the commendable policy of guarding the integrity of the adversarial system.[49] In *Massiah*, the Court rejected the government's contention that Massiah, unlike Spano, was not in custody or subjected to "of-

---

46. *Id.* at 444.

47. *See* U.S. Const. amend. VI ("In all criminal prosecutions, the accused shall [...] have the Assistance of Counsel for his defence.").

48. Massiah, 377 U.S. 201 (1964). *See also id.* (the Supreme Court, relying on the concurrence in *Spano v. New York*, 360 U.S. at 327 (Stewart, J., concurring), stressed the impropriety of police eliciting a confession after a defendant had been indicted); Escobedo v. Illinois, 378 U.S. 478 (1964) (excluding defendant's confession after repeated requests by the defendant to consult with retained counsel were refused, and after his attorney had actually been turned away at the police station).

49. *See* Brewer v. Williams, 430 U.S. 387, 398 (1977) (citing Powell v. Alabama, 287 U.S. 264, 270) (1980) (The right, "guaranteed by the Sixth and Fourteenth Amendments, is indispensable to the fair administration of our adversary system of criminal justice" and "vital" at the pretrial stage.). *See generally* Yale Kamisar, *Equal Justice in the Gatehouses and Mansions of American Criminal Procedure*, Criminal Justice in our Time 11-38 (A. Howard ed., 1965) (discussing policies behind the Sixth Amendment as extended to pretrial practices); Amy D. Ronner, Law, Literature, and Therapeutic Jurisprudence 104–108 (Carolina Academic Press 2010) (discussing policies behind the Sixth Amendment and explaining that "while the government could indeed investigate a suspect's criminal activities after the indictment, it could not fairly and constitutionally use unlawfully obtained criminal statements as evidence against him at his trial").

ficial pressure" and, instead, founded its decision on precepts of fair play.[50] But although not as expressly stated in the Sixth Amendment, as opposed to the *Miranda* context, there is nevertheless at least an implicit hope on the part of the Court that the *Massiah* doctrine will help promote uncoerced and rational decisionmaking.

In *Massiah*, the Court said that a "Constitution which guarantees a defendant the aid of counsel at […] a trial could surely vouchsafe no less to an indicted defendant under interrogation by the police in a completely extrajudicial proceeding."[51] The Sixth Amendment thus does not just encompass the right to have an advocate at trial; it also extends to pre-trial, recognizing that charged individuals will, and should, engage in strategizing with their counsel, which, of course, helps foster adequate representation.[52] If defendants relinquish information to the prosecution while they have their attorney by their side, it is more likely that this will happen by choice, after a reasoned weighing of options. On the other hand, interrogation of a lone defendant in an "extrajudicial proceeding" is more likely to reduce freedom and incite a less rational decision.[53]

In *Brewer v. Williams*, a post-*Massiah* case, the Court clarified that deliberate elicitation on the part of state actors violates the Sixth Amendment.[54] *Brewer* involved the murder of a child, Pamela Powers, who vanished while attending an event at the YMCA in Des Moines, Iowa. Williams, an escapee from a mental hospital and resident at the YMCA, was spotted absconding with a big bundle. After issuance of an arrest warrant, Williams placed a long-distance call to a Des Moines attorney, Henry McKnight, who advised Williams to turn himself in to the Davenport police. Once Williams surrendered, was booked, and received *Miranda* warnings, McKnight, again conferring with his client, told him not to talk to Des Moines officers about Pamela Powers. The police also gave their word that they would not question Williams on the drive back to Des Moines.

---

50. Massiah, 377 U.S. at 206.

51. *Id.* at 204.

52. *See generally* Powell v. Alabama, 287 U.S. 45 (1932) (The Supreme Court, overturning the convictions of nine uneducated African American youths, accused of raping two white women, found that the tardy appointments were constitutionally infirm, depriving the defendants of legal advice "during perhaps the most critical period of the proceedings against [them] … from the time of their arraignment until the beginning of their trial, when consultation, thorough-going investigation and preparation were vitally important.").

53. Massiah, 377 U.S. at 204.

54. 430 U.S. 387 (1977). *See also* Fellers v. United States, 540 U.S. 519 (2004) (upholding the deliberate-elicitation standard in the Sixth Amendment area and finding that the absence of "interrogation" does not foreclose a claim that statements should be suppressed).

Post-arraignment, the judge again administered *Miranda* rights and another lawyer, Kelly, warned Williams not to say anything until he could consult with his Des Moines lawyer. When the detective and his colleague arrived to pick up Williams, they met with Kelly and repeated the *Miranda* warnings. Kelly also reminded the detective that Williams was not to be questioned about Pamela Powers until he had consulted with McKnight in Des Moines. After sensing "some reservations" on the part of the detective, Kelly "firmly stated that the agreement with McKnight was to be carried out" and that there was to be no questioning.[55] Moreover, Kelly's request to accompany Williams in the police car was rebuffed.

On the way to Des Moines, the detective, who knew that Williams had mental problems and was deeply religious, delivered what has become the notorious "Christian burial speech," in which he commented on the bad weather, referred to the arduous task of finding the body, and pressed that the child's parents deserved a proper "Christian burial" for their little girl.[56] In response, Williams self-incriminated by describing the body's location.

The Supreme Court, declining to review the lodged *Miranda* violation, reversed the murder conviction solely on the basis of the *Massiah* doctrine.[57] The Court found that the Sixth Amendment attached at arraignment, and that Williams had not "intentionally relinquished" his right to counsel before the police "deliberately elicited" admissions from him.[58] With respect to the "Christian burial speech," the officers knew that two lawyers were representing Williams, and yet "purposely sought" to "obtain as much incriminating evidence as possible" during his isolation in the police car.[59] Further, the Court found "no rea-

---

55. *Id.* at 392.

56. *Id.* at 392–93. The detective said:

And since we will be going right past the area on the way into Des Moines, I feel that we could stop and locate the body, that the parents of this little girl should be entitled to a Christian burial for the little girl who was snatched away from them on Christmas [E]ve and murdered. And I feel we should stop and locate it on the way in rather than waiting until morning and trying to come back out after a snow storm and possibly not being able to find it at all.

Id.

57. In *Massiah*, the Supreme Court rejected the government's argument that Massiah was not in custody or subjected to "official pressure," and instead based the decision on basic notions of fair play. 377 U.S. at 206. The Court made it clear that, although the government could indeed pursue an investigation of the suspect's criminal activities after the indictment, it could not fairly and constitutionally use "his own incriminating statements" as evidence against him at his trial. *Id.* at 206–207.

58. Brewer, 430 U.S. at 397.

59. *Id.*

sonable basis" for inferring waiver of counsel, because Williams had both expressly and impliedly invoked this right repeatedly throughout his interactions with law enforcement.[60]

In later decisions, like *United States v. Henry*[61] and *Kuhlman v. Wilson*,[62] which strain to justify opposite results based on virtually identical facts, the Court sought to further define "deliberate elicitation."[63] Once again the key, having little to do with the confessant's mindset (or even that of the elicitors), is the behavior of others, who interpose themselves between the accused and counsel in an ongoing prosecution. The query is whether a reasonable person would find it likely that the state's planned course of conduct would lead to the elicitation of incriminating information from the formally charged individual.

In *Henry*, the Court applied *Massiah* to incriminating statements made to a jailhouse snitch. The Court found a violation of the *Massiah* rule because the informant had engaged the defendant in dialogue and "had developed a relationship of trust and confidence with [the defendant] such that [the defendant] revealed incriminating information."[64] The Court deemed reasonable the lower courts' findings that the informant "deliberately used his position to secure incriminating information" at a time when defendant's counsel was absent.[65] In *Henry*, the informant had apparently not questioned the defendant, but rather just "stimulated" conversations.[66] The Court analogized this to the *Massiah* facts because it was tantamount to "indirect and surreptitious interrogation."[67] In the Court's eyes, the *Henry* informant became too active, too deliberate.

Kuhlmann, on nearly identical facts which also involve incriminating statements made to a jailhouse informant, comes out the other way—no Sixth

---

60. *Id.*

61. 447 U.S. 264 (1980).

62. 477 U.S. 435 (1986).

63. *See, e.g., Henry*, 447 U.S. at 270 ("The question here is whether under the facts of this case a Government agent 'deliberately elicited' incriminating statements from Henry within the meaning of *Massiah*."); *Kuhlman*, 477 U.S. at 457 ("The Court in *Massiah* adopted the reasoning of the concurring opinions in *Spano* and held that, once a defendant's Sixth Amendment right to counsel has attached, he is denied that right when federal agents 'deliberately elicit' incriminating statements from him in the absence of his lawyer."). *See also* Fellers v. United States, 540 U.S. 519 (2004) (putatively distinguishing Sixth Amendment "deliberate elicitation" from Fifth Amendment interrogation).

64. *Henry*, 447 U.S. at 269.

65. *Id.* at 270.

66. *Id.* at 273.

67. *Id.*

Amendment violation. In *Kuhlmann*, the defendant was arraigned and incarcerated with another prisoner, Lee, who agreed to assist in the investigation. When the defendant began talking to Lee about the robbery, reciting the same litany that he had given the police, Lee said that it "didn't sound too good."[68] Over the next few days, the defendant tweaked his story. Then, after a visit from his brother, who told him that family members were upset by the murder, the defendant gave damning details.

This time, the Court, disagreeing with the conclusion below that the prosecution violated the right to counsel, faulted the federal appellate court for failing to accord the state court's findings the requisite presumption of correctness. In the Court's view, the federal appellate court should have deferred to state court findings that purportedly distinguish the circumstances *sub judice* from those in *Henry*: namely, that the police in *Kuhlmann* already had "solid evidence" of defendant's complicity in the crime, and that Lee obeyed instructions to just listen to the "spontaneous" and "unsolicited" narrative without injecting questions.[69]

In concurrence, Chief Justice Burger stressed that the case is "clearly distinguishable" from *Henry* in that there is "a vast difference between placing an 'ear' in the suspect's cell and placing a voice in the cell to encourage conversation for the 'ear' to record."[70] According to Burger, the state court got it right when it found the informant to be an innocuously passive, non-deliberate "ear."[71] For Dostoevsky, the question of whether some recipient of a confession is a passive "ear" or active "voice" is a distinction without a difference.[72] For him, most of us have a deliberate elicitor as cellmate, imprisoned in our very souls and psyches. He also knew that the informer and defendant's narratives could be fabricated, misinterpreted, or both.[73]

B. Commentators

What makes suspects waive their *Miranda* rights and confess? Numerous theories abound: for example, Stephen Schulhofer, blaming loose lips on at-

---

68. Kuhlman, 477 U.S. at 439–40.

69. *Id.* at 460.

70. *Id.* at 461 (Burger, J. concurring).

71. *Id. See also* Fellers v. United States, 540 U.S. 519 (2003) (emphasizing that deliberate elicitation is not equivalent to custodial interrogation within the meaning of the Fifth Amendment).

72. *Id.*

73. *See generally* Welsh S. White, *Interrogation Without Questions*: Rhode Island v. Innis *and* United States v. Henry, 78 Mich. L. Rev. 1209 (1980) (discussing the difficulties in assessing the credibility of the informer or defendant).

titude, believes that "confessions are now mostly the result of persuasion and the suspect's overconfidence, not of pressure and fear," and that confessants tend to be cocksure of their own ability to "talk their way out of trouble."[74] Professor Peter Arenella, rebutting Schulhofer, asserts that "when the efficacy of the police confidence game depends so heavily on police custodial control of the suspect in a very hostile, threatening environment," it might be impossible to "distinguish between persuasion and fear."[75]

Most commentators, siding with Arenella, opine that the interrogation environment, along with judicially condoned police tactics, is the veritable culprit.[76] As Professors Daniel J. Seidmann and Alex Stein explain, police still "interrogate virtually all suspects in a hostile environment, subjecting them to physical and psychological pressures designed to make the suspects' choices irrational."[77] Many suspects believe, and are made to believe, that silence, sig-

---

74. Stephen J. Schulhofer, Miranda's *Practical Effect: Substantial Benefits and Vanishingly Small Costs*, 90 Nw. U.L. Rev. 500, 561–62 (1996).

75. Peter Arenella, Miranda *Stories*, 20 Harv. J.L. & Pub. Pol'y 375, 385–86 (1997).

76. *See, e.g.*, Barry Friedman, *The Wages of Stealth Overruling (With Particular Attention to Miranda v. Arizona)*, 99 Geo. L. J. 1 (2010) (explaining that the exceptions to *Miranda* are so numerous that *Miranda* has been overruled by stealth); Mark A. Godsey, *Reformulating the Miranda Warnings in Light of Contemporary Law and Understandings*, 90 Minn. L. Rev. 781, 789–90 (2012) (discussing the litany of cases that have retreated from *Miranda* protections); Rinat Kitai-Sangero, *Respecting the Privilege against Self-Incrimination: a Call for Providing Miranda Warnings in Non-custodial Interrogation*, 42 N.M. L. Rev. 203, 204 (2012) (analyzing how "*Miranda's* holding has been eroded over time as courts have admitted evidence gained in the absence of the warnings"); Irene Merker Rosenberg and Yale L. Rosenberg, *A Modest Proposal for the Abolition of Custodial Confessions*, 68 N.C.L. Rev. 69, 81 (1989) (explaining how the "Court has undercut the [*Miranda*] decision, hollowing out its core while maintaining a pretext of viability," which "facilitates confessional evidence"); Starr, *supra* note 39, at 42 (describing the basic Reid & Associates training course, which teaches post-*Miranda* law enforcers how to effectively extract a confession); Charles D. Weisselberg, *Mourning Miranda*, 96 Cal. L. Rev. 1519, 1524 (2008) (concluding, after researching "police training materials, social science literature and post-*Miranda* decisions," that "little is left of *Miranda's* vaunted safeguards and what is left is not worth retaining"); Jonathan Witmer-Rich, *Interrogation and the Roberts Court*, 63 Fl. L. Rev. 1189, 1192 (2011) (discussing how commentators have realized that "the Supreme Court ... seems to be shaping interrogation law to facilitate the admission of custodial confessions by creating 'safe harbor' rules that are relatively clear and simple for police to satisfy").

77. Daniel J. Seidman and Alex Stein, *The Right to Silence Helps the Innocent: A Game-Theoretic Analysis of the Fifth Amendment Privilege*, 114 Harv. L. Rev. 430, 450 (2000). *See also* Richard A. Leo, Peter Neufeld, Steven A. Drizin, and Andrew E. Taslitz, *Promoting Accuracy in the Use of Confession Evidence: An Argument For Pretrial Reliability Assessments to Prevent Wrongful Convictions*, 85 Temp. L. Rev.759, 764 (2013) (discussing the case of Bruce Godschalk, who falsely confessed to and was convicted of two rapes and how it "illustrates

naling guilt, can and will be used against them.[78] Police still fruitfully wield promises, threats, and trickery, in mimicry of the very tactics that the *Miranda* Court condemned and felt warranted prophylaxis.[79] In fact, Douglas Starr, who enrolled in the basic Reid & Associates training course in effective interrogation techniques, points out that the "company says that the people it trains get suspects to confess eighty per cent of the time."[80]

Self-incrimination occurs quite frequently, in spite of *Miranda* and other putative protections, and legal critics offer multiple, intertwined reasons for this.[81] For one, the *Miranda* warnings, which have moldered into sonorous wallpaper, akin to elevator music, are often ignored and also, any confession, given in their wake, is almost always admissible evidence.[82] Cognizant of this, in-

---

how readily an innocent suspect can be induced to give a false confession, indeed multiple false confessions"). Leo, et. al, explain "how readily police interrogators can 'contaminate'— i.e., leak or disclose nonpublic details to—an innocent suspect" and "how readily a contaminated suspect can be led to incorporate those nonpublic crime details into his confession narrative, and how the presence of these nonpublic crime facts can be used to create the illusion that a completely false confession is verifiably true." *Id.*

78. *See, e.g.*, Godsey, *supra* note 76, at 793 ("While many reasons certainly contribute to the willingness of Mirandized suspects to talk to the police, a major factor undoubtedly is that many suspects naturally believe, albeit incorrectly, that remaining silent will make them 'look guilty' and will be used against them as evidence of guilt.").

79. *See supra* notes 39–44 and accompanying text (discussing the kind of techniques, fleshed out in police manuals, which the *Miranda* Court condemned and felt necessitated the implementation of safeguards).

80. Starr, *supra* note 39, at 42.

81. *See generally* Richard A. Leo, *Questioning the Relevance of* Miranda *in the Twenty-first Century*, 99 MICH. L. REV. 1000, 1003 (2001) ("[D]espite the fourfold warnings, suspects frequently waived their *Miranda* rights and chose, instead, to speak to their interrogators."). *See also* Starr, *supra* note 39, at 45 ("Leo has reported that the Miranda decision, which is supposed to shield suspects from involuntary confessions, generally does not: more than eighty percent decline their *Miranda* rights ...").

82. When *Miranda* issued, it aimed to supplement—not replace—the voluntariness inquiry of the due process cases. *See generally* Edwin D. Driver, *Confessions and the Social Psychology of Coercion*, 82 HARV. L. REV. 42, 60 (1968) ("The *Miranda* warnings of course do not directly affect the limits set by 'voluntariness' on permissible tactics, but merely add several safeguards."). In today's practice, *Miranda* has replaced the due-process-inquiry: that is, once an interrogator recites the *Miranda* buzz words, a trial court typically skips the voluntariness inquiry and admits the evidence. *See* Dickerson, 530 U.S. 535 (conceding that when police obey *Miranda*, there will rarely be a colorable claim that the confession was compelled in violation of the Due Process Clause). *See generally* Leo, *supra* note 81, at 1025 (explaining that *Miranda* has "shift[ed] the legal inquiry from whether the confession was voluntarily given to whether the *Miranda* rights were voluntarily waived," and that "defendants will rarely succeed in arguing that their self-incriminating statement was

terrogators can, and do, perfunctorily drone through the *Miranda* script, thus imparting what has become reality—namely, that this is just inane formality, and the rights themselves mere nullities.[83] Moreover, as discussed in greater depth in the next chapter, the Supreme Court has butchered *Miranda* to such an extent that the prosecution can almost always secure a loophole to excuse compliance with *Miranda*, except themselves from its dictates, or foist the evidentiary fruit of a violation into the trial.[84]

With respect to the exclusionary rule, it is practically extinct, and today, numerous confessions, true or false, come into evidence.[85] As the next chapter also reveals, the Supreme Court has effectually handed police a fresh box of tricks, including that of interrogate-now-warn-later, or the redundant ques-

---

compelled"); Weisselberg, *supra* note 76, at 1523 ("[I]t turns out that following *Miranda's* hollow ritual often forecloses a searching inquiry into the voluntariness of a statement.").

83. *See generally* Leo, *supra* note 81, at 1003 (explaining that there are many theories with respect to why suspects waive their *Miranda* rights, including "the manner in which detectives deliver[] ... the warnings[,] ... the failure of suspects to understand the meaning or significance of their ... rights[,]" and the fact that "the tactics and techniques of police interrogation" have not changed as a result of *Miranda*").

84. *See supra* note 76 (giving examples of legal commentary on the many exceptions to *Miranda*). *See also infra* note 85 and accompanying text (examples of how the Court has eviscerated the exclusionary rules) and Chapter IV (Prisons of Coercion: *Notes from the House of the Dead*) (explaining how the Supreme Court has slaughtered *Miranda* and essentially deemed it inapplicable to prisoners).

85. In many cases involving confessions, the exclusionary rule is inapplicable, limited, or riddled through with exceptions. *See, e.g.,* Kansas v. Ventris, 556 U.S. 586 (2009) (Incriminating statements given to a jailhouse informant in violation of the *Massiah* doctrine were admissible to impeach the defendant's trial testimony); United States v. Patane, 52 U.S. 630 (2004) (The failure to give *Miranda* warnings does not mandate suppression of the physical fruits of a suspect's unwarned but voluntary statements); Oregon v. Elstad, 470 U.S. 298 (1985) (holding that when police, acting without bad faith, violate *Miranda* during an interrogation, a confession following a subsequent proper interrogation is not the inadmissible fruit of the initial violation); Nix v. Williams, 467 U.S. 431 (1984) (The fruits of self-incriminating statements given in violation of the Sixth Amendment right to counsel can be admitted at trial if the government can show, by a preponderance of the evidence, that the evidence would have inevitably been discovered through means completely independent of the illegality); Oregon v. Hass, 420 U.S. 714 (1975) (When a police officer violated *Miranda* by interrogating the defendant after he received warnings and invoked the right to counsel, the incriminating statements could be introduced at trial for impeachment purposes); Harris v. New York, 401 U.S. 222 (1971) (An incriminating statement obtained without *Miranda* warnings was admissible on cross-examination to show inconsistency between it and the defendant's trial testimony); Wong Sun v. United States, 371 U.S. 471 (1963) (Where defendant had initially been arrested without probable cause, his subsequent confession is attenuated from the illegality and can come in as evidence).

tion-release-question-again game, which is now permissible (and even implicitly encouraged) in the prisons.[86] Such devices make suspects, especially those who are already incarcerated, feel that invocation of *Miranda* rights is perilous and futile.[87] Dostoevsky, understanding that confessions can be unreliable and fail to facilitate truth finding, has suggested that such evidence has no place in an earthly justice system.[88]

Now, with DNA exoneration, scholars, officers in the criminal justice system, and the public are cognizant of the staggering number of wrongful convictions, many of which are based on false confessions.[89] For this, experts blame

---

86. *See generally* Oregon v. Elstad, 470 U.S. 298 and Missouri v. Seibert, 542 U.S. 600 (2004), which together permit the admission of a confession made after a *Miranda*-defective confession as long as the failure to warn was not done in bad faith and the second confession does not proceed directly from the first. In *Maryland v. Shatzer*, 130 S. Ct. 1213 (2010), the Court held that, where an inmate invokes counsel and there is a fourteen day break in custody, incriminating statements made, without counsel present, in a second interrogation are admissible. In *Howes v. Fields*, 132 S. Ct. 1181 (2012), the Court held that an incarcerated individual is not always in custody within the meaning of *Miranda* any time he or she is being interrogated. Under *Shatzer*, when prisoners request counsel, the interrogator need only ship them back to their cell and then, fourteen days later, start over without counsel present. Under *Fields*, interrogators can dispense with the *Miranda* warnings altogether if they question an inmate in an average-sized, well-lit room, swing open the door every now and then, refrain from physical restraint or direct threats, offer food and water, and tell the inmate that he or she can return to the cell. *See also infra* Chapter IV (Prisons of Coercion: *Notes from the House of the Dead*)(discussing the *Shatzer* and *Fields* decisions, along with other instances in which the Supreme Court has either deemed *Miranda* inapplicable or carved out an exception).

87. *See supra* note 86 (giving some examples of the *Miranda* loopholes); *infra* Chapter IV (Prisons of Coercion: *Notes from the House of the Dead*) (analyzing how the cases, which have obliterated *Miranda*, generate a feeling of futility).

88. *See generally infra* Parts III (discussing Dostoevsky's confessant gene) and IV (concluding issues).

89. *See generally* Starr, *supra* note 39, at 42 ("Of the three hundred and eleven people exonerated through post-conviction DNA testing, more than a quarter had given false confessions—including those convicted in such notorious cases as the Central Park Five."). Starr discusses the case of Darrel Parker, who "[a]fter nine hours of interrogation, ... broke down and confessed." *Id.* Although he "recanted the next day, ... a jury found him guilty of murder and sentenced him to life in prison." *Id.* In 1988, another man in the Nebraska State Penitentiary confessed to the crime, after which Parker obtained a pardon and later, when Parker was eighty years old, he received an award of damages from the state. *Id.* at 49. *See also* Barry Scheck & Peter Neufeld, *DNA and Innocence Scholarship*, in WRONGFULLY CONVICTED 241 (Westervelt & Humphreys eds., 2001) and Innocent Project.com, http://www.innocenceproject.com (giving the ever-rising number of DNA exonerations). *See also* Steven A. Drizin & Richard A. Leo, *The Problem of False Confessions in the Post-DNA World*, 82

outside forces, like coercion or deliberate elicitation on the part of interrogators, who isolate and overwhelm an already terrified accused.[90] Dostoevsky, knowing that nearly every human being has internalized his or her coercer, realizes that individuals, at least on an unconscious level, are primed and eager to oust secrets—and this is true well before the elicitor or interrogator converges on the scene to shove them under hot lights.

III. Dostoevsky's Confessant Gene

Jurisprudence does not have a monopoly on confession, a phenomenon that for ages has fascinated multiple theologians, philosophers, and artists. Dostoevsky, of course, knew of religious communities, like the Roman Catholic Church, which institutionalized the ritual.[91] His character, Fyodor Pavlovich Karamazov ("Fyodor"), the reviled buffoon in *The Brothers Karamazov*, sputters his version of the history behind the Russian Orthodox sacrament:

> Confession is a great mystery before which I stand in awe and am ready to bow down, and here suddenly everyone in the cell falls on his knees and confesses out loud. Is it proper to confess out loud? The Holy Fathers instituted whispered confession, only then is there any mystery in it, and that has been so since olden times.[92]

Not surprisingly, like just about all else, Fyodor has it ass-backwards: for the first centuries of Christianity, confession was public, but by the thirteenth century, it had transformed into a private act, one even transpiring behind the

---

N.C.L. Rev. 891 (2004) (discussing how the innocent are wrongfully convicted); Brandon L. Garrett, *The Substance of False Confessions*, 62 Stan. L. Rev. 1051 (2010) (analyzing wrongful convictions); Leo, et al, *supra* note 77, at 764 (explaining how "the law may fail to protect contaminated false confessors against the fate of wrongful conviction and incarceration, despite the many constitutional safeguards of the American criminal justice system"); Witmer-Rich, *supra* note 76, at 1237 (discussing the "trend of DNA exonerations of convicts").

90. *See supra* notes 76-87 and accompanying text (commentators and cases addressing permissible interrogation tactics and the numerous *Miranda* loopholes).

91. *See* Brooks, *supra* note 3, at 90 ("Other religious traditions, including the Judaic, have ... emphasized the avowal of sin to the deity, but the Roman Church institutionalized and ritualized the practice in ways that had a momentous cultural impact.")

92. Dostoevsky, *supra* note 10, at 88.

grille of a confessional.[93] In old Russia, sinners often confessed openly to the soil, rather than to priests, but this too underwent change.[94] Incidentally, some Slavic literature scholars consider Zosima, the esteemed elder in *The Brothers Karamazov*, who worships mother earth and all holy creation, as an animistic, pantheistic, Christian alloy, one atavistically suggestive of that old ritual of bowing to breathe one's sins into the ears of Russian *terra firma*.[95]

During Dostoevsky's time, in Russian Orthodox tradition, with its monasteries and elders, who were the spiritual guides, confession was venerated. But it also fueled controversy. In *The Brothers Karamazov*, the narrator, elaborating on the elder, "who takes your soul, your will into his soul and into his will," explains that "[a]ll disciples accept an eternal confession to the elder, and an indissoluble bond between the one who binds and the one who is bound."[96] The elders, feared as too powerful, initially met with persecution, and as their popularity amongst the people grew, so did criticism, which primarily targeted confession:

> [C]ommon people as well as the highest nobility flocked to the elders of our monastery so that prostrating before them, they could confess to them their doubts, their sins, their sufferings, and ask for advice and admonition. Seeing which, the opponents of the elders shouted, among other accusations, that here the sacrament of confession was being arbitrarily and frivolously degraded, although a disciple's or lay-

---

93. Fyodor Dostoevsky, The Brothers Karamazov 81. n. 5 (W.W. Norton & Co., Inc. 2011) (1979–80) ("Confession was public for the first centuries of Christianity, so Fyodor Pavlovich has it wrong: private confession is the more recent innovation."). *See also* Roger B. Anderson, *Mythical Implications of Father Zosima's Religious Teachings*, in Dostoevsky, *id.* at 733 (explaining that Zosima "expresses a disturbing tendency, by Christian standards, to worship the earth and all forms of creation as being endowed with holy meaning" and that Russian critic R. Pletnev aligns the monk with "anthropomorphism and pantheism" and "considers Dostoevsky to be close to the *Strigol'niki* heresy, the old Russian practice of confessing to the soil rather than to Christian priests"); Brooks, *supra* note 3, at 90 (With respect to the Roman Catholic Church, there was "a change from an emphasis on public penance, as a manifestation of one's sin and need for restoration to the Christian community, to an emphasis on the verbal act and fact of confession itself, and the corresponding speech act of absolution.").

94. *See supra* note 93.

95. *See* Anderson, *supra* note 93. *See also* Miller, *supra* note 8, at 31 ("Dostoevsky was one of the founders of the *pochvennichestvo* movement[, and thus,] when his characters express the desire to kiss the earth and water it with their tears, they are echoing a fundamental belief of their creator.").

96. Dostoevsky, *supra* note 10, at 27–28.

man's ceaseless confession of his soul to the elder is not at all sacramental.[97]

Dostoevsky's narrator alludes to these kinds of accusations in the scandal, in which Zosima's opportunistic enemies, capitalizing on the stink emanating from the elder's corpse, "malicious[]ly whisper" that the newly departed ... had "abused the sacrament of confession."[98]

Dostoevsky was conversant with the theological and philosophical debates of his day, along with the genre of confession literature, which includes the works of ancient Christian Latin writer Saint Aurelius Augustinus, and the eighteenth century French genius Jean-Jacque Rousseau, both of whom authored *Confessions*.[99] Professor Robin Feuer Miller, noting this, sees Dostoevsky as straddling the fence: he "was both attracted and repelled by the act of confession—attracted by its moments of rare and precious authenticity, repelled by the many self-justificatory and arrogant uses to which it could be put."[100] Unlike the Supreme Court and legal commentators, who prescribe tests and rules, Dostoevsky, humbled by what he knew to be impenetrable mystery,

---

97. *Id.* at 28–29.

98. *Id.* at 333. *See also* Anderson, *supra* note 93, at 735 ("The early decomposition of the elder's body, of course, is testimony to many that Zosima had strayed far from the regular teachings of the church, that the rapid corruption of the body revealed his spiritual 'corruption' while alive.").

99. *See* Letter from Fyodor Dostoevsky to Nikolay Strakhov (May 18, 1877) in III Dostoevsky Letters 1868–1871, at 360 (David Lowe ed. & trans., Ardis Publishers 1990) [hereinafter III Letters] (discussing Rousseau and "the dream of recreating the world anew through reason and knowledge (positivism)"). *See generally* Martinsen, *supra* note 3, at 92 ("Dostoevsky's experiments in confession ... manifest his lifelong polemic with Rousseau."); Miller, *supra* note 8, at 61 (explaining that much of [Dostoevsky's] fiction can be read as a veiled polemic with that archetypal master of the confessional genre, Jean Jacques Rousseau, author of *Confessions* (1781)"). *See also* Coetzee, *supra* note 3 (discussing "confessional fictions" in Dostoevsky, which consist, for the greater part, of representations of confessions of abhorrent acts committed by their "narrators" within the Augustine and Rousseau genre); Kantor, *supra* note 3, at 10 ("It is no coincidence that the Book of Job has been the favorite book of St. Augustine (he wrote *Notes on Job*) and of Dostoevsky, who made frequent references to Job"); *id.* at 13 ("Dostoevsky was probably familiar with St. Augustine, for the blessed Augustine was recognized by Orthodoxy and Orthodox writers referred to him."); Miller, *supra* note 3, at 83 (explaining that "despite Dostoevsky's sustained critique—through parody and polemic—of Rousseau's *Confessions*, he felt, throughout his entire career, a continued attraction to the confessional mode and always had a predilection for first person narratives both in his short stories and in his longer fiction").

100. Miller, *supra* note 8, at 30.

understood that confession, with its jillion inducements and manifestations, could not be tested, regulated, or explained. While in criminal procedure, the exegesis and panacea focus on physical conditions and third-party conduct, Dostoevsky looked elsewhere. He scoured the psychological, spiritual, metaphysical landscape to locate coercion in the recesses of each soul and psyche. For him, moreover, confession tends to serve no purpose, salutary or otherwise, in courts of law.

Dostoevsky, himself once a suspect, convict, and resident in a Siberian prison, who experienced firsthand interrogation and saw torture, of course disapproved of police overreaching and recoiled at the resultant phenomenon of false convictions.[101] He, however, did not believe that interrogators or torturers were the real causal factors. According to Professor Peter Brooks, Dostoevsky's characters demonstrate that "[g]uilt can in any event always be produced to meet the demand for confession, since there is always more than enough guilt to go around, and its concealment can be a powerful motive for confession."[102] Brooks' theory, one in which Dostoevsky would acquiesce, is that what compels confession are "inextricable layers of shame, guilt, contempt, self-loathing, attempted propitiation, and expiation."[103] For Dostoevsky, all people possess a confessant gene, replete with interminable, refractory, emotive layers. Dostoevsky's characters, like those in *Crime and Punishment* and *The Brothers Karamazov*, can be obsessive compulsive or self-flagellating divulgers, and one lone confessant can present all or multiple genotypes.

A. The Compulsive Self-Incriminator

In Dostoevsky's *Crime and Punishment*, Rodion Raskolnikov slaughters an old woman, a moneylender. When the victim's step-sister unexpectedly barges in, Raskolnikov, again wielding his axe, makes it a double murder and pockets the valuables. About twelve days later, Raskolnikov surrenders to police.

---

101. *See generally* DOSTOEVSKY, *supra* note 2. In *Dead House*, the narrator, commenting on the man wrongfully convicted of parricide, who "had suffered ten years of penal servitude for no reason," says, "[n]o need to expatiate on the tragic profundity of this case, on the young life ruined by such a dreadful accusation." *Id.* at 303. *See also infra* Chapter IV (Prisons of Coercion: *Notes from the House of the Dead*) (discussing the inmates in *Dead House*, including the gentleman wrongfully convicted of parricide).

102. BROOKS, *supra* note 3, at 21.

103. *Id.* at 6.

While the novel entails a brutal murder of two women, the real focus is not on
the crime itself, but on its aftermath, on Raskolnikov's psychological anguish,
and on what eventually preempts all else—the murderer's need, or rather obsessive compulsion, to confess.[104]

Freud proposed that unconscious guilt can spawn a crime in order to assure punishment as satisfaction of the guilt.[105] In essence, Dostoevsky gives us
a psychological portrait of someone who, although a unique human being, is
also a species of offender, the kind who so intensely craves mollification of
guilt, acceptance of responsibility, and spiritual regeneration that he actually
offends to pour content into his confession. For Raskolnikov, this is evident before the crime, during the crime, and after the crime.

1. Confession as Motive

For a long time, scholars have asked why Raskolnikov did what he did, and
have answered by adopting one of the perpetrator's spurious rationalizations
for his offense. The scholarship on and the novel itself proffer, essentially,
four possible motives, and as Dostoevsky intended, each one is discredited.[106]
Raskolnikov's first putative motive is personal: he murders Alyona Ivanovna
because he detests her, which the novel substantiates to some extent. When
we first see her through the starving ex-student's eyes, Alyona is repulsive and
cadaverous: "a tiny, dried-up little old woman of about sixty, with sharp, hostile eyes, a small sharp nose and no head covering."[107] Her "whitish hair" is "abun-

---

104. *See generally* Letter from Fyodor Dostoevsky to Mikhail Katkov (Sept. 27, 1865
Draft), in II Dostoevsky Letters 1860–1867, at 174–75 (David A. Lowe ed. & trans., Ardis
Publishers 1989) [hereinafter II Letters]. Dostoevsky, who was in the process of writing
Crime and Punishment, says that "[i]t is the psychological account of a crime" in which "[a]
young man, expelled from the university, petit-bourgeois by social origin, and living in extreme poverty, after yielding to strange, 'unfinished' ideas floating in the air, has resolved,
out of light-mindedness and out of the instability of his ideas, to get out of his foul situation at one go." *Id.* at 174.

105. Sigmund Freud, *Criminals from a Sense of Guilt* in 14 The Standard Edition of
the Complete Psychological Works of Sigmund Freud, at 332–33 (James Strachey, ed.
Hogarth Press, 1974). *See also* Brooks, *supra* note 3, at 21 (applying Freud's theory to confessions). Brooks also points out that "Talmudic law has recognized for millennia [that]
confession may be the product of the death-drive, the production of incriminating acts to
assure punishment or even self-annihilation, and hence [is] inherently suspect because [it
is] in contradiction to the basic human instinct of self-preservation." *Id.*

106. *See generally* Ronner, supra note 49, at 117–22 (discussing the putative motives for
Raskolnikov's crime in the context of confession and therapeutic jurisprudence).

107. Dostoevsky, *supra* note 1, at 9.

dantly smeared with oil," and her "long, thin neck ... resemble[s] the leg of a chicken."[108]

It is indeed litotes that Raskolnikov is not particularly fond of her. But it is more accurate to say, as Raskolnikov does to Sonya, that Alyona is just a "loathsome, useless, harmful louse," someone whom he negates as human.[109] After Sonya admonishes, "[b]ut that louse was a human being," Raskolnikov concedes that Alyona "wasn't really a louse," and that he is prattling "nonsense."[110] He admits: "I simply killed; I killed for my own sake, for no one but myself."[111] In short, Raskolnikov's animosity toward his chosen victim is dissociated from his crime.

A second, but related, theory is one that seduces some psychologists and psychiatrists. They attribute the murder to Raskolnikov's conflicted feelings towards his mother. For example, Kathleen Garber explains that Raskolnikov, viewing the "harsh, miserly old woman" as "the bad mother ... who treats her step-sister shamefully," needs to "project inner destructiveness (death instinct) and finds the old pawnbroker suitable for this purpose."[112] Thus, Raskolnikov, loving and abhorring his mother, unconsciously welds her to the despicable, ruptured facet of the self. But Alyona is not the only candidate for the office of maternal scapegoat. Rather, as Louis Breger has pointed out, *Crime and Punishment* is chock full of mothers, like the landlady, the "bad" mother, the "source of food, shelter, and comfort, [...] whose care is bound up with anger, fear and guilt" and the landlady's maid, the "good" mother, who "attends to [Raskolnikov's] needs in a simple and straightforward manner."[113] If

---

108. *Id. See also* II, LETTERS, *supra* note 104, at 174 (Raskolnikov "has resolved to murder an old woman, a titular counselor who lends money at interest[, who is] stupid, deaf, sick, greedy ... malicious and preying on someone else's life by tormenting her younger sister.").

109. DOSTOEVSKY, *supra* note 1, at 497.

110. *Id.*

111. *Id.* at 500.

112. Kathleen Donnellan Garber, *A Psychological Analysis of a Dostoyevsky Character: Raskolnikov's Struggle for Survival*, 14 PERSPECTIVES IN PSYCHIATRIC CARE 16, 16 (1976). Garber explains that "[i]t was not [the pawnbroker's] death he really sought so much as relief from his intolerable rage at the introjected 'bad mother' from whom he learned the concept of 'bad self' and self-contempt." *Id.*

113. LOUIS BREGER, DOSTOYEVSKY: THE AUTHOR AS PSYCHOANALYST 23 (1989). *See also* Jeffrey C. Hutzler, *Family Pathology in* Crime and Punishment, 38 AM. J. OF PSYCHOANALYSIS 337 (1978) ("[A]fter murdering the pawnbroker and her daughter [sic] (symbolically mother and sister?), Raskolnikov realizes that in this act he has cut himself off from his mother and sister."); David Kiremidjian, Crime and Punishment: *Matricide and the Woman Question*, 33 AM. IMAGO 403 (1976) (Raskolnikov acts out his matricidal impulses.); Robert B. Lower, *On Raskolnikov's Dreams in Dostoyevsky's* Crime and Punishment, 17 J. AMER-

matricidal rage were the real trigger, Raskolnikov might have embarked on a spree to serially exterminate a whole female coterie of St. Petersburg society.

The third putative motive assigned to the impoverished Raskolnikov is monetary.[114] Raskolnikov tries to persuade himself that murder plus robbery equals economic escape hatch. Some scholars, like Dr. Atkin, who call this a "social crime," argue that, "[h]ad Raskolnikov not been a ragged, starving ex-student whose sister was about to prostitute herself for his benefit, no murder would have been committed, and his youthful ambitions would have taken a different course altogether."[115] For Atkin and others, Raskolnikov, who has "already been reduced to the lowest level of poverty," feeling "driven into a cage like a rat to starve to death," believes that only Alyona's bounty can free him.[116] Over time, however, Dostoevsky makes readers realize that the economic motive is just a red herring.

Even before the crime, Raskolnikov's physical and mental conditions are so deplorable that he needs to heal, integrate the self, and reconnect with the human race.[117] Raskolnikov is a threadbare, starving ex-law student, whose saintly sister, Dunya, is on the brink of prostituting herself for his benefit by marrying an evil man with some wealth and social standing. Raskolnikov's living quarters (if you can call them that) consist of a "room … situated right under the roof of a tall, five-story tenement" and "sooner resemble[s] a closet

---

ICAN PSYCHOANALYTIC ASSOC. 728 (1969) (Raskolnikov lives a sadomasochistic oedipal fantasy.).

114. *See generally* I. Atkin, *Raskolnikov: The Study of a Criminal*, 5 J. OF CRIMINAL PSYCHOPATHOLOGY 255 (1943) (analyzing Raskolnikov as a "living being who is at odds with his environment," discussing the "social determinants of crime," and attributing the crime to poverty).

115. *Id.* at 256–57.

116. *Id.* at 365. *See also* II LETTERS, *supra* note 104, at 174 (Dostoevsky, discussing the crime as putative economic escape hatch, proposes that Raskolnikov "decides to murder … and rob … in order to make his mother, who lives in the provinces, happy; to deliver his sister, who lives as a hired companion for certain landowners, from the lascivious attentions of the head of the landowner household—attentions that threaten her with ruin; and to finish the university, go abroad, and then for his whole life long to be honest, firm, unswerving in fulfilling his 'humanitarian duty to humanity,' …"). In one of his interviews with Raskolnikov, Porfiry, the examining magistrate, suggests a monetary motive for the crime. *See* DOSTOYEVSKY, *supra* note 1, at 315 ("[T]hen is it really possible that you might also have decided—oh, because of some everyday setback or financial difficulty, let's say, … to step across an obstacle? … Well, by robbing and murdering someone, for example? …").

117. *See* II, LETTERS, *supra* note 104, at 175 (Dostoevsky describes his Raskolnikov as "compelled to denounce himself" and "[c]ompelled, so as to become linked to people again.").

than a place of habitation."[118] Because Raskolnikov is unemployed, in debt, and in arrears on his rent, his daily life consists of dodging his landlady and the maid, who live on the floor below.

Raskolnikov is not just trapped by poverty, squalid living conditions, and uncooperative people. Raskolnikov, who is "in a tense, irritable state of mind that verged on hypochondria," also suffers from disorienting seizures and severe anguish.[119] In fact, Raskolnikov's name says it all because, in Russian, *raskol* means split or schism.[120] The Raskolnikov enigma, and the reason that he is so difficult to pin down, is that he is indeed split, at war with himself at all times and in all things. Whatever you can say about him, you can easily say the contrary, and whatever Raskolnikov does, he seeks to retract. Torn asunder by a conterminous need for isolation and companionship, he presents as a caricature of self-contradiction. At least on an unconscious level, Raskolnikov, intuiting his own need of peace and self-reconciliation, knows that no wad of stolen lucre can bestow salvation.

While in the throes of planning the murder, Raskolnikov eavesdrops on a conversation in which men postulate killing Alyona and disseminating her wealth to the poor, sick, and needy.[121] Raskolnikov, interpreting this as "predestination," states that "inside his own head there had been engendered ... *precisely those very same thoughts.*"[122] In so doing, he adopts the banter as his own thoughts and thus, momentarily, subscribes to the altruistic justification that his scheme is for the betterment of humankind.[123] This too proves false because Raskolnikov does nothing for himself, or anybody else, with the stolen property.

---

118. DOSTOEVSKY, *supra* note 1, at 5.

119. *Id.*

120. David McDuff, *Introduction to* Crime and Punishment, *in* DOSTOYEVSKY, *supra* note 1, at xxvii (noting that *Raskol* means schism, which indicates "[o]ne aspect of Raskolnikov's revolt against God ... [because it] is the term used to describe the split that took place in the Russian Orthodox Church in the mid seventeenth century...."). *See also* William Burnham, *The Legal Context and Contributions of Dostoyevsky's* Crime and Punishment, 100 MICH. L. REV. 1231 (2002) ("Raskolnikov gets his name from the Russian word *raskol*, which means a split or schism, and represents the conflict between his intellectual justifications for the crime and the moral revulsion he feels.")

121. DOSTOYEVSKY, *supra* note 1, at 80 ("Hundreds, possibly even thousands of lives that could be set on the right road; dozens of families saved from poverty, breakup, ruin, depravity, the venereal hospitals—and all of that with her money.").

122. *Id.* at 81.

123. *See* Burnham, *supra* note 120, at 1231 (discussing the "selfless theory" behind the crime and suggesting that "Raskolnikov figures that since the pawnbroker is old and rich from preying on human suffering, there is nothing wrong with killing her so that he can use her money to relieve suffering").

Further, Raskolnikov's behavior throughout the book rebuts any conceivable presumption that his crime is driven by lust for lucre. One of the few consistent things that can be said about Raskolnikov is that the destitute scholar, donned in rags and residing in a suffocating box, is not materialistic. Whenever he manages to get his hands on a few copecks, he either gives or tosses them away.[124] Sonya underscores the trait, when she hypothetically asks Raskolnikov: "how could you give away the last copeck you had, yet murder someone in order to rob her?"[125] Further, in the murder's aftermath, Raskolnikov exhibits little interest in the spoils: he hides the purse and valuables under a brick and never bothers to retrieve them. At his trial, it emerges that Raskolnikov failed to "remember the details of any of the goods he had stolen" and was "even mistaken as to their number."[126] In fact, he had never once deigned to peek in the purse, and after he abandoned it, "the largest denominations had suffered serious water damage."[127] Yes, Raskolnikov put himself through living hell for something, but surely it was not for his own, or humanity's, enrichment.

The fourth putative motive is philosophical—Raskolnikov's Napoleonic theory—likely borrowed from Napoleon III's book, *The Life of Julius Caesar*, which was popular among the Russian intelligentsia at the time Dostoevsky was writing *Crime and Punishment*.[128] Commentators have suggested that Raskolnikov, suffering from deep-seated feelings of inferiority, confiscated an ideology prefiguring Nietzsche and murdered to assert his own greatness and superiority.[129] In an article that Raskolnikov penned after leaving the university, he theorizes that there are certain people in the world who "have a perfect right to commit all sorts of atrocities and crimes and that it's as if the law did not apply to them."[130] Porfiry, the examining magistrate, taunting Raskol-

---

124. *See, e.g.,* DOSTOYEVSKY, *supra* note 1, at 140 ("Making an automatic movement with his hand, he suddenly felt the twenty-copeck piece that was clutched in it. He unclenched his fist, stared fixedly at the little coin and, with a swing of his arm, hurled it into the water....").

125. *Id.* at 492.

126. *Id.* at 638.

127. *Id.*

128. *See* Burnham, *supra* note 120, at 1231 (suggesting that the "selfish" or "Napoleonic" theory comes from Napoleon III's 1865 book).

129. *See* Atkin, *supra* note 114, at 271 (suggesting that we follow the "fuller development of Raskolnikov's ideas by Nietzsche[,]" who "also envisages a society which is divided into two distinct classes, an aristocratic ruling caste (the 'free spirits') and an inferior slave class," and that Raskolnikov's theory is thus seen as "a foreshadowing of the ideology of a fascist society").

130. DOSTOYEVSKY, *supra* note 1, 307 (Porfiry's summary of Raskolnikov's ideas).

nikov with these ideas, teases that he might have committed a crime to prove himself to be that extraordinary Napoleonic man:

> What I mean is, sir, that when you were writing your article, it couldn't just possibly have been, could it—ha, ha!—that you too considered yourself—oh, just the merest bit—to be one of the "extraordinary" people who can say *a new* word—in the sense you've explained.[131]

Dostoevsky has Raskolnikov echo Porfiry to mock this hypothetical motive. This occurs when Sonya seeks an explanation of the Napoleonic doctrine, and Raskolnikov, like his nemesis Porfiry, proclaims that "all of what I've been telling you is nonsense, almost pure drivel."[132] Through the dialogue with Porfiry and with Sonya, we come to see that the crime was neither a personal nor matricidal episode, and it was surely not monetarily, altruistically, or philosophically driven. Raskolnikov's crime is inextricable from the confessional compulsion that predates his crime. Significantly, before ever conceiving of the attack on Alyona, he had anticipated his own cathartic confession by putting his self-incriminating Napoleonic ponderings out there for all to find.

2. The Crime as Confession

During the murder, Raskolnikov makes mistakes, yet clumsily charges forth to make more mistakes, unconsciously propelled by the need to get caught and have that confession squeezed out of him.[133] After bashing in Alyona's head, Raskolnikov starts fumbling for her keys and haphazardly grabbing at valuables. Despite all of his supposed meticulous planning, which included arrival at a time when Alyona's step-sister would be absent, Lizaveta unexpectedly barges in to become an unintended victim. Rather than dash out instantly, Raskolnikov, confused, fails to efficiently confiscate the spoils, and instead freezes, obsessing over the blood on his weapon, hands, and clothes. In the

---

131. *Id.* at 315.

132. *Id.* at 496.

133. *See* II LETTERS, *supra* note 104, at 174 ("[S]uch crimes are terribly difficult to commit—that is, people almost always leave threads crudely sticking out, clues and so forth, and leave terribly much to chance, which almost always gives away the guilty parties."). *See also* DOSTOYEVSKY, *supra* note 1, at 181 (Razumikhin, discussing the crime, says: "[I]n my opinion, he's neither skilled nor experienced, and he's probably a first-timer.... If, on the other hand, you assume he was inexperienced, it looks as though it was only chance that saved him from disaster.")

delay, two men startle him by banging on the apartment door. Raskolnikov nearly gets caught but, in a near euphoric paralysis, manages to hunker down until the men leave.

Although the whole thing is awkward and amateurish, Raskolnikov might have gotten away with it.[134] But Raskolnikov made a serious, although not necessarily fatal, mistake: he failed to consider that the miser might maintain a customer list, and that police would use it to schedule interviews. While the mere fact of being the victim's customer is not enough by itself for a conviction, it would at least guarantee that Raskolnikov would have a chance to wrangle with police, who might, in turn, help him consummate what he most desires—confession.

After the crime, Raskolnikov, tormented by his need to get caught, becomes even more of a self-saboteur, and starts to flaunt his guilt. Significantly, some of Raskolnikov's episodic self-incriminations occur even before the official interrogator, Porfiry, enters the stage and begins his cat and mouse game with the suspect. Right after the crime, Raskolnikov returns the weapon to its niche under the bench, but admits that if the yard keeper had been there to greet him, "he would probably have simply handed him the axe."[135] Before he decides to stuff the loot under a rock, Raskolnikov, brain storming, comes up with crannies that are likely to be discovered, like the household stove, "the first place they'll start rummaging about in."[136] He is unconsciously compelled to plant evidence against himself and self-entrap.

Police initially summon Raskolnikov to the station, which, unbeknownst to him, has nothing to do with the murder, but rather involves his debt to the landlady. Here, Raskolnikov decides that he might just get it over with, and tell the official "everything that had happened the day before, down to the last detail, and then tak[e] him to his lodgings and show[] him the gold objects in the corner, inside the hole."[137] In fact, his urge to self-incriminate is "so strong" that, after merely hearing mention of the murder, he suspiciously swoons.[138] When Raskolnikov exits the station, triumphant, expecting that he has secured that promotion to suspect status, he both relishes and fears the inevitable room search.

From there on, he is consumed with a desire to be cornered and forced to confess, and Raskolnikov's behavior becomes increasingly reckless and self-

---

134. *See* II LETTERS, *supra* note 104, at 174–75 (Dostoevsky says of his Raskolnikov that "he manages in an absolutely accidental way to accomplish his undertaking both quickly and successfully.")

135. DOSTOYEVSKY, *supra* note 1, at 106.

136. *Id.* at 112.

137. *Id.* at 127.

138. *Id.*

condemning. Raskolnikov meets a police clerk in a bar, sardonically admits to the crime, and then pretends that it just was a joke. Unable to leave well enough alone, Raskolnikov visits the crime scene, goes right up to the workmen repairing Alyona's apartment, questions them about blood, and makes a memorable ruckus, which he secretly hopes will be reported to police. In fact, after that episode, Raskolnikov is relieved, "know[ing] for a certainty that it would all very soon be over."[139]

Although Porfiry, a natural psychologist, plays a role in, and arguably contributes to, Raskolnikov's surrender, he cannot take credit. Other agents, mostly Raskolnikov himself, but also Sonya and Svidrigailov, help jog out the confession. In fact, the coercive forces within Raskolnikov's psyche well exceed any that the plucky examining magistrate can ever apply. Although Raskolnikov professes to loathe him, he nevertheless cannot stop flirting with Porfiry. He cannot resist ascertaining whether Porfiry knows that "[he] went to that old witch's apartment … and asked about the blood," and commands Porfiry to interrogate him by shouting, "to put it bluntly: be so good as either to ask your questions or let me go, this instant … and if you are going to question me, then do it according to the proper form, sir."[140] In crescendo, Raskolnikov, actually pleading for arrest and prosecution, states and reiterates, "[i]f you believe that you have the right to prosecute me, then please do so; if you are going to arrest me, arrest me."[141] As such, it is Raskolnikov who recruits Porfiry's service as coercive catalyst.

In the jousting between Raskolnikov and Porfiry, the examiner may have his tool kit, stocked with psychological methodology, but none of that is what really ousts the confession. Porfiry tellingly likens suspects, like Raskolnikov, to moths at a "lighted candle" that are "hovering, circling around [him]."[142] What is coercing the suspect here is an internecine Porfiry, drawing him toward the flesh-and-blood Porfiry, with Raskolnikov hoveringly circling toward destination disclosure.[143] Significantly, Raskolnikov never does confess to his investigator, but delivers the fruit of Porfiry's toil first to Sonya, and then to some

---

139. *Id.* at 210.

140. *Id.* at 293, 399. *See generally* Harriet Murav, Russia's Legal Fictions 26 (The University of Michigan Press, 1955) (Speaking of legal reform of 1864, she points out that "[p]retrial criminal investigations retained some features of the inquisitorial principle" and that "[a]n examining magistrate interrogated suspects without the presence of an attorney.")

141. Dostoevsky, *supra* note 1, at 408.

142. *Id.* at 405. According to Porfiry, a suspect will eventually "come to the station himself and ask: 'Why are they taking so long to arrest me?'" *Id.* at 408.

143. *See* II Letters, *supra* note 104, at 175 (Dostoevsky describes Raskolnikov as "*compelled* to denounce himself.").

generic official. In so doing, Dostoevsky denigrates the efficacy of outside agents in a genuine, fluid, regenerative process, one in which confession is just a start.

3. The Confession

Sonya, whose role is far more important than Porfiry's, is the first to hear the whole truth. Raskolnikov, sensing that the prostitute is his salvation and that she will raise him, like Lazarus, from the dead, promises to tell her, and her alone, the murderer's identity:

> I know and I'll tell you.... You I'll tell, and you alone! I've singled you out. I won't come to ask you to forgive me, I'll simply tell you. I singled you out a long time ago as the person to tell this to. I thought of it back at the time when your father spoke about you and when Lizaveta was still alive.[144]

Feeling that he "must" confess to Sonya, and that he could not put it off any longer, Raskolnikov keeps his word and identifies himself as the murderer.[145] Once Sonya learns the truth, she does not shun Raskolnikov, but "move[s] toward him, ... seize[s] both his hands" and then "thr[ows] herself on his neck, embracing him and gripping him as hard as she could in her arms."[146] She tells Raskolnikov what he already knows—that "[t]here's no one, no one in the whole world more unhappy than you are now."[147] Sharing his agony and sense of isolation, Sonya vows, "I'll never leave you, no matter where you go! ... I'll follow you everywhere."[148] Through this, Sonya intimates that, if he decides to do what he needs to do—to confess and accept responsibility—he will not bear it alone. She prescribes the next step:

> Go immediately, this very moment, go and stand at the crossroads, bow down, first kiss the ground that you've desecrated, and then bow to the whole world, to all four points of the compass and tell everyone, out loud: "I have killed!" Then God will send you life again.[149]

Sonya's *elixir vitae*, implicating neither Porfiry nor legal constructs, consists of faith in God, repentance, and redemptive suffering. While Raskolnikov

---

144. Dostoyevsky, *supra* note 1, at 393.
145. *Id.* at 485.
146. *Id.* at 490–91.
147. *Id.* at 491.
148. *Id.*
149. *Id.* at 501.

is not yet ready to "stand at the crossroads," his regeneration is inchoate in his acceptance of Sonya's cross so that, one day, they can together "bear crosses" and "pray and take the road together."[150]

Sonya's influence, incubating in Raskolnikov's soul, prompts him to cast aside the lethal solution that Svidrigailov has chosen for himself.[151] Before committing suicide, Svidrigailov, Dunya's former employer and spurned suitor, confesses to Raskolnikov, narrating his lecherous life story, replete with multiple offenses against women and girls.[152] Realizing that Svidrigailov's inner torment parallels his own, Raskolnikov repudiates self-annihilation and instead marches off to the police station to accept Sonya's life affirming antidote.[153] For Raskolnikov, his obsessive compulsive need to come clean motivated his crime and filled his confession with content, which inaugurated his "gradual renewal, ... gradual rebirth, ... gradual transition from one world to another."[154] No coercive tactics from outside the self, and no implemented safeguards, could have staved off the inevitable—his confession—which served not as prosecutorial fodder, but significantly, as the first tiny step on a long path to redemption and reunion with humanity.[155]

B. The Self-Flagellating Confessant

In expounding his Napoleonic theory, Raskolnikov tells Porfiry that only ordinary folks make mistakes when "a certain capriciousness of temperament"

---

150. *Id.* at 504.

151. *See* Breger, *supra* note 113, at 42–49 (analyzing Svidrigailov and explaining that "[o]ther characters in the novel can be seen as aspects of Raskolnikov—Marmeladov his masochistic side, Porfiry his accusing conscience—but Svidrigailov is the most explicit 'double'; he floats into the action as if he were part of Raskolnikov's mind").

152. *Id.* at 44 (discussing Svidrigailov's "sexual depravity" and calling him a "Don Juan, an expert at the seduction of women ... [with] a particular sexual perversion: he is drawn to young girls").

153. *Id.* at 49 ("The path of Svidrigailov has led to death, Raskolnikov is now left with the road that has beckoned him for so long, and which he has been so reluctant to follow: that represented by Sonya.").

154. Dostoyevsky, *supra* note 1, at 656.

155. *See generally* Miller, *supra* note 3, at 98 (For Dostoevsky, "the confession of one's transgression before a good soul is only a first step, as Rasknolikov ... learn[s]" and "the genuine confession always serves to reunite man with other men and with the whole universe."). *See also* II Letters, *supra* note 104, at 175 (Raskolnikov, who is "[c]ompelled ... to become linked to people again, even at the price of perishing at penal servitude" experienced "the feeling of separation and alienation from humanity that came over him immediately after committing the crime.").

deludes them into believing that they are one of the extraordinary kind.[156] But he says that that breed does not "represent any significant threat" because of their tendency toward self-flagellation:[157]

> One doesn't need a whip-master for the job—they'll whip themselves, because they're very well-behaved; some of them will perform this service for one another, while others do it for themselves with their own hands.... Moreover, they impose various public acts of penitence on themselves—the effect is both splendid and edifying and, in short, you have nothing to worry about.[158]

Near the close of an interview between Raskolnikov and Porfiry, there is a *deus ex machina* reprieve in the form of just such a self-flagellator, who dashes into the station. Nikolai, the apartment painter, insists on confessing to Raskolnikov's crime and Porfiry, forced to shift ken to this false-confessant, releases Raskolnikov and says, "we'll be seeing each other again."[159] Porfiry, wiser (and likely more ethical) than some of today's interrogators, intuits that innocent Nikolai is unreliably boasting about a crime that he did not commit. Porfiry (and Dostoevsky as well) senses that the Nikolai species imperils criminal investigations by effectually painting over truth. The examining magistrate, who denominates Nikolai as someone who just "wants to 'accept his suffering,'" knows that he is "not our man."[160] Nikolai, a member of Raskolnikov's theoretical race of "ordinary" men, compelled to be his own "whip-master … impose[s] various acts of penitence" on himself.[161] But his modality is punishment minus crime.

Although masterful, Porfiry is tethered to the shortcomings of criminal justice and he knows it. He understands that confessions are deceptive and that his task, that of sifting genuine from ersatz, can be tedious and unproductive. After encountering the false confessant, Raskolnikov tells his agitator that his job is "comical" because, after Nikolai claims to be murderer, Porfiry is duty bound to "pick[] him to little pieces again, telling him that he's lying, that he

---

156. DOSTOYEVSKY, *supra* note 1, 311–12.

157. *Id.* at 312.

158. *Id.*

159. *Id.* at 421.

160. *Id.* at 543. *See also* BROOKS, *supra* note 3, at 6 ("Unless the content of the confession can be verified by other means, thus substantiating its trustworthiness, it may be false—false to fact, if true to some other sense of guilt. The law records many instances of false confessions—and no doubt many have gone unrecorded."). *See also supra* notes 89–90 and accompanying text (discussing convictions based on false confessions).

161. DOSTOYEVSKY, *supra* note 1, at 311–12.

is not the murderer."[162] Porfiry, all too-familiar with that fiasco, knows that, although he has been handed that "direct and irrefutable proof" in the form of Nikolai's admissions, the evidence is cheap lacquer, and he must start chipping away at it.[163]

Nikolai and Raskolnikov are kith and kin, in that both are compulsive self-incriminators. But unlike Raskolnikov, Nikolai, who does not need to offend in order to pour content into his confession, can do his atoning by merely pilfering another's crime. Also, if Porfiry had not had the wherewithal to intercede, an erroneous conviction, along with years of penal servitude, could have ensued. While we never discover precisely what demons within Nikolai spur his self-flagellation, Dostoevsky gives us access to the psyches and souls of Mitya and Ivan Karamazov, whose burning shame and spiritual crisis respectively galvanize true confessions, which, "incomprehensible and impossible" in legal proceedings, paradoxically end up obfuscating truth and derailing justice.[164]

1. Mitya's Confession: Purgation of Shame

Mitya Karamazov is consumed with unbearable shame, which he struggles to hide and yet wants to expose for public reprobation. His fear is that the beast, thrashing about in his own breast, will escape to commit heinous deeds.[165] He dreads loss of self-control with its resultant public degradation, which counterintuitively makes Mitya yearn to bring it on, get it over with, and disgrace himself before the world. Like Raskolnikov, for Mitya, confession is a step toward healing. It is also Mitya's way to start reining in his destructive impulses, connect with other human beings, and halt that self-perpetuating cycle

---

162. *Id.* at 421–22. *See also* BROOKS, *supra* note 3, at 6 ("What is the truth of confession? ... You may find yourself confessing to something else, something other than the supposed referent of your confession. You may damn yourself even as you seek to exculpate yourself.").

163. DOSTOYEVSKY, *supra* note 1, at 403.

164. DOSTOEVSKY, *supra* note 10, at 686. *See also infra* note 451 and accompanying text (discussing the judge's reaction to Ivan's true testimony).

165. See VICTOR TERRAS, READING DOSTOEVSKY 113, 128 (University of Wisconsin Press, 1998) (speaking of the "subtext, intertext, and ambiguity" in *Brothers Karamazov* and pointing out that "Fiodor Pavlovich, old Adam, carries in his lustfulness the seed of the personalities of his three sons: Ivan, whose passion is intellectual, Dmitry, whose passion is sensual, and Aliosha, whose passion is spiritual") *But see* MILLER, *supra* note 8, at 29 ("It is common place to discover in the three Karamazov brothers an allegory about spirit (Alyosha), mind (Ivan), and body or heart (Mitya)[, b]ut this classification becomes woefully inadequate and thin once one takes more than a cursory glance at them.").

of throbbing shame. In *Brothers Karamazov*, the narrator tells readers that a justice system incapable of descrambling such a genuine, heartfelt struggle, is simply foredoomed to get it wrong.

a. Confession to Alyosha

Mitya's tripartite confession to half-brother, Alexei Fyodorovich ("Alyosha"), who, like Sonya, is a worthy recipient, begins in the secret venue of a gazebo in a "completely deserted garden" where his whisper escalates into a shout, "I'm here in secret, I'm guarding a secret."[166] The preamble bares Mitya's confessant gene, his craving to reveal information and explore his own inner struggle. At first, Mitya stalls by quoting writers, like the nineteenth-century Russian poet Nikolai Nekrasov and the German Friedrich Schiller, which is suggestive of Mitya's desire to embellish, stretch it out, savor the onset of catharsis.[167] He even says, "Don't be in a hurry, Alyosha … There's no rush now."[168] Mitya, ardently yearning for expulsion, vows, "I'm going to tell you *everything*. For I surely must tell at least somebody," and then candidly brands himself "a babbler."[169]

In his preamble, this "babbler" gives Alyosha (and readers) a peek at his internecine battle with the beast. He says, "I'm just a brute of an officer who drinks cognac and goes whoring," who can "sink into the deepest, the very deepest shame of depravity."[170] He, "a Karamazov," both blasts and cherishes his inner devil, with its humiliating smirk:

> [W]hen I fall into the abyss, I go straight into it, head down and heels up, and I'm even pleased that I'm falling in just such a humiliating position, and for me I find it beautiful. And so in that very shame I suddenly begin a hymn. Let me be cursed, let me be base and vile, but let me also kiss the hem of that garment in which my God is clothed.[171]

---

166. DOSTOEVSKY, *supra* note 10, at 103. *See also* MILLER, *supra* note 8, at 22 (explaining that "Alyosha is the perfect repository for the confessions of his brothers and would seem to have the makings of an ideal future 'elder'").

167. MILLER, *supra* note 8, at 29 ("Dmitri shrewdly prefaces his own achingly personal confession with a literary preamble in which he quotes many of Dostoevsky's favorite writers.").

168. DOSTOEVSKY, *supra* note 10, at 105.

169. *Id.* (emphasis added).

170. *Id.* at 107.

171. *Id.*

Mitya, reviling while indulging his own Dr. Jekyll and Mr. Hyde, proclaims, "let me be following the devil at the same time, but I am still also your son, Lord."[172] He talks about the "'insects'… to whom God gave sensuality" and calls himself "that very insect."[173] In noting that "here the shores converge, here all contradictions live together," he acknowledges the conflict and stresses that "[h]ere the devil is struggling with God and the battlefield is the human heart."[174] For Mitya, confession can begin to placate that painful tension.

Before getting to the near nub, Mitya reminisces about his bacchanalian era of "thr[owing] fistfuls of money around" and bringing in "music, noise, gypsy women."[175] He, "speaking allegorically," claims to have always "liked the back lanes, dark and remote little crannies, away from the main square" where "there lay the unexpected nuggets in the dirt."[176] His admission that he not only "loved depravity," but also "the shame of depravity," conveys that shame is his guilty pleasure.[177] While Mitya's "base desires" and "insect" sensuality thwart his ambition to be perceived as the commensurate gentleman, they also help sate his need to self-shame.[178] Significantly, we learn that unlike his other half-brother, Ivan, Mitya is acutely aware of the distinction between desiring something and actually doing it.[179] In fact, Mitya habitually tries on behavioral options in the wardrobe of his mind before selecting one to sport before society.[180] Ultimately, this quirk will do him in at his trial, which occurs when Katerina furnishes the court with Mitya's drunken scribblings, in which he scripted his unexecuted plot to murder his father.[181]

While tautologically insisting that he is not "dishonorable," Mitya narrates a tri-lemma he once faced while serving as a seamy lieutenant in a small

---

172. *Id.*

173. *Id.* at 108.

174. *Id.*

175. *Id.* at 108–109. It is just a "near" nub, because Mitya does not tell Alyosha the complete truth. *See infra* notes 198, 210, 245, 253–64 and accompanying text (addressing the information that Mitya does not disclose to Alyosha).

176. DOSTOEVSKY, *supra* note 10, at 109.

177. *Id.*

178. *Id.* at 108.

179. *See infra* notes 282–83 and accompanying text (discussing Ivan's proclivity to blur together desire and conduct).

180. *See* MILLER, *supra* note 8, at 32–33 (Readers "witness at firsthand the struggle between God and the devil in Mitya's heart. Mitya crisply presents that amorphous conflict in terms of three potential scenarios that occur to him during his moment of crisis.").

181. *See infra* notes 414–36 and accompanying text (describing the trial scene and Ivan's mental breakdown on the stand).

town.[182] During that time, he learned that his colonel, Katerina Ivanovna's father, had appropriated 4,500 rubles of government funds. He hinted to his friend, Agafya, that he might be willing to give her half-sister, Katerina, the money if she would come to him "secretly."[183] The crisis unfolds when Katerina, the "beauty of beauties," appears in Mitya's room, prepared to sacrifice herself in exchange for the rubles.[184]

In his idiosyncratic way, Mitya mentally tests out alternative modes — that of insect, merchant, or nobleman. His first was "a Karamazov thought," that of a "bedbug and scoundrel."[185] "Breathless" and ablaze with an impulse to seduce her right then and there, he tempers that with a pact that he would propose marriage the next day.[186] He then realizes, however, that if he were to come to offer Katerina his hand, she would refuse to see him and even have him ejected. Such a prospect, infuriating him, propels him from the insect to the second, mercantile mode: he contemplates "pull[ing] some mean, piggish merchant's trick" and "giv[ing] her a sneering look."[187] He envisions the cruel, sarcastic mouth of a tradesman spewing, "[b]ut four thousand is much too much! Perhaps two hundred, even gladly with pleasure, but four thousand — it's too much money, miss, to throw away on such trifles."[188] He is so enthralled with this *modus vivendi* that he comes perilously close to actually implementing it, and although he thinks that "such infernal revenge would be worth it all," he would spend the rest of his life "howling with remorse."[189]

After purportedly casting aside the "bedbug" or "evil tarantula" frocks, the third suit, that of the nobleman, is the one that Mitya actually decides to don.[190] Mitya, who has six thousand rubles from his father as a final settlement, "silently" extricates a five thousand ruble bank note, "hand[s] it to [Katerina,] open[s] the door to the hallway for her, and, stepping back, bow[s] deeply to

---

182. Dostoevsky, *supra* note 10, at 109 ("[T]hough I have base desires and love baseness, I'm not dishonorable.").

183. *Id.* at 112.

184. *Id.* at 111.

185. *Id.* at 113–14.

186. *Id.* at 114.

187. *Id. See also* Miller, *supra* note 8, at 33 ("The Karamazov idea modulates into the tradesman's idea ... [and s]ensuality governs this idea as profoundly as it does the first, for Mitya realizes that the ecstasy of that moment of delicious 'infernal revenge' would be worth a lifetime of regret.") (quoting *Dostoevsky, supra* note 10, at 114).

188. Dostoevsky, *supra* note 10, at 114.

189. *Id.*

190. *Id.* at 113–14.

her, with a most respectful and heartfelt bow."[191] When Katerina, reciprocating, bows with "her forehead to the ground" and exits, Mitya pulls his sword from its scabbard, kisses it, and replaces it.[192] His gesture, with its phallic implications, imparts libidinous lust, along with, albeit temporary, self-control and putatively civilized repression.[193]

Significantly, right before handing over the rubles, there is an "ecstatic" instant in which anti-points converge: Mitya feels such "terrible hatred" of "the kind ... that is only a hair's breadth from love, the maddest love," and when he touches his forehead to the "frozen" window glass, "the ice burned [his] forehead like fire."[194] This oxymoronic spasm suggests that Mitya, the very bundle of antipodal impulses, is equally proficient at doing the "tarantula" sting or the "respectful" bow: in fact, he can conterminously perform both — that is, bow while stinging or sting while bowing.[195] In conceding to Alyosha that it might seem as if was "telling about all these agonies," and "filling them out a little, to praise [himself]," Mitya implies that he likes to primp, posture, and impress others.[196] As such, his honorable poses can and do invert into dishonorable, self-interested deeds: they are at times neither "respectful" nor "heartfelt," but calculated to manipulate others and self-aggrandize.[197]

The final piece of his confession to Alyosha, revolving around the three thousand rubles that Katerina entrusts to Mitya, mostly concerns his self-besmirched honor. We can detect, however, that Mitya is not giving Alyosha (or the readers) the entire picture and as such, his confession, which is incomplete, neither induces healing nor sates him. In fact, the longer he nurses that burning secret, the part he desperately needs to share but nevertheless

---

191. *Id.* at 114.

192. *Id.* (Mitya explains that her bow to the ground was "not like an institute girl but like a Russian woman."). *See supra* notes 93–95 and accompanying text (discussing the significance of bowing to the earth). *See also* Edward Wasiolek, *Dmitry and Katerina*, in DOSTOEVSKY, *supra* note 93, at 719 (explaining that "the hate and contempt that [Katerina] ascribes to Dmitry is the hate and contempt she herself feels for him"). According to Wasiolek, the hatred Katerina feels started with "his bow, out of respect to her," which "hurts." *Id.* "For with the bow, Dmitry changes from one who abases and humiliates to one who respects and forgives[, and] she hates the long low bow she must return, for it acknowledges his triumph over her." *Id.*

193. *See* MILLER, *supra* note 8, at 90 ("Mitya had, in a gesture loaded with phallic significance, pulled his sword from its scabbard, kissed it, and replaced it" which "embodied both his lust and honorable repression of it.").

194. DOSTOEVSKY, *supra* note 10, at 114–15.

195. *Id.* at 114.

196. *Id.* at 115.

197. *Id.* at 114.

withholds, the worse it gets, and will get, for Mitya. It is essentially his stymieing of full disclosure that rankles and will ultimately subsidize his own destruction. That is, in his trial, there are no witnesses to attest to the once buried facts, which are the very ones that might have exonerated Mitya of parricide.[198]

As told to Alyosha, Katerina suddenly came into an inheritance, returned the rubles that Mitya had given her, and sent Mitya a love letter, offering to be his fiancée. In replying, Mitya slips, by "mention[ing] that she was now rich and had a dowry, and [he] was just a poverty-stricken boor."[199] Mitya's mention of money reminds him of that vulgar tradesman persona he had rejected before handing Katerina the five thousand rubles and infuses him with "eternal" shame. [200] Then, after agreeing to be Katerina's fiancé and even vowing "to reform," Mitya begins to fan the fires of shame.[201] Katerina entrusts Mitya with three thousand rubles to bring secretly to Agafya. Instead, Mitya becomes romantically involved with Agrafena Alexandrovna Svetlova ("Grushenka") and whisks her off to Mokroe, where they squander the rubles in wild revelry, replete with partying "gypsy women" and "champagne."[202] Later, in one of his typical fibs, Mitya tells Katerina that he delivered the money and would bring her a receipt.

Miller aptly notices that Mitya "is more tormented by his squandering of Katerina Ivanovna's money than he is by his terrible treatment of her."[203] Before his interrogation, trial, and resolve to seek exile in America, Mitya, in a primitive stage of evolution and missing something, can see one thing and one thing only—Mitya. He is oblivious to Katerina's feelings and to those of the many others whom he has hurt. In fact, his behavior repeatedly bears this out: for example, Mitya seizes his father's agent, Snegiryov, by the beard in a tavern, drags him into the street, and beats him publicly.[204] The victim's humiliation spirals out to lacerate an already destitute and ailing family.[205] Similarly,

---

198. *See infra* notes 406–407 and accompanying text (explaining that the sole corroboration of the remaining fifteen hundred rubles is Alyosha's sudden recollection on the witness stand of Mitya's chest-beating gesture).

199. DOSTOEVSKY, *supra* note 10, at 116.

200. *Id.*

201. *Id.* at 117.

202. *Id.* at 118.

203. MILLER, *supra* note 8, at 35.

204. DOSTOEVSKY, *supra* note 10, at 72 (Mitya's father, Fyodor, exclaims, "[t]hink how he must treat others!" and elaborates: "three years ago our Dmitry Fyodorovich seized [the poor captain] by the beard in a tavern, dragged him by that same beard into the street, and there in the street publicly thrashed him …").

205. *Id.* at 193 (Katerina describes Mitya's "rash and unjust act" of seizing Snegiryov's beard). She explains that when Mitya "seized [the captain] by the beard in front of every-

Mitya whacks the old servant, Grigory, with all his might, and later smashes his skull with a brass pestle. He also brutalizes his own father by "seiz[ing] the old man by the two surviving wisps of hair on his temples … and smash[ing] him against the floor."[206] Then, in an encore of "kick[ing] the fallen man in the face two or three times with his heel," he vows to return to kill him.[207] Throughout all of these outbursts, reckless Mitya, neglecting to consider other people and the consequences of acting on his impulses, frets only over *his* wounds, *his* libidinous needs.

It is significant that Mitya vacillates between self-incrimination and exculpation: "I can be a mean man, with passions mean and ruinous, but a thief, a pickpocket, a pilferer, that Dimitri Karamazov can never be!"[208] After muttering, "I am a little thief, a pickpocket and pilferer" and "a base sensualist, a mean creature with irrepressible passions," who spent the money because "he couldn't help himself, like an animal," he rebuts, "[b]ut he is not a thief."[209] Here, Mitya repeatedly stops short of holding himself in full contempt, which should make an attentive reader surmise that he might be hiding something, like a little key that he is saving for redemption. It is only later that readers learn the hush-hush detail that Mitya did not spend *all* of Katerina's money, but instead kept half of it in a ragged pouch, nestled against his breast.[210]

After dodging the consummation of a full and true confession, Mitya strays to a related topic, one involving his lascivious father, who is in pursuit of Grushenka. In an envelope, "tied crisscross with a red ribbon" (like Mitya's pouch), Fyodor has his own three thousand rubles, which he promised to give Grushenka if she comes to him in the night.[211] Mitya, in the throes of a potentially

---

one, led him outside in that humiliating position, and led him a long way down the street, … the captain's son, who goes to the local school, just a child, saw it and went running along beside them, crying loudly and begging for his father, and rushing up to everyone asking them to defend him, but everyone laughed." *Id.* She adds that Snegiryov is "very poor" and "he and his family, a wretched family of sick children and a wife—who, it seems, is insane—have fallen into abject poverty." *Id.* at 193–94. The incident—"one of those acts that [Mitya] alone could bring himself to do"—damages Snegiryov's family and causes his son to be bullied and teased. *Id.* at 193.

206. *Id.* at 139.

207. *Id.* (Mitya cries, "'Serves him right! … And if I haven't killed him this time, I'll come back and kill him. You can't save him.'").

208. *Id.* at 119.

209. *Id.*

210. *See infra* notes 253–64 and accompanying text (Mitya's admission to his interrogators after being accused of parricide).

211. *Id.* at 120.

lethal oedipal triangle, tells Alyosha that he wants to kill, and might not be able to resist killing, his father.[212] Mitya is similarly torn over the unspent fifteen hundred rubles, that confessional tidbit which he desperately needs to share and yet refrains from sharing. At this juncture, for an unevolved Mitya, entertaining parricide and squandering rubles are in parity.

When Mitya later meets Alyosha, he supplements his confession with kinesics, and thus digs a smidgen deeper toward excavating interred shame. Mitya calls himself a "scoundrel" and says, "right here, do you see, right here a horrible dishonor is being prepared."[213] The narrator gives us the clue that will later figure into the epiphany Alyosha has during Mitya's trial: "as he said 'right here,' Dimitry Fyodorovich struck himself on the chest with his fist, and with such a strange look as though the dishonor was lying and being kept precisely there on his chest, in some actual place, maybe in a pocket, or sewn up and hanging around his neck."[214] Mitya says that "nothing can compare in baseness with the dishonor I am carrying, precisely now, precisely at this moment, here on my chest, here, right here, which is being enacted and carried out, and which it is fully in my power to stop."[215] Subsequently, after bootlessly begging Madame Khokhlakova for three thousand rubles, Mitya reenacts that chest-beating:

> He walked like a madman, beating himself on the chest, on that very place on his chest where he had beaten himself two days before, with Alyosha, when he had seen him for the last time, in the evening, in the darkness, on the road. What this beating on the chest, *on that spot* meant, and what he intended to signify by it—so far was a secret that

---

212. *See* SUSANNE FUSSO, DISCOVERING SEXUALITY IN DOSTOEVSKY 113–14 (Northwestern University Press 2006) (explaining how "Dmitri and Fyodor are locked in a fierce struggle over Grushenka," a "relationship … often called 'Oedipal,' with the Freudian sense of the term in mind"). Fusso points out that "Dostoevsky's version of the father-son rivalry is closer to the original myth of Oedipus (and its treatment in the tragedy of Sophocles) than to Freud's version." *Id.* at 114. She adds: "[i]t is Laius's abandonment of Oedipus that makes psychologically possible the realization of the prophecy he fears [and] Oedipus kills a father who is not really a father (and marries a mother who is not really a mother) in Fetiukovich's sense." *Id. See infra* notes 443–48 and accompanying text (describing Fetyukovich's closing argument). *See also* Chapter I (Inexpressible Ideas: A Multifaceted Life and Legal Lens) (discussing Freud's analysis of Dostoevsky and the commentators that debunk it).

213. DOSTOEVSKY, *supra* note 10, at 156.

214. *Id. See also infra* 406–407 notes and accompanying text (describing Alyosha's epiphany on the witness stand at Mitya's trial).

215. *Id.*

no one else in the world knew, which he had not revealed then even to Alyosha, but for him that secret concealed more than shame, it concealed ruin and suicide.[216]

b. Confession to his Interrogators

The second confessional episode begins with officials cornering Mitya to charge him with murder. They employ nearly every trick in the book to coerce and deliberately elicit information out of their suspect, and these old-fangled Russian tactics prefigure the ones in the pre-and post-*Miranda* tool kit.[217] As is similar to the facts in the *Ashcraft* and *Spano* cases, the Russian authorities keep applying pressure while Mitya is in custody and incommunicado for a prolonged period without sleep or rest.[218] Significantly, however, their coercive machinations, ones the early Supreme Court case law would likely find violative of the due process clause, are not *the* operative provocateurs of the very confession that Mitya is determined to expel.

The Russian interrogators even deliver some *Miranda*-like admonitions that Mitya need not speak and can approve everything they put writing, but their words are vacuous and inefficacious. Mitya, so weary of "beating himself on the chest," is primed, ready, and eager to expel that "secret that no one else in the world knew."[219] Self-coerced to purge his shame, he will, in due time, launch what *he* feels *he* needs—namely, that public, humiliating, flogging. Mitya, in fact, bellows, "come, gentlemen, crush me, punish me, decide my fate!"[220]

Right off the bat, Mitya admits to *almost* everything. Although, yes, he desired his father's death and "wanted to kill him," no, he is not guilty of murder.[221] In contrast to Ivan, Mitya does discern that boundary between desire and deed.[222] Mitya also owns up to bad conduct, like beating and nearly killing fa-

---

216. Dostoevsky, *supra* note 10, at 388.

217. *See supra* II. A. 1 (discussion of the Due Process clause and the totality-of-the-circumstances test) and 2 (discussion of *Miranda* what amounts to inherent coercion). *See also* Murav, *supra* note 140, at 55 (discussing how after the legal reforms of 1864, interrogations of suspects still occurred without the presence of their attorneys).

218. Ashcraft v. Tennessee, 322 U.S. 143 (1944) and Spano v. New York, 360 U.S. 315 (1959). *See also supra* II. A. 1 (Due Process: Totality of the Circumstances) (describing factors in cases in which the Supreme Court found that state agents violated the Due Process Clause).

219. Dostoevsky, *supra* note 10, at 388.

220. *Id.* at 458.

221. *Id.* at 461.

222. *See infra* notes 282–83 and accompanying text (discussing Ivan's tendency to blur together desire and conduct).

ther, and then swearing before witnesses that he would return to finish the job. After speaking of brutally bludgeoning and killing the servant, Grigory, the prosecutor, Ippolit Kirillovich ("Ippolit") informs Mitya that the old man had actually recovered. Mitya, who is still the primitive Mitya, finds greater joy in the fact that he, no longer "sinner and evildoer," can more easily realize his dream of marrying Grushenka than in the fact of Grigory's seemingly miraculous rebirth.[223]

It is telling that, after urging the officers to put it in writing that "within himself, too, inside, in the bottom of his heart, he is guilty," he reverses, saying that "there's no need to write that down."[224] Mitya challenges them to gouge away and extract the shame at his heart's bottom. What he seeks to still conceal, and yet wants to publicize, is the existence of, and inner turmoil over, the unspent rubles. On an unconscious level, Mitya hopes that, after poking and prodding, the officers will force him to publicize what he believes is his most heinous deed, and then indelibly immortalize it in ink.

One thing readers should detect is that Mitya bears more guilt and shame over Katerina's rubles than he does over wishing his father dead, beating him, and nearly killing the old servant, his surrogate father, who "carried Mitya in his arms ... [and] washed [him] in a tub when [he] was a three-year-old child and abandoned by everyone."[225] In confessional foreplay, Mitya keeps protesting that "it is a noble man, you are speaking with, a most noble person."[226] After admitting that he has "done a world of mean things," Mitya insists that he has always "remained a most noble person."[227] Like a toreador taunting a bull with a red banner, Mitya defies his bullies to charge, grab him, and gore his ignoble, insectile core.

Mitya's words, "don't go digging around in my soul so much, don't torment it with trifles," belie the fact that that "digging" and "tormenting" is precisely what Mitya covets with every fiber of his soul.[228] Mitya even spurs them on: "I'm the wolf, you're the hunters—so hunt the wolf down."[229] When the prosecutor asks Mitya why he needed three thousand rubles, Mitya initially teases him with generic evasion: "I wanted to repay a debt, a debt of honor, but to whom

---

223. *Id.* at 458.

224. *Id.* at 460.

225. *Id.* at 459. *See* Miller, *supra* note 8, at 96 ("We learn that Mitya is more tortured by the thought that he has been a thief than by the thought that he might have, in a fit of fury, murdered Grigory.").

226. *Id.* at 462.

227. *Id.*

228. *Id.* at 464.

229. *Id.* at 471.

I won't say."[230] Here, the prosecutor, sensing and seeking to exploit the ambivalence, appears to steal from the very manuals discussed in the *Miranda* decision.[231]

In *Miranda*, the Supreme Court, reviewing popular techniques aimed to undermine the right to silence, explains that trainers tell police "how to handle the individual who refuses to discuss the matter entirely."[232] They advise the examiner to at first "concede him the right to remain silent," which will "disappoint" the suspect in his "expectation of an unfavorable reaction," and likewise "impress ... [him] with the apparent fairness of his interrogator."[233] Immediately "after this psychological conditioning, however, the officer is told to point out the incriminating significance of the suspect's refusal to talk."[234]

Dostoevsky's prosecutor, Ippolit Kirillovich, could be the poster child for the tactics censured in the *Miranda* decision. He concedes that Mitya has "every right not to answer the questions that are put to [him]," and that the interrogators, "on the contrary, have no right to extort answers."[235] Then, in a monologue of the kind that prompted the birth of the *Miranda* safeguards, Ippolit Kirillovich underscores the "incriminating significance" of Mitya's silence: "[o]n the other hand, in such a situation, it is our business to point out to you and explain the full extent of the harm you will be doing yourself by refusing to give this or that evidence."[236]

After Mitya is reminded that witnesses saw him with a wad of ruble bills in his "blood-stained hands," he still refuses to address the source of the money.[237] Shortly thereafter, the examiner bludgeons him with another tactic that resembles one described in *Miranda*, asking:

---

230. *Id.* at 468.

231. *See generally infra* II A. 2 (discussing the kind of tactics that necessitate the *Miranda* safeguards).

232. Miranda, 384 U.S. at 453.

233. *Id.* at 453–54.

234. *Id.* at 454 ("Suppose you were in my shoes and I were in yours ... and I told you, 'I don't want to answer any of your questions[,]' [y]ou'd think I had something to hide and you'd probably be right in thinking that."). *See also supra* II. B (discussing techniques that extract confession, even after implementation of the *Miranda* safeguards).

235. DOSTOEVSKY, *supra* note 10, at 468.

236. *Id. See also* Miranda, 384 U.S. at 584; DOSTOEVSKY, *supra* note 10, at 479 ("The prosecutor intervened and again reminded him that a man under interrogation was of course at liberty not to answer questions if he thought it more beneficial, and so on, but in view of the harm the suspect might do himself by keeping silent ..."); *infra* note 238 and accompanying text (another suggestion by interrogators that silence is damaging to the accused).

237. *Id.* at 479.

[b]ut could you not, without in the least violating your determination to keep silent on this main point, could you not at the same time give us at least some slight hint as to precisely what sort of compelling motives might force you to keep silent at a moment so dangerous for you in your evidence?[238]

Although putatively potent, and aimed to extract that parricide admission, the examiner's message does not have its anticipated impact on a suspect, who is hell-bent on publicly flagellating himself for a different, but uncharged, offense, one which, for him, is far more iniquitous than murdering one's father. It is here that Mitya moves closer to realizing his goal by letting his "cat out of the bag."[239]

The Supreme Court has discussed the "cat out of the bag" metaphor: "after an accused has once let the cat out of the bag by confessing, no matter what the inducement, he is never thereafter free of the psychological and practical disadvantages of having confessed. He can never get the cat back in the bag."[240] Interrogators are thus taught to secure a "tactical advantage" by pushing the "cat out of the bag," and reaching what is referred to as the point of "breakthrough" or "beachhead."[241] In Dostoevsky's view, confessants often force their own "cat[s] out of the bag," and for Mitya, his feline escapes as his effort to justify silence:[242]

> I keep silent, gentlemen, because it involves a disgrace for me. The answer to the question of where I got this money contains such a disgrace for me as could not be compared even with killing and robbing my father, if I had killed and robbed him. That is why I cannot speak. Because of the disgrace.[243]

---

238. *Id.* at 480.

239. *See generally* Oregon v. Elstad, 470 U.S. 298, 311 (1985) (discussing the Oregon court's identification of a "lingering compulsion, the psychological impact of the suspect's conviction that he has let the cat out of the bag and, in so doing, has sealed his own fate") and *infra* notes 240–42 (explaining the metaphor).

240. Oregon v. Elstad, 470 U.S. at 311 (quoting United States v. Bayer, 331 U.S. 532, 540–41 (1947)).

241. Elstad, 470 U.S. at 328 ("Interrogators describe the point of the first admission as the 'breakthrough' and the 'beachhead'… which once obtained will give them enormous tactical advantages.") (J. Brennan, dissenting) (quoting R. Royal & S. Schutt, The Gentle Art of Interviewing and Interrogation: A Professional Manual and Guide 143 (1976) and F. Inbau & J. Reid, Criminal Interrogation and Confessions 82 (2d ed. 1967)).

242. Elstad, 470 U.S. at 311.

243. Dostoevsky, *supra* note 10, at 480.

Mitya, baiting his examiners to press on, subliminally ties the "disgrace" that commands his silence to that which urges, and will unleash, speech.[244] In a scene reminiscent of his earlier chest-beating, Mitya uses body language to self-incriminate: he empties his pockets and blurts, "here it is, my money, here, count it, take it."[245] From this, the prosecution calculates that Mitya originally had only about fifteen hundred rubles. Ironically, Mitya's surrender of the evidence of what he feels is *his* worst crime disappoints his legal examiners because it is not what they consider *their* perfect evidence. Thus, they feel duty bound to deploy more interrogation weapons.

The *Miranda* Court noted that, according to police manuals, the key to fruitful interrogation is the creation of an environment that makes the subject feel alone, powerless, and vulnerable.[246] This "subjugate[s] the individual to the will of [the] examiner[,] … carries its own badge of intimidation[,]" and destroys "human dignity."[247] Mitya's examiners resort to an approach aimed to accomplish this, but here, it is overkill. The team, abrading Mitya's Achilles heel of desired-feared shame, orders him to strip, which causes him to reflect that, "[i]f everyone is undressed, it's not shameful, but when only one is undressed and the others are all looking—it's a disgrace."[248] He then relishes and agonizes over each stratum of his unveiling:

> But to take his socks off was even painful for him: they were not very clean, nor were his underclothes, and now everyone could see it. And above all he did not like his own feet; all his life for some reason he had found both his big toes ugly, especially the right one with its crude, flat toenail, somehow curved under, and now they would all see it.[249]

This disrobing, which he professes to hate, excites such "unbearable shame" that he is "suddenly" inspired to exacerbate his own misery by tearing off his own shirt.[250] In so doing, he literally and figuratively tries to bare his breast and then, effectually prolonging the demeaning dishabille, initially declines the offered replacement garments. Although horrified at the prospect that others might notice his dirty undergarments, Mitya makes certain that these are

---

244. *Id.*

245. *Id.* at 481.

246. Miranda, 384 U.S. 436. *See also supra* II.A. 2 (discussing techniques interrogators used to make their suspects feel alone, powerless, and vulnerable).

247. Miranda, 384 at 458.

248. DOSTOEVSKY, *supra* note 10, at 484.

249. *Id.*

250. *Id.*

indeed noticed when he gripes, "[h]e examined my socks too closely, and had them turned inside out … he did it on purpose, to show everyone how dirty my underwear is!"[251] Shortly thereafter, Mitya, reaching what is, and has been all along, *his* unconsciously appointed "breakthrough" or "beachhead," caves: "I will reveal my secret to you, … reveal my disgrace."[252]

When Mitya unloads his complete true secret, it essentially falls on deaf ears, doing him nothing but disservice. Mitya explains that the money came from around his neck, where it was "sewn up in a rag," and where he had been carrying it for about a month "with shame and disgrace."[253] The first time he took Grushenka to Mokroe, he only "squandered half of that cursed three thousand" and hid the rest on his breast "in place of an amulet."[254] In his last binge with Grushenka, he depleted half of that half as well. At this juncture, Ippolit Kirillovich, who fancies himself to be the preeminent psychologist, simply cannot fathom why Mitya would "attach such extraordinary secrecy to this fifteen hundred, … [and] connect[] this secret … with some kind of horror," and finds it "incredible that such a secret should cost [him] such torment in confessing it."[255]

From there, the confessional process can be likened to the slow peeling of an onion, whereby Mitya, becoming his own interrogator, whittles away, layer by layer, into his soul's pith in a fruitless effort to make his oppressors grasp his plight. Like the earlier account to Alyosha about his gift of rubles to Katerina, Mitya projects alternatives that he had entertained, but he does it with respect to that albatross-pouch that once dangled from his neck.[256] For Mitya, the safeguarding of a portion of Katerina's money had dual import: it served both as a premeditated stab at quasi-redemption and as a self-imposed hair shirt. Mitya scripts the hypothetical return of the unspent rubles:

> I go on a spree and spend only … half…. The next day I go to her and bring her the other half: "Katya, take this half back from me, a villain and a thoughtless scoundrel, because I've already squandered one

---

251. *Id.* at 485. *See also id.* ("Well, what now, do you start flogging me with a birch, or what?").

252. Elstad, 470 U.S. at 328. DOSTOEVSKY, *supra* note 10, at 489. *See also supra* note 241 and accompanying text (describing "breakthrough" and "beachhead").

253. DOSTOEVSKY, *supra* note 10, at 490.

254. *Id.* at 490–91.

255. *Id.* at 491.

256. *See supra* note 185–93 and accompanying text (discussing Mitya's proclivity to entertain alternative scenarios before acting and giving an example from his confession to Alyosha).

half, therefore I'll also squander the other, so put me out of harm's way!" … She would see at once that if he's brought her the one half, he'll also bring her the rest, the part he squandered, he'll spend his life looking for it, he'll work, but he will find it and give it back.[257]

But, as always for Mitya, there is a glitch: from the get go, his act of setting aside the money, although somewhat expiatory, was nevertheless "calculated" and "base."[258] When however, Mitya actually tapped into that mitigative ruble-reserve, he vanquished the only thing that could conceivably elevate him from "vile thief" to mere "scoundrel."[259] Realizing that his interrogators neither get it nor believe it, and being utterly "horrif[ied] by [their] lack of understanding," Mitya, paring it down further, closes in on the *mea culpa* nub:[260]

> All the while I carried that fifteen hundred sewn up on my chest, I kept saying to myself every day and every hour: "You are a thief, you are a thief!" And that's why I raged all month, that's why I fought in the tavern, that's why I beat my father, because I felt I was a thief! I could not bring myself, I did not dare to reveal anything about the fifteen hundred even to Alyosha, my brother: so much did I feel myself a scoundrel and a pickpocket.[261]

By squandering half of the half and tossing the pouch's ragged sheath into the gutter, Mitya forfeits both his mode of self-laceration and his last shred of potential atonement. In his mind, this issues as a life sentence or, as he put it, he thus "became a final and indisputable thief … for the rest of [his] life."[262] While the wily prosecutor contends that he is "beginning to understand," it is apparent that he does and does not.[263] Despite the fact that his suspect has just proclaimed himself to be the proverbial seeker of torment, the prosecutor purports to not understand why Mitya would fail to return the fifteen hundred rubles to Katerina and thus spare himself such torment. Intuiting, however, what could devastate his victim the most, the prosecutor asks why Mitya did not just tell all to Katerina and then, knowing of her generosity, ply her for more rubles to fund his next romp with Grushenka. Here, Mitya, jabbing at

---

257. *Id.* at 492.
258. *Id.* ("'I set it aside out of baseness—that is, out of calculation, because calculation in this case is baseness …'").
259. *Id.*
260. *Id.* at 493.
261. *Id.*
262. *Id.* at 493–94.
263. *Id.* at 494.

the very ganglion, avulses his deepest, unabated shame—namely, that he had actually considered just such a vile option:

> Yes, gentlemen, I, too, had that thought during this cursed month, so that I almost resolved to go to Katya, so base I was! But to go to her, to announce my betrayal to her, and for that betrayal, to carry through that betrayal, for the future expenses of that betrayal, to ask money (to ask, do you hear, to ask!) from her, from Katya, and immediately run off with another woman, with her rival, with her hater and offender ...[264]

Mitya's earlier shout, "I've found out more in this one cursed night than I'd have learned in twenty years of living," vaticinates what is in the works.[265] After the confession, when all layers are stripped away, readers can detect change (albeit still miniscule) in Mitya, who experiences an empathic twinge. Prior to full confession, Mitya, preoccupied with Mitya and myopically fixated on his own "respectful" and "heartfelt" bows in his role as knight of honor, stayed callously indifferent to the pain he had inflicted on his jilted fiancée and others.[266] It is only after unburdening his guilty shame that the feelings of other people begin to infiltrate his awareness. For a flash, Mitya can actually feel what Katerina might have felt had he asked her to finance her own betrayal.

Readers here can detect another related, but equally inchoate, change in Mitya. Mitya, who tended to fudge the line between truth and untruth, begins to see that such a proclivity can hatch disaster. When the prosecution reminds the accused that he himself was "spreading" rumors and "even shout[ing] everywhere about the three thousand [he] had spent ... and not fifteen hundred" and that there were "dozens" who could attest to this, Mitya sees the inherent fecundity of prevarication.[267] Here, Mitya exclaims, "[i]t means nothing, I lied, and everyone started lying after me" and then adds, "so I lied, and that's it, I lied once and then I didn't want to correct it."[268] Implicit in his question—

---

264. *Id.* at 495.

265. *Id.* at 486. *See also* Letter from Fyodor Dostoevsky to Nikolay Lyubimov (Nov. 16, 1879) in V DOSTOEVSKY LETTERS, 1878–1881, at 165 (David Lowe ed. & trans., Ardis Publishers 1991) [hereinafter V LETTERS] (Mitya "experiences a purification of his heart and conscience under the storm of misfortune and false accusation" and "[h]is moral purification begins during the several hours of preliminary investigation.").

266. DOSTOEVSKY, *supra* note 10, at 114. *See also supra* notes 185–93, 195–97 and accompanying text (describing Mitya's poses); note 203 and accompanying text (addressing Mitya's indifference to Katerina's feelings).

267. DOSTOEVSKY, *supra* note 10, at 496.

268. *Id.*

"[w]hy does a man lie sometimes"—is a miniscule seed of spiritual evolution, the onset of a new Mitya, who is starting to posit questions that matter.[269]

In the aftermath of his true and genuine confession, Mitya seems to intuit that what he has revealed is neither enough nor believed.[270] His oppressors, with their prosecutorial reflex, find it incredible that not one witness knew about the money in Mitya's pouch and embark on poking holes in Mitya's facts. In this regard, the interrogators miss the mark on multiple fronts. They pat themselves on their backs, deluding themselves into believing that Mitya's admissions were the fruit of their own dexterous moves. What is irrebuttable, however, is that the only moves of importance were those of Mitya himself. It was Mitya who ended up expelling what he needed and intended to expel *ab initio*. In fact, he ends up thanking his oppressors for taking a "burden from [his] soul."[271] On top of this, the prosecution instantly brainwashes itself that Mitya's "facts," so preposterous and unsubstantiated, will actually bolster the parricide conviction. While their strategy literally prevails, it loses in a broader sense, by deflecting truth. That is, their hubristic faith in their own skill at excavating valuable evidence reveals one thing and one thing only—namely, that fools tend to find fool's gold.

Unlike a confession bestowed on a worthy soul, like a Sonya, who is adept at steering Raskolnikov toward faith and spiritual rebirth, Mitya's confessors are unworthy players in a paltry game of earthly justice. In this regard, Dostoevsky suggests that law enforcers (and later counsel, judge and jury) are ill equipped to decipher confessions and assess their veracity. The prosecutor, along with his cronies, haven't a clue what to do with the real deal, with confessions of authenticity. Tragically, in all of the jousting between suspect and examiners, Mitya inadvertently entrusts the prosecution with the rarest of rubles, the one that could and should have solved the crime. When it emerged that Smerdyakov was the "only one" who knew the whereabouts of Fyodor's hid-

---

269. *Id. See also* FYODOR DOSTOEVSKY, A WRITER'S DIARY 269 (Kenneth Lantz trans., Northwestern University Press 1994) (1873–78) (asking, "[w]hy is it that all—every single one of us—tell lies?"). He states that "among other nations, ... only worthless people lie" and do it "for practical advantage ... with criminal intent." *Id.* He adds: "[b]ut in Russia the most honest people can lie for no reason whatsoever and with the most honorable intentions," and explains that the "vast majority of our lies are told for the sake of sociability ... to produce an aesthetic impression on the listener, to make him feel good, and so people lie, even sacrificing themselves to the listener." *Id.*

270. DOSTOEVSKY, *supra* note 10, at 498 ("'I see very well that you don't believe me! Not a word, not a bit! It's my fault, not yours, I shouldn't have stuck my neck out. Why, why did I defile myself by confessing my secret! And you think its funny, I can see by your eyes.'").

271. *Id.* at 499.

den envelope, the perpetrator's identity should have been plain as day.[272] Like Katerina's rubles, Mitya's entrustment of that gem of truth to the prosecution is squandered, becoming "like pearls before swine."[273]

2. Ivan's Confession: Spiritual Crisis

In *The Brothers Karamazov*, Smerdyakov, the murderer, comes clean to Ivan, but not to atone, appease his conscience, or accept responsibility.[274] Smerdyakov, the non-repentant confessant, aims, among other things, to aggravate Ivan's pre-existing guilt, charge him with murder, and pulverize his already imperiled mental state. He indicts: "You killed him, you are the main killer, and I was just your minion ... and I performed the deed according to your word."[275] He reasons that Ivan, by knowing of the parricide plot and choosing not to stay and stop it, effectively perpetrated the crime.[276] Smerdyakov's twisted rheto-

---

272. *Id.* at 488.

273. *Matthew* 7:6 ("Give not that which is holy unto the dogs, neither cast ye your pearls before swine, lest they trample them under their feet, and turn again and rend you."),

274. *See generally* DOSTOEVSKY, *supra* note 10, at 99 (Smerdyakov, was the son of "stinking Lizaveta," and when she became pregnant, "a strange rumor spread all over town that the offender was none other than Fyodor Pavlovich [Karamzov]"). Many commentators see Smerdyakov as the personification of evil. *See, eg., supra* note 3, at 25 n. 19 ("Smerdyakov himself makes a kind of confession when he finally acknowledges that he killed Fyodor Karamazov but, in a profound inversion of Dostoevsky's view of the proper spirit of a confession, Smerdyakov's confession comes out as an accusation."); Vladimir Kantor, *Pavel Smerdyakov and Ivan Karamazov: The Problem of Temptation* in DOSTOEVSKY, *supra* note 93, at 697–98 ("[U]nlike Ivan, who tries to weigh and evaluate in his heart the pro as well as the contra, Smerdyakov is monosemantic and pronounces an apologia to perfidy, his own sort of justification of evil" and "[i]t is not by chance ... that Ivan swings between Alyosha and Smerdyakov, who are 'firm orientation points of good and evil.'").

275. DOSTOEVSKY, *supra* note 10, at 623.

276. *See generally* Horst-Jurgen Gerigk, *Dialogue and Pseudo-Dialogue*, in ART, CREATIVITY, AND SPIRITUALITY, *supra* note 3, at 29, 43 ("Ivan[,] who obeyed Smerdyakov by leaving town, ... has to see himself as the lackey of the devil[, and] Ivan is tortured by the thought that Smerdyakov used their tacit agreement quite for his own design to kill the father."); MURAV, *supra* note 140, at 208 (It is "Smerdiakov, [who] hates Russia, ... resembles a eunuch, is unclean, ... and suffers from epilepsy, a disease associated with demonic possession," and it is he, who "literalizes Ivan's hypothesis that 'all is permissible.'"). *See also* Letter from Fyodor Dostoevsky to Ye. N. Lebedeva (November 8, 1879) in V LETTERS, *supra* note 265, at 164 (discussing how "the old man was killed by the servant Smerdyakov"). In that letter, Dostoevsky elaborates:

> Ivan ... participated in the murder only obliquely and remotely, only by (intentionally) keeping from bringing Smerdyakov to his senses during the conversation with him before his departure for Moscow and stating to him clearly and categorically his repugnance for the crime conceived by him (which Ivan ... clearly saw and had

ric, equating nonfeasance with deed, hits its mark by eliciting Ivan's pre-confession and coaxing what is already imminent—a mental breakdown:

> [P]erhaps I, too, was guilty, perhaps I really had a secret desire that my father ... die, but I swear to you that I was not as guilty as you think, and perhaps I did not put you up to it all. No, no, I did not! But, anyway, I shall give evidence against myself tomorrow, in court, I've decided! I shall tell everything, everything. But we shall appear together![277]

Significantly, this prequel to Ivan's decision to testify jolts forth in increments that will rhyme with his subsequent courtroom testimony: it starts with disclosure of Ivan's secret, the desire for his father's death, but initially, that is tempered with a partial not-guilty plea. But then, in a blurted admission, Ivan says that "whatever you say against me in court, whatever evidence you give—I accept, and ... shall confirm it all!"[278] He then lunges beyond mere *respondeat superior* to accept direct liability: "I alone shall confess."[279] By looking "sick" and jaundiced, so much so that his eyes "are quite yellow," Ivan's demeanor reflects his inner crisis, which will culminate in his public confession on the stand.[280]

As Professor Terras explains, *The Brothers Karamazov* interweaves multiple thematic strands:

> [One is] the novelistic strategy to show some men who believe in God and in immortality, and who are willing to accept the teaching of Christ; and some other men who reject God's world, Christ, and immortality, and who would rather create a world based on human reason; and then let the practical consequences of their attitudes speak for themselves.[281]

---

a premonition of) and thus *seemed to permit* Smerdyakov to commit the crime. The *permission* was essential for Smerdyakov.
Id.

277. DOSTOEVSKY, *supra* note 10, at 631.

278. *Id.*

279. *Id.*

280. *Id.*

281. VICTOR TERRAS, A KARAMAZOV COMPANION 48 (University of Wisconsin Press, 2002). *See also* Letter from Fyodor Dostoevsky to Pavel Pototsky (June 10, 1876), in IV FYODOR DOSTOEVSKY COMPLETE LETTERS (1872–1877(at 287 (David A. Lowe, ed. & trans., Ardis Publishers 1991) [hereinafter IV LETTERS] (speaking of "men and women who seek something superior ... [b]ut after leaving their homes, they wind up in circles of people who assure them that there is no spiritual life and that spiritual life is a fairy tale and not realism.")

Ivan's problem is that he embodies both men (believer and rejecter) at once, and thus endures excruciating cognitive dissonance. Part of Ivan wants to reason his way to a world without God, but he cannot. This brings pain and guilt. Part of Ivan wants to have faith in God, but he cannot. This brings more pain, more guilt. In fact, the resulting impasse heaps on even more layers of abrading guilt.

With respect to Ivan, Brooks attributes his eventual confession to the "blurring" of the distinction between "thoughts and deeds."[282] There is no question that Ivan's guilty conscience, his "psychic parricide," helps prompt not just his resolve to testify, but also his self-conflagration on the stand.[283] This "blurring," however, is not the sole provocateur: combatants for good and evil, God and the devil, vie for Ivan, and each alone and both together pile on toxic stress. Ivan's lectures on Euclidean geometry, theodicy, and the Grand Inquisitor, along with his chat with the devil, are quadrate events that elucidate a confession born of an individual spiritual crisis. Unfortunately, as with Mitya, Ivan's testimony finds vent in an earthly justice system, which is the very one foredoomed to miscarry.

a. Euclid

First, Ivan's rebellion surfaces in his Euclidean discussion with Alyosha, who again serves as repository for confession.[284] Ivan talks about those "geometers and philosophers," who "dare to dream that two parallel lines, which according to Euclid cannot possibly meet on earth, may perhaps meet somewhere in infinity."[285] From there, he presents two equations: non-Euclidean geometry, accounting for God's justice, and Euclidean geometry, accounting for earthly justice.[286] After insisting that his is a "Euclidean mind, an earthly mind, and …

---

282. BROOKS, *supra* note 3, at 59 ("[W]hereas Mitya is forever making distinctions between thoughts and deeds, Ivan's confession thoroughly blurs them, offering Smerdyakov's deed as a version of his own thoughts, and indeed of *everyone's* thoughts.").

283. *Id.* at 56.

284. MILLER, *supra* note 8, at 26 (describing Alyosha as "loved as an angel and chosen as the interlocutor for confessions," who is "described as having the same potential for sensuality as his unruly brothers").

285. DOSTOEVSKY, *supra* note 10, at 235.

286. *See* MILLER, *supra* note 8, at 59 (describing Ivan's discussion of Euclidean and non-Euclidean geometry as "an instance of reason being counterposed against God's world"); TERRAS, *supra* note 281, at 42 ("Human reason—called 'Euclidean reason' by Ivan Karamazov … perceives the world as absurd, sees no justice but only self-interest effectively protected and conceives of the beautiful as that which pleases the senses."). Terras explains that "man also possesses higher, divine reason, which affirms all that his lower reason denies: harmony, justice and beauty." *Id.* at 42. According to Terras, "the encounter between intellectual bril-

[that] it is not for us to resolve things that are not of this world" and counseling Alyosha to "never think about ... whether God exists or not," he implies and does the opposite.[287] As Professor Miller points out, Ivan, by "both introduce[ing] and grant[ing] the existence of non-Euclidean geometry as well as of God's justice ... creates the equation only to show that it cannot encompass his whole reality."[288] Moreover, Ivan is the chronic contemplator of "things that are not of this world" and of the exact issues he bans as taboo—those of "whether God exists or not"—and thus, he embodies that which he tells his brother not to be or do.[289]

Ivan pledges allegiance to the power of his own free will: "[l]et the parallel lines even meet before my own eyes ... I shall look and say, yes, they meet, and still I will not accept it."[290] He pays lip service to the apothegm that non-acceptance of divine justice is a matter of choice and that he can, through sheer volition, refuse to "accept" a truth, even one that unequivocally materializes before his very eyes.[291] Ivan, simultaneously jerked in the dissenting direction, mistrusts his lifeline of free choice, reason, and earthly justice, which betray not only him, but the entire human race.

b. Theodicy

Second, Ivan's diatribe on theodicy similarly harbors implacable discord, but here, what emerges is self-contempt. In negating God's existence and envisioning a world ruled by free will and reason, Ivan ends up painting the an-

---

liance and simple Christian wisdom is a central theme in *The Brothers Karamazov*," and Dostoevsky has "no faith in the former." *Id.*

287. DOSTOEVSKY, *supra* note 10, at 235.

288. MILLER, *supra* note 8, at 59–60.

289. DOSTOEVSKY, *supra* note 10, at 235.

290. *Id.* at 236. In a letter, Dostoevsky writes, "to believe that there is nothing more beautiful, more profound, more attractive, more wise, more courageous and more perfect than Christ, and what's more, I tell myself with jealous love, there cannot be." Letter from Fyodor Dostoevsky to Natalya Dmitrievna Fonvizina (end of January, third week of February, 1854), in I DOSTOEVSKY LETTERS 1832–1859, at 193, 195 (David Lowe & Ronald Meyer eds. & trans., Ardis Publishers 1988) [hereinafter I LETTERS]. Dostoevsky adds, "if someone proved to me that Christ were outside the truth and it *really* were that the truth lay outside Christ, I would prefer to remain with Christ rather than with the truth." *Id.* at 195. *See also* MILLER, *supra* note 8, at 60 (Speaking of that letter to Madame Fonzina in which "Dostoevsky affirmed that his love for Jesus was even greater than his love for truth" and explaining that "Ivan divides his universe into two camps as well," she says that "like Dostoevsky, he maintains that something is more valuable to him than truth; but it is not Jesus, it is his own right not to accept that truth.").

291. DOSTOEVSKY, *supra* note 10, at 235.

tipodal picture of mean-spirited, unfree irrationality. That is, in "reduc[ing] the scope of [his] argument" to the suffering of children, Ivan bombards Alyosha with inexplicable acts of mutilation, lashings, and torture. Significantly, his brooding over the surrounding cruelty compels him to introspect and self-indict.[292]

Ivan assails Christianity and faith in a God who lets innocent children suffer.[293] He tells of a retired general who strips a child naked and commands his pack of wolfhounds to "hunt him down before his mother's eyes" and then has his dogs rip the child to shreds.[294] Ivan's grisly anecdotes are interspersed with editorials on the voluptuous pleasure that child abusers experience. For example, while describing the Turks, who "start[] with cutting [babies] out of their mothers' wombs with a dagger, and end[] with tossing nursing infants up in the air and catching them on their bayonets before their mothers' eyes," Ivan ejaculates: the "Turks ... have ... taken a delight in torturing children."[295]

In a similar vein, after Ivan narrates the saga of a couple with a little five-year-old daughter, who "beat her, flogged her, kicked her, not knowing why them-

---

292. *Id.* at 237. *Cf.* Deborah A. Martinsen, *Ingratitude and the Underground*, XVII Dostoevsky Stud. 7, 20 (2013) (pointing out that the "underground man sees humans as ungrateful in part because he projects his self-image onto others").

293. *See generally* Letter from Fyodor Dostoevsky to Nikolay Lyubimov (May 10, 1879), in V Letters, *supra* note 265, at 82–83(describing Book 5 of *The Brothers Karamazov* for the upcoming issue of *The Russian Herald*). Dostoevsky elaborates on Ivan, who "takes up a theme that *I think* irrefutable—the senselessness of the suffering of children—and derives from it the absurdity of all historical reality," and adds:

Everything that my protagonist says in the text that has been sent off to you is based on reality. All the stories about the children occurred, took place, were printed in the newspapers, and I can show where. Nothing has been invented by me. The general who hunted down the child with dogs, and the whole fact is a real occurrence, was published this winter ... My protagonist's blasphemy, however, will be solemnly refuted in the following ... issue, for which I am now working with fear, trepidation, and reverence, since I consider my task (the rout of anarchism) a civic feat.

Id. at 83. *See also* Frank, *supra* note 8, at 449–50 (describing the rape of Dostoevsky's childhood playmate). This little girl was a "delicate, grateful child of nine ... And some disgraceful wretch violated the girl when drunk and she died, pouring out blood." *Id.* (quoting S.V. Belov, *Z.A. Trubetskaya Dostoevsky i A. P. Filosofova*, 3 Russkaya Literatura 117 (Moscow 1973)). For Dostoevsky, this "memory ... haunted [him] as the most frightful crime, the most terrible sin, for which there is not, and cannot be, any forgiveness." *Id.* at 450.

294. Dostoevsky, *supra* note 10, at 243.

295. *Id.* at 238.

selves, until her whole body was nothing but bruises," he gasps that these parents "attained the height of finesse" when they forced her to eat excrement and smeared her face with it.[296] He describes a brutal flogging of a seven-year-old girl with a birch, which, "covered with little twigs," make it "smart more," and climactically exclaims: "I know for certain that there are floggers who get more excited with every stroke, to the point of sensuality, literal sensuality, more and more, progressively for five minutes, they flog for ten minutes—longer, harder, faster, sharper."[297] At one point, he distills the aphrodisiac down to the "defenselessness of these creatures that tempts the torturers, the angelic trustfulness of the child, who has nowhere to turn and no one to turn to—that is what enflames the vile blood of the torturer."[298]

Ivan's treatise on the release derived from child abuse is rife with insistence that the perpetrators are, in all other respects, normal, humane, and not infrequently exceptional. For example, that retired general, who sicced his dogs on the little boy, is "wealthy" with "high connections."[299] He introduces one set of floggers as "an intelligent, educated gentleman and his lady," and another as "most honorable and official people, educated and well-bred."[300] He maintains that "these same torturers look upon all other examples of humankind even mildly and benevolently, being educated and humane Europeans, but they have a great love of torturing children, they even love children in that sense."[301] Ivan postulates that "this peculiar quality exists in much of mankind—this love of torturing children, but only children," and that "[t]here is, of course, a beast hidden in every man, a beast of rage, a beast of sensual inflammability at the cries of the tormented victim, an unrestrained beast let off the chain, a beast of diseases acquired in debauchery—gout, rotten liver, and so on."[302] Ivan's outburst, not unlike what happens periodically with Mitya, rises from the suspicion that that "beast of sensual inflammability" thrashes about within himself as well.[303]

Dostoevsky, moreover, corroborates that suspicion: Ivan "admits" that he "never could understand how it's possible to love one's neighbors" and he, the adult,

---

296. *Id.* at 242.
297. *Id.* at 241.
298. *Id.*
299. *Id.* at 242.
300. *Id.* at 241.
301. *Id.*
302. *Id.* at 241–42.
303. *Id.* at 242. *See supra* notes 170–77 and accompanying text (describing Mitya's acknowledgement of his inner Karamazovian beast).

automatically belongs to the caste he deems "disgusting" and unworthy of love.[304] This is borne out when, en route to Ivan's "last meeting with Smerdyakov," Ivan commits an act of brutality. He encounters a "solitary drunk little peasant in a parched coat, … feel[s] an intense hatred for him … [and] an irresistible desire to bring his fist down on him."[305] When the "little peasant, staggering badly, suddenly lurche[s] full force into Ivan[, t]he latter furiously shove[s] him away."[306] Beholding the "motionless, unconscious" peasant on the "frozen ground," Ivan, although surmising that "[h]e'll freeze" to death, abandons him while he bolts into lamplessness to consort with the diabolical Smerdyakov.[307] Although later he makes amends to this bashed peasant, Ivan, by periodically affixing the "Karamazovian" name to "cruel" and "carnivorous" impulses, acknowledges and vents his lethal tendencies.[308] Further, as Terras points out, "[o]n the psychological level, Ivan will readily believe that his brother Dmitry is a scoundrel and murderer because deep inside he knows that he himself is."[309]

Ivan, believing that "man has … created [the devil] in his own image and likeness," aligns the human race (which naturally includes Ivan) with blighted evil.[310] Alyosha, interrupting the sermon, tells Ivan, "You have a strange look as you speak…as if you were in some kind of madness."[311] What is sickening Ivan is not that cruel, godless reality, in which children are forced to suffer, but rather the inkling that he himself, the "Karamazovian," is evil incarnate. In essence, Ivan's atheistic fixation, which draws him to the Grand Inquisitor and devil, also make him vulnerable to Smerdyakov, who leads Ivan by the nose into a lightless vortex.

c. Grand Inquisitor

Third, Ivan's prose-poem about the Grand Inquisitor's encounter with Jesus in the sixteenth century shows not just inner conflict and contradiction, but also a soul torn between salvation and disaster. Dostoevsky, who despised

---

304. DOSTOEVSKY, *supra* note 10, at 236–37.

305. *Id.* at 621.

306. *Id.*

307. *Id.* When Ivan leaves Smerdyakov he finds the "little peasant … still lying in the same spot, unconscious and not moving," but manages to carry the peasant to the police station and "have him examined … by a doctor," which took "almost a whole hour." *Id.* at 634.

308. *Id.* at 236.

309. TERRAS, *supra* note 281, at 52. *See also* Martinsen, *supra* note 292 (discussing the underground man and how he tends to project onto the world his own flaws).

310. DOSTOEVSKY, *supra* note 10, at 239.

311. *Id.* at 238.

Catholics (and especially Jesuits), made Ivan's Inquisitor a Jesuit.[312] In so doing, he intended his readers to penetrate Ivan's rhetoric and brand his creed loathsome.

In the prose-poem, Ivan's Inquisitor reproaches Jesus for returning to earth to unravel what he and Roman Catholics have accomplished over the last millennium and a half. As the prose-poem progresses, Ivan and Inquisitor merge, as do Alyosha and Jesus.[313] While the Inquisitor pays lip service to humanity's well-being, he, reminiscent of Ivan's inability to love his neighbors, feels nothing but contempt for individuals. Ivan, like the Inquisitor, does all the talking, while Alyosha, like the prose-poem's Jesus, silently listens. More broadly, the Inquisitor articulates what is raging within Ivan's soul—his doubts, self-disgust, and spiritual anguish.

The Inquisitor gives his version of New Testament events from the gospels of Matthew and John, in which the devil approaches Jesus with three temptations. One, the devil urges Jesus to turn stones into bread so that " 'mankind will run after you, like sheep, grateful and obedient, though eternally trembling lest you withdraw your hand and your loaves cease for them.' "[314] The devil, speaking through the Inquisitor, chastises Jesus: " 'But you did not want

---

312. *See* Letter from Fyodor Dostoevsky to Apollon Maykov (December 23, 1868) in III Dostoevsky Letters 1868–71, at 113 (David A. Lowe ed. and trans., Ardis Publishers 1990) [hereinafter III Letters] (speaking of plans to write an "enormous novel called *Atheism*," about a character who "loses his faith in God[,] ... checks out the new generations, atheists, Slavs and Europeans, Russian fanatics and anchorites, priests[, and] gets hooked, strongly, by the way, by a Jesuit, a propagator, a Pole[, who] sinks from him into the depths of flagellantism—and at the end finds both Christ and the Russian land"); Letter from Fyodor Dostoevsky to Nikolay Strakhov (May 18 1871) in *id.* at 360 ("[I]n the West Christ has been lost (through the fault of Catholicism), and because of that the West is declining."). *See also* Denis Dirscherl, Dostoevsky and the Catholic church 121 (Loyola University Press, 1986) (explaining how others have called Dostoevsky the enemy of Jesuits); Miller, *supra* note 8, at 45 ("Dostoevsky scathingly indicts, through Smerdyakov, the kind of reasoning applied to theological issues that he believed to be typical of the Jesuits, whom he despised.")

313. *See* Miller, *supra* note 8, at 65 (discussing the "complex interplay... between Alyosha as listener (audience) and sometimes critic and Ivan as author and sometimes critic[,]" which "becomes even more complex as the reader begins to discern the similarities between Ivan and his Grand Inquisitor and between Alyosha and Jesus").

314. Dostoevsky, *supra* note 10, at 252. *See* Letter from Fyodor Dostoevsky to Vasily Alexeev (June 7, 1876) in IV Letters, *supra* note 281, at 284–85 (Responding to a question about "[s]tones and loaves" in *The Diary of A Writer*, Dostoevsky explains: "[g]ive them all food, *provide* for them, give them such a social system that they will always have bread and order."). *See also id.* at 285 ("Today's *socialism* in Europe and with us too, eliminates Christ everywhere and worries first of all about *bread* ...").

to deprive man of freedom and rejected the offer, for what sort of freedom is it, you reasoned, if obedience is bought with loaves of bread?' "[315]

When the Inquisitor imparts that the masses are "incapable of being free, because they are feeble, depraved, nonentities and rebels," it meshes with Ivan's earlier ideas on theodicy and denunciation of people as weak, cruel, and despicable.[316] In a totalitarian vein, the Inquisitor explains that he and his church, by tending to the weak and lying to them, are showing greater love for humanity than did Jesus.[317] Here, he invokes one of Ivan's quandaries: "[t]here is nothing more seductive for man than the freedom of his conscience, and there is nothing more tormenting either."[318] Freedom of conscience, along with a life in which "everything is permitted," is Ivan's stalking seductress.[319]

Two, the devil urges Jesus to fling himself from the Temple's pinnacle to demonstrate his faith that God would not let him fall. The Inquisitor (and devil) mocks Jesus' rejection of this temptation:

> Oh, you knew then that if you made just one step, just one movement towards throwing yourself down, you would immediately have tempted the Lord and would have lost all faith in him and been dashed against the earth you came to save, and the intelligent spirit who was tempting you would rejoice. But, I repeat, are there many like you?[320]

The Inquisitor tells Jesus that his hopes that "man too would remain with God, having no need of miracles" are absurd, and that humans were not born "to reject the miracle, and in those terrible moments of life, the moments of the most terrible, essential, and tormenting questions of the soul, to remain only with the free decision of the heart."[321] The Inquisitor foreshadows what will

---

315. DOSTOEVSKY, *supra* note 10, at 252. *See* Letter from Fyodor Dostoevsky to Vasily Alexeev (June 7, 1876) in IV LETTERS, *supra* note 281, at 285 ("Christ was hungry and the Devil advised him to take a stone and order it to become bread—the proof is precisely the fact that Christ replied ... : 'Man does not live by bread (that is, like animals) alone.'").

316. DOSTOEVSKY, *supra* note 10, at 253.

317. *See* MILLER, *supra* note 8, at 67 ("The Grand Inquisitor repeats the rationale that virtually every totalitarian system has used to justify its rule, but he also, paradoxically, repeats the beliefs of many benevolent social thinkers and philanthropists.").

318. DOSTOEVSKY, *supra* note 10, at 254.

319. *Id. See also infra* notes 483–87 and accompanying text (describing the oppositional philosophies in *The Brothers Karamazov*).

320. DOSTOEVSKY, *supra* note 10, at 255.

321. *Id.*

become the "terrible moment[ ] of [Ivan's] life" and "the most terrible, essential, and tormenting question" of his soul: Ivan will stand at the crossroads, before a Grand-Inquisitor alley and the alternate path, paved with faith, where he can either seal his lips or speak in a "free decision of the heart."[322]

After the second temptation, the Inquisitor, along with Ivan and the devil, congeals into a grotesque troika as Alyosha doubles with Jesus.[323] When the Inquisitor asks, "why are you looking at me so silently and understandingly with your meek eyes," he captures Alyosha, Ivan's silent audience.[324] Then, in one full-swoop, the Inquisitor shackles himself, along with the Roman Church, to the devil's hoof: "We are not with you, but with *him*; that is our secret."[325] In the wake of this, the Inquisitor, conceding that he (and the Church) had accepted temptation number three, states that "we took Rome and the sword of Caesar from him, and proclaimed ourselves sole rulers of the earth, the only rulers."[326]

For Ivan's Inquisitor, there are "only three powers on earth, capable of conquering and holding captive forever the conscience of these feeble rebels, for their own happiness—these powers are miracle, mystery, and authority."[327] The Inquisitor informs Jesus that, had he taken the devil's offerings, he "would have furnished all that man seeks on earth, that is: someone to bow down to, someone to take over his conscience, and a means for uniting everyone at last into a common, concordant, and incontestable anthill."[328] From there, the Inquisitor-Ivan-devil trinity, "flushed … from speaking with such enthusiasm," proudly unveils his project, and it sure as hell looks like hell on earth—an abode of slavery, slaughter, and inequity.[329] The Inquisitor brags that enslaved chattel will be persuaded that "they will only become free when they resign their freedom to us, and submit to us."[330] In the process, some will "exterminate" themselves and each other, while others will "crawl" to his feet and "cling …

---

322. *Id. See also infra* notes 385–88 and accompanying text (Alyosha describing what awaits Ivan before Mitya's trial).

323. *See* MILLER, *supra* note 8, at 69 ("As Ivan's narrative continues, the doubling between him and his Inquisitor and between Alyosha and Jesus grows more intense.").

324. DOSTOEVSKY, *supra* note 10, at 257. *See also* MILLER, *supra* note 8, at 69 (With respect to this line, she says that "it is the image of Alyosha sitting silently before Ivan that comes to mind.").

325. DOSTOEVSKY, *supra* note 10, at 257.

326. *Id.*

327. *Id.* at 255.

328. *Id.* at 257.

329. *Id.* at 260.

330. *Id.* at 258.

in fear, like chicks to a hen."[331] Everything will be permitted, or, as the Inquisitor boasts, "[w]e will tell them that every sin will be redeemed if it is committed with our permission ... and as for the punishment for these sins, very well, we take it upon ourselves."[332]

Ivan, wracked with doubt, cannot fully ratify Inquisitor-ism, as becomes apparent when his supposed utopia devolves into a depicted inferno. That is, the hideousness of the Inquisitor creed flip-flops into an implicit endorsement of Jesus. Alyosha, realizing this, exclaims, "[y]our poem praises Jesus, it doesn't revile him ... as you meant to."[333] The implication here is that Ivan's godless field is somehow fertile and has planted in it a small seed of faith. In fact, this is suggested even before his theodicy diatribe, when Ivan, smiling "like a meek little boy," said to Alyosha, "perhaps I want to be healed by you."[334]

In the prose-poem, Ivan and Inquisitor conjoin, and Alyosha, who intuits this, interjects, "[y]our Inquisitor doesn't believe in God, that's his whole secret," and shortly thereafter, revises this to, "*[y]ou* don't believe in God."[335] The ligature between Ivan and Inquisitor also manifests itself in the form of parallel farewells. Prior to his exodus, Ivan's Christ, sensing that the Inquisitor will "hold[] to his former idea ... approaches the old man in silence and gently kisses him on his bloodless, ninety-year-old lips."[336] In an addendum, Ivan says that "[t]he kiss burns in [the Inquisitor's] heart."[337] Before the brothers part, there is déjà vu: Alyosha "st[ands] up, [goes] over to [Ivan] in silence ... to gently kiss him on the lips," and Ivan's reaction—"[l]iterary theft"—intimates not only that Alyosha and Jesus are plagiaristic couplings, but also that his brother's kiss can potentially "burn" in his heart as well.[338]

In analyzing this scene, Miller suggests that "Alyosha may, through his loving kiss, be sowing in Ivan the seed of his own redemption" and notes "that the kiss actually originates in Ivan's sensibility; it is he who has created the parable of a Jesus who kissed the old sinner; it is he who describes how the kiss glowed in the old atheist's heart."[339] Although Jesus's quiet love for the Inquisitor might augur potential redemption for Ivan, the brothers' conversation in the hiatus between the fictive and real kiss suggests that if such

---

331. *Id.* at 258–59.
332. *Id.* at 259.
333. *Id.* at 260.
334. *Id.* at 236.
335. *Id.* at 261–62 (emphasis added).
336. *Id.* at 262.
337. *Id.*
338. *Id.* at 262–63.
339. MILLER, *supra* note 8, at 70.

reunification with God is, at the very least, embryonic, it will not become viable without lots of helter-skelter.

In the conversation, Ivan tells Alyosha that he just wants to "drag on until [he is] thirty, and then—smash the cup on the floor!"[340] Alyosha, seeing the "hell in [Ivan's] heart and in [his] head," reminds his brother of the "sticky little leaves and the precious graves, and the blue sky and the woman [he] love[s]" and asks, "[h]ow will you live, what will you love them with?"[341] Ivan, with a "cold smirk" suggestive of Smerdyakov's diabolical countenance, extols "the force of the Karamazov baseness," and relishes "drown[ing] in depravity" and "stif[ling his soul] with corruption."[342] Ivan refuses to "renounce" that lethal sound bite, "everything is permitted."[343] Here, momentarily, the devil holds sway: when Ivan left, a "sad and sorrowful" Alyosha, noticing a slight fiendish gait, saw "that his brother Ivan somehow swayed as he walked, and that his right shoulder, seen from behind, appeared lower than his left."[344]

d. The Devil

In the fourth collinear episode, the devil visits Ivan, who, now "on the verge of brain fever," teeters on the edge of collapse.[345] In a scene evoking the disquieting ambiguity of *The Double*, Ivan, fighting to stave off the "madhouse," tries to parse multi-horned queries: does the devil objectively exist?[346] Is he "a

---

340. DOSTOEVSKY, *supra* note 10, at 263.

341. *Id.*

342. *Id.*

343. *Id.*

344. *Id. See also* TERRAS, *supra* note 281, at 382 (suggesting that when Smerdyakov pokes around in his stocking to extract the 3,000 rubles, Ivan fears the exposure of a cloven hoof, which is associated with the devil).

345. DOSTOEVSKY, *supra* note 10, at 634. *See also* Letter from Fyodor Dostoevsky to Nikolay Lyubimov (August 10, 1880, in V LETTERS, *supra* note 265, at 262 ("My hero [Ivan], of course, sees hallucinations too, but confuses them with his nightmares. It's not just a physical (diseased) trait here, when a person begins at times to lose the distinction between the real and the unreal (which has happened to almost every person at least once in his life), but a spiritual trait as well, which coincides with the hero's character ... ")

346. DOSTOEVSKY, *supra* note 10, at 637. *See also supra* Chapter II (The Impenetrable Mental Capacity Doctrine: *The Double*) (discussing the ambiguity in Dostoevsky's *The Double*). *See* Letter from Fyodor Dostoevsky to Alexander Blagonravov (a doctor) (Dec. 19, 1880) in V LETTERS, *supra* note 265 at 303 (thanking the doctor "for ... informing [him] of the accuracy of [Ivan's] mental illness [as] depicted" and saying that "[a]n expert's opinion will support me, and you have to agree that under the circumstances ... Ivan ... could not have had any hallucination other than that one.")

lie," a mere emanation from Ivan's illness?[347] Is he hallucination? While it is characteristic of Dostoevsky not to appease readers with pat answers,[348] what he does here is give readers a glimpse of the coercive demons that will ultimately oust Ivan's courtroom confession.

Ivan strives to convince himself that the devil is hallucination, or as he puts it, "the embodiment of myself, but of just one side of me ... of my thoughts and feelings, but only the most loathsome and stupid of them."[349] Ivan reasons that he can do this by proving that the devil is a plagiarist, "not capable of telling [him] anything new."[350] In dissembling cooperation, the devil reacts by echoing Ivan's Euclidean geometry of earthly justice: "like you, I myself suffer from the fantastic, and that is why I love your earthly realism." The devil adds, "[h]ere you have it all outlined, here you have the formula, here you have geometry, and with us it's all indeterminate equations."[351]

The devil, in the guise of co-conspirator, assures his host that he is just Ivan, "only with a different mug."[352] In retraction similar to the predominant device at work in *The Double*, the devil casts doubt by parodying an aphorism from Terence, one which Ivan had never before considered and which, for at least a nanosecond, makes Ivan buy into the devil as reality apart from himself.[353] But, like a shot out of hell, the devil soothes with hooey: "Though I am your hallucination, even so, as in a nightmare, I say original things, such as never entered your head before, so that I am not repeating your thoughts at all, and yet I am merely your nightmare and nothing more."[354] The devil's methodology, one of tautological giveth and taketh away, duplicates Ivan's idiosyncratic vacillation from one extreme to another, from belief to disbelief. Ivan, constantly shifting, accuses the devil of just that: "[y]our goal is precisely to convince me that you are in yourself and are not my nightmare, and so now you yourself assert that you're a dream."[355]

---

347. Dostoevsky, *supra* note 10, at 637.
348. *See generally supra* Chapter II (The Impenetrable Mental Capacity Doctrine: *The Double*). (discussing Dostoevsky's technique of obfuscation and retraction in *The Double*).
349. Dostoevsky, *supra* note 10, at 637.
350. *Id.* at 638.
351. *Id.*
352. *Id.*
353. *Id.* at 639, 793 n. 5 ("the devil adapts a famous line from the Roman playwright Terence (190-159 B.C.): *homo sum, humani nihil a mea alienum puto*" ("I am a man, nothing human is alien to me")). *See also supra* Chapter II (The Impenetrable Mental Capacity Doctrine: *The Double*) (discussing the doubt and ambiguity in *The Double*).
354. Dostoevsky, *supra* note 10, at 639.
355. *Id.*

As the scene builds, the devil starts administering homeopathic doses of Ivan's own elixir.[356] Earlier, Ivan had renounced non-Euclidean justice, and the devil, following suit, likewise refuses to cotton to non-Euclidean theories. In so doing, the devil recalls his own journey through space and time to a "diplomatic soiree" in his "evening dress, white tie [and] gloves" and does it with parodic, Euclidean flair.[357] Because he was not properly attired for the weather, the devil, adding satire, wound up with an all-too-earthly cold. Similarly, the devil confides in his host that his "dream [is] to become incarnate, so that it's final, irrevocable, in some fat, two-hundred-and-fifty pound merchant's wife, and to believe everything she believes."[358] His "incarnation," evocative of Ivan's Inquisitor prose-poem, deprecates that holy union of divinity and humanity in Jesus Christ. But there is another, more confuting, facet to this. For the fat "merchant's wife," who eats, sleeps, attends church, and lights her little candle, life is scripted and quite simple.[359] Thus, the devil's dream, another antinomy, exposes Ivan's lust for a contrary state of existence, one of simplicity, an incarnated peace with undoubting faith: as the devil says, what would "put an end to my sufferings" is to attain that "ideal" of "go[ing] into a church and light[ing] a candle with a pure heart—by God it's true."[360]

---

356. *See generally* ROBIN FEUER MILLER, DOSTOEVSKY'S UNFINISHED JOURNEY 167–70 (Yale University Press 2007) (discussing the devil's "claims to practice metaphysical homeopathy").

357. DOSTOEVSKY, *supra* note 10, at 640. *See generally* Deborah A. Martinsen, *The Devil Incarnate* in ART, CREATIVITY & SPIRITUALITY, *supra* note 3, at 45, 46 (explaining how "the devil dwells on the literal to explain the metaphysical" and "accentuates the physical details of catching cold to explain the suffering caused by his alienation [from God]").

358. DOSTOEVSKY, *supra* note 10, at 639. *See also id.* at 642 ("[But] I will repeat to you once more that I would give all of that life beyond the stars, all ranks and honors, only to be incarnated in the soul of a two-hundred-and-fifty-pound merchant's wife and light candles to God."). *See also* Martinsen, *supra* note 357, at 50 (explaining that this is "an even more extreme physical cure for his alienation from God").

359. DOSTOEVSKY, *supra* note 10, at 639. A. Gerasimova, wrote to Dostoevsky and "complained that her life in her parents' home gave her no spiritual satisfaction" and that "she dreamed of a career in medicine so as to be able to help others." Letter from Fyodor Dostoevsky to A. Gerasimova (March 7, 1877), in IV LETTERS, *supra* note 281, at 357 n. 4. She also said that she did not want to settle into "becom[ing] the wife of a 'fat merchant.'" *Id.* at 360 n.11. Dostoevsky assured her: "[w]ith your mood and view, being the wife of a merchant, of course, is impossible." *Id.* at 360.

360. DOSTOEVSKY, *supra* note 10, at 639. *See generally* Martinsen, *supra* note 357, at 51 (discussing the devil's "church-going, candle-light merchant's wife"). Martinsen suggests, *inter alia*, that "[p]ositing a candle-lighting woman of the merchant class can suggest a caricatured piety that is superstitious, materialistic, and earthbound, or a sincere piety that

When Ivan hits his visitor with the penultimate question—"[i]s there a God, or not"—the devil, as noncommittal as Ivan, replies, "I just don't know."[361] Ivan, hearing himself parroted, asks, "[y]ou don't know, yet you see God?"[362] These words echo Ivan's earlier assertion that, through sheer will, he can disavow Euclidean justice, even when it is proven right before his very eyes.[363] Because the devil is his near-mirror image, he temporarily confirms Ivan's belief that his visit is "fantasy," provoking his statement, "[n]o, you are not in yourself, you are *me, me* and nothing else!"[364] But not surprisingly, the devil has another trick up his sleeve to nudge Ivan in the opposite direction, establish his own existence, and defeat Euclidean logic. He mesmerizes Ivan with a non-Euclidean parable starring miracles and paradise.

The story, one created by Ivan when he was seventeen years old, portrays a man, like adult Ivan, who is a doubting "thinker here on … earth, who 'rejected all—laws, conscience, faith,' and above all, the future life."[365] Upon death, this rebel was "sentenced to walk in darkness a quadrillion kilometers … and once he finished that quadrillion, the doors of paradise would be opened to him and he would be forgiven everything."[366] The rebel initially refuses to go "on principle," but instead, after lying on a road for almost a thousand years, eventually rises and "start[s] walking."[367]

In the midst of this, Ivan cuts in with a Euclidean sound bite and "burst[ing] into nervous laughter," says: "[i]sn't it all the same whether he lies there forever or walks a quadrillion kilometers? It must be about a billion years' walk!"[368] The devil, tip toeing toward the non-Euclidean point, agrees that "if [they] had a pencil and paper, [they] could work it out" and then says that the rebel "arrived long ago, … [which] is where the anecdote begins."[369] The tale ends with the protagonist in paradise, but "before he had been there two seconds," he has the epiphany: "for those two seconds it would be worth walking not

---

combines faith and materialism, transcendence and immanence, divine soul and human body, or both." *Id.*

   361. Dostoevsky, *supra* note 10, at 642.

   362. *Id.*

   363. *See supra* notes 290–91 and accompanying text.

   364. Dostoevsky, *supra* note 10, at 642.

   365. *Id.* at 643.

   366. *Id.*

   367. *Id.* at 643–44.

   368. *Id.* at 644.

   369. *Id.*

just a quadrillion kilometers, but a quadrillion quadrillion, even raised to the quadrillionth power!"[370]

The parable, now coursing through Ivan's bloodstream, has a potent, twofold effect: Ivan's sudden recollection that the story originated with him (and not the devil) does what Ivan craves and establishes the devil as fantasy. But the obstructive devil also rouses Ivan's dormant faith. Significantly, when Ivan all-too-zealously denies that he has "the hundredth part" of faith inside of him, the devil divulges his "homeopathic" methodology, the motto of which is "*Similia similibus currentur* ('let likes be cured with likes')."[371]

In her description of the devil as homeopathic practitioner, Miller explains that the "science of homeopathy, both popular and discredited in the nineteenth century, maintained that illness was best cured by giving medicines that mimicked rather than masked the symptoms of disease."[372] As she puts it, the underlying theory is that "[t]he symptoms of illness should be simulated, according to homeopathic wisdom, for they are not part of the disease itself, but rather evidence of the body's attempt to cure itself."[373] By duplicating his patient's symptoms and inoculating him with Euclid, atheism, and doubt, the devil supplies a diagnosis and induces healing:

> [H]esitation, anxiety, the struggle between belief and disbelief—all that is sometimes such a torment for a conscientious man like yourself ... Precisely because I knew you had a tiny bit of belief in me, I let in some final disbelief by telling you that anecdote. I'm leading you alternatively between belief and disbelief, and I have my own purpose in doing so. A new method, sir: when you've completely lost faith in me, then you'll immediately start convincing me to my face that I am not a dream but a reality—I know you now; and then my goal will be achieved.[374]

---

370. *Id.*

371. *Id.* at 645. *See also* MILLER, *supra* note 356, at 167.

372. MILLER, *supra* note 356, at 167.

373. *Id.* She points out that "[t]he devil, whether he is a hallucinatory or a truly demonic double, homeopathically duplicates the symptoms of Ivan's disease; he mimics and mocks Ivan's own words, ideas, doubts." *Id.* Here there is hope, however: namely, that "Ivan, by recoiling from this toxic doubling of himself, might, according to the principles of homeopathy, begin to heal himself." *Id. See also* Letter from Fyodor Dostoevsky to Yekaterina Yunge (April 11, 1880) in V LETTERS, *supra* note 265 at 189–90 (After Yunge had written Dostoevsky that she suffered from "duality," he says that the "*split* in you is exactly the way it is in me and has been all my life," recommends "believ[ing]" in Christ and in His promises" and explains that "[i]f you believe (or very much want to believe), then give yourself over to Him completely, and the torments from that split will be greatly assuaged.")

374. DOSTOEVSKY, *supra* note 10, at 645.

The devil, after noting his patient's gyration between "belief and disbelief," and admitting to inducing those vertiginous symptoms, tells Ivan that "[h]e will sow just a tiny seed of faith in [him], and from it an oak will grow."[375] The devil, spooning out allusions to the meeting between Jesus and Grand Inquisitor, gives the prognosis that Ivan, who "secretly ... want[s salvation] ver-ry, ver-ry much ... will drag [himself] to the desert to seek [it]."[376]

Before all of this, Ivan, even with his internally repugnant theories about theodicy, Euclid, and Grand Inquisitor, had a handle on reality. With all of the fog—his rebellion, scorn of God's justice, and atheistic protestations—Ivan, still with a moral compass, could locate a boundary between good and evil. Now, confounded by the two-faced devil, who claims to be "the only man in all of nature who loves the truth and sincerely desires good," who himself dreams of reconciliation with God and of walking the "quadrillion," Ivan, with an "unbearable," "agonizing," "throbbing in [his] brain," starts to implode.[377] The devil drivels on, feverishly, hysterically, and, here and there, incoherently. While praying for reunification with good and God, he, in refutation, champions evil incarnate—the man-god.[378] When the devil starts droning the Karamazovian mantra—"everything is permitted," Ivan, like "Luther" with his "inkstand," hurls (or might not have hurled) a glass at his guest.[379]

But when Alyosha knocks, things go from bad to worse. Ivan, now apoplectically ill, feels as if his "legs and arms" are bound.[380] His context, "one in which the glass he had just thrown at his visitor stood before him on the table" and with an empty sofa, suggests that what transpired (and what readers witnessed) was a hallucination.[381] Despite the fact that hallucination was precisely the resolution Ivan had sought throughout, he asserts the opposite: "That was no dream! No, I swear it was not dream, it all just hap-

---

375. *Id.*

376. *Id.*

377. *Id.* at 647–48

378. *See* MILLER, *supra* note 8, at 124 ("The devil ... punctuat[es] his desire for reunification with God with his opposing desire to bring about the appearance of the man-god, a figure who, throughout Dostoevsky's canon, has always represented the antithesis of God.")

379. DOSTOEVSKY, *supra* note 10, at 659. *See also id.* at 794 n. 25 ("[I]t is said that Martin Luther (1483–1546) was tempted by the devil while translating the Bible and threw his inkstand at him.").

380. *Id.* at 650. *See generally* Martinsen, *supra* note 357, at 55 ("Dostoevsky uses the devil's disappearance to signal the profoundly private nature of Ivan's hallucination: he dissipates as soon as the external world, in this case Alyosha's knock on the window, obtrudes on his interiority.").

381. DOSTOEVSKY, *supra* note 10, at 650.

pened!"[382] For him, the border between reality and fantasy, between subjective and objective venues, has vanished.

But here, the author conveys that Ivan's disease is far more insidious. In relating to Alyosha his meeting with the devil, it becomes apparent that Ivan's doubt, inner contradictions, and self-disdain have swollen into an all-consuming tsunami. Ivan, reverting to his symptomatic waffling, insists that "it was not a dream," that "he was here, sitting here, on that sofa," and then follows that with the contrarian postulate: "*he*—is me, Alyosha, me myself. All that's low, all that's mean and contemptible in me!"[383] For Ivan, polar opposites are concentrically swirling together, such that subjective and objective spheres, the dream and awake states, hallucination and reality, converge in one indiscriminate murk. Ivan, sensing his own rack and ruin, complains, "I sometimes have dreams now, ... yet they're not dreams, but reality" repeating, "It's as if I'm awake in my sleep ... I walk, talk, and see, yet I'm asleep."[384]

Like a Matryoshka doll, paradox within paradox nests inside Ivan. As Ivan tells Alyosha about his meeting with the devil, it becomes apparent that the details impugn what readers witnessed. For example, Ivan tells his brother that the devil ridiculed his reasons for deciding to confess at trial and says that the devil had already told him about Smerdyakov's suicide. The implication here is that the fractured shards in Ivan's psyche are themselves fracturing and that Ivan's hallucinations are themselves spawning hallucinations. Ivan, no longer able to parse reality from delusion, has also lost the ability to distinguish his hallucinations from their hallucinatory imposters.

On the eve of trial, Alyosha, acknowledging that justice here on earth is flawed, foresees that, "with Smerdyakov dead, no one will believe Ivan's testimony; but he will go and testify."[385] He forecasts "Ivan's illness ... [t]he torments of a proud decision, a deep conscience" while figuratively detecting Jesus' kiss burning on Ivan's lips: Alyosha thinks that "God, in whom [Ivan] did not believe, and his truth were overcoming his heart, which still did not want to

---

382. *Id. See also* Letter from Fyodor Dostoevsky to Nikolay Lyubimov (August 10, 1880) in V LETTERS, *supra* note 265, at 262 ("[I]n denying the reality of the phantom, [Ivan] defends its reality when the phantom disappears. *Tormented by lack of faith, he (unconsciously) wishes at the same time that the phantom were not imaginary, but something real.*").

383. DOSTOEVSKY, *supra* note 10, at 652.

384. *Id.*

385. *Id.* at 655. *See generally* Martinsen, *supra* note 357, at 70–71 ("Once [Ivan] decides to confess publicly, to open his private thoughts to public inspection, in short, to face the shame of self-exposure in order to serve justice and clear his brother Dmitry, Ivan casts aside his Inquisitor's mantle and joins the community of brotherhood.").

submit."[386] That prognostication, however, rooted in non-Euclidean soil, is ambiguous and irresolute. While Alyosha optimistically conjectures that "God will win," he qualifies that with pessimism: "[Ivan] will either rise into the light of truth, or perish in hatred, taking revenge on himself and everyone for having served something he does not believe in."[387] As courtroom confessant, Ivan effectually validates both postulates: that is, he "ris[es] into the light of truth" *and* "tak[es] revenge on himself."[388]

C. Miscarriage of Justice

In *Crime and Punishment*, Raskolnikov's confession inaugurates spiritual rebirth. As Sonya knows, confession is not just evidence that closes a court file, but more significantly, it serves as catalyst for healing. This comes across in the form of Raskolnikov's changes while he is in prison.

When Raskolnikov first arrives in Siberia, he is still tormented: he feels "no remorse for his crime" and heaps abuse on Sonya, treating her with "scornful and crudely insulting behavior."[389] While writing the novel, Dostoevsky commented in a letter that "the feeling of separation and alienation from humanity that came over [Raskolnikov] immediately after committing the crime" compels him to "denounce himself ... so as to become linked to people again, even at the price of perishing at penal servitude."[390] This alienation continues in prison, where Raskolnikov is estranged from the community of convicts, who, "dislike[] him[,] ... avoid him," and even "gr[ow] to hate him."[391]

But here, Raskolnikov incrementally reforms. It begins after an illness, when he dreams that the whole world is afflicted with "some strange, unheard of

386. Dostoevsky, *supra* note 10, at 655.

387. *Id. See infra* notes 414–36 and accompanying text (discussing Ivan's testimony at trial).

388. Dostoevsky, *supra* note 10, at 655.

389. Dostoevsky, *supra* note 1, at 647. In a letter to a journalist and writer, who was convicted of forgery and fraud and sentenced to four years in a convict labor gang, he "had defended his actions with a utilitarian argument close to the one used by Raskolnikov in *Crime and Punishment*." Letter from Fyodor Dostoevsky to Arkady Kovner (February 14, 1877) in IV Letters, *supra* note 281, at 352 n. 8. Dostoevsky writes to Kovner, who had stolen 168,000 rubles, "I do not at all like the two lines in your letter when you say that you don't feel any repentance for the deed done by you at the bank." *Id.* at 352. Kovner had also "take[n] issue with Dostoevsky's contention that without a belief in God and the immortality of the soul one cannot find any sense or logic to life or the world." *Id.* at 351 n. 3.

390. *See generally* Letter from Fyodor Dostoevsky to Mikhail Katkov (September 1865, Draft) in II Letters, *supra* note 104, at 175.

391. Dostoevsky, *supra* note 1, at 650.

and unprecedented plague" and that entire populations are rabid, with people "kill[ing] one another in a kind of senseless anger."[392] Such symptoms reflect Raskolnikov's destructive state, along with his self-imposed isolation and claims of superiority. He believes, due to the infection, that "no one could under-stand anyone else ... [and] each person thought that he alone possessed the truth."[393] After practically everything is ravaged, the chosen few escape to "usher in a new life, to renew the earth and render it pure." Raskolnikov likewise com-mences his own Lazarus-like rebirth.[394]

Once Raskolnikov recuperates, readers detect changes. For the first time, cog-nizant of another being, Raskolnikov actually notices that he hasn't seen Sonya in a while. Worrying about someone other than himself, he realizes that he is "waiting for her with anxious concern," and inquires about her condition.[395] When Sonya, who was ill, discovers that Raskolnikov "was so dejected and wor-ried for her sake," she sends him a note that arouses emotion, making "his heart beat violently and painfully."[396] The glacier is melting, and Raskolnikov begins to feel, and to care for another being. After Sonya recovers and rejoins Raskol-nikov, "he [is] hurled to her feet, and ends up weeping and hugging her knees."[397]

This moment is the milestone, and Sonya, whose "eyes beg[in] to shine with infinite happiness," knows it. Raskolnikov also realizes that he has "recovered ... completely with the whole of his renewed being."[398] He relinquishes "those tor-ments of the past" and opens the *New Testament*.[399] He does not just reach for faith, but also, while planning his future with Sonya, reconnects with humanity. With respect to other inmates, the narrator tells readers that the dynamics here have altered: "all the convicts, his former enemies, now looked upon him dif-ferently," and Raskolnikov "had actually begun to talk to them, and they had replied to him in kindly tones."[400] The confession inducts what Dostoevsky

---

392. *Id.* at 651–52.

393. *Id.* at 652.

394. *Id. See also id.* at 386 (After Raskolnikov spots a Russian translation of the New Testament on a chest of drawers, which was Lizaveta's gift to Sonya, he urges Sonya to read him that "bit about the raising of Lazarus."); *id.* at 388, 390 (Sonya, with "shaking hands and chest constricted," complies with Raskolnikov's request until she reaches the part, "'*And he that was dead came forth,*'" which she read loudly and ecstatically shaking and shiv-ering as though she were seeing it in real life.").

395. *Id.* at 653.

396. *Id.*

397. *Id.* at 654.

398. *Id.* at 655.

399. *Id.*

400. *Id.*

calls a "new story ... of a man's gradual renewal, his gradual rebirth, his gradual transition from one world to another."[401]

In contrast to *Crime and Punishment*, in which the trial is quite svelte, *The Brothers Karamazov* proceedings are drawn out, filling almost one-hundred-and-fifty pages, and Mitya and Ivan's disclosed truths play pivotal roles in the miscarriage of justice.[402] Together, *Crime and Punishment* and *The Brothers Karamazov* dispatch the message that, while confessions can and sometimes do have a vital place in the individual, spiritual tribunal, they (like those of Ivan and Mitya) tend to be misplaced, misunderstood, or even mephitic in a plebian courtroom.

Before Ivan takes the stand, things are going decently for Mitya, despite his recurrent outbursts.[403] Although witnesses Grigory and Dr. Herzenstube attest to Mitya's guilt, they, inadvertently assist the defense by stirring compassion through their memories of the accused as toddler. In particular, Herzenstube, who recalls feeling sorry for the forgotten child, "running in the dirt without any shoes and just one button on his little britches," ended up buying him a gift—a pound of nuts.[404] According to Herzenstube, twenty three years later, Mitya, still savoring that one act of kindness, came to thank him. This anecdote, which makes both doctor and defendant weep, has a "favorable" impact on the public, and by implication, on the jury as well.[405]

---

401. *Id.* at 656.

402. *Compare id.* at 637-42 (Raskolnikov's trial) *with* DOSTOEVSKY, *supra* note 10, at 656-753 (Mitya's trial). *See also* Letter from Fyodor Dostoevsky to Nikolay Lyubimov (Sept. 8, 1880) in V LETTERS, *supra* note 265, at 274-25 (Speaking of the trial scene in *The Brothers Karamazov*, Dostoevsky states that he "consulted beforehand with two prosecutors in Petersberg" and that "both the defense attorney and the prosecutor in my presentation are partly representative types from our contemporary justice system (although, they're not copies of anyone personally), with their mores, liberalism, and view of their role.").

403. *See, e.g.*, DOSTOEVSKY, *supra* note 10, at 661 ("But most striking was Mitya's outburst: as soon as the report on Smerdyakov was made, he exclaimed from his seat so that the whole courtroom could hear: 'The dog died like a dog!'"); *id.* at 666 ("Mitya cried loudly ...'For combing the lice out of my hair, I thank him; for forgiving me my blows, I thank him; the old man has been honest all his life, and was as faithful to my father as seven hundred poodles.'"); *id.* at 668 ("Mitya shouted in a booming voice: 'He kept hitting me for loans, even in prison! A despicable Bernard and careerist, and he doesn't believe in God, he hoodwinked His Grace!'"); *id.* at 673 ("'Bravo, leech!' Mitya cried from his place. 'Precisely right!'"); *id.* at 681 ("'Katya, why have you ruined me!' And he burst into loud sobs that could be heard all over the courtroom."); *id.* at 688-89 ("Mitya suddenly yelled. 'I looked into your eyes, knowing that you were dishonoring me, and yet I took your money! Despise the scoundrel, all of you, despise me, I deserve it!'"); *id.* at 689 ("'It's mine, mine!' cried Mitya. 'If I hadn't been drunk, I'd never have written it ... !'").

404. *Id.* at 674.

405. *Id.* at 675.

As expected, Alyosha, with unrivaled credibility, is instrumental to the defense: he firmly avows that "it was *not he* who killed my father," and by harkening back to the image of the accused beating his own breast, Alyosha furnishes sole corroboration for Mitya's story about that little pouch of unspent rubles on his neck.[406] Also, the fact that Alyosha spontaneously comes to his realization about the significance of that breast-beating gesture while he is on the stand ostensibly adds drama and credence.[407] In fact, Alyosha's testimony fortifies some of the more effective techniques of Mitya's defense counsel, Fetyukovich.

Fetyukovich, whose appellation means "blockhead," is based on V.D. Spasovich, a famous Russian lawyer and law professor at the University of St. Petersburg.[408] Despite his unflattering name and Dostoevsky's disparagement of prototype Spasovich, his Fetyukovich, a mixed bag, initially does an able job by discrediting prosecution witnesses.[409] Fetyukovich, by getting Grigory to admit that he was drunk as a skunk, casts doubt on his damaging testimony about the open garden door and then punctuates that with a humorous biblical allusion: after "[a] tumbler and a half of pure spirits" anyone "might see 'the doors of heaven open,' not to mention the door to the garden."[410] Equally skilled in impeaching Rakitin, "one of the most important witnesses" for the prosecution, he exploits a testimonial "slip" to expose hostility and bias.[411] He further impresses the jurors with the fact that Trifon Borisovich, "one of the most dangerous witnesses brought forward by the prosecution," is dishonest when it comes to money.[412] After Fetyukovich is done with this innkeeper, the witness "leav[es] under suspicion ... with his reputation rather besmirched."[413]

After all of these positive developments, what goes so horribly wrong? Although this might sound counter-intuitive, the glitch boils down to one thing— an overabundance of truth. When truth spews from the mouth of Ivan, it turns

---

406. *Id.* at 676.

407. *Id.* 677 ("'I now recall one circumstance I had quite forgotten; it was not at all clear to me then, but now ...' And Alyosha excitedly recalled, obviously having just hit upon the idea himself, how during his last meeting with Mitya, in the evening, by the tree, on the road to the monastery, Mitya, hitting himself on the chest.")

408. *See* MILLER, *supra* note 8, at 126 (discussing Spasovich). *See also supra* Chapter I (Inexpressible Ideas: A Multifaceted Life and Legal Lens) (discussing Spasovich and the Kronenberg case).

409. *See supra* Chapter I (Inexpressible Ideas: A Multifaceted Life and Legal Lens) (discussing Dostoevsky's treatment of Spasovich).

410. DOSTOEVSKY, *supra* note 10, at 665.

411. *Id.* at 666–67.

412. *Id.* at 670.

413. *Id.*

the tide to foment a lie in the form of an erroneous verdict. When Ivan takes the stand, he is, as Dostoevsky once said about Raskolnikov, trapped and "*compelled* to denounce himself."[414] Of course, Ivan is literally free to leave, which is underscored by the fact that, at one point, he pulls a characteristic Ivan, changes his mind, and "turn[s] and start[s] out of the courtroom."[415] But Ivan's coercive demons lurch him back to "his former place again."[416] Ivan, making light of his own erraticism, recites a folk custom with a peasant girl teasing, " 'I'll jump if I want, I won't if I don't.' "[417] This jingle belies Ivan's indecision: "I want," "I won't," "I don't."[418] As readers see, Ivan eventually commits to want, will, and do.

After handing the stolen money to the bailiff, Ivan comes clean: "I got it from Smerdyakov, the murderer, yesterday. I visited him before he hanged himself. It was he who killed father, not my brother. He killed him on my instructions.... Who doesn't wish for his father's death?"[419] As mentioned above, his testimony adheres to the pattern of his earlier utterances to Smerdyakov.[420] That is, Ivan discloses his guilt and his desire for his father's death, but at first, tempers it by identifying Smerdyakov as the perpetrator. Then, lickety-split, Ivan vicariously owns the blame by equating his omission to stop murder with conduct of "instructing" it.[421] When he finally blurts, "I'm simply a murderer," Ivan, transcending mere *respondeat superior* status, accepts direct criminal liability.[422] In so doing, he erases that crucial line between wishing it and making it so.

The problem is that Ivan's confession—all too true and genuine—exposes his every raw nerve, along with the pangs, strife, and doubt that surfaced in his theodicy lecture, Grand Inquisitor prose-poem, dialogue with the devil, and Euclidean commentary. In his theodicy lecture, Ivan expressed his fear that all of the enveloping evil was likewise part and parcel of his own soul.[423]

---

414. *See supra* II Letters, note 104, at 175.
415. Dostoevsky, *supra* note 10, at 685.
416. *Id.*
417. *Id.*
418. *Id.*
419. *Id.* at 686.
420. *See supra* notes 277–80 and accompanying text (describing Ivan's admissions to Smerdyakov).
421. Dostoevsky, *supra* note 10, at 686. *See also supra* notes 277–80 and accompanying text (words to Smerdyakov).
422. Dostoevsky, *supra* note 10, at 686. *See also supra* notes 277–80 and accompanying text (words to Smerdyakov).
423. *See supra* notes 302–303 and accompanying text.

By asking "[w]ho doesn't wish for his father's death" and answering "[e]very-one wants his father dead," he does not merely prick a Freudian nerve.[424] What Ivan does is glue his personal guilt onto collective guilt, which results in a fusion that effaces boundaries between the inner-self and outer-others.

In the Grand Inquisitor prose-poem, the devil, urging Jesus to miraculously turn stones into bread, mocks Christ for believing "that man does not live by bread alone" and envisions an uprising, the slogan of which is "[f]eed them first, then ask virtue of them."[425] On the witness stand, Ivan goes there, bellowing, "Circuses! Bread and Circuses!"[426] His words invoke his Inquisitor-devil's temptations and allude to the Caesars, who appeased the citizenry of Imperial Rome by giving them bread and circuses.[427] Ivan, now momentarily with "God, in whom he did not believe," and with "truth … overwhelming his heart," begs for "water" and shouts, "Give me a drink, for Christ's sake!"[428] Through the juxtaposition of bread and water, Ivan conjures disparate images, loaves of materialism and the "living water" of Christian faith, thus blurring together the worldly and holy.[429]

In response to the judge's demand for evidence, Ivan searches for *his* witness, his devil, who is "sure to be here somewhere."[430] Ivan, convinced that he is "there, under the table with the material evidence," regresses to the delusional state he had endured during and after his chat with the "wretched, paltry devil."[431] For Ivan, reality and fantasy merge, and then, on the stand, Ivan, as he last did with Alyosha, recounts words that fail to match the ones that readers heard: "I told him [the devil] I would not keep silent, and he started telling me about the geological cataclysm …"[432] Ivan has not only dissolved the

---

424. DOSTOEVSKY, *supra* note 10, at 686. *See also* MILLER, *supra* note 8, at 91 (describing Mitya coming to kill his father with the brass pestle in his pocket as a "fraught, Freudian, Oedipal moment" with "a shocking phallic icon: the young son drawing his pestle from his pocket to do battle with his father"); *supra* Chapter I (Inexpressible Ideas: A Multifaceted Life and Legal Lens) (discussing Freud's perspective on Dostoevsky).

425. DOSTOEVSKY, *supra* note 10, at 252-53.

426. *Id.* at 686.

427. *See* DOSTOEVSKY, *supra* note 93, at 577 n. 3 (citing John 4:10) ("The Caesars provided bread and circuses (*panem et circenses*) to the people of Imperial Rome to keep them content.")

428. DOSTOEVSKY, *supra* note 10, at 686.

429. DOSTOEVSKY, *supra* note 93, at 577 n.3 (citing John 4:10) ("The juxtaposition of bread and water is significant, signaling the distinction between materialism (bread) and the 'living water' of Christian faith.")

430. DOSTOEVSKY, *supra* note 10, at 687.

431. *Id.*

432. *Id. See also supra* notes 380–84 and accompanying text (Ivan's inaccurate account to Alyosha of the devil's visit).

membrane between reality and hallucination, but once again cannot differentiate the hallucinations from their hallucinatory offspring.

In his Euclidean speech, Ivan explained how such geometry accounts for earthly justice and proclaimed that he epitomizes the rational, Euclidean "earthly mind."[433] Ivan, purportedly as earthly as earthly can be, boasted that even if the non-Euclidean theory is proven before his very eyes, he still would not accept it.[434] The problem is that when he confesses the whole truth and nothing but the truth in the earthly courtroom, Ivan's Euclid throws Ivan to the dogs. After the judge asks, "[h]ow can you confirm such a confession," Ivan caves: "[t]hat's the trouble, I have no witnesses. That dog Smerdyakov won't send you evidence from the other world ..."[435] At this juncture, still unable to accept the possibility of non-Euclidean justice where parallel lines can meet somewhere else, what is demonstrated right before Ivan's eyes is that there is no rational justice here on earth.[436] This, leaving him with nothing, becomes the final snap.

When Katerina, initially Mitya's friendly witness, testified the first time, the accused prophetically shouted, "Katya, why have you ruined me."[437] When Ivan opens his mouth, that prophesy comes to fruition. After Ivan, the man Katerina truly loves, incriminates himself, she swoops in to save him, brandishing an epistolary sword against Mitya. She delivers Mitya's letter, one composed in a drunken stupor, in which he "described beforehand" his plan to kill father.[438] What Katerina says about herself and her dysfunctional relationship with Mitya is accurate, and the document sure looks like that irrefutable, "mathematical," proof against the accused.[439]

Perversely, Katerina, the only participant fearing that Ivan is guilty, helps secure a guilty verdict against Mitya, whom she does not think is guilty.[440] The

---

433. Dostoevsky, *supra* note 10, at 235. *See also supra* notes 285–91 and accompanying text (Ivan's thoughts on Euclid).

434. *See supra* notes 285–91 and accompanying text (Ivan's thoughts on Euclid).

435. Dostoevsky, *supra* note 10, at 686.

436. *Id.* at 235. *See also supra* notes 285–91 and accompanying text (Ivan's thoughts on Euclid).

437. Dostoevsky, *supra* note 10, at 681.

438. *Id.* at 689.

439. *Id.* at 688 ("The paper she handed over was that same letter Mitya had written from the 'Metropolis' tavern, which Ivan Fyodorovich referred to as a document of 'mathematic' importance," and "it was acknowledged precisely as mathematic, and had it not been for this letter, Mitya would perhaps not have perished, or at least not have perished so terribly!").

440. *See* Miller, *supra* note 8, at 128–29 ("The dreadful irony of this scene is that, to defend Ivan, Katerina Ivanovna makes her consummate accusation of Mitya at the very moment when she believes (all of a sudden) that it is Ivan who is guilty.").

defense counsel, Fetyukovich, can share blame for the miscarriage of justice as well. In flagrant breach of his duty to zealously advocate on behalf of his client, he helps seal Mitya's doom. Concededly, Fetyukovich starts off effectively, by essentially proving his thesis that "psychology, … though a profound thing, is still like a stick with two ends," and deftly deflates each of the prosecutor's psychological theories.[441] Although asserting that "[t]here is an overwhelming totality of facts against the defendant," Fetyukovich, honoring his promise, shows that "there is not one fact that will stand up to criticism, if it is considered separately, on its own."[442]

Later, modulating to a "new, heartfelt voice, quite unlike the one in which he had been speaking so far," Mitya's advocate, becoming his "blockhead" namesake, snatches defeat from the jaws of any conceivable victory.[443] Fetyukovich, who never believed in his client's innocence, commits misfeasance when he lets these feelings leak to the jury. It occurs when he finesses a fallback position, one that not only is not necessary, but also undermines his earlier, more compelling closing statements. After conceding that homicide, especially parricide, is horrific, Fetyukovich goes where he ought not go by positing hypothetical guilt: "what *if* [Mitya] did kill him and goes unpunished."[444] After reviewing Fyodor's reprehensibility, Mitya's tragic childhood, and the events on the night of the murder, Fetyukovich suggests that, *if* Mitya did kill, it was due to understandable, unpremeditated indignation:

> [H]e did not break into his house in order to kill him, oh, no. A feeling of hatred took hold of him involuntarily, unrestrainably; to reason was impossible: everything surged up in a moment! It was madness and insanity, a fit of passion, but a natural fit of passion, avenging its eternal laws unrestrainably and unconsciously, like all things in nature.[445]

Suddenly catching himself, Fetyukovich tries to un-ring the bell by asserting, "[b]ut even then the killer did not kill."[446] From there, he embellishes his sophistic sequitur: since "such a father as the murdered old Karamazov cannot and does not deserve to be a father," it thus follows that "such a murder is

---

441. Dostoevsky, *supra* note 10, at 727.

442. *Id.* at 726.

443. *Id.* at 741. *See also supra* note 408 and accompanying text (Fetyukovich's name—"Blockhead").

444. Dostoevsky, *supra* note 10, at 742.

445. *Id.* at 746.

446. *Id.*

[neither] murder" nor parricide.[447] What comes across in the oratory is disbelief in his client's innocence and the implication that Mitya did it. Ironically,
Fetyukovich, who had faulted opposing counsel for pretending be both "prosecutor and defender," turns into the pot calling the kettle black by serving as
prosecutor himself.[448]

Fetyukovich's jab, in conjunction with Katerina's sandbag, fuels what is,
and has been, inevitable from day one—that miscarriage of justice. Brooks
attributes the problem, at least partially, to the fact that "Ivan's confession is
too true to be believed."[449] The same could be said of all of Mitya's attestations,
like the shame he attached to the remnants of Katerina's rubles, his "drunkenness
and depravity," and his innocence of the crime with which he has been charged.[450]
Things go so awry not just because of an over-abundance of all-too-true truth,
but rather because a mortal construct, like the legal system, is simply not designed to, and cannot, accommodate genuine confessions. The judge, telling
Ivan, "your words are incomprehensible and impossible in this place," delivers
that message loud and clear.[451]

When the legal system latches onto something so rare as a bona fide confession, be it compelled by shame or borne of spiritual struggle, it is fated to
ignore, misunderstand, or misinterpret it. In fact, today in America and in
Dostoevsky's Russia, there have been erroneous convictions and instances
where a false or unreliable confession is used to convict, while the true one is
cast aside.[452] Like the Russian novelist, some members of the United States

---

447. *Id.* at 744, 747. *See also* Letter from Fyodor Dostoevsky to an Unidentified Ad-
dressee (March 27, 1878), in V LETTERS, *supra* note 265, at 25 (While explaining what it
really means to be a parent and giving advice on child rearing, he recommends that the
mother "acquaint [the eight-year old] with the Gospel [and] teach him to believe in God
strictly according to the law."). He adds:

> Imagine that your child, grown to be fifteen or sixteen, comes to you ... and asks you
> or his father a question such as 'Why should I love you and why ought I to make
> that an obligation for myself?' Believe that at that point no knowledge or questions
> will help, and besides. There won't even be any point in answering him. And there-
> fore you need to manage it so that *he doesn't even come to you* with such a question.
> *Id.*

448. DOSTOEVSKY, *supra* note 10, at 742 ("[I]n his ardent speech my esteemed oppo-
nent...exclaimed several times...'No, I shall not turn over the defense of the accused to anyone, I shall not yield his defense to the defense attorney from Petersburg—I am both
prosecutor and defender!'").

449. BROOKS, *supra* note 3, at 60.

450. DOSTOEVSKY, *supra* note 10, at 661.

451. *Id.* at 686.

452. *See generally* LOUISE MCREYNOLDS, MURDER MOST RUSSIAN: TRUE CRIME AND

Supreme Court have similarly expressed distrust of confessional evidence. One prime example is in the *Connelly* case, in which the record was "barren of any corroboration of the mentally ill defendant's confession," and lacked "a shred of competent evidence … linking the defendant to the charged homicide."[453] But even with "overwhelming evidence in the record point[ing] to the unreliability of … [his] delusional mind," Connelly, a diagnosed, chronic paranoid schizophrenic, is convicted on the sole basis of words from his own mouth.[454] The *Connelly* dissenters, acknowledging "distrust for reliance on confessions," said that the matter *sub judice* "starkly highlights the danger[s]."[455]

Unlike what happened to Connelly, when Ivan speaks with raw candor, he is branded the unreliable madman, deemed incredulous, and ejected from the courtroom. In *The Brothers Karamazov*, there is an analogue to this in elder Zosima's autobiographical recollection of confessant Mikhail, who had murdered a woman for rejecting his marriage proposal. Unlike Zosima, who comes to believes the confession, when Mikhail furnishes the same statement to the authorities, along with plentiful, tangible corroborating evidence that he had saved for fourteen years, the legal institution rejects it all, and issues the "verdict that the unfortunate man had gone mad."[456] Even after the "authenticity" of his evidence is verified, the case languishes, "destined to be left unfinished."[457]

Dostoevsky lets us know, however, that Mikhail's confession, although discredited and ignored by the earthly justice system, secures a place elsewhere. As Professor Louise McReynolds points out, in Russia there is the "cultural as well as the philological difference that separated the two words for 'confession,' the religious *ispoved* that asked for forgiveness, and *soznanie*, the admission of

PUNISHMENT IN LATE IMPERIAL RUSSIA 104 (Cornell University Press, 2013) (explaining how the Russian "public's attitude toward the judicial process itself reflected mistrust of the prosecutorial system, and not necessarily the law" and that "[f]ear of committing a 'judicial mistake' was regularly invoked as an appeal for clemency, exemplified early by a booklet from 1874 'dedicated to jurors,' warning them with examples from the British courts of convictions of the innocent").

453. Connelly, 479 U.S. at 183 (Brennan J., dissenting). *See also supra* notes 23–32 and accompanying text (discussing *Connelly*).

454. Connelly, 479 U.S. at 183. *Cf.* MCREYNOLDS, *supra* note 452, at 47–48 (describing an actual case in Russia, which occurred shortly after Dostoevsky's death, in which a young woman turned herself in and confessed to a murder, and then, after being "committed to a psychiatric hospital, … recanted her confession").

455. Connelly, 479 U.S. at 183.

456. DOSTOEVSKY, *supra* note 10, at 311.

457. *Id.*

having committed the crime."[458] On his death bed, Mikhail, who sought for-giveness, "feel[s] joy and peace for the first time after so many years" and speaks of it to Zosima:

> I at once felt paradise in my soul, as soon as I had done what I had to do. Now I dare to love my children and kiss them. No one believes me, neither my wife nor the judges; my children will never believe me ei-ther. In that I see the mercy of God towards my children. I shall die and for them my name will remain untainted. And now I am looking to-wards God, my heart rejoices as in paradise ... I have done my duty.[459]

In some ways, Mikhail and Raskolnikov are kindred spirits. In *Crime and Punishment*, Dostoevsky does not inordinately dwell on Raskolnikov's trial or internment, which, for all intents and purposes, are irrelevant. The author in-dicates that what imbues Raskolnikov's confession with meaning has nothing to do with the justice system, but instead, has all to do with its function as preliminary step along a highly individual spiritual trajectory.[460] In a letter, Dostoevsky shared his plans to include in *Crime and Punishment* "a hint at the idea that legal punishment imposed for a crime frightens the criminal much less than lawmakers think, in part because [the criminal] himself psycholog-ically demands it."[461] For this reason, the writer refrained from protracting the Siberian penal phase, and instead got right to the nitty-gritty, the reprisal, which Raskolnikov himself "psychologically demands" and executes.[462]

Although Mitya's decision to dodge his Siberian sentence and instead seek exile in America poses a conundrum for some readers, it makes sense as the tem-pered middle ground.[463] Mitya, who admitted guilt for all sorts of heinous

---

458. MCREYNOLDS, *supra* note 452, at 92.

459. DOSTOEVSKY, *supra* note 10, at 311–12.

460. *See supra* notes 154–55 and accompanying text (discussing Raskolnikov's confes-sion as a starting point in the process of a spiritual rebirth).

461. Letter from Fyodor Dostoevsky to Mikhail Katkov (October 22, 1865) in II LET-TERS, *supra* note 104, at 175 (letter to Mikhail Katkov while Dostoevsky is writing *Crime and Punishment*).

462. *Id.*

463. *See generally* Paul J. Contino, *Incarnational Realism and the Case for Casuistry: Dmitry Karamazov's Escape*, in ART, CREATIVITY, AND SPIRITUALITY, *supra* note 3, at 131 (dis-cussing the debate over whether Mitya "[s]hould accept his sentence in Siberia or escape to America with Grushenka" and concluding that Mitya's ultimate decision is "a good one"). *But see* GARY ROSENSHIELD, WESTERN LAW, RUSSIAN JUSTICE: DOSTOEVSKY, THE JURY TRIAL AND THE LAW 211 (University of Wisconsin Press, 2005) ("Alyosha's words [in defending es-cape] are essentially a paraphrase of the Devil's (Fetyukovich's) words on spiritual resurrection."); Carol Flath, *The Passion of Dmitrii Karamazov*, 58 SLAVIC REV. 595 (1999) ("[I]t is incon-

deeds, did not kill his father. Alyosha advises him to not take on more than he can bear, and Mitya knows full well that he is not built to bear that Siberian "martyr's cross" with floggings and no Grushenka.[464] Alyosha concurs:

> But you're innocent and such a cross is too much for you. You wanted to regenerate another man in yourself through suffering; I say just remember that other man always, all your life, and wherever you escape to—and that is enough for you. That you did not accept that great cross will only serve to make you feel a still greater duty in yourself, and through this constant feeling from now on, all your life, you will do more for your regeneration, perhaps, than if you went *there*.[465]

Both Mitya and Dostoevsky, who himself experienced self-imposed exile, knows that being uprooted from Russian soil is not a cakewalk.[466] For someone like Russia-loving Mitya, who as an adult indulged in creature comforts, physical toil "in solitude, in some remote place" will flog him enough to meet his "psychological[] demands."[467]

---

ceivable that Dmitry should accede to the pressure to flee to America; instead he must go, into Siberian exile, go below the earth (in an analogy to Christ's time spent in the tomb, or perhaps to his entire life spent 'below,' here on earth).")

464. DOSTOEVSKY, *supra* note 10, at 763.

465. *Id. See also* Contino, *supra* note 463, at 148 (asserting that "[t]hough guilty of much, Mitya is innocent of the murder of his father" and that "considerations of proportion and readiness must enter into his decision"). Contino explains that "[t]wenty years in Siberia, bereft of Grushenka, would be a disproportionate punishment, and given his impulsive character, an imprudent burden for him to shoulder." *Id.*

466. *See generally* Letter from Fyodor Dostoyevsky to Apollon Maykov (August 16, 1867), in II LETTERS, *supra* 104, at 251 (describing his self-imposed exile abroad during the time he sought to escape his creditors in Russia). Dostoevsky writes:

> I have landed, in addition, in an alien land, where not only is there not a Russian face, Russian books, or Russian thoughts and cares to be found, but not even a friendly face! Really, I can't even understand how a Russian abroad, if only he has feelings and sense, can fail to notice this and feel it painfully ... And how can one spend one's life abroad? Without one's native land it's suffering, honest to God! ... But to go the way I have, without knowing and without foreseeing when I'll return, is very bad and distressing.

Id.

467. DOSTOEVSKY, *supra* note 10, at 765. See also *supra* note 461, and accompanying text (referring to Dostoevsky's letter to Mikhail Katkov).

IV. Conclusion: The "Experience of Active Love"

In the due process and *Miranda* contexts, the Court aims to ensure that confessions are the product of free and rational choices.[468] In Sixth Amendment decisions, which purport to protect the integrity of the adversarial process, the freedom and rationality behind confession are also aspirational.[469] Confession jurisprudence is all about externalities, with relevant factors being the conduct of state agents, coercive techniques, or deliberate elicitation tactics.[470] While the Supreme Court has touted the value of confessions, it has also expressed mistrust of such evidence.[471]

Dostoevsky, writing on an entirely different page, could not be more mistrustful of confessions, especially ones that stray into criminal prosecutions. According to him, confessions are an elusive phenomenon of infinite variety, and the psychological and spiritual forces that coerce them tend to be *unfree* and *ir*rational. Furthermore, he would find the Supreme Court's concern with outer coercers as fatuous as some of Fyodor Karamazov's notions, and the installed *Miranda* safeguards as inutile as Doctor Herzenstube's placebos.[472] Dostoevsky believed that, in the justice system, confessions are not just valueless, but frequently do more harm than good by actually derailing the putative truth-finding process. Even "blockhead" Fetyukovich seems to get that.[473]

In one of his better moments, Fetyukovich suggests that confessions should not be determinative without ample corroboration. In his closing statement, Fetyukovich, talking anecdotally about a boy accused of killing a shopkeeper and robbing him of fifteen hundred rubles, describes the evidence:

> About five hours later he was arrested, and … the entire fifteen hundred was found on him. Moreover, the shop clerk, who returned to the shop after the murder, informed the police not only of the amount

---

468. *See supra* II. A. 1 & 2 (summarizing seminal Supreme Court decisions on confessions under the Due Process Clause and *Miranda*).

469. *See supra* II. A. 3 (summarizing seminal Supreme Court confession cases under the Sixth Amendment).

470. *See supra* II. A. (Supreme Court confession cases).

471. *See generally* II. A. *See also supra* notes 453–55 (discussing the *Connelly* decision).

472. *See supra* notes 92–93 and accompanying text (describing Fyodor Karamazov's incorrect pontification on the history of confessions). As for Doctor Herzenstube, as Madame Khokhlakov keeps pointing out, he is "terrible and eternal," his treatments don't work, and he "always comes and says he can make nothing of it." DOSTOEVSKY, *supra* note 10, at 181. Madame Khokhlakov's daughter, Lise, agrees: "Your Herzenstube will come and say he can make nothing of it!" *Id.* at 182.

473. *See supra* note 408 and accompanying text (discussing "blockhead").

stolen, but also of what sort of money it consisted—that is so many hundred-ruble bills, so many fifties, so many tens, so many gold coins and precisely which ones—and then precisely the same bills and coins were found on the arrested murderer.[474]

After explaining that "*[o]n top of that* there followed a full and frank confession from the murderer that he had taken that very money," Fetyukovich exclaims, "[t]his, gentlemen of the jury, is what I call evidence."[475] Of course, if there is such ample evidence to support a conviction, then the confession, mere surplusage, need not be introduced at all, and Dostoevsky would likely concur with that proposition.[476]

Throughout Dostoevsky's novels, loquacious people admit to things they did or did not do. *The Brothers Karamazov* is set in Skotoprigonevsk, a town in which just about everyone is coming clean. As to be expected, elder Zosima has his flock of confessants, like the peasant sharing her grief after the burial of her three-year-old son, and the mother anguished over her adult son's neglecting to keep in touch. He also hears Madame Khokhlakova's confession that she "suffers from ... lack of faith," as well as that of a "wasted, consumptive-looking" peasant woman with "two burning eyes," who whispers her offense against her abusive husband.[477]

Similarly, Alyosha gets an earful: on top of Mitya's and Ivan's confessions, Katerina tells Alyosha that she knew all along that Mitya had failed to deliver the rubles, and that she would endure anything from, or for, her faithless fiancé. Grushenka, confessing to being as "wicked as can be," admits to the young monk that she wanted to ruin him and had promised Rakitin twenty-five rubles, if he would deliver the prey to her door.[478] Kolya relates the details of his bond

---

474. DOSTOEVSKY, *supra* note 10, at 730–31.

475. *Id.* at 731 (emphasis added). *See also* BROOKS, *supra* note 3, at 153 ("Perhaps the only truly probative way to detect and exclude the false confession would be insistence that the alleged crime be convincingly substantiated by other means (apparently the procedure in German courts).") Brooks adds, "But taken to its logical conclusion, this would be tantamount to saying that we do not need to use confessions in criminal procedure." *Id.* 153–54. *But see* Leo, et. al, *supra* note 77, at 764–65 (proposing a solution whereby "judges ... take a more active role in preventing false confessions from being introduced into evidence at trial by considering the reliability of confession evidence at a pretrial hearing").

476. *See* BROOKS, *supra* note 3, at 153–54. *Cf.* MCREYNOLDS, *supra* note 452, at 43 (explaining how Russian legal "reformers added the article that confession was to be but one piece of the evidence").

477. DOSTOEVSKY, *supra* note 10, at 55, 51.

478. *Id.* at 353.

with Ilyusha, which ruptured when, upon Smerdyakov's urging, his friend tortured the stray dog Zhuchka by feeding him bread with a pin in it.[479] Kolya, in fact, flashes more—his "egoistic vanity and base despotism," which have plagued him his whole short life and, for a time, forestalled his visit to his dying companion.[480]

Enlightened Alyosha is not himself devoid of the confessant gene, which readers learn through secrets bandied back and forth between him and his betrothed, Lise Khokhlakov: Alyosha tells Lise that his "brothers are destroying themselves" and confesses that he might not "even believe in God."[481] Later, after Lise confesses to Alyosha that she hates happiness, "want[s] someone to torment [her]," would like to "set fire to the house" or "kill somebody," and has vile dreams of devils and of "abusing God out loud," he ponies up to having had the same dreams.[482]

In Skotoprigonevsk, the popular pastime is not only confession, but also the pontification of various philosophies, of which the two most prominent are diametrically opposed. On one end of the spectrum resides the cannibalistic credo that "everything is permitted."[483] Pyotr Alexandrovich summarizes the idea that devilishly torments Ivan and sporadically ensnares others as well:

> There is decidedly nothing in the whole world that would make men love their fellow men; that there exists no law of nature that man should love mankind, and that if there is and has been any love on earth up to now, it has come not from natural law but solely from people's belief in their immortality ... [W]ere mankind's belief in its immortality to be destroyed, not only love but also any living power to continue the life of the world would at once dry up in it. Not only

---

479. *Id.* at 535 (Ilyusha "had somehow managed to make friends with Smerdyakov ... [who] ... had taught the little fool a silly trick—that is, a beastly trick, a vile trick—to take a piece of bread, the soft part, stick a pin in it, and toss it to some yard dog, the kind that's so hungry it will swallow whatever it gets without chewing it ...").

480. *Id.* at 556.

481. *Id.* at 220.

482. *Id.* at 581, 83. *See also id.* at 40 (Fyodor Karamazov confesses to being a "buffoon."); *id.* at 407 (Pyotr Ilych confesses to Mitya that he stole twenty kopecks from his mother when he was nine.); *id.* at 440 (Inebriated Grushenka confesses to the partying Poles that she is "wicked" and asks for forgiveness).

483. *Id.* at 263. *See also supra* notes 340–44 and accompanying text (discussion between Ivan and Alyosha after recitation of Grand Inquisitor prose-poem); *infra* note 484 and accompanying text.

that, but then nothing would be immoral any longer, everything would be permitted, even anthropophagy.[484]

At the other end of the spectrum is what Zosima calls the "experience of active love," which he endorses:

> Try to love your neighbors actively and tirelessly. The more you succeed in loving, the more you'll be convinced of the existence of God and the immortality of your soul. And if you reach complete selflessness in the love of your neighbor, then undoubtedly you will believe, and no doubt will even be able to enter your soul.[485]

---

484. DOSTOEVSKY, *supra* note 10, at 69. *See also id.* at 82 (Rakitin discussing Ivan says, "did you hear his stupid theory just now: 'If there is no immortality of the soul, then there is no virtue, and therefore everything is permitted.'"); *id.* at 263 (Alyosha asks Ivan if he plans to "drown in depravity,..stifle [his] soul in corruption" and live as if "'everything is permitted.'"); *id.* at 313, 317 (In the "Talks and Homilies of the Elder Zosima," there is a question: "in the end man will find his joy in deeds of enlightenment and mercy alone, and not in cruel pleasures as now—in gluttony, fornication, ostentation, boasting, and envious rivalry with one another?"); *id.* at 577 (defining the insanity defense or "[a] legal fit of passion" as something "for which they forgive everything. Whatever you do—you're immediately forgiven"); *id.* at 589 (Mitya explains: "[w]ithout God and the future life? It means everything is permitted now, one can do anything?"); *id.* at 593 (Mitya, discussing Ivan with Alyosha, mentions that Ivan believes in "everything is permitted" and said that "'our papa ... was a little pig[,] but his thinking was right.'"); *id.* at 604 ("Smerdyakov even managed to insult Ivan ... in this first meeting, telling him abruptly that he was not to be suspected or questioned by those who themselves assert that 'everything is permitted.'"); *id.* at 625. (Smerdyakov says to Ivan: "[y]ou used to be brave once, sir, you used to say, 'Everything is permitted.'"); *id.* at 632 (Smerdyakov tells Ivan, "I did have ... a dream sir and even more so as 'everything is permitted'" and asks, "[y]ou yourself kept saying then that everything was permitted, so why are you so troubled now ... ? You even want to go and give evidence against yourself."); *id.* at 649 (The devil repeats "everything is permitted" and explains, "[w]here God stands—there is the place of God! Where I stand, there at once will be the foremost place ... 'everything is permitted,' and that's that!"); *id.* at 696–97 (In his speech the prosecutor says, that "Ivan ... had horrified [Mitya] with his spiritual unrestraint" and "[e]verything, according to him, is permitted ... and from now on nothing should be forbidden.").

485. *Id.* at 56. *See also id.* at 217 (Alyosha tells Lise that "we are just the same, not better," and "my elder said once that most people need to be looked after like children, and some like the sick in hospitals."); *id.* at 289 (Elder Zosima's brother realizes that "each of us is guilty before everyone, for everyone and everything," and says, "let me also be the servant of my servants, the same as they are to me."); *id.* at 298 (After striking his servant, Zosima had a question that "pierced" him: "[m]other, heart of my heart, truly each of us is guilty before everyone and for everyone, only people do not know it, and if they knew it, the world would be at once paradise."); *id.* at 303 (The "mysterious visitor" tells Zosima, "'as

For Dostoevsky, the whole object is to get from one pole to the other, to recede from "everything is permitted" and not just embrace, but actually become and be "active love."[486] In this journey alone, confession has a potentially salutary role, and can help begin to propel an individual soul from one end of the spiritual trajectory toward the other. But, contrary to one of Ivan's delusions, desire alone does not make it so. Rather, Dostoevsky (and Zosima) clarifies that active love is an "experience," and that a qualifying deed, one Grushenka calls "an onion," must requite desire.[487]

---

for each man being guilty before all and for all, beside his own sins, your reasoning about that is quite correct, and it is surprising that you could suddenly embrace this thought so fully'" and "'indeed it is true that when people understand this thought, the Kingdom of Heaven will come to them no longer in a dream but in reality.'"); *id.* at 318–19 ("Brothers, do not be afraid of men's sin, love man also in his sin, for this likeness of God's love is the height of love on earth. Love all of God's creation, both the whole of it and every grain of sand."); *id.* at 319 ("Brothers, love is a teacher, but one must know how to acquire it, for it is difficult to acquire, it is dearly bought, by long work over a long time, for one ought to love not for a chance moment but for all time."); *id.* at 520 ("There is only one salvation for you: take yourself up, and make yourself responsible for all the sins of men."); *id.* at 507 (In his epiphany dream, Mitya asks, "'why are these burnt-out mothers standing here, why are the people poor, why is the wee one poor, why is the steppe bare, why don't they embrace and kiss, why don't they sing joyful songs ... why don't they feed the wee one?'"); *id.* at 591 (Mitya explains, "'everyone is guilty for everyone else. For all the "wee ones," because there are little children and big children. All people are "wee ones."'")

486. *Id.* at 69, 56. *See also supra* notes 484–885 (giving examples of how the two polar opposite approaches to life are reiterated throughout the novel). Dostoevsky explains that he "quite share[s] the ideas that [Zosima] expresses," and adds: "if I personally were expressing them, *on my own behalf*, I would express them in a different form and a different language," but Zosima "*could not* have expressed himself in either a language or a *spirit* other than the one I gave him." Letter from Fyodor Dostoevsky to Nikolay Lyubimov (August 7, 1879), in V LETTERS, *supra* note 265, at 130–31. *See generally* Deborah A. Martinsen, *Introduction* in NOTES FROM UNDERGROUND, THE DOUBLE AND OTHER STORIES xxxvi (Barnes & Noble Books 2003) (Speaking of *Notes From Underground*, she points out that "[t]o debunk contemporary theories of rational or enlightened egoism, Dostoevsky proposes acts of love and compassion.").

487. DOSTOEVSKY, *supra* note 10, at 56 ("experience of active love") and 352 (Grushenka's "onion"). *See also supra* note 485 (giving examples of how the theme of active love runs throughout the novel); *infra* notes 488–89 and accompanying text (describing Grushenka's "onion" fable). Dostoevsky requests that Nikolay Lyubimov "specially ... do a good job of proofing the legend about the onion" and adds that "[i]t's a gem, was written down by me from the words of a peasant woman, and, of course, is *recorded for the first time.*" Letter from Fyodor Dostoevsky to Nikolay Lyubimov (Sept. 16, 1879), in V LETTERS, *supra* note 265, at 160.

In *The Brothers Karamazov*, Grushenka recalls the "onion" fable from child-hood, which is about a woman who was "wicked" to the bone.[488] After that woman died and devils tossed her into a "lake of fire," her "guardian angel" told God about her one good deed: namely, that "she once pulled up an onion and gave it to a beggar."[489] In the novel, other figurative "onions" materialize, but unlike the one in Grushenka's tale, they do not become squandered op-portunities.[490] There is the money Katerina gives to Snegiryov to compensate him for the humiliation he endured at the hands of Mitya; the consolation that Grushenka bestows on grieving Alyosha; and pancakes and salmon to be savored by mourners at Ilyusha's memorial dinner.

Incidentally, quite a few onions are those conferred on Mitya, like that pound of nuts, the kindness Mitya remembers his entire adult life, or the pil-low anonymously placed under his sleeping head after the dreadful interroga-tion. His dream of "the wee one," however, is the iconic onion, which figures prominently in Mitya's rebirth.[491] In his "strange dream," there is a "bony" woman with her breasts "all dried up, not a drop of milk in them" and a baby in her arms "crying, crying, reaching out its bare little arms, its little fists some-how all blue from the cold."[492] Mitya repeatedly asks, "[w]hy are they crying," and a peasant replies—"the wee one."[493] Once pressed, the peasant elaborates: "[t]he wee one's cold, its clothes are frozen, they don't keep it warm."[494] Like what transpired within Raskolnikov, the glacier begins to thaw and Mitya feels a "tenderness such as he has never known before surging up in his heart," which, in turn, makes him yearn to give an onion:

> He wants to do something for them all, so that the wee one will no longer
> cry, so that the blackened, dried up mother of the wee one will not cry

---

488. DOSTOEVSKY, *supra* note 10, at 352.

489. *Id.*

490. In the "onion" fable, the woman fails the test: God gives her "that same onion" and if she can hold onto it and her guardian can "pull her out of the lake, she can go to para-dise, but if the onion breaks, she can stay where she is." *Id.* When her guardian "had almost pulled her all the way out, … other sinners in the lake saw her being pulled out and all began holding on to her so as to be pulled out with her." *Id.* According to Grushenka, "the woman..[as] wicked as could be, … began to kick them with her feet: 'It's me who's getting pulled out, not you; it's my onion, not yours.'" *Id.* At this point "the onion broke[, a]nd the woman fell back into the lake and is burning there to this day." *Id.*

491. *Id.* at 507.

492. *Id.*

493. *Id.*

494. *Id.*

either, so that there will be no more tears in anyone from that moment on, and it must be done at once, at once, without delay …[495]

The dream, occurring in the wake of his confession, begins to extricate him
from "everything is permitted" and inches him a smidgeon closer to Zosima's
"experience of active love."[496] Moreover, he has an epiphany, like the one Zosima
had as a child while his brother lay dying: namely, that "we are all responsible
for everyone and everything."[497] The dream (Mitya's onion) enkindles his
"whole heart, [which] blazed up and turned toward some sort of light, and
he wanted to live and live, to go on and on along some path, towards the new
beckoning light."[498] This non-Euclidean passage, like "walking … a quadrillion
kilometers," is "incomprehensible and impossible" in an earthly tribunal.[499]

This chapter opened with Dostoevsky's near anomaly, Sonya, who, when
confronted with concrete evidence against her, does not confess.[500] Unlike
Raskolnikov, she lacks that compulsive need to self-incriminate, and unlike
the two Karamazov brothers, she is neither consumed by shame nor enduring
a prolonged dark night of the soul. Sonya, nearly *sui generis*, lacks the confessant gene, the one omnipresent in residents of Skotoprigonevsky and in just about
the entire human race. Beyond that, she intuits that the slanderer Luzhin, the
extractor Pyotor Petrovich, and the judgmental spectators have no right to
constitute her tribunal. Sonya, along with her author, knows that mortals tend
to create scandals, be they in the earthly courthouse or in the worldly parlor,
and that in such venues, confessions wreak havoc or simply come to naught.
Through silence, Sonya delivers Dostoevsky's message that mortal interrogators, judges, or juries have no business meddling in immortal affairs between
individual souls and their God.

---

495. *Id.* at 508.

496. *Id.* at 69, 56. *See also supra* notes 483–86 (giving examples of how polar opposite
philosophies are reiterated throughout the novel.).

497. *See generally* Ralph E. Matlaw, *On Translating* The Brothers Karmazov, DOSTO-
EVSKY, *supra* note 93, at 671, 672 ("Since the leading idea of the novel is that we are all responsible for everyone and everything, it would not have done to translate the word
'responsible' as 'guilty,' for that would both limit the meaning and introduce an unwarranted
legal note, perhaps also a more specifically psychiatric connotation than Dostoevsky may
have intended."). *See also* DOSTOEVSKY, *supra* note 10, at 289 (The dying brother speaks:
"you must know that verily each of us is guilty before everyone, for everyone and everything.
I do not know how to explain it to you, but I feel it so strongly that it pains me.").

498. DOSTOEVSKY, *supra* note 10, at 508.

499. *Id.* at 644, 686. *See also supra* note 451 and accompanying text (describing Judge's
reaction to Ivan's confessional testimony).

500. *See supra* note 1.

Chapter Four

Prisons of Coercion: *Notes from The House of the Dead*

I. Introduction

In Fyodor Dostoevsky's *Notes from the House of the Dead* (*Dead House*),[1] officials flog prisoners to the brink of death in calculated intervals:

> If the crime entailed a large number of strokes, so many that the victim could not take them all at once, the flogging divided into two or even three parts, depending on the doctor's opinion, once the flogging had got under way, as to whether the man would be able to go on walking up and down the line, or whether this would put his life at risk. Sentences of five hundred, a thousand or even fifteen hundred strokes were normally taken in one go; but if the sentence called for two or three thousand, its execution would be divided into two or even three parts.[2]

The beating "hurts like nothing on earth" and "feels like a fire burning you … as if your back [is] being roasted in the hottest of fires."[3]

Although Dostoevsky created a fictional narrator, Aleksandr Petrovich Goryanchikov, to depict life (or rather non-life) in Dead House, the novel is

---

1. FYODOR DOSTOEVSKY, THE HOUSE OF THE DEAD (David McDuff, trans. 2003) (1862) [hereinafter DEAD HOUSE]. Whenever the author is referring to the novel, she will use the italicized *Dead House*. When, however, she is referring to the prison itself, she will use the unitalicized version—Dead House. This chapter is a substantially revised and expanded version of Amy D. Ronner, *Recreating Dead House: The Ouster of* Miranda *from our Prisons*, originally published in 50 CRIMINAL LAW BULLETIN 1 (2014)(with permission of Thomson Reuters).

2. *Id.* at 239–40.

3. *Id.* at 241.

definitely autobiographical.[4] After Nicholas I commuted Dostoevsky's death sentence to a term of hard labor and exile in Siberia, Dostoevsky served his time and eventually returned to St. Petersburg.[5] In the aftermath, he published *Dead House*, his account of life in a Siberian prison. While throughout his career, Dostoevsky displayed brilliant insight into the workings of criminal justice and the psyches of people, who either commit crimes or are punished for crimes they did not commit,[6] there is nothing more penetrating, intense, and rattling than his *Dead House*: it foists us, as readers, into the confines of Omsk prison and forces us to reside in fetters, in close proximity with ordinary and political offenders.[7]

Dostoevsky's novel takes place in the mid-nineteenth century in a remote region of Russia and we, as readers, tend to comfort ourselves with its temporal

---

4. *See* Joseph Frank, Dostoevsky: A Writer in His Time 185–222 (2010) (describing the four years Dostoevsky spent in prison camp and how it shaped *Dead House*); John Jones, Dostoevsky 129–71 (2002) (discussing how *Dead House* is far more autobiographical than Dostoevsky's other fiction); Nancy Ruttenburg, Dostoevsky's Democracy (2008) (discussing how the Siberian prison inspired *Dead House* and affected Dostoevsky's philosophy and view of society). *See also* David McDuff, *Translator's Introduction*, Dead House, *supra* note 1, at 15 (explaining how *Dead House* is "essentially autobiographical reminiscence").

5. *See generally supra* Chapter I (Inexpressible Ideas: A Multifaceted Life and Legal Lens) (summarizing Dostoevsky's life and the events that precipitated his arrest). *See also* Frank, *supra* note 4, at 129–44 (describing Dostoevsky's involvement in the Petrashevsky Circle, which brought about his arrest); *id.* at 174 ("Dostoevsky, initially condemned to eight years of hard labor instead of outright execution, enjoyed a reduction in his period of penal servitude to four years, after which he was ordered to serve in the Russian Army for an indeterminate time.")

6. *See generally supra* note 4 (various commentators discussing the impact prison camp had on Dostoevsky and how it shaped his understanding of convicts and others). *See also* Amy D. Ronner, Law Literature, and Therapeutic Jurisprudence 89–149 (2010) (analyzing Dostoevsky's insights into criminals, convicts, and confessions); William Burnham, *The Legal Context and Contributions of Dostoevsky's Crime and Punishment*, 100 Mich. L. Rev. 1227, 1228–29 ("[T]e experience in Siberia threw [Dostoevsky] together for several years with a wide variety of ordinary and political offenders. This experience undoubtedly informed him well and piqued his curiosity about the nature of both crime and its punishment."); McDuff, *supra* note 4, at 7 (noting that Dostoevsky wrote to his brother Mikhail, "I had got to know something of the convict population back in Tobolsk; here in Omsk I was to live for four years in close proximity to it" and discussing how Tolstoy considered *Dead House* "the finest work in all of modern Russian literature"). *See also infra* notes 342–43 and accompanying text (Dostoevsky acknowledged that there were innocent men in prison, and gave as an example the nobleman who, after serving ten years, turned out to be innocent when the true perpetrators came forth.).

7. *See infra* Part II (describing the attributes of Dostoevsky's Dead House).

and geographical distance. That is, we handle the prison atrocities and horrors by telling ourselves, at least on an unconscious level, that it all happened way back when and that Siberia, so many light years away, could almost be another planet. If, however, we are gritty enough to banish denial, we likely know in our heart of hearts that Dostoevsky has a salient message, one which pertains to today and the very prisons in our own backyard.

On its broadest level, this chapter aims to show how the United States Supreme Court is effectually recreating Dead House through its post-*Miranda* decisions.[8] The chapter, divided into six parts, builds to an exploration of recent confession decisions, like *Maryland v. Shatzer*[9] and *Howes v. Fields*,[10] and their impact on prison inmates. It aims to reveal how the Supreme Court condones and even promotes tactics that resemble the dehumanization that once presided over Dostoevsky's notorious torture chamber.

Part II begins with *Dead House* itself, anatomizing the prison environment that conspires to strip Siberian inmates of free will and human dignity. Dostoevsky's Dead House is a hell, comprised of excessive regulation, coercion, and futility. Its inhabitants endure prolonged cognitive dissonance, in which they are lonely, but never alone. Compounding that, prisoners are fettered, sometimes chained to the wall, and redundantly lashed in a manner preordained to pulverize body and soul.

Part III, shifting from Dostoevsky's Russia to the United States, reviews the rise and fall of free will and human dignity under seminal Due Process Clause and the *Miranda* cases. This part briefly revisits the policies behind early landmark cases, along with *Miranda* itself, to show how the Court once aspired to safeguard our fair accusatorial process, distinguish our system from those of less civilized nations, and maximize respect for the individual. It also summarizes the progressive dismemberment of *Miranda*, which denigrates the very goals behind its once sacrosanct protections. It is significant that the interrogations in those decisions obliterating *Miranda* do not transpire in prison, where the Fifth Amendment and its prophylactic safeguards are absolutely essential.

Part IV examines the cases that do take place within the prison and discusses how the Supreme Court, at least initially, deemed inmates entitled to the paltry remnants of the *Miranda* safeguards. From there, the chapter summa-

---

8. Miranda v. Arizona, 384 U.S. 436 (1966). *See also infra* Parts III and IV (analyzing *Miranda*, and decisions in its wake which essentially demolished it).

9. Maryland v. Shatzer, 559 U.S. 98 (2010). *See infra* Parts IV. B and V (discussing *Shatzer*).

10. Howes v. Fields, 132 S. Ct. 1181 (2012). *See infra* Parts IV. C and V (discussing *Fields*).

rizes the more recent decisions, *Shatzer* and *Fields*, which have the combined effect of expelling *Miranda* from our prisons.[11]

Part V, taking the next step, juxtaposes *Shatzer* and *Fields* with *Dead House* in an attempt to show how these decisions implicitly commend the conditions that made Dostoevsky's Siberia into Dead House hell. Through its effectual overruling of *Miranda*, along with its total ouster from our prisons, the Supreme Court, in fact, invites the intensification of Dead House elements, like regulation, coercion, and futility. The Court encourages tactics that exploit the prisons' paradoxical loneliness with no aloneness and endorses a species of torture that resembles the Siberian lashings.

Part VI, the Conclusion, revisiting the overarching thesis in Dostoevsky's *Dead House*, discloses how the effects of the Supreme Court's post-*Miranda* prison decisions are not confined to our penal system. Rather, they transmit a message, which imprisons, detriments, and flogs us all.

II. *Dead House*: Stripped of Free Will and Human Dignity

When Dostoevsky entered prison at Omsk, Western Siberia, to begin his four-year term of penal servitude, he felt like he was being buried alive. After release, Dostoevsky wrote to his younger brother, Andrey:

> And those 4 years, I consider a time during which I was buried alive and locked up in a coffin. I can't even tell you, my friend, what a horrible time that was. It was inexpressible, unending suffering, because every hour, every minute weighed on my soul like a stone.[12]

It was not just physical discomfort that plagued Dostoevsky. What compounded his agony was that rules and regulations dictated every facet of day and night. These rules forbade the possession of books (except for the Bible) and imposed the most draconian prohibition on the Russian novelist: he was barred from writing.[13] Despite being divested of his *raison d'etre*, Dostoevsky

---

11. *See supra* notes 9 & 10 (referring to analysis of the ouster of *Miranda* from prison); *supra* part IV (discussing the prison cases).

12. Letter From Fyodor Dostoevsky to Andrey Dostoevsky November 6, 1854) in I Dostoevsky Letters (1832–1859), at 20 (David Lowe and Ronald Meyer, eds., Ardis Publishers 1988) [hereinafter I Letters].

13. *See* Dostoevsky, *supra* note 1, at 137 (Goryanchikov describes how his only book, *The Bible*, was stolen from him by another convict, who secretly sold it to buy vodka).

conceived of *Dead House* while in prison. Apparently, during a hospital stay, Dr. Troitsky let Dostoevsky jot notes and these, mingled with memories, were later woven into the autobiographical masterpiece.[14] In *Dead House*, we share Dostoevsky's observations of human beings gutted of free will and human dignity. In short, the Russian author gives us a guided tour through hell and parses the formula that makes hell a hell.

A. No Free Will

In *Dead House*, inmates are systematically stripped of free will, a process that Dostoevsky distills into three elements: excessive regulation, coercion, and futility.

Possibly because Dostoevsky was unable to confront such unspeakable pain by writing his novel in the first person, he created his fictitious narrator, former inmate Goryanchikov, a nobleman, who had murdered his wife out of jealousy.[15] Through Goryanchikov, Dostoevsky artfully paints a dismal picture of the physical plant, which serves as the objective correlative of the misery housed within:

> Imagine a large courtyard, two hundred yards long and a hundred and fifty yards wide, completely enclosed all round by a high stockade in the form of an irregular hexagon, that is a fence of high posts (pales), driven vertically deep into the earth, wedged closely against one another in ribs, strengthened by cross-planks and sharpened on

---

14. *See* McDuff, *supra* note 4, at 2–3 (discussing how Dostoevsky started planning the novel while he was still in prison, and how the kindly hospital doctor facilitated the process); FRANK, *supra* note 4, at 193–94 (describing how Dostoevsky "would have suffered more if not for the kindness of the head of the fortress hospital, Dr. Troitsky" and how Dostoevsky "kept a notebook in the hospital in which he jotted down phrases and expressions"). LINDA IVANITS, DOSTOEVSKY AND THE RUSSIAN PEOPLE 39 (Cambridge Univ. Press 2008) ("Though Dostoevsky was not permitted to write while in prison, thanks to the good auspices of Doctor Troitsky and his assistant A.I. Ivanov, during his stays in the hospital he managed to compile a notebook of roughly 500 popular sayings and turns of speech that caught his attentive ear.").

15. *See* McDuff, *supra* note 4, at 14 ("The intensity of the suffering undergone by the writer seems to have been such that he was unable to approach its recollection in personal terms" and "[i]n order to write his memories down, he had to construct a 'novel,' with a fictitious narrator-hero.") *But see* FRANK, *supra* note 4, at 364 ("The more convincing accepted view is that Dostoevsky introduced Goryanchikov primarily as a means of avoiding trouble with the censorship, and that he did not expect his readers to take him as more than a convenient device.").

top: this was the outer enclosure of the prison. In one of the sides of the enclosure a sturdily constructed gate was set; this was always kept closed and was guarded by sentries at every hour of the day and night; it was opened on demand in order to let men out to work.[16]

The prison, with its courtyards, enclosures, stockades, pales, cross-planks, gates, guards, and sentries, governed by "[its] own laws, [its] own dress, [its] own manners and customs," contrasts with "the bright world of freedom where people live like everyone else."[17] Dostoevsky, moreover, clarifies that it is not just the facade that makes this "the house of the living dead."[18] It is the Dead House trilogy that conspires to pulverize the human spirit.

One, there is copious regulation. Goryanchikov tells us that the real "enclosure with a sturdily constructed gate" is the fact that "no one dared to rebel against the endogenous and accepted rules of the prison; everyone submitted to them."[19] It is a venue where "[s]earches were frequent, unexpected and no joking matter," and where "punishments were severe."[20] This tends to seemingly tame all, including the most vicious, violent, and unruly:

> There were violently unusual characters, who submitted with difficulty and effort, but submit they did, nevertheless. To the prison came men who had gone too far, had overstepped the limit when they had been free, so that in the end it was as if their crimes had not been committed by them personally, as if they had committed them without knowing why, as if in some fever or daze, often out of vanity, raised in them to an extraordinary degree. But in our prison they were soon brought to heel, in spite of the fact that some of them, before they came here, had been the terror of whole villages and towns.[21]

The narrator does not equate submission with rehabilitation or repentance: the doomed "gathered together ... against their will," working under the "threat of the stick," without "the slightest trace of repentance [and] not one sign that their crime weighed heavily on their conscience."[22] Goryanchikov stresses that if the inmates "had not been depraved before they came to prison, they be-

---

16. DOSTOEVSKY, *supra* note 1, at 27.

17. *Id.*

18. *Id.*

19. *Id.* at 27, 32.

20. *Id.* at 35.

21. *Id.* at 32–33.

22. *Id.* at 33, 35.

came so here."[23] Rules, punishments, and other practices, including forced labor and solitary confinement, "achieve only a spurious, deceptive, external goal" and "suck[] the vital sap from a man, enervate[] his soul, weaken[] it, intimidate[] it and then present[] the withered mummy, the semi-lunatic as a model of reform and repentance."[24] The narrator explains that, out of the blue, an inmate, even a model one, will just snap, explode in rage, and embark on a violent rampage.[25]

Two, Dead House is all about coercion that expunges life even more efficiently than the barrage of despotic rules. In one of the most haunting parts of the novel, Goryanchikov, contemplating the impact of penal labor, attributes misery not to the unalleviated difficulty of the task itself, but to the fact of "its being *forced*, compulsory, done under the threat of the stick."[26] He elaborates:

> It is probable that the peasant in freedom works incomparably harder and longer, sometimes even at night, especially in the summer; but he works on his own account, with a reasonable end in view, and this makes it far easier for him than for the convict with his work that is compulsory and quite without use to him.[27]

Not only are prisoners required to endure penal labor in cumbersome fetters, but endemic to Dead House is another facet of coercion, which is "more

---

23. *Id.* at 33.

24. *Id.* at 36.

25. *See id.* at 35 ("[A] convict is obedient and submissive to a certain degree; ... there is no phenomenon more curious than these strange outbursts of impatience and obstinacy. Often a man will suffer in patience for several years, resign himself, endure the most savage punishments, and then suddenly erupt over some trifle, some piece of nonsense, almost over nothing at all. In one view, he may be termed insane; and is indeed considered so by many."). *See also id.* at 59 (Although Gazin is "quiet when he's sober[,] when he gets drunk it all comes out; he goes for people with a knife."); *id.* at 79 ("Reduced to the last stages of terror by the punishment that awaited him, ... the day before he was to run the gauntlet he took a knife and went for the duty officer who had entered his barrack."); *id.* at 110 ("The prison administrators are sometimes surprised that one convict or another can have lived quietly for several years, a model of good behavior, even being made a head prisoner for good conduct, when suddenly for no apparent reason whatever—as if the devil had got into him—he starts to behave waywardly, to go on binges, get mixed up in brawls, and sometimes even takes the risk of committing a criminal offense.").

26. *Id.* at 43.

27. *Id.*

powerful than all of the others"—namely *"forced communal existence."*[28] Incarcerated in choiceless fraternity, "human beings are herded together by force, against their will," and this breeds hatred, enmity, and violence.[29] Here there is no egress: resistance can only trigger more penalties, aggravate coercion, and expedite inevitable despair.

Three, futility mingles with drudgery, menacing the only glimmer that sustains these men—namely, hope. Goryanchikov tells us that from day one, he "began to dream about freedom."[30] For him, it "became [his] favourite occupation to calculate, using a thousand different measurements and methods, how long it would be before my years of imprisonment were over."[31] Admitting that he didn't know whether "other convicts thought and calculated" in that exact way, what struck Goryanchikov as universal was "the astonishing lightheadedness of their hopes."[32]

Goryanchikov likens most Dead House hopes to pipe dreams. By way of example, there is prisoner Nurra, one of the Caucasian mountain tribesmen, who survives on a diet of hope. He was "resolutely convinced that when he had served out his prison sentence he would be returned to his home in the Caucasus, and he lived in the hopeful expectation of that day."[33] Goryanchikov acknowledges that if Nurra "had been deprived of this hope he would have died."[34] There are others, incarcerated for the most heinous offenses, who, surviving for five to ten years literally chained to a wall, relentlessly ponder mirages of relative reprieve. These were men who knew full well that when they were "released from their chains," they would be kept in prison "for the rest of their days, until they died, wearing fetters."[35] If, however, these prisoners had been stripped of this one prospect of promotion to mere fetter-status and their goal of "serv[ing] out their enchainment as quickly as possible," they would "die or go out of their minds."[36]

---

28. *Id.* at 44.

29. *Id.* at 325.

30. *Id.* at 127.

31. *Id. Cf.* Letter from Fyodor Dostoevsky to Mikhail Dostoevsky (December 22, 1849) in I. LETTERS, *supra* note 12, at 179 ("[T]o be a human being among people and to remain one forever, no matter in what circumstances, not to grow despondent and not to lose heart—that's what life is all about, that's its task.")

32. DOSTOEVSKY, *supra* note 1, at 127.

33. *Id.* at 87.

34. *Id.*

35. *Id.* at 128.

36. *Id.* at 128–29.

Dostoevsky's narrator knows that "[n]o man can live without some goal to aspire towards," and "[i]f he loses his goal, his hope, the resultant anguish will frequently turn him into a monster."[37] By way of example, there is "the old man from the Starodubye settlements" with "tell-tale signs" that his "inner state of mind was atrocious," who, praying feverishly, became obsessed with the "idea of martyrdom."[38] Another "who had given up every last hope[,] ... who went mad, who used to read the Bible and went for the Major with a brick," ended up replacing hope with a "voluntary, almost artificial martyrdom."[39] He rationalized that "he had gone for the Major quite without malice, solely out of a desire to take suffering upon himself."[40] It is apparent that quashed dreams morph into madness or death.

In the novel, Dostoevsky seamlessly transitions from a central motif, the life raft of hope, to its very nemesis—futility. As biographer Joseph Frank explains, this is a signature Dostoevsky technique:

> Dostoevsky's imagination at this point could not resist taking the eschatological leap that was to become so characteristic for him—the leap to the end condition of whatever empirical situation he is considering—and so, in order to dramatize the supreme importance of hope for human life, he deliberately *invents* a situation in which it is systematically destroyed.[41]

Here, Goryanchikov explores what it is that deflates hope and defeats the human spirit:

> The thought once occurred to me that if one wanted to crush and destroy a man entirely, to mete out to him the most terrible punishment, one at which the most fearsome murderer would tremble, shrinking from it in advance, all one would have to do would be to make him do work that was completely and utterly devoid of usefulness and meaning ... [I]f, let us say, he was forced to pour water from one tub

---

37. *Id.* at 305. *See also* RUTTENBURG, *supra* note 4, at 56 ("[H]ope is the expression of a futile dream of freedom that for the prisoner's sake must be viciously suppressed yet cannot be completely extinguished without risking an extinction of the self.").

38. DOSTOEVSKY, *supra* note 1, at 305. *See also id.* at 94 (Calling the "old man from the Starodubye settlement" an "assiduous and dogmatic[] literal reader[] of the Bible.")

39. *Id.*

40. *Id.*

41. FRANK, *supra* note 4, at 219.

into another and back again, time after time, to pound sand, to carry a heap of soil from one spot to another and back again—I think that such a convict would hang himself within a few days or commit a thousand offences in order to die, to escape from such degradation, shame and torment.[42]

While Goryanchikov finds prison work "reasonable enough," with some "purpose," he knows that it still has that Sisyphean quality due to the fact that it is coerced.[43] As he says, since "there is an element of this kind of torture, pointlessness, degradation and shame in all forced labour, the work that convicts do is vastly more unpleasant than any work done in freedom, simply because it is forced."[44] For Dostoevsky, debasing futility leads to despair. Frank, commenting on this portion of the novel, says that "[n]ot to believe in God and immortality, for the later Dostoevsky, is to be condemned to live in an ultimately senseless universe, and the characters in his great novels who reach this level of self-awareness inevitably destroy themselves because, refusing to endure the moment of living without hope, they have become monsters in their misery."[45]

Dead House meaninglessness, however, is more abysmal than forces that poison other Dostoevsky characters, like, inter alia, Kirillov, Stavrogin, Smerdyakov, Svidrigailov, and Nastasya, who are catapulted toward possible or actual suicides.[46] At least, in other masterpieces, the "condemned" struggle,

---

42. Dostoevsky, *supra* note 1, at 43. *See also* James E. Robertson, *Houses of the Dead: Warehouse Prisons, Paradigm Change, and the Supreme Court*, 34 Hous. L. Rev. 1003, 1004–1005 (1997) (explaining how "[m]any contemporary prisons do little more than warehouse their human residents by subjecting them to coerced and regimented idleness[,]" which "denies [them] a humane and productive purpose.").

43. Dostoevsky, *supra* note 1, at 43. In Greek mythology, Sisyphus was once King of Corinth, who was punished in Hades for betraying a secret of Zeus, and thus sentenced to forever roll a stone up a hill, only to have it roll back down. *See generally* Edith Hamilton, Mythology 298 (1969). *See also* The Ultimate Encyclopedia of Mythology 83 (1999) ("Zeus ... condemned Sisyphus to Tartarus to pay for his lifelong impiety" and "[f]or the rest of eternity he had to roll a block of stone to the top of a hill only to see it roll back again as it reached the crest."). *But see* Albert Camus, *The Myth of Sisyphus*, Albert Camus, The Myth of Sisyphus and Other Essays, 1, 91 (1955) ("Each atom of that stone, each mineral flake of that night-filled mountain, in itself forms a world. The struggle itself toward the heights is enough to fill a man's heart. One must imagine Sisyphus happy.").

44. Dostoevsky, supra note 1, at 43–44.

45. Frank, *supra* note 4, at 219–20.

46. *See* Fyodor Dostoevsky, Demons (Richard Pevear and Larissa Volokhonsky, trans., 1995) (1871–72) (Kirillov, along with Stavrogin, a conceivable pedophile and sadist, are characters in the novel); Fyodor Dostoevsky, The Brothers Karamazov (Richard Pevear and Larissa Volokhonsky, trans., 1990) (1879–1880) (Smerdyakov, the illegitimate son,

grapple with theodicy, and make choices.[47] That is, each in their own way navigate their course, even if their free will becomes lethal or concentrically spirals them into an inferno.[48] In contrast, Dead House tenants, coerced and chained to futility, do not get to choose or navigate, but instead push inane boulders up futile mountains, only to have them tumble down again and again.[49] This, for Dostoevsky, is the pit, the hell of a non-life, one "completely and utterly devoid of usefulness and meaning."[50]

---

and character in novel); FYODOR DOSTOEVSKY, CRIME AND PUNISHMENT (David McDuff ed., 2003) (1866) (Svidrigailov, a sociopathic landowner, who commits suicide) FYODOR DOSTOEVSKY, THE IDIOT (David McDuff, ed., 2004) (1868) (Nastasya, one of Prince Myshkin's two loves). *See also* Fyodor Dostoevsky, *A Gentle Creature* in GREAT SHORT WORKS OF FYODOR DOSTOEVSKY , 667-714 (George Bird et al. eds., 1968) (1876) [hereinafter GREAT SHORT WORKS] (The young seamstress, despairing about her life on earth, jumps to her death from a window.); Fyodor Dostoevsky, *The Dream of a Ridiculous Man*, in *id.* (1877), at 717–38 (Character becomes obsessed by the thought of suicide.). *See generally* FRANK, *supra* note 4, at 581 (describing Nastasya's "suicidal flight with Rogozhin" and "[a] mysterious coda to her tragic destiny provided by Myshkin's finding a copy of *Madame Bovary* in her abandoned rooms, the tale of another hopeless suicide ..."); Yannis Kakridis, *Smerdjakov's Suicide Note*, 14 DOSTOEVSKY STUD. 145 (2010) (discussing the "well-calculated ambiguity in Smerdjakov's [suicide] note").

47. *See supra* note 46 and accompanying text. *See also* FRANK, *supra* note 4, at 868–69 (discussing Ivan Karamazov's "searing indictment of God" and how he "does not believe in God as more than a hypothesis"); *supra* Chapter III (The Confessant Gene: *Crime and Punishment* and *The Brothers Karamazov*) (analyzing Ivan Karamazov's spiritual struggle); RONNER, *supra* note 6 (describing Raskolnikov's struggle before, during, and after the crime, and his eventual spiritual regeneration).

48. *See supra* notes 46–47. *But see* FRANK, *supra* note 4, at 663 ("Nor is Kirillov's eerie death the triumphant assertion of a total self-will; it is, rather the demented act of a crazed and terrified subhuman creature" and "[l]ike Raskolnikov's crime, Kirillov's suicide is the self-negation and self-refutation of his own grandiose ideas.").

49. *See supra* note 43 (discussing Sisyphus and his eternal punishment).

50. DOSTOEVSKY, *supra* note 1, at 43. *See also id.* at 304–05 ("The good-natured convicts—a tiny bunch—kept quiet, nursed their hopes to themselves, and were, needless to say, more inclined than the morose ones to believe in the possibility of their realization. But it seemed to me that there was yet another category of convicts; the ones who had given up all hope."). *Cf.* MIKHAIL BAKHTIN, PROBLEMS OF DOSTOEVSKY'S POETICS 172 (Caryl Emerson, ed. & trans., 1984) ("Juxtapos[ing] the game of roulette [in *The Gambler*] with penal servitude [in *Dead House*]," he states that "[b]oth the life of convicts and the life of gamblers—for all their differences in content—are equally 'life taken out of life' (that is, taken out of common, ordinary life) ... [a]nd the *time* of penal servitude and the *time* of gambling are—for all their profound differences—an identical *type of time*, similar to the 'final moments of consciousness' before execution or suicide, similar in general to the time of crisis.").

B. No Human Dignity

In Dead House, a paradoxical form of solitude, along with restraints and redundant torture, strips prisoners of all vestiges of human dignity.

It is not just "forced communal existence" that torments inmates, but the fact that they must suffer relentless contradiction—loneliness with no aloneness.[51] Goryanchikov describes his barracks, crammed with assorted inhabitants. Along with the "dogmatically literal readers of the Bible,"[52] like the old man from the Starodubye settlement, there were:

> Two or three Ukranians, dreary men; a young convict with a thin face and a thin nose, aged about twenty-three, who had already murdered eight people; a group of forgers, one of whom was the life and soul of the whole barrack; and finally a few gloomy, morose individuals who were unshaven and disfigured, close-jawed and envious, looked distrustfully and with hatred around them, and did so intentionally; who would remain frowning, close-jawed and full of hatred for long years to come—for the entire duration of their imprisonment.[53]

For Goryanchikov, such bunkmates blend with the backdrop of omnipresent fear "smoke and soot, ... foul air, ... clanking of fetters, curses and shameless laughter," and there is no exit.[54] Goryanchikov finds it unprecedented to be assigned a society in which it is next to impossible to grab a snippet of alone time or sit silently with the clamor of one's own thoughts:

> I could never have conceived how terrible and agonizing it would be not once, not even for one minute of all the ten years of my imprisonment, to be alone. At work to be constantly under guard, in the barracks to be with two hundred other convicts and not once, never once to be alone! [55]

---

51. Dostoevsky, *supra* note 1, at 44.
52. *Id.* at 94.
53. *Id.*
54. *Id.* at 78. *See also id.* ("The fear that convicts inspire is to be found wherever there are convicts ... Every convict, no matter how bold and cheeky, is afraid of everything in prison.").
55. *Id.* at 30. *See also* Letter from Fyodor Dostoevsky to Natalya Fonvizina (January 1854) in I LETTERS, *supra* note 12, at 195 ("I haven't been alone for a single hour. To be alone is a normal need, like drinking and eating, otherwise in this forced communism you'll become a misanthrope."); Letter from Fyodor Dostoevsky to Mikhail Dostoevsky (July 30, 1854), in *id.* at 199 ("I live here in solitude; as is my custom, I hide from people ... I was

But this is not the whole problem. Pitted against this unrequited lust for solitude is an equal and opposite, but just as unsated, craving for communion with another being. Goryanchikov's isolation is, of course, exacerbated by his nobleman status, which automatically alienates him from the peasants, commoners, and those of Russia's lower castes.[56] He realizes that, no matter what he does, the "gentleman" will never be considered by these others as "one of *their own*."[57] He grasps that, "[n]o matter how fair-minded, good-natured and intelligent he is, the other convicts will continue to hate and despise him for years on end ... [and h]e will never be their friend and companion."[58]

While Goryanchikov's rank erects an extra bulwark between him and others, all residents endure partitions and loneliness. Throughout the novel, we see inmates, famished for friendship, trying desperately, through blurting confessions or straining conversation, to be heard and forge connection.[59] These

---

under guard for five years, and therefore it's the greatest pleasure for me to find myself alone sometimes.")

56. DEAD HOUSE, *supra* note 1, at 305 ("I found at the beginning of my time in the prison that I was unable to penetrate the inner fabric of this life, and was indeed incapable of doing so ... I sometimes found myself hating these fellow-sufferers of mine ... [and] I envied them because they were among their own kind, were companions to another and understood one another ..."). *See also* Letter from Fyodor Dostoevsky to Mikhail Dostoevsky (January 30, 1854) in I LETTERS, *supra* note 12, at 186 ("They are coarse people, irritable and spiteful. Their hatred of the nobility exceeds all bounds."); Letter from Fyodor Dostoevsky to Eduard Totleben (March 24, 1856), in *id.* at 251 ("I did not see and could not see for all of these 4 years anything cheerful, besides the blackest, most hideous reality. I had not a single being at my side with whom I could exchange even a single sincere word ... and ... my thieving comrades ... took vengeance because I was from the nobility and an officer.").

57. DEAD HOUSE, *supra* note 1, at 307.

58. *Id. See also* RUTTENBURG, *supra* note 4, at 44 (describing Goryanchikov as "[e]ntirely cut off from his former life as a nobleman and landowner" and as "existing in a state of oppositional solitude ... utterly estranged from those around him and thus as disarticulated from the social body").

59. While in Dead House it is apparently taboo for inmates to discuss their crimes, they tend to do that anyway and divulge all kinds of personal information. *See e.g.*, DOSTOEVSKY, *supra* note 1, at 37 (A man, falsely accused of parricide, talked about his father, and the "healthy constitution that was hereditary in his family."); *id.* at 51–52 (Russian nobleman, who "lost no time in telling [Goryanchikov] about his case"); *id.* at 90 (Aley goes on about his mother: "Oh, what are you saying? She's probably died of a broken heart thinking about me by now. I was her favourite son."); *id.* at 141 (Goryanchikov "lay idly and miserably on [his] plank bed" and heard the "story ... about how this man ... for no other reason but his own satisfaction, had *wiped out* a certain major."); *id.* at 159 (Inmate Baklushin tells the story of murder and how in the "middle of a [love] affair [he] did shoot one of the Ger-

men, pushed together and never alone, relish the chance to ritualistically bond in the bath house or embrace the reprieve of a collective Christmas festivity.[60] These are humans, who ache with chronic cognitive dissonance, where, on the one hand, they hunger to escape "forced communal existence," and, on the other hand, are famished for companionship.[61] Because of the very nature of the Siberian prison, neither antipodal craving can ever be appeased. In essence, loneliness with no aloneness is a genotype of torture, which conceivably extracts as much (if not more) pain than fetters, chains, or even the dreaded birch.

There exist other Dead House indignities, which exceed what Goryanchikov euphemizes as "discomforts," like "the filthiness of one's living conditions, the iron grip of one's captors, ... the meager, ill-prepared food" and "soup with cockroaches floating in it."[62] These are physical oppressors, like the fetters, which

---

mans...with a pistol."); *id.* at 179–82 (Varlamov tells his life story while being followed by "a tiny convict with a large head," who keeps interrupting and saying " '[w]hatever he says, he's lying, lying, lying."); *id.* at 258–69 (While in the hospital, Goryanchikov hears the story of Akulka's husband, and how a man tortures and murders his wife.); *id.* at 285–86 (The Lomovs, accused of killing their farmhands, "themselves told the story, and the whole prison knew it.")

60. In the "cramped" bath house, Goryanchikov describes how Petrov "did not leave [his] side," and "without [his] having to ask…, leapt to [his] assistance and even offered to wash [him]. "*Id.* at 153. Goryanchikov elaborates:

> When he finished washing me, he delivered me back to the antechamber…, supporting me and warning me at every step as if I were made of porcelain; he helped me to put on my underwear, and only when he had quite finished with me did he rush back into the bath to steam himself.

Id. at 157. Also, in Dead House, there are Christmas festivities, along with a stage show, in which the men become friendly, civil, and considerate. Goryanchikov remarks:

> All that was needed was for these poor men to be allowed to live in their own way for a bit, to enjoy themselves like human beings, to escape from their convict existence just for an hour or so—and each individual underwent a moral transformation, even if it only lasted for a few moments.

Id. at 203.

61. *Id.* at 44. *See also* JONES, *supra* note 4, at 145 (Dostoevsky's "[p]rison life, imagined and realized, sometimes contracts into absolute embattled solitude.")

62. DEAD HOUSE, *supra* note 1, at 307. *See also* Letter from Fyodor Dostoevsky to Mikhail Dostoevsky (January 30, 1854) in I LETTERS, *supra* note 12, at 187 (describing the physical discomforts in which his "foot got frostbitten," he "lived in a heap, all together, in one barracks," in which "in the summer the stuffiness is unbearable, in the winter the cold beyond enduring," and they were "like herring in a barrel," where "there's no room to turn around[,] ... [and a]ll prisoners stink like pigs ... shiver the whole night" with "[m]ountains of fleas, lice, and cockroaches").

literally thwart mobility. The mandatory fetters, affixed upon arrival, are "regarded ... as an accomplished fact with which it was useless to argue" and "after a few years of wearing [them,] a man's legs begin to wither."[63] Each convict had to buy at his own expense accessory straps, which were vital, because without them, it was impossible to walk: "the iron ring knocks and rubs against one's ankle, and in one day a convict without fetter straps can rub his legs raw."[64]

Oddly enough, Siberian fetters accomplish nothing. They do not even purport to block escape, but are affixed solely as a "public dishonor, a disgrace, and a shameful physical and moral burden."[65] Even those inmates, apoplectic, with spindly legs, who lay dying in the hospital, remain fettered until officials excise the bonds from their naked corpses.[66] As already mentioned, there were prisoners who actually craved betterment by donning the fetters, because they had to live like beasts on "seven-foot-long chains."[67] While all Dead House restraints maul flesh, they are most adept at digging deeper, at gouging psyche and soul.

Dead House floggings are so graphic that readers either recoil or skip pages. Here, punishment methodically includes psychological stress through anticipation, hiatus, and redundancy. Specifically, before flogging, there is "pre-sentence detention," in which officials stick the men in the guardhouse, creating a vigil which is "much worse than prison itself."[68] Goryanchikov explains that the period "before a beating or flogging is a cruel one, so cruel that [he is] perhaps wrong to call this fear faintheartedness and cowardice."[69] Goryanchikov recalls men "who themselves asked to be discharged as soon as possible, even though their backs had not yet healed from the first part of their punishment, in order to receive the rest of their strokes and thus be released from pre-sentence

---

63. DEAD HOUSE, *supra* note 1, at 219. *See* Letter from Fyodor Dostoevsky to Mikhail Dostoevsky (January 30, 1854) in I LETTERS, *supra* note 12, at 184 ("I put on irons for the first time. They weighed about 10 pounds and it was extraordinarily awkward walking.").

64. DOSTOEVSKY, *supra* note 1, at 153–54.

65. *Id.* at 220.

66. Goryanchikov points out that "[e]ven the consumptive patients died before my very eyes wearing their fetters," and that the officials would only remove the fetters from one consumptive patient, Mikhailov, after he was dead. *Id.* at 219. Goryanchikov recalls the "fetters ... jangling on the floor amidst the silence, still attached to the dead man," and the "duty sergeant ... sending someone off to get the smith" so that the "corpse would have its fetters removed." *Id.* at 222–23.

67. *Id.* at 128.

68. *Id.* at 228.

69. *Id.*

detention."[70] Also, as mentioned above, officers mete out beatings in intervals to allow for a little healing, and then start anew, while flesh is still raw and afire. Hospital doctors, standing by, signal when the victim verges on death:

> Those men, once their backs had healed after the first part of their sentence, left hospital in order to receive its second part, were usually morose, sullen and unsociable on the day of their discharge. They would display a kind of stupefaction, a weird absent-mindedness. Such men would not enter into conversation and normally never uttered a word.[71]

Such floggings, which "hurt[] like nothing on earth,"[72] transmit a "terror that is involuntary and inexorable," one which "overwhelms a man's entire moral being."[73] Not all men, of course, contend with torture in the same way. Orlov, "a fiery, volatile individual," who did not believe he could survive the first round, emerged in relatively good spirits even though he had the worst wounds that Goryanchikov had ever seen.[74] But, with hope as his balm, Orlov, "already beginning to dream of the road, of escape, of freedom, the fields and woods," perished after the next installment.[75]

In Dead House, with excessive regulation, coercion, futility, loneliness with no aloneness, and redundant torture, the men, stripped of free will and human dignity, "seem[] to grow more and more gloomy and melancholy," with "[d]ejection and anguish ... eating [them] up."[76] The nocturnal howls speak for themselves: "[n]early all the convicts talked and raved in their sleep at night ... 'We're beaten men,' th[ey] used to say, 'we've had the insides beaten out of us, that's why we cry out at night.' "[77] Such "howls," and the horrors that precipitate them, occur in secrecy, inside an "irregular hexagon," guarded by detested, mistrusted officials, who abuse and lie to their captives.[78]

---

70. *Id.*

71. *Id.* at 239–40.

72. *Id.* at 241

73. *Id.* at 239.

74. *Id.* at 240.

75. *Id.*

76. *Id.* at 333.

77. *Id.* at 37.

78. *Id.* at 27. *See supra* note 16 and accompanying text (Goryanchikov's description of the Dead House facility).

III. The Rise and Fall of Free Will and Human Dignity Under the Due Process Clause and *Miranda*

It used to be of concern to the Supreme Court whether a confession was voluntary or coerced. In early cases, decided under the Due Process Clause, and later under *Miranda*, the Court did not just focus on voluntariness. It also aimed to safeguard the fairness of our accusatorial process for its own sake, and because it is a feature distinguishing us from other nations.

A. *Due Process Before* Miranda

The Due Process cases, already discussed in the prior chapter, are significant because, as the Supreme Court buries *Miranda*, they re-emerge as the sole, but frail, allies for an accused seeking to exclude a confession.[79] In these early Due Process cases, the unreliability of a coerced confession was a concern, but it wasn't the only one. Cases, like *Ashcraft v. Tennessee*[80] and *Spano v. New York*,[81] indicate that the Supreme Court once cared just as much about the importance of instilling confidence in a fair criminal justice system.

1. Free Will and Human Dignity

Initially, the Supreme Court turned to the Due Process Clause to ban confessions extracted through physical torture. For example, in *Brown v. Mississippi*, police officers brutally beat defendants until they confessed to dictated

---

79. *See generally* Richard A. Leo, *Questioning the Relevance of Miranda in the Twenty-First Century*, 99 MICH. L. REV. 1000, 1025 (2001) (pointing out that *Miranda* has "shift[ed] the legal inquiry from whether the confession was voluntarily given to whether the Miranda rights were voluntarily waived," and that "defendants will rarely succeed in arguing that their self-incriminating statement was compelled"). *See also infra* notes 157–62 and accompanying text (discussing how *Miranda* has almost eviscerated the involuntariness argument, while indicating that the involuntariness is the only recourse for an accused seeking to exclude a confession). For a more in-depth discussion of the early Due Process cases and their facts, see *supra* Chapter III (The Confessant Gene: *Crime and Punishment* and *The Brothers Karamazov*).

80. Ashcraft v. Tennessee, 322 U.S. 143 (1944).

81. Spano v. New York, 360 U.S. 315 (1959).

statements.[82] In overturning the convictions under the Due Process Clause, the Court said that such confessions tend to be unreliable. The Court later expanded the concept of torture to include coercion, which can depend on factors like the conduct of officials, the characteristics of the defendant, and the circumstances surrounding the confession.[83] In *Ashcraft* and *Spano*, the Court considered whether the methods used to extract confessions comport with our definition of a fair process.[84] In such cases, the Court, equating coercion with torture, proscribed police overreaching even if it did not make, or could not have made, an innocent person falsely confess.

For example, in *Ashcraft*, Ashcraft successfully argued that his alleged confession was "extorted" from him in violation of due process.[85] In finding that if Ashcraft confessed, it was not voluntary, the Court said that such methodology "is so inherently coercive that its very existence is irreconcilable with the possession of mental freedom by a lone suspect against whom its full coercive force is brought to bear."[86] In his decision, Justice Black worried not just about the unreliability of compelled evidence, but also about how psychological tor-

---

82. Brown v. Mississippi, 297 U.S. 278 (1936) (It was undisputed that defendants were repeatedly whipped, and one was even strung up in a mock lynching and repeatedly choked.). *See also* Wakat v. Harlib, 253 F.2d 59, 61–62 (7th Cir. 1958) (noting that the defendant was beaten by police, had multiple bruises and broken bones, and spent months in the hospital); People v. Matlock, 336 P.2d 505, 511–12 (Cal. 1959) (finding that the defendant was interrogated under sleep deprivation tactics and put on an icy board when he got sleepy); Bruner v. People, 156 P.2d 111, 120 (Colo. 1945) (The defendant was not allowed to eat for fifteen hours, deprived of the use of the toilet, and held for over two months.); Kier v. State, 132 A.2d 494, 496 (Md. 1957) (Defendant was strapped naked to a chair, and police indicated that they would take skin and hair scrapings from his body.); People v. Portelli, 205 N.E. 2d 857, 858 (N.Y. 1965) (Suspect was beaten and tortured until he gave incriminating confession.). *See generally* Steven Penney, *Theories of Confession Admissibility: A Historical View* 25 AM. J. CRIM. L. 309, 333 (1998) (discussing *Brown* and judicial responses to such police interrogation).

83. *See* Penney, *supra* note 82, at 337–41. *See generally* Aurora Maoz, *Empty Promises: Miranda Warnings in Noncustodial Interrogations*, 110 MICH. L. REV. 1310, 1314–15 (2012) (discussing the "voluntariness inquiry," which "examines the totality of the circumstances, including the physical and mental characteristics and abilities of the suspect"); Welsh S. White, *What Is an Involuntary Confession Now?*, 50 RUTGERS L. REV. 2001 (1998) (discussing voluntariness and applying it in a post-*Miranda* world).

84. *See generally* Amy D. Ronner, *Dostoevsky and the Therapeutic Jurisprudence Confession*,40 J. MARSHALL L. REV. 41, 57–62 (2006) (discussing confessions and the Due Process Clause). *See also* RONNER, *supra* note 6, at 93–98.

85. Ashcraft, 322 U.S. at 145.

86. *Id.* at 154.

ture sullies our judicial system and disfigures the very face that we, as Americans, present to the world:

> There have been, are now, certain foreign nations with governments dedicated to an opposite policy: governments which convict individuals with testimony obtained by police organizations possessed of an unrestrained power to seize persons suspected of crimes against the state, hold them in secret custody, and wring from them confessions by physical or mental torture. So long as the Constitution remains the basic law of our Republic, America will not have that kind of government.[87]

Kindred concerns surfaced in *Spano*, a case in which the Court, considering "all the facts in their post-indictment setting," found that Spano's "will was overborne by official pressure, fatigue and sympathy falsely aroused."[88] While the Court did not believe that law enforcement made Spano admit to something he did not do, Chief Justice Warren's decision clarified that "the use of involuntary confessions does not turn alone on their inherent untrustworthiness."[89] He made it plain that the decision "also turns on the deep-rooted feeling that the police must obey the law while enforcing the law," and "that in the end life and liberty can be as much endangered from illegal methods used to convict those thought to be criminals as from the actual criminals themselves."[90] As in *Ashcraft*, the *Spano* Court annexed coercion to torture because it undermines free will and human dignity, the preservation of which is essential to a civilized system and our national decency.[91]

2. The Denigration of Free Will and Human Dignity

While obtaining reliable evidence was one of the salutary aspirations in *Ashcraft* and *Spano*, it is here that the Supreme Court has apparently reneged. What makes this disappointing is that, after what has become *Miranda*'s effectual demise, defense counsel must typically establish that a confession is in-

---

87. *Id.* at 155. *See also* Penney, *supra* note 82, at 341–46 (discussing *Ashcraft* and the era between 1944–1949, in which the Supreme Court was increasingly concerned with "the means by which confessions are obtained—a concern that is independent of the desire to prevent the admission of untrustworthy confessions"); Ronner, *supra* note 84, at 59–60 (analyzing *Ashcraft* and explaining that reliability was not the Court's only concern).

88. Spano, 360 U.S. 323.

89. *Id.* at 320.

90. *Id.* at 320–21.

91. *See supra* notes 84–90 (The Supreme Court's concerns in the early due-process-voluntariness inquiry).

voluntary in order to get it excluded.[92] As such, the weakening of what undergirds the totality-of-the-circumstances inquiry blunts what is practically the only constitutional sword the defense bar has in its sheath. *Colorado v. Connelly* is one example of the Court's retreat from the goal of reliability and the aspiration of preserving free will, which were the core policies in the due process analysis.[93] In *Connelly*, this becomes apparent in the contrasting approaches of the state courts and the Supreme Court.

On the basis of the psychiatrist's testimony that Connelly had a psychosis, impairing his ability to make free and rational choices, the state trial court found both the initial statements and custodial confession to be "involuntary."[94] The court, apparently not convinced of the reliability of the confession, suppressed it, even though the police had not done anything tricky, improper, or coercive. The court simply felt that Connelly's mental illness, vitiating his free will, negated his waiver of both the right to counsel and privilege against self-incrimination. The Colorado Supreme Court affirmed, but the United States Supreme Court reversed and remanded.[95]

The Supreme Court concluded that there was no constitutional violation because of the absence of coercive police activity, which is "a necessary predicate to the finding that a confession is not 'voluntary.' "[96] In also faulting the Colorado court for finding an invalid *Miranda* waiver, the Supreme Court said that "notions of 'free will'... have no place [in constitutional law]."[97] For the Court, Connelly's "perception of coercion flowing from the 'voice of God,' however important or significant such a perception may be in other disciplines, is a matter to which the United States Constitution does not speak."[98]

The *Connelly* decision shrivels not just *Miranda*, but also due process protection, which is essentially *the* lone post-*Miranda* survivor. While the Court

---

92. *See infra* notes 157–62 and accompanying text (discussing the Court's implicit nullification of the voluntariness argument).

93. Connelly, 479 U.S. 157 (1986).

94. *Id.* at 162. The Colorado Court in *People v. Connelly*, 702 P.2d 722 (1985), relying on the decisions in *Townsend v. Sain*, 372 U.S. 293 (1963) and *Culombe v. Connecticut*, 367 U.S. 568 (1961), said that a confession is admissible only if it ensues from rational intellect and free will. *See also supra* Chapter III (The Confessant Gene: *Crime and Punishment* and *The Brothers Karamazov*) (providing a more detailed discussion of *Connelly* and the facts in the case).

95. Connelly, 702 P.2d 722 (1985) (the affirmance).

96. Connelly, 479 U.S. at 167. See also Chapter III (providing a more detailed discussion of *Connelly* and the facts in the case).

97. Connelly, 479 U.S. at 169–70.

98. *Id.* at 170–71.

in *Ashcraft* and *Spano* suggested that voluntariness is not *just* about gathering reliable evidence, it still kept reliability and free will as factors in the calculus.[99] The *Connelly* decision, however, eliminates, or at least demotes, such concerns.[100] It indicates that the Constitution might condone even an untrustworthy confession, as long as the officers themselves did not misbehave to cause the confession.

Connelly is disturbing for what it does not recognize: namely, the fact that state action in the form of introducing a potentially unreliable confession into evidence, which then is used to convict, undermines fairness and confidence in our justice system as much as, if not more than, police overreaching. Justice Brennan surely knew this, and objected to the *Connelly* Court's finding that the absence of police misconduct is determinative.[101] He, dissenting, was deeply troubled by the record, which was "barren" of any "indicia of reliability" and "of any corroboration of the mentally ill defendant's confession."[102] Justice Brennan was just as irritated by the Court's "refusal to acknowledge free will as a value of constitutional consequence."[103] As Brennan admonished, our commitment to fundamental fairness means that individuals, like Mr. Connelly, retain their human dignity along with the "right to make a vital choice

---

99. *See supra* notes 84–91 and accompanying text.

100. *See* George E. Dix, *Federal Confession Law: The 1986 and 1987 Supreme Court Terms* 67 Tex. L. Rev. 231, 232 (commenting on *Connelly* as the "rejection of reliability as a relevant consideration" for determining the admissibility of a confession); Irene Merker Rosenberg and Yale L. Rosenberg, *A Modest Proposal For the Abolition of Custodial Confessions*, 68 N.C.L. Rev. 69, 107 (1989) (discussing how "the *Connelly* Court rejected a free will rationale and required that government coercion be present to establish involuntariness or to invalidate a waiver of the fifth amendment privilege"). *But see* Peter Brooks, Troubling Confessions: Speaking Guilt In Law and Literature 170 (2000) (suggesting that *Connelly* may, because of its special facts, be something of an aberration in Supreme Court rulings on confessions, "[b]ut it once again points to, and creates, an unease about confessional speech and the wisdom of holding it to a standard of 'voluntariness' that seems better designed for almost any kind of speech").

101. Connelly, 479 U.S. at 172 (Justice Brennan, with whom Justice Marshall joins, dissenting).

102. *Id. But see* Brooks, *supra* note 100, at 170 (asking: "Is the psychotic's discourse voluntary?" and answering, "Is that of any criminal suspect? Do we care?"). According to Brooks, "what we learn about confession from literature, from religious tradition, and from the psychotherapeutic culture, suggests that where confession is concerned, the law needs to recognize that its conceptions of human motivation and volition are particularly flawed, even perhaps something of a fiction." *Id.* at 5. He suggests that the "heavy reliance on confessions in criminal justice creates a certain unease." *Id. See also supra* Chapter III (The Confessant Gene: *Crime and Punishment* and *The Brothers Karamazov*).

103. Connelly, 479 U.S. at 172.

with a sane mind."[104] For Brennan, voluntariness and the credibility of our nation's accusatorial process are inextricable, and thus, permit introduction only of those confessions that are the product of free will. His implication here is that such values, entwined with our collective moral-cultural fibers, set us apart from the kind of dehumanization portrayed in Dostoevsky's *Dead House*.[105]

B. Miranda *Protection*

The due process analysis proved time consuming, impractical, and unwieldy.[106] It became difficult, if not impossible, for courts to assess what really happened because confessions were typically extracted in that "irregular hexagon" of secrecy.[107] Also, courts rendered ostensibly inconsistent results, affording little to no guidance for law enforcement.[108] In the mid-1960s, the United States Supreme Court turned to the Fifth Amendment privilege against self incrimination as a basis for regulating police extraction of incriminating statements from suspects.[109] Not long after *Miranda* emerged, however, the Court began to hack it to pieces.[110]

---

104. *Id.*

105. *See supra* Part II (dissecting *Dead House*).

106. *See generally* Barry Friedman, *The Wages of Stealth Overruling (With Particular Attention to* Miranda v. Arizona), 99 Geo L.J. 1, 17–18 (2010) (discussing how the totality of the circumstances test proved "problematic" because "[c]onfessions were obtained out of sight of judicial officers[, d]etermining what had happened often involved a swearing contest between police and suspects[,]" there was "deeply troubling" evidence about the interrogation tactics in use, and "Supreme Court review on a case-by-case basis was doing little to offer clear guidance to police or the lower courts"); Leo, *supra* note 79, at 1021–22(analyzing how "*Miranda* has helped law enforcement by de facto displacing the case-by-case voluntariness standard as the primary test of a confession's admissibility"); Rosenberg and Rosenberg, *supra* note 100, at 75 (discussing how "*Miranda* recognized that a per se remedy, rather than an ad hoc totality-of-the-circumstances test, was the best method of preserving the privilege against self-incrimination").

107. Dostoevsky, *supra* note 1, at 27.

108. *See supra* note 106 (commentary on the failings of the case-by-case approach under the Due Process Clause).

109. *See supra* note 106 (discussing why the Supreme Court turned to *Miranda* to alleviate the difficulties of the totality-of-the-circumstances test).

110. *See generally* Friedman, *supra* note 106, (explaining that *Miranda* has been stealth overruled instead of overruled expressly and honestly); Mark A. Godsey, *Reformulating the Miranda Warnings in Light of Contemporary Law and Understandings*, 90 Minn. L. Rev. 781, 789 (2006) (describing how, "[s]hortly after *Miranda* was decided, the Court retreated from its 'compulsion' theory as originally delineated in *Miranda*."); Rinat Kitai-Sangero, *Respecting the Privilege against Self-Incrimination: a Call for Providing Miranda Warnings in Non-*

1. Free Will and Human Dignity

In *Miranda v. Arizona*, the Court said that prosecutors "may not use" statements "stemming from custodial interrogation" in the absence of "procedural safeguards effective to secure the privilege against self-incrimination."[111] The safeguards are, of course, the *Miranda* warnings, now indelibly engrained in our media and conflated with American culture.[112]

Under *Miranda*, the right to silence and to an attorney is serious business: "[i]f the individual indicates in any manner, at any time prior to or during questioning, that he or she wishes to remain silent, the interrogation must cease."[113] Similarly, when an individual requests an attorney, "the interrogation must cease until an attorney is present."[114] The Court, stressing that, since the right to have such counsel present at the interrogation is an "indispensable" Fifth Amendment protection, the failure to ask for a lawyer "does not constitute a waiver."[115]

For the prosecution, proving waiver is not designed to be lenient. With the right to remain silent, "a valid waiver will not be presumed simply from the silence of the accused after warnings are given or simply from the fact that a confession was in fact eventually obtained."[116] When, after invoking counsel, interrogation proceeds without counsel and the defendant gives a statement,

---

Custodial Interrogation, 42 N.M. L. Rev. 203, 204 (2012) (explaining how "*Miranda*'s holding has been eroded over time as courts have admitted evidence gained in the absence of the warnings"); Rosenberg & Rosenberg, *supra* note 100, at 81 (describing how "the Court has undercut the [*Miranda*] decision, hollowing out its core while maintaining a pretext of viability"); Jonathan Witmer-Rich, *Interrogation and the Roberts Court*, 63 Fl. L. Rev. 1189, 1192 (2011) (arguing that "*Miranda*'s original motivating purpose—protecting vulnerable suspects—appears to have entirely vanished, prompting a number of academic-style funerals for *Miranda*"). *But see* Kit Kinports, *The Supreme Court's Love-Hate Relationship with Miranda*, 101 J. Crim. L & Criminology 375 (2011) (arguing that the "Supreme Court's recent attitude towards its landmark ruling in *Miranda* ... seems to be one of studied ambivalence," and that while it has "ruthlessly cut back on *Miranda*, ... it has resisted blatant attempts to subvert [it]").

111. Miranda, 394 U.S. at 444. *See also supra* Chapter III (The Confessant Gene: *Crime and Punishment* and *The Brothers Karamazov*) (discussing the *Miranda* rules and warnings in greater depth).

112. *See generally* Dickerson v. United States, 530 U.S. 428 (2000) (recognizing that *Miranda* warnings are ingrained in American culture).

113. Miranda, 394 U.S. at 474.

114. *Id.*

115. *Id.* at 469–70.

116. *Id.* at 475.

"a heavy burden rests on the government to demonstrate that the defendant know-ingly and intelligently waived his privilege against self-incrimination and his right to retained or appointed counsel."[117] The *Miranda* Court admonished, "any evidence that the accused was threatened, tricked, or cajoled into a waiver will … show that the defendant did not voluntarily waive privilege."[118]

Chief Justice Warren explained that the Fifth Amendment privilege applied to the stationhouse and "all settings in which [an individual's] freedom of ac-tion is curtailed in any significant way."[119] The Court reasoned that, because custodial interrogation employs "inherently compelling pressures," it triggers the Fifth Amendment ban on compelled self-incrimination.[120] Here, the Court saw that coercion, like torture, need not manifest itself as a literal beating with a birch, but can be psychological as well.

Although the Court tipped its hat to the value of trustworthy or reliable confessions, the focus was mainly on the apodictic truth that "custodial inter-rogation exacts a heavy toll on individual liberty and trades on the weakness of individuals."[121] In this vein, the *Miranda* Court reiterated the concern that also resides in the due process decisions—namely, how respect for free will and human dignity distinguish us as a civilized nation:

> Th[e interrogative] atmosphere carries its own badge of intimidation. To be sure, this is ot physical intimidation, but it is equally destruc-tive of human dignity. The current practice of incommunicado in-terrogation is at odds with one of our Nation's most cherished principles—that the individual may not be compelled to incriminate himself. Unless adequate protective devices are employed to dispel the compulsion inherent in custodial surroundings, no statement ob-tained from the defendant can truly be the product of his free choice.[122]

The Court, elevating the Fifth Amendment privilege to "the essential mainstay of our adversary system," said that it is about honoring the "dignity and integrity of its citizens" and protection of "the inviolability of the human personality."[123]

---

117. *Id.*

118. *Id.* at 476.

119. *Id.* at 467.

120. *Id.*

121. *Id.* at 455. *See also id.* at 456 n. 24 (mentioning the problem of false confessions). *See generally* Friedman, *supra* note 106, at 17 ("Although the Court mentioned a concern for trustworthy or reliable confessions, it is an aside in a footnote.")

122. *Miranda*, 394 U.S. at 457–58.

123. *Id.* at 460. The Court explained that the privilege, which protects "the inviolabil-ity of the human personality" and "our accusatory system of criminal justice," means that

2. The Denigration of Free Will and Human Dignity

Congress enacted a statute replacing *Miranda* with the totality-of-the circumstances approach of the due process era.[124] In *Dickerson v. United States*, the Supreme Court deemed *Miranda* a constitutional decision, declined to overrule it, and invalidated the statute.[125] In spite of *Dickerson's* ostensible apotheosis of *Miranda*, the Supreme Court dedicated itself to *Miranda's* nullification.[126]

In the post-*Miranda* world, the Supreme Court does not merely allow, but effectually encourages, police to circumvent the Self Incrimination Clause by condoning a meshwork of *Miranda* loopholes.[127] These exceptions are so com-

---

the "government seeking to punish ... individual[s] [must] produce the evidence against [them] by its own independent labors, rather than by the cruel, simple expedient of compelling it from [their] own mouth[s]." *Id.*

124. 18 U.S.C. § 3501. *See* Dickerson v. United States, 530 U.S. at 435 (2000). In *Miranda*, the Court said that the decision "in no way creates a constitutional straitjacket," and "encourage[d] Congress and the States to search for effective ways of protecting [individual] rights." *Miranda*, 384 U.S. at 467.

125. *Dickerson*, 530 U.S. 428 (2000).

126. *See id.* at 437 (admitting that the Court has "created several exceptions to *Miranda's* warnings requirement and [has] repeatedly referred to the *Miranda* warnings as 'prophylactic' ... and 'not themselves rights protected by the Constitution'") (citing New York v. Quarles, 467 U.S. 649, 653 (1984); Michigan v. Tucker, 417 U.S. 433, 444 (1974). *See also Dickerson*, 530 U.S. at 438 n.2 (listing other cases in which the Court had diminished *Miranda's* Constitutional Status); Yale Kamisar, *Miranda's Reprieve*, 92 A.B.A. J. 48, 51 (2006) ("[T]he Supreme Court has now made it clear that what it reaffirmed in *Dickerson* was not the *Miranda* doctrine as it burst onto the scene in 1966, but rather *Miranda* with all its post-Warren court exceptions frozen in time.").

127. *See generally* Friedman, *supra* note 106 (arguing that the exceptions are so extensive that they are overruled by stealth); Godsey, *supra* note 110, at 789–90 (discussing the litany of cases that have retreated from *Miranda*); Jonathan Wilmer-Rich, *supra* note 110, at 1192 (discussing how commentators have realized that "the Supreme Court ... seems to be shaping interrogation law to facilitate the admission of custodial confessions, by creating 'safe harbor' rules that are relatively clear and simple for police to satisfy"). Some commentators, like Professor Cassel, would be happy to see *Miranda* overruled and have zealously supported this. *See* Paul G. Cassell, *Miranda's 'Negligible' Effect on Law Enforcement: Some Skeptical Observations*, 20 HARV. J. L. PUB. POL'Y 327 (1997) (blaming *Miranda* for decreasing the amount of successful interrogations, lowering police clearance rate for violent offenses, and increasing the crime rate itself); Paul G. Casell & Brett S. Hayman, *Police Interrogation in the 1990s: An Empirical Study of Miranda*, 43 UCLA L. REV. 839, 843 (1996) (reporting a study's conclusion that "the *Miranda* decision, despite the promises of the Court and its defenders, has yet to be empirically justified as the proper balance between the competing interests of criminal suspects and society at large"). *But see* Stephen Schulhofer, *Bashing Miranda is Unjustified—and Harmful*, 20 HARV. J.L. & PUB. POL'Y 347 (1997) (praising *Miranda* as the benefactor

prehensive that scholars, like Professor Barry Friedman, have denominated the process "stealth overruling."[128] For example, in *New York v. Quarles*, the Court adopted a public safety exception, permitting officers to skip the warnings if they need to get at a fact (like the location of a gun) necessary to protect the public from harm.[129] In other cases, the Court found admissible the evidentiary fruit of a *Miranda* violation, like a third-party witness or physical evidence, as long as it is not the confession itself.[130] In practice, such decisions let law enforcement off the hook. Because many prosecutions are all about drugs and weapons, often all that is needed for a conviction is the contraband itself.[131] In such instances, browbeating without *Miranda* warnings

---

of all of the legal actors in the criminal justice system); Stephen J. Schulhofer, Miranda's *Practical Effect: Substantial Benefits and Vanishingly Small Costs*, 90 NW U.L. Rev. 500, 563 (1996) (rebutting Cassell and arguing that "*Miranda* is—and deserves to be—here to stay"). *See also* Peter Arnella, Miranda *Stories*, 20 Harv. J.L. & Pub. Pol'y 375 (1996–1997) (analyzing the Cassell-Schulhofer debate and arguing that Schulhofer is correct); Charles D. Weisselberg, *Mourning Miranda*, 96 Cal. L. Rev. 1519, 1524 (2008) (A "long advocate of the Miranda decision, [who] ... has changed his beliefs," after researching "police training materials, social science literature, and post-*Miranda* decisions," has "concluded that little is left of Miranda's vaunted safeguards and what is left is not worth retaining.").

128. Friedman, *supra* note 106, at 5 (contending that "'stealth overruling' is a misnomer" and that "[i]n reality, what disturbs critics is the disingenuous treatment of precedents in a manner that obscures fundamental change in the law" and that "[e]xisting precedents are not given their logical scope, or are trimmed to almost nothing, without sufficient (or any) explanation").

129. *Quarles*, 467 U.S. 649 (1984).

130. In Michigan v. Tucker, 417 U.S. 433 (1974), the police discovered the identity of a prosecution witness when they obtained a statement without full compliance with *Miranda*. In finding that the introduction of the third-party witness testimony did not violate the Fifth Amendment, the Court eroded *Miranda's* exclusionary rule. *See* Kamisar, *supra* note 126, at 50 ("Another Rehnquist opinion that built on *Tucker* was New York v. Quarles, 467 U.S. 649 (1984) ... [which] recognized a public safety exception to the need for *Miranda* warnings in a prosecution of defendant who answered a question by police officers who had chased him into a supermarket."). In United States v. Patane, 542 U.S. 630 (2004), the Court found that the failure to give *Miranda* warnings did not require suppression of physical evidence, like a gun, which was the fruit of the suspect's statements. Both cases give police license to fish around, unencumbered by *Miranda* safeguards, so that they can secure admissible third-party witnesses or physical evidence. *See* Kamisar, *supra* note 126, at 51 ("A majority of the [*Patane*] Court (including Rehnquist) seemed to attach no significance whatever to the fact that only a few years earlier, Rehnquist, speaking for the Court, had told us that *Miranda* had 'announced a constitutional rule.'").

131. *See generally* Friedman, *supra* note 106, at 51 (explaining that, "[i]n many drug and weapons cases, all that is needed to convict is the contraband itself," and that "[f]ind-

is without consequence, and can be potentially dispositive for the prosecution.[132]

The confession itself, moreover, can often come in as well. In *Harris v. New York*[133] and *United States v. Havens*,[134] the Court held that the prosecution can use even the incriminating statements themselves, the very ones taken in violation of *Miranda*, to impeach the credibility of suspects who elect to testify at trial on their own behalf.[135] There is also the *Elstad-Seibert* loophole, which, reaching beyond impeachment, can inject the confession into the case in chief.[136] That is, in spite of the fact that the *Miranda* Court sought to protect suspects against inherent coercion, later cases deemed confessions admissible even when law enforcement concocted ploys to trick, threaten, deceive, and coerce.[137] Ironically such ratified methods resemble the very ones the Court had criticized in *Miranda* and deemed the impetus for its decision.[138]

Specifically, under *Oregon v. Elstad*, police can first question suspects without *Miranda* warnings, and then, delivering warnings after the suspects have already confessed, lead them to repeat their self-incriminating statements. While the unwarned statements themselves are excluded, if suspects later putatively waive their rights and repeat the statements after proper warnings, they are admissible. This gives law enforcement a way to side-step *Miranda*, because suspects who have already confessed are likely to feel that there is nothing to be

---

ing out where it is located does the trick, so the result in *Patane* encourages foregoing *Miranda* warnings").

132. *See supra* note 131 and accompanying text.

133. Harris v. New York, 401 U.S. 222 (1971).

134. U.S. v. Havens, 446 U.S. 620 (1980). *See also* Kansas v. Ventris, 556 U.S. 586 (2009) (holding that incriminating statements obtained by a jailhouse informant in violation of the *Massiah* doctrine, which were deliberately elicited from an accused, were admissible to impeach the defendant's trial testimony).

135. In both *Harris*, 401 U.S. 222, and *Havens*, 446 U.S. 620, the Court indicated that the only way the impeachment exception will not apply is if suspects' statements are coerced or involuntary.

136. Oregon v. Elstad, 470 U.S. 298 (1985) and Missouri v. Seibert, 542 U.S. 600 (2004). *See generally* Rosenberg & Rosenberg, *supra* note 100, at 95 (discussing *Elstad* and how "it is no longer true that police need even administer the *Miranda* warnings initially to assure admissibility of subsequent statements"); Friedman, *supra* note 106, at 21 (discussing *Elstad* and *Seibert*, and how "the fractured opinions in effect instructed police on how to ignore *Miranda*").

137. *See generally Miranda*, 384 U.S. 436 (elaboration on successful law enforcement tactics and tricks to extract incriminating statements from suspects). *See also* Weisselberg, *supra* note 127 (discussing how the Supreme Court's post-*Miranda* decisions are used to give police the very tactics to obtain confessions).

138. *See supra* note 137.

gained if they later heed the warnings and seal their lips.[139] The *Elstad* Court rationalized that it was not "condon[ing] inherently coercive police tactics or methods offensive to due process that render the initial admission involuntary and undermine the suspect's will to invoke his rights once they are read to him."[140] Therefore, individuals with *Elstad*-like fact patterns must depend solely on a due process challenge to get "post-warning" confessions excluded.

Elstad still controls because, in *Missouri v. Seibert*, the Court, expressly declining to overrule *Elstad*, indicated that this two-step method of extracting the confession will be invalid only if police use it as deliberate subterfuge.[141] The *Seibert* Court found impermissible a question-first-Mirandize-later tactic because it "effectively threaten[ed] to thwart *Miranda's* purpose of reducing the risk that a coerced confession would be admitted."[142] A glimpse at the *Seibert* facts reveals how easy it is to replicate *Elstad* and dodge *Seibert* to get such confessions into evidence.[143] When the state charged Seibert with first-degree murder, she, like Elstad, sought to exclude both her pre-and post-warning statements.

---

139. *See generally Elstad*, 470 U.S. at 321 (Brennan J. dissenting) ("Today's decision, in short, threatens disastrous consequences far beyond the outcome in this case."). Brennan states: "One of the factors that can vitiate the voluntariness of a subsequent confession is the hopeless feeling of an accused that he has nothing to lose by repeating his confession, even where the circumstances that rendered his first confession illegal have been removed." *Id.* at 325. *See also id.* at 365 (Stevens, J., dissenting) (accusing the Court of "denigrat[ing] the importance of one of the core constitutional rights that protects every American citizen from the kind of tyranny that has flourished in other societies").

140. Elstad, 470 U.S. at 317.

141. Seibert, 542 U.S. 600.

142. *Id.* at 617.

143. *Seibert* arose when Seibert's child, Jonathan, who had cerebral palsy, died in his sleep. Fearing that she would be charged with neglect because of Jonathan's bedsores, Seibert, together with her teenage sons and their friends, devised a scheme to incinerate the body by torching the mobile home. Donald, a mentally ill teenager, was also living with Seibert, and the team planned to abandon him in the burning house so that it would not appear that Jonathan had been left unattended. Five days later, the police entered the picture. Police awakened Seibert at about three in the morning and arrested her. The officer, who was trained to delay in giving Seibert *Miranda* warnings, left her alone for a while. An officer then questioned Seibert without *Miranda* warnings for about thirty to forty minutes, while continually squeezing her arm and reiterating, "[The victim] was also to die in his sleep." *Id.* Once Seibert blurted admissions, the officer rewarded her with coffee and a cigarette. After that, the officer turned on a tape recorder and gave *Miranda* warnings, and Seibert signed the waiver. Once the officer resumed questioning and confronted her with her pre-warned retorts, Seibert re-incriminated herself.

For the prosecution, the botch was that, at the suppression hearing, the officer told the truth and admitted that he consciously withheld the *Miranda* warnings to do what he had been trained to do—question first and warn later.[144] It thus became undisputed that the two-step technique, already gaining popularity in police departments, aimed to render *Miranda* warnings ineffective and divest suspects of a meaningful choice between speech and silence.[145] The *Elstad-Seibert* combo implicitly instructs the police to perform, and the prosecution to finesse, the two-step process as a blunder, as a good faith failure to warn, and thus, to conceal the belly of the beast—the use of a coercive ploy deliberately aimed at thwarting *Miranda*.[146]

In two even more recent decisions, *Berguhis v. Thompkins*[147] and *Florida v. Powell*,[148] the Supreme Court ablated *Miranda*'s safeguards for the rights to silence and counsel. In *Thompkins*, after the police had recited the warnings, Thompkins neither said nor indicated that he wished to waive. Moreover, he endured a near three hours of questioning while he sat silently in a hard chair. When asked whether he "pray[ed] to God to forgive [him] for shooting that boy down," Thompkins uttered, "Yes."[149] In a 5-4 vote, the Court held that the police did not violate Thompkins' rights. According to the Court, once told of the right to remain silent, the onus was on the accused to indicate that he was availing himself of that right.[150] The police need not inform him that vo-

---

144. *Seibert*, 542 U.S. 611 & n.3 (describing question-first interrogations, and citing cases in which police departments trained officers in that tactic). *See also Friedman, supra* note 106, at 21 (discussing how "[s]ome police and prosecutors took *Elstad* as a license to develop policies involving deliberate use of 'question-first' tactics ... [whereby] police intentionally failed to deliver *Miranda* warnings, obtained a confession, then read the warnings and obtained a second (ostensibly admissible) statement"); Charles D. Weisselberg, *Saving* Miranda, 84 CORNELL L. REV. 109, 132–40 (1998) (discussing training materials on this tactic); Weisselberg, *supra* note 127, at 1592 (describing *Seibert-Elstad* tactics as the "Missouri two-step," and explaining that "the Court has issued decisions that tolerate tactics that diminish *Miranda*'s effectiveness and officers have predictably been trained to use these tactics").

145. *See supra* note 144.

146. *See generally* Weisselberg, *supra* note 127, at 1552–3 (While police training states that the "two-step approach used by police in *Seibert* has been officially disapproved," they "tend to emphasize the deliberate conduct of the officers in *Seibert*, distinguishing *Elstad* as a good faith mistake.").

147. Berghuis v. Thompkins, 560 U.S. 370 (2010).

148. Florida v. Powell, 559 U.S. 50 (2010).

149. *Thompkins*, 130 S. Ct. at 2257.

150. *Id.* at 2255, 2260.

calization is required, nor do they have to get a waiver on the record before interrogating.[151]

Justice Sotomayor's branding of the decision as a "substantial retreat" from *Miranda* is litotes:[152] *Thompkins* is more aptly likened to *Miranda*'s extinction, not only because it dissipates the right to silence, but also because it legitimates manipulation, one of the very things that the *Miranda* Court censured. Post-*Thompkins*, police can badger away, without bothering to get waiver on the record, and nevertheless emerge with admissible evidence. As such, police tenacity can trample the right to silence and still lead to something a court is willing to bless as a "waiver."[153]

The *Powell* decision dilutes the *Miranda* obligation to "clearly inform" suspects of "the right to consult with a lawyer and to have the lawyer with him during interrogation."[154] In *Powell*, the Justices found adequate a police instruction that, although including the right to consult with a lawyer, omitted the right to have that lawyer present during the interrogation.[155] Although the Court seemed to limit its decision to the efficacy of the words in the record, in

---

151. *Id.* at 2263–64. *See also* Salinas v. Texas, 133 S. Ct. 2174 (2013) (court rejected Fifth Amendment claim of defendant, who did not expressly invoke the privilege against self-incrimination in response to the officer's question, all of which occurred prior to custody, arrest, and *Miranda* warnings).

152. *Thompkins*, 130 S. Ct. at 2266 (Sotomayor, J. dissenting).

153. *See generally* Kinports, *supra* note 110, at 375 (discussing how *Berghuis* "allow[s] law enforcement officials to do a complete end run around *Miranda*, reducing the Warren Court's decision to a formalistic requirement that warnings be read and otherwise reinstating the voluntariness due process test"); Witmer-Rich, *supra* note 110, at 1240 (In *Berghuis*, "the Court removed a barrier that might prevent police from reaching the Miranda safe harbor, by eliminating the requirement that police elicit a distinct waiver from the suspect separate from and before any admissible confession.").

154. *Miranda*, 384 U.S. at 471.

155. *Powell*, 130 S. Ct. at 1204–06. The *Powell* Court relied on its own precedent in California v. Prysock, 453 U.S. 355 (1981) and Duckworth v. Eagan, 492 U.S. 195 (1989), and said that both cases "inform our judgment here." *Powell*, 130 S. Ct. at 1204. In those cases, the *Powell* Court explained that it had declined to "dictate[] the words" police had to use in the Miranda warnings and in those cases the accused were clearly informed of their rights. *Id. See also Duckworth*, 492 U.S. at 209 (*Miranda* requires that "the suspect be informed, as here, that he has the right to an attorney before and during questioning."); *Prysock*, 453 U.S. at 361 (quoting United States v. Noa, 443 F.2d 144, 146 (9th Cir. 1971)) (stating that this "'is not a case in which the defendant was not informed of his right to the presence of an attorney during questioning … or in which the offer of an appointed attorney was associated with a future time in court'").

the post-*Powell* world, the police can muddle counsel warnings by simply pla-giarizing the one delivered and approved in *Powell*.[156]

When it was born, *Miranda* aimed to supplement, not replace, the volun-tariness inquiry of the due process era.[157] In case after case, the Court, indi-cating that today's linchpin is voluntariness, has resuscitated the due process analysis as *the* ticket to exclusion.[158] In this regard, the Supreme Court has fos-tered an oxymoronic vicious cycle: it pays lip service to the reactivation of the voluntariness approach while, in reality, foreclosing just such an inquiry in ac-tual practice. Today, if a trial court finds that law enforcement has obeyed *Mi-randa* rules, it typically refrains from engaging in the voluntariness inquiry and simply admits the evidence.[159] But even if a court does genuinely entertain

---

156. *See generally* Friedman, *supra* note 106, at 23 ("Although the Court purported only to be analyzing ex post whether a warning given ex ante was enough to inform that partic-ular suspect, one can anticipate police now getting the message about what is (or is not) re-quired."); Witmer-Rich, *supra* note 110, at 1240 (explaining how the "Roberts Court has made it much easier for police to reach that safe harbor" and how "*Powell* ... imposed a relatively simple requirement on police (recite some version of the warnings) instead of the more dif-ficult task of ensuring that a possibly uneducated, scared, defensive, or confused suspect truly comprehends her rights in the interrogation setting").

157. *See generally* Edwin D. Driver, *Confessions and the Social Psychology of Coercion*, 82 HARV. L. REV. 42, 60 (1968) ("The Miranda warnings of course do not directly affect the limits set by 'voluntariness' on permissible tactics, but merely add several safeguards."); Au-rora Maoz, *supra* note 83 at 1318 (explaining that, after *Miranda,* "lower courts ... still have to decide whether a statement was voluntarily given regardless of whether the *Miranda* dic-tates were followed").

158. *See generally supra* notes 127–57 and accompanying text (discussing those cases eroding *Miranda,* but which purport to leave the voluntariness inquiry intact).

159. *See Dickerson,* 120 S. Ct. at 2336 (Where police have "adhered to the dictates of *Miranda,*" a defendant can rarely make a "colorable argument that his self-incriminating statement was compelled."). *See generally* Leo, *supra* note 79, at 1025 (explaining that "there is to date support for [the] view [that as long as *Miranda* warnings were given, courts ig-nored interrogation misconduct, freeing the police to coerce suspects as long as they had first Mirandized them"); Maoz, *supra* note 83, at 1318–19 ("[T]he *Miranda* doctrine was meant to supplement, not supplant, the voluntariness inquiry in lower courts" but "it ap-pears ... that rather than engage in both inquiries, some lower courts have used *Miranda* as a substitute."); Welsh S. White, Miranda's *Failure to Restrain Pernicious Interrogation Prac-tices*, 99 MICH. L. REV. 1121, 1220 (2001) ("A finding that the police have properly informed the suspect of his *Miranda* rights thus often has the effect of minimizing the scrutiny afforded interrogation practices following the *Miranda* waiver."); Weisselberg, *supra* note 127, at 1523 ("[I]t turns out that following *Miranda's* hollow ritual often forecloses a searching in-quiry into the voluntariness of a statement.") *But see* Mincey v. Arizona, 437 U.S. 385 (1978) (an older case, in which the Court found a confession involuntary, and that it could not be

a due process challenge, the *Connelly* decision eliminates, or at least demotes, reliability as a factor.[160] Beyond that, due to the fact that the *Dickerson* Court slapped its wrist when it tried to regulate police interrogation, it is highly unlikely that Congress will try again to implement a *Miranda* substitute.[161] As such, the Supreme Court has commanded the defense bar to use the Due Process Clause for excluding confessions. At the same time, *Miranda* progeny have conterminously eradicated *Miranda* and rendered ineffectual its putative due process supplement. Interestingly, commentators have discussed and advocated videotaping as a viable solution, a way to discourage and fix police overreaching.[162] The videotapes, however, would not always benefit the accused, because in many instances, all they would likely show is a trained interrogator carefully dancing around *Miranda* to perform one or several of the legalized exceptions in the post-*Miranda* repertoire.[163] Before *Shatzer* and *Fields*, however, there was at least a sliver of good news: namely, none of the anti-

---

used for impeachment purposes where the defendant was in pain in the hospital intensive care unit and repeatedly asked for the interrogation to stop until he could secure an attorney). *See* Rosenberg & Rosenberg, *supra* note 100, at 101 (discussing *Mincey* as exemplifying the proposition that "when the Court does find a due process violation, the nature of its inquiry suggests that the governing standard is rather primitive").

160. *See supra* Part III.A.2 (discussing Colorado v. Connelly, 479 U.S. 157 (1986) and how it indicates that an unreliable confession might be admissible). *See also supra* Chapter III (The Confessant Gene: *Crime and Punishment* and *The Brothers Karamazov*) (discussing *Connelly*).

161. *See supra* note 124–26 and accompanying text (discussing Dickerson v. United States, 530 U.S. 428 (2000)). *Cf.* Weisselberg, *supra* note 127, at 1523 (discussing how, since *Miranda*, the Court has "frozen legislative and other efforts to regulate police interrogation practices").

162. *See generally* Godsey, *supra* note 110, at 815 (suggesting that "the police should be required to videotape the interrogation and inform the suspect that if she speaks, the entire interview will be recorded"). According to Godsey, "[a] suspect who knows that the interrogation is being videotaped and that the videotape will be admissible in court will have substantially less fear that the police will engage in third-degree tactics and will know that her statement will be accurately recorded." *Id.* He also points out that, "[b]ecause the voluntariness test considers the totality of the circumstances, videotaping provides the perfect prophylactic safeguard, as it captures the nuances and subtleties of interrogations." *Id. See also* Leo, *supra* note 79 (elaborating on the mandatory videotaping of police interrogation); Wayne T. Westling & Vicki Waye, *Videotaping Police Interrogations: Lessons from Australia*, 25 Am J. Crim. L. 493 (1998) (discussing the benefits of videotaping).

163. With respect to the teenagers wrongfully convicted of raping and beating a female jogger in New York's central park, the police manipulated them into making false confessions and had it all on videotape. *See* Mick Lasalle, *The Lie was Big, the Truth Ignored*, The Miami Herald, December 21, 2012, at 13G (discussing the recent film, *The Central Park Five*, about the boys who spent about thirteen years in prison for a crime they did not com-

Miranda fact patterns, discussed above, took place in prison, which, as Dostoevsky knew, is the proverbial venue of inherent compulsion.

IV. The Ouster Of *Miranda* From The Prison

Although the Court has chopped *Miranda* to smithereens, what little was left once did apply to inmates. In two decisions, however, *Maryland v. Shatzer*[164] and *Howes v. Fields*,[165] the Supreme Court categorically ousted *Miranda* from our prisons.[166]

A. Miranda *Once Applied*

Under two older cases, *Mathis v. United States* [167]and *Illinois v. Perkins*,[168] inmates had the same, but already tapered, *Miranda* protections as people on the outside. In *Mathis*, an Internal Revenue Service agent, removing an inmate from the general population, questioned him about tax violations allegedly occurring outside of the prison.[169] After the agent failed to warn Mathis of his *Miranda* rights, Mathis implicated himself in the crime. In his trial for knowingly filing false claims, Mathis unsuccessfully sought suppression of the evidence, and the appellate court affirmed.

The Supreme Court, agreeing with Mathis, said that *Miranda* safeguards govern individuals who, while "in custody[, are] interrogated by officers about matters that tend to incriminate [them]."[170] The Court rejected the government's contention that a "routine tax investigation where no criminal proceedings might even be brought" should be immune from *Miranda*.[171] While the Court acknowledged that tax investigations differ from those of "murder, robbery, and other crimes," it noted that they frequently (and actually did in

---

mit). *Cf. infra* notes 342–43 and accompanying text (discussing the nobleman in *Dead House*, who spent time in prison for a crime he did not commit).

164. Shatzer, 130 S. Ct. 1213 (2010).

165. Fields, 132 S. Ct. 1181 (2012).

166. *See infra* Part IV. C and V (discussing how the Court has made *Miranda* inapplicable to prisoners).

167. 391 U.S. 1 (1968).

168. 496 U.S. 292 (1990).

169. *Mathis*, 391 U.S. 1.

170. *Id.* at 3.

171. *Id.* at 4.

the *Mathis'* case) lead to prosecutions.[172] The Court, moreover, stressed that the custodial interrogation happened only eight days before the onset of the "full-fledged criminal investigation."[173]

In *Mathis*, the Court also declined the government's invitation to narrow *Miranda* by finding that it only applies to interrogation of a suspect whose custody is connected to the case under investigation. In declaring such an exception to be inappropriate, the Court said that the mandatory warnings do not hinge upon "the reason why the person is in custody."[174] Significantly, the Court adhered to the unremarkable proposition that custody is custody, and interrogation, even about things unrelated to the prison sentence, is still interrogation.

Although in *Perkins*, the Supreme Court found no constitutional violation, it upheld *Mathis*, still endorsing the applicability of *Miranda* to in-prison custody.[175] Perkins, like Mathis, was in jail pending trial on an aggravated-battery charge. When another inmate told police that Perkins might have been involved in an unrelated, unsolved murder, they slipped an undercover agent into the cell-block with Perkins and the snitch. Eventually, the agent, participating in an elaborate charade, gained Perkins' trust and got him to describe the murder.[176]

After the trial court granted Perkins' motion to suppress his in-jail statements on the basis of *Miranda* and the appellate court affirmed that ruling, the Supreme Court reversed. Significantly, the Court did not find prison to be noncustodial, but rather treated custody *sub silentio* as a given. What the decision hinged on was the fact that the interrogator's identity was disguised. That is, the issue was whether the suspect knew that the repository of his confession was a state actor or believed that he was just another inmate. The Court reasoned that "conversations between suspects and undercover agents do not implicate the concerns underlying *Miranda* ... because compulsion [is] not present when an incarcerated person speaks freely to someone that he believes to be a fellow inmate."[177] The Court, still sticking to its guns, confirmed

---

172. *Id.*

173. *Id.*

174. *Id.*

175. 496 U.S. 292.

176. When police suspected that Perkins was involved in a murder, they placed an agent, John Parisi, in the cellblock with Perkins and Charlton, and "Parisi and Charlton were instructed to engage [Perkins] in casual conversation and report anything he said about the murder." *Id.* at 294–95. Parisi, "using the alias 'Vito Bianco' and Charlton, both clothed in jail garb," began to plot an escape. *Id.* at 295. In the course of planning and discussion, Perkins "describe[d] at length the events of the ... murder," and did so without *Miranda* warnings. *Id.*

177. *Id.* at 297–98.

that prison is custody: "the danger of coercion results from the interaction of *custody* and official interrogation. We reject the argument that *Miranda* warnings are required whenever a suspect is *in custody* in a technical sense and converses with someone who happens to be a government agent."[178] For the Court, the state courts erred not by finding custody, but by "assum[ing] that because the suspect was *in custody*, no undercover questioning could take place."[179]

In distinguishing *Mathis*, the *Perkins* Court found that the only real difference was that Mathis, unlike Perkins, "was aware that the agent was a governmental official."[180] This, unlike what occurred in *Perkins*, triggered *Miranda*'s concern with an inherently coercive, "police-dominated atmosphere."[181] In a parenthetical, the Court said that the *Perkins* case presented "the bare fact of custody."[182] The Court framed as unripe the question of whether custody alone always mandates *Miranda* warnings, even in those situations in which the suspect knows that he is speaking to law enforcement.[183] In so doing, the *Perkins* Court foreshadowed the ouster of *Miranda* from Dead House.

B. Inmates Don't Always Get *Miranda*

A potent *Miranda* offshoot, the one conceived in *Edwards v. Arizona*,[184] automatically excludes confessions if police initiate re-interrogation of a suspect

---

178. *Id.* at 297 (emphasis added by author).

179. *Id.* (emphasis added by author). By applying *Hoffa v. United States*, 358 U.S. 293 (1966), the *Perkins* Court did not retract, but actually solidified, the principle that prison equals *Miranda* custody. In *Hoffa*, the merely detained suspect divulged his attempts to bribe jurors to an undercover agent, who to him seemed simpatico. The Court found that such facts did not "affect the voluntariness of [his] statements." *Id.* at 304. In discussing *Hoffa*, the *Perkins* Court reasoned that the "only difference between [*Perkins*] and *Hoffa* is that [Perkins] was incarcerated" and intimated that the particular custodial setting is, for all intents and purposes, immaterial. *Perkins*, 496 U.S. at 299–300. For the Court, what mattered was the common denominator in *Perkins* and *Hoffa*—that both suspects confessed to a "friend" who turned out to be an agent. *Id.* at 300.

180. *Perkins*, 496 U.S. 299.

181. *Id.* at 296.

182. *Id.* at 299.

183. *Id.* ("The bare fact of custody may not in every instance require a warning even when the suspect is aware that he is speaking to an official, but we do not have occasion to explore that issue here.").

184. *Edwards*, 451 U.S. 477. *See also infra* notes 246–63 and accompanying text (discussing *Edwards* and its policies).

who has previously invoked the right to counsel. In *Maryland v. Shatzer*,[185] the Supreme Court debilitated the *Edwards* rule, and did it in the worse place possible—the penitentiary.

Shatzer arose when an officer tried to question Shatzer about alleged sexual abuse of his own son. At the time, Shatzer was serving a sentence for an unrelated child-sexual abuse offense. When Shatzer invoked his right to counsel, the detective stopped, released Shatzer back into the general prison population, and closed the investigation. Two and a half years later, when new information came to light, another detective, reopening the investigation, tried to re-interrogate Shatzer, who was still incarcerated. This time, Shatzer, without counsel, self-incriminated.[186]

Shatzer, moving to suppress, relied on *Edwards*, but the trial court, finding a "break" in custody, denied his motion.[187] After Shatzer's conviction for sexual child abuse, the state appellate court reversed, holding that *Edwards* protections do not expire with time.[188] Alternatively, the appellate court found that, even if there is a time limit, Shatzer's "release" back into the general prison population did not qualify as a break in custody.[189] The Supreme Court reversed, and in its decision, authored by Justice Scalia, concluded that Shatzer's release back into the general prison population amounts to a break in *Miranda* custody. The Court even legislated a time frame for such a qualifying "break."[190] Because Shatzer experienced a break of more than two weeks between the first and second interrogations, the Court deemed the confession admissible.

---

185. *Shatzer*, 130 S. Ct. 1213 (2010).

186. Initially Shatzer "denied ordering his son to perform fellatio on him, but admitted to masturbating in front of his son" and agreed to a polygraph examination. *Id.* at 1218. When detectives met with Shatzer five days later, he "became upset, started to cry, and incriminated himself by saying, 'I didn't force him. I didn't force him.'" Id.

187. *Id.*

188. *Id.*

189. *Id.*

190. *Id.* at 1222–23 ("It is impractical to leave the answer to that question for clarification in future case-by-case adjudication; law enforcement officers need to know, with certainty and beforehand, when renewed interrogation is lawful."). In *Shatzer*, Justice Thomas (concurring in part and concurring in the judgment), agreed "that release into the general prison population constitutes a break in custody," but disagreed with the Court's "decision to extend the [*Edwards*] presumption of involuntariness ... for 14 days after custody ends." *Id.* at 1227. He argued that the Court incorrectly "extends the presumption of involuntariness ... to interrogations that occur after custody ends" and adds that such "bright-line rules are not necessary to prevent Fifth Amendment violations." *Id.* at 1227–28.

As developed more below, the *Shatzer* decision gives law enforcement a method to evade *Edwards*.[191] When prisoners request counsel, all the interrogator needs to do is ship them back to their cell, count fourteen days, and then start over without counsel present.[192] Despite the *Shatzer* Court's statement that "[n]o one questions that Shatzer was in custody for *Miranda* purposes during the interviews," the case set the stage for the *Fields* decision, which, evicting *Miranda* from prisons, endorsed the kind of conditions that once existed in Dostoevsky's Siberia.[193]

C. Inmates Never Get Miranda

The *Howes* v. *Fields* decision, stretching further than *Shatzer*, makes not just *Edwards*, but *Miranda* itself, unavailable to inmates.[194] In *Fields*, the investigation focused on Randall Fields, who was serving time for disorderly conduct. One evening, a corrections officer, removing Fields from his cell, led him down a floor, through a locked door, and into a conference room.[195] Once there, two armed deputies questioned him into the night and early morning.[196]

Fields did not seek this interview and, at the start, no one told him that he had the right to decline to speak.[197] Shut in with armed officers, Fields felt "trapped."[198] Even when the officers said that he could return to his cell if he refused to cooperate, Fields believed that the deputies would have kept him there.[199] At the suppression hearing, Fields testified that, although he had said several times that he did not want to talk, he did not specifically ask to go back

---

191. *See infra* notes 246–66 and accompanying text (discussing the policies behind *Edwards* and how they can now be ignored).

192. *See infra* notes 246–66 and accompanying text (discussing the policies behind *Edwards* and how they can now be ignored).

193. *Shatzer*, 130 S. Ct. at 1224. *See infra* Part V (discussing how *Shatzer* contributes to the recreation of Dead House).

194. *Fields*, 132 S. Ct. 1181.

195. *Id.* at 1185–86. Fields "had to go down one floor and pass through a locked door that separated two sections of the facility," and he "arrived at the conference room between 7 p.m. and 9 p.m." *Id.* at 1186.

196. Fields "testified that he left his cell around 8 p.m. and that the interview began around 8:30 p.m." *Id.* at 1186 n. 1 (citing App. To Pet for Cert. 77a). He was "questioned for between five and seven hours." *Id.* at 1186.

197. *Id.* at 1195 (Ginsburg, J. concurring in part and dissenting in part) (citing App. To Pet. For Cert. 71a).

198. *Id.*

199. *Fields*, 132 S. Ct. 1186 (citing App. To Pet. For Cert 71a, 72a).

to his cell before the session's end.[200] Fields had other issues, which made the ordeal especially grueling: each night, Fields took an antidepressant and, because he had a kidney transplant, needed antirejection medications as well.[201] The officials gave Fields water, but did not administer his meds.[202]

When deputies questioned him about accusations that, prior to prison, he had engaged in sexual conduct with a 12-year-old boy, Fields "became agitated and began to yell."[203] According to Fields's testimony, one of the deputies, using an expletive, said that "if [he] didn't want to cooperate, [he] could leave."[204] Eventually, Fields confessed, after which the authorities had Fields wait an additional twenty minutes or so while they secured a corrections officer to escort him back to his cell.[205] Fields did not return to his cell until more than an hour after he was accustomed to retiring.[206] Throughout the entire session, no one administered *Miranda* warnings or told Fields that he did not have to speak to the deputies.[207]

When the State of Michigan charged Fields with criminal sexual conduct, Fields unsuccessfully sought suppression, but in habeas proceedings, the federal courts granted Fields relief.[208] In a reversal, authored by Justice Alito, the Supreme Court scolded the Sixth Circuit for utilizing what it characterized as a categorical rule. But it was the Supreme Court that did precisely that: the

---

200. *Id.* at 1186 (citing App. To Pet. For Cert. 92a, 93a).

201. *Id.* 1195 & n.* (Ginsburg, J. concurring and dissenting) (citing App. To Pet. For Cert. 79a).

202. *Id.* at 1195.

203. *Fields*, 132 S. Ct. at 1186.

204. *Id.*

205. *Id.*

206. *Id.* at 1186 n. 3 ("Fields testified that his normal bedtime was 10:30 p.m. or 11 p.m.").

207. *Id.* at 1186.

208. When the State of Michigan charged Fields with criminal sexual conduct, he moved to suppress his confession on the basis of *Miranda*. *Id.* After his motion to suppress and renewed defense objections to state testimony were denied, the jury convicted Fields of two counts of third-degree criminal sexual conduct. *Id.* The judge sentenced him to a term of 10 to 15 years in prison. The Michigan Court of Appeals affirmed, and the Michigan Supreme Court denied discretionary review. The Federal District Court, however, granted Fields habeas corpus relief, and the Sixth Circuit Affirmed. In so doing, the courts found that Fields's isolation from the prison population, plus the fact that the questioning focused on conduct that occurred outside of the prison, makes the interrogation custodial. The court reasoned that *Mathis*, 391 U.S. 1, established that "'*Miranda* warnings must be administered when law enforcement officers remove an inmate from the general population and interrogate him regarding criminal conduct that took place outside the jail or prison.'" *Fields*, 132 S. Ct. at 1187 (quoting Fields v. Howes, 617 F.3d 813, 820 (6th Cir. 2010)).

Court adopted a categorical rule effectually stripping inmates of all *Miranda* safeguards.[209]

The *Fields* Court used precedent, like *Mathis*, *Perkins*, and *Shatzer*, to bolster its theory that prison is not custody.[210] As discussed above, in *Mathis*, the Supreme Court held that *Miranda* applied to an inmate removed from the general prison population and interrogated about criminal conduct occurring outside of the jail.[211] *Mathis* was, in fact, the fulcrum of the federal appellate decision, because the significant facts in *Fields* matched those in *Mathis*: Fields, like Mathis, was extricated from the general population and interrogated about conduct occurring outside of the jail.[212] The Supreme Court, accusing the Sixth Circuit of "misreading" *Mathis*, contorted *Mathis* into a rejection of the factors that the *Mathis* Court had deemed determinative.[213] The *Fields* Court said that, in *Mathis*, it specifically found that a "prisoner is not taken outside the scope of *Miranda* by either of the two factors on which the Court of Appeals had relied."[214] Under *Fields*, being removed from the prison population and interrogated about conduct outside of the prison does not trigger *Miranda* protection. The Court said that *Miranda* is inapplicable when the " 'inherently compelling pressures' of custodial interrogation" are not present.[215]

As also discussed above, the *Perkins* Court said that "[t]he bare facts of custody may not in every instance require a warning *even when the suspect is aware that he is speaking to an official, but we do not have occasion to explore that issue here.*"[216] The *Fields* Court, plucking that language, construed it as indicating that *Miranda* warnings are not mandated "whenever a suspect is in custody in a technical sense and converses with someone who happens to be a government agent."[217] The Court, ignoring what was undisputed in *Perkins*—the existence of custody— somehow recruited *Perkins* as an ally for the axiom that prison is not custody.[218]

---

209. *See infra* Part V (discussing how *Fields* creates a categorical rule).

210. *See supra* Part IV. A & B (discussing the prior cases and their reasoning).

211. See *supra* Part IV. A (discussing *Mathis*, 391 U.S. 1).

212. *Fields*, 132 S. Ct. 1187. ("Because Fields was isolated from the general prison population and interrogated about conduct occurring in the outside world, the Court of Appeals found the state court's decision was contrary to clearly established federal law....")

213. *Id.* at 1188.

214. *Id.*

215. *Id.*

216. *Id.* at 1187 (emphasis by Court). *See also Perkins*, 496 U.S. at 297; *supra* notes 175–88 and accompanying text (discussing *Perkins*).

217. *Fields*, 132 S. Ct. at 1187.

218. *See supra* notes 175–83 and accompanying text (discussing the *Perkins* decision and what it really says).

The *Fields* Court, revisiting *Shatzer*, said that the case had rejected all bright-line rules for *Miranda* safeguards: it felt that, in *Shatzer*, it had recognized that incarceration does not necessarily constitute *Miranda* custody, and said that custody "depends upon whether [incarceration] exerts the coercive pressure that *Miranda* was designed to guard against."[219] While the *Shatzer* Court had chiseled away primarily at *Edwards*, the *Miranda* offshoot, it had stopped short of holding that *Miranda* protections are *per se* unavailable to inmates.[220] The *Shatzer* Court said point blank that "[n]o one questions that Shatzer was in custody for *Miranda* purposes."[221] The *Fields* Court, however, brushed that language aside as indicating that "the issue of custody was not contested before [it]."[222]

The *Fields* Court further found that the facts before it did not amount to custody. In so doing, it essentially foreclosed *Miranda* safeguards in the prison context.[223] After branding the Sixth Circuit formula as wrongly "categorical," the Court categorically ruled that imprisonment plus private interrogation about events allegedly occurring outside of or within prison does not equal custody.[224] After *Fields*, officers need only duplicate the *Fields* facts to free themselves of *Miranda*.[225]

V. The Recreation of Dead House

In Dostoevsky's time, offenders, some innocent, were exiled to serve hard time in remote Siberia, far from homes, families, and communities.[226] Un-

---

219. *Fields*, 132 S. Ct. at 1188. The *Fields* Court also relies on the inapposite case, Berkemer v. McCarty, 468 U.S. 420 (1984), in the which the Court held that roadside questioning of a motorist, pulled over in a routine traffic stop, did not constitute custodial interrogation because, *inter alia*, it is "temporary" and "relatively nonthreatening." *Id.* at 437. While one could, of course, disagree with the reasoning in *Berkemer*, it is even easier to balk at the Court's equating a traffic stop detention on a public road with being yanked out of a jail cell, secreted to a separate chamber, and questioned there by authorities.

220. See *supra* Part IV. B (discussing the *Shatzer* decision).

221. *Shatzer*, 130 S. Ct. at 1224.

222. *Fields*, 132 S. Ct. at 1188.

223. *See infra* notes 302–307 and accompanying text (discussing how the *Fields* facts are going to match virtually all prison interrogation facts).

224. *Fields*, 132 S. Ct. at 1187. *See infra* notes 302–307 and accompanying text (discussing how the *Fields* facts create a categorical rule).

225. *See infra* notes 302–307 and accompanying text (discussing how *Fields* can be used to help police to evade *Miranda* in the prison context.).

226. In *Dead House*, there is one man who is accused and convicted of murdering his father so that he can "get his hands on his inheritance." DOSTOEVSKY, *supra* note 1, at 37.

derstandably, today's *Dead House* readers tend to relegate the novel to the genre of historical anomaly, or as a portrayal of an archaic penal system, worlds apart from our own. Such thinking is delusion or denial, a way to deflect the unsettling likeness between Dostoevsky's Omsk fortress and our own prisons. Recently, the Supreme Court, by divesting from inmates what little is left of the *Miranda* safeguards, has effectually encouraged the recreation of the kind of conditions that defined Dead House. This is no trivial matter: our prison population, with over 2.3 million people confined in state and federal facilities, is enormous.[227]

A. No Free Will

In *Dead House*, Dostoevsky shows how inmates are stripped of free will, a process that narrator Goryanchikov breaks down into excessive regulation, coercion, and futility.[228] While these elements, transcending time and place, had already existed in modern-day prisons, the Supreme Court, through its anti-*Miranda* rulings, has intensified them.

Goryanchikov, along with his colleagues, endures the "endogenous and accepted rules of the prison" which "suck[] the vital sap" of the men.[229] Every facet of daily life is "*forced*, compulsory, done under the threat of a stick."[230] An omnipresent sense of futility reigns, rendering Dead House residents powerless to make choices or effectuate change.[231] While they desperately cling to evanescent dreams of freedom, to visions of a future with choices, which keep

---

His father's "body was found in a ditch" and "[i]t was dressed and neatly arranged, the grey-haired head had been cut off and laid against the torso" and "under the head the murderer had placed a pillow." *Id.* The convict "had made no confession; had been stripped of his nobility and government service rank, and had been sentenced to twenty years' deportation and penal servitude." *Id.* It later turned out, however, that although "the facts were so clear that there could be no doubt about [his guilt],"this convict was innocent: "the true perpetrators of the crime had apparently been found and had confessed" after the one that was falsely convicted "had [already] suffered ten years of penal servitude for no reason." *Id.* at 391–92. The narrator exclaims that there is "[n]o need to expatiate on the tragic profundity of this case, on the young life ruined by such a dreadful accusation." *Id.* at 392. *See also infra* notes 342–43 and accompanying text.

227. *See generally* Sharon Dolovich, *Teaching Prison Law*, 62 J. LEGAL. EDUC. 218, 218 (2012).

228. *See supra* Part II. (describing the components of Dead House).

229. DOSTOEVSKY, *supra* note 1, at 32, 36.

230. *Id.* at 32–33.

231. *See supra* Part II. (describing the atmosphere in Dead House).

them alive or sane, futility competes to dissolve what sustains them.[232] The guards dominate, search, abuse, and lie. Dead House victims are gutted of free will and choice in every facet of their routine.[233]

Dead House regulations, coercion, and futility are so all-pervasive that men, risking death, even maneuver their way into a mephitic hospital just "to have a rest" and get a modicum of reprieve.[234] To them, the hospital represents an upgrade, even though it is bristling with contagion, fevers, sores, venereal diseases, tuberculosis, and lacks sanitation. Goryanchikov makes that point by showing how the hospital, failing to disinfect, recycles filthy, smelly gowns from one patient to the next. In one of the most memorable scenes, Goryanchikov recalls a chronic sneezer, who "would open his handkerchief out and closely examine the abundant gobbets of snot in it, whereupon he would immediately smear it all over his brown prison dressing gown, so that all the snot stayed on the dressing gown and the handkerchief was left only slightly damp."[235] The narrator notices that this "drew not the slightest protest from the other patients, even though one of them would have to wear the dressing gown after him."[236] Readers realize that while the hospital is quite vile, it is the doctors' relative benevolence that makes it better than the coerced fortress of futility, "guarded by sentries at every hour of the day and night."[237]

What does a snotty hospital gown, or any of this, have to do with *Shatzer* and *Fields*? Justice Stevens, likely cognizant of why Dead House inmates might opt for a hospital stay, posits an answer: In words reminiscent of Goryanchikov's, Stevens explains that "[a] prisoner's freedom is severely limited and his entire life remains subject to government control" and that it "is not like a normal situation in which a suspect 'is in control and need only shut his door or walk away to avoid police.' "[238] Justice Steven's point is that the erosion of *Edwards* in the

---

232. *See supra* Part II.(discussing how Dead House inmates cling to hope).

233. *See generally supra* Part II (elaborating on Dostoevsky's depiction of Dead House).

234. Dostoevsky, *supra* note 1, at 213.

235. *Id.* at 214.

236. *Id. See also* Ruttenburg, *supra* note 4 at 153 ("The gown is an instrument of revelation: it is able to bridge the impassable abyss between Gorianchikov and the peasant-convicts because its significance is entirely adequate to and can be immediately apprehended in its materiality, the bodily fluids with which it is saturated and the bodily warmth which distils and releases them.").

237. Dosteovsky, *supra* note 1, at 27.

238. *Shatzer*, 130 S. Ct. at 1233 (Stevens, J. concurring) ("Such an environment is not conducive to shak[ing] off any residual coercive effects of his prior custody.").

prison context is to delete it precisely where it is essential. While American prisons vary with respect to levels of confinement, they share attributes.[239] In the *Miranda* lexicon, prison "deprive[s] [inmates] of their freedom in a significant way."[240] Prisoners are typically physically confined in a limited space and can only go places and act with permission.[241] In addition, prisoners have a reduced expectation of privacy and, like Dead House residents, can be searched, exposed to constant surveillance, and reasonably feel that the government is not just watching, but monitoring, their every move.[242] Naturally, those incarcerated do not feel at liberty to rebel against or decline authoritative "requests."[243] In fact, pressure to comply is greater where, as is often the case, cooperation factors into parole hearings.[244]

The effect of the *Shatzer* and *Fields* decisions, which magnify the restraint already extant in our prisons, promotes added regulation, coercion and futility. As discussed above, in *Shatzer*, the Court held that the prisoner's release back into the general population qualified as a break in *Miranda* custody and legislated a 14-day time frame for the expiration of the *Edwards* rule.[245] Two aspects of the *Shatzer* Court's reasoning—the dilution of the *Edwards* rule and the Court's misrepresentation of prison life—bring our prisoners closer to their burial in Dead House.

---

239. *See generally* Brief of Amicus Curiae National Association of Criminal Defense Lawyers in Support of Respondent, Maryland v. Shatzer, 2009 WL 1611722 (U.S.) at *25 (U.S. June 5, 2009) (describing the restraint on freedom in prisons).

240. *Miranda*, 384 U.S. at 478.

241. *See generally* Brief, *supra* note 239.

242. *See id. See also* Hudson v. Palmer, 468 U.S. 517, 526 (1984) ("[W]e hold that society is not prepared to recognize as legitimate any subjective expectation of privacy that a prisoner might have in his prison cell and that, accordingly the Fourth Amendment proscription against unreasonable searches does not apply within the confines of the prison cell."); Florence v. Board of Chosen Freeholders of County of Burlington, 131 S. Ct. 1816 (2011) (holding that even detainees admitted to a prison's general population are required to submit to mandatory strip searches in the name of "Jail security.").

243. *See generally* Brief, *supra* note 239; *Shatzer*, 130 S. Ct. at 1233 (Stevens, J., concurring) ("Prison guards may not look kindly upon a prisoner who refuses to cooperate with police.").

244. *See generally* Brief, *supra* note 239; *Shatzer*, 130 S. Ct. at 1233 (Stevens, J. concurring) (citing Code of Md. Regs., tit. 12, §08.01.18(A)(3) (2009) (naming "[t]he offender's behavior and adjustment" and "[t]he offender's current attitude toward society, discipline, and other authority," as considerations for parole).

245. *See supra* Part IV. B (discussing *Shatzer*). *See also infra* notes 246–66 and accompanying text (discussing *Edwards*, 451 U.S. 477 (1981)).

First, post-*Shatzer*, inmates can no longer rely on *Edwards*. The *Edwards* rule fortifies the *Miranda* Court's mandate that "[i]f ... individual[s] state that [they] want an attorney, the interrogation must cease until an attorney is present."[246] In *Edwards*, the defendant said, "I want an attorney before making a deal" and the police stopped.[247] But, returning the next morning, the police told the defendant that he "had to" talk to them.[248] Edwards, eventually waiving, incriminated himself. The Court invalidated the alleged waiver because the police had initiated the second interrogation. The *Edwards* Court clarified that the only true waiver is, and has to be, a product of free will. That is, the arrestees themselves, choosing freely, must be the ones to "initiate further communication, exchanges, or conversations with the police" after invoking the right to counsel.[249]

The *Edwards* rule, with its bright-line stature, has been the fair-haired child in the family of *Miranda* cases.[250] The Court has blessed the request for counsel more than the sibling invocation of the right to silence.[251] The *Edwards*'

---

246. *Miranda*, 384 U.S. at 128. *See supra* Part III. B. 1 (discussing *Miranda*).

247. *Edwards*, 451 U.S. at 479.

248. *Id.*

249. *Id.* at 484–85.

250. Even in the post-*Miranda* world, many attempts to get around *Edwards* have failed. *See e.g.*, Arizona v. Roberson, 486 U.S. 675, 687 (1988) (The Court applied *Edwards* to interrogations concerned with unrelated offenses, barring police from questioning a suspect if he had asserted his right to counsel during a prior interrogation for an unrelated offense.). *See also* Minnick v. Mississippi, 498 U.S. 146 (1990) (The Court applied *Edwards* when a suspect had the opportunity to consult with counsel, but did not have counsel present for questioning.). *But see* Davis v. United States, 512 U.S. 452 (1994). During a police interview, Davis said, "Maybe I should talk to a lawyer." *Id.* at 555. The interviewers testified that they asked Davis whether he meant that he wanted a lawyer and Davis answered, "No, I'm not asking for a lawyer." *Id.* After a short break, the interview continued for another hour until Davis said, "I think I want a lawyer before I say anything else." *Id.* Davis argued in support of suppression that his statement, "Maybe I should talk to a lawyer," constituted an invocation of his right to counsel. *Id.* at 459. The Supreme Court, disagreeing, said that interrogations may continue unless a suspect clearly and unequivocally requests counsel. *Id.* at 460–61. *See generally* Thomas N. Radek, Note, Arizona v. Roberson: *The Supreme Court Expands Suspects' Rights in the Custodial Interrogation Setting*, 22 J. Marshall L. Rev. 685, 686 (1989) (discussing how *Roberson* strengthens *Edwards*). *See also* Marcy Strauss, *The Sounds of Silence: Reconsidering the Invocation of the Right to Remain Silent Under* Miranda, 17 Wm. & Mary Bill Rts. J. 773, 1022 (2009) (In various challenges to *Edwards*, "the Court was concerned with preserving the clear, bright-line nature of the *Edwards* decision.").

251. *Compare Edwards*, 451 U.S. at 484–85 (holding that, when a suspect invokes the right to counsel, the interrogation must cease until counsel is made available or the suspect initiates discussion), *with* Michigan v. Mosley, 423 U.S. 96, 102–04 (1975) (holding that, when a suspect asserts the right to remain silent, the interrogation must cease immediately,

cases, reiterating that the right to counsel must be scrupulously honored, make it more difficult to waive than the right to silence.[252] The Court has given sound reasons for this: normatively, suspects requesting counsel tend to feel powerless or overmatched and thus choose not to interact *pro se* with police.[253] In such a situation, it is unlikely that individuals would later, doing a complete about face, elect for just such an uncounseled exchange with interrogators.[254] For these reasons, under strict *Edwards*, if the police (not the suspect) re-initiate interrogation after the suspect has invoked the counsel right, the confession is out.[255] This is so even if the state can show that the defendant knew his or her rights and voluntarily waived them.[256]

---

it does not follow that law enforcement may not resume questioning two hours later). In *Mosley*, the Court held that *Miranda* did not require a *"per se* proscription of indefinite duration" upon police interrogation after a suspect invoked the right to remain silent. *Id.* Rather, as the *Mosley* Court put it, all *Miranda* requires is the "scrupulous honor[ing]" of the "right to cut off questioning." *Id.* For the *Mosley* Court, *Miranda's* goal was to make police respect the suspect's invocation of the right to silence and to give the suspect control over the time of the interrogation, its subject, and its duration. *Id.* The Court reasoned that when police resume questioning after the invocation of the right to silence it does not necessarily impair those goals. *Id. See also Godsey, supra* note 110 at 804 ("[W]hen a suspect invokes her right to counsel, the rules regarding when the police can reengage the suspect are more protective than when a suspect merely invokes the right to remain silent."); Rosenberg & Rosenberg, *supra* note 100, at 88–89 (discussing the different rules for when a suspect invokes the right to counsel as opposed to the right to silence and that "[i]nvocation of the right to silence has not resulted in either a per se prohibition of further interrogation or any other measures designed to overcome the effects of continued detention and resumption of questioning"); Strauss, *supra* note 250, at 818–19 (explaining how the invocation of the right to counsel has more consequences for law enforcement than does the assertion of the right to remain silent).

    252. *See supra* notes 246–51 and accompanying text.

    253. *See supra* notes 246–51 and accompanying text. *See also Shatzer*, 130 S. Ct. at 1230-31 (Stevens, J. concurring) A suspect requesting counsel " 'signals his inability to cope with the pressures of custodial interrogation' " and " 'considers himself unable to deal with the pressures of custodial interrogation without legal assistance.' ") (quoting *Roberson*, 486 U.S. at 683, 686)

    254. *See generally Edwards*, 451 U.S. at 484–85. *See also Roberson*, 486 U.S. at 681 (Under *Edwards*, once a suspect indicates that "he is not capable of undergoing [custodial] interrogation without advice of counsel, ... any subsequent waiver that has come at the authorities' behest, and not at the suspect's own instigation, is itself the product of the 'inherently compelling pressures' and not the purely voluntary choice of the suspect.")

    255. *See supra* notes 246–54.

    256. *See supra* notes 246–54.

The *Edwards* rule has practical and psychological benefits.[257] By guiding law enforcement and limiting the amount of suppression hearings, it, of course, aims to promote judicial economy.[258] Essentially, *Edwards*, with its presumption of involuntariness, like *Miranda* itself, aspires to relieve courts of the task of engaging in multiple ad hoc voluntariness inquiries.[259] Beyond that, and more importantly, the *Edwards* cases seek to preserve the integrity of individual choice.[260] The Court has acknowledged that suspects, asking for a lawyer, express vulnerability and signal their own "inability to cope with the pressures of custodial interrogation."[261] The *Edwards* rule prevents police from badgering and extinguishing free will, especially when individuals have voiced susceptibility to coercion.[262]

The *Edwards* decision, aligned with *Miranda*, sees coercion for what it is—namely, as the proficient shape shifter that can materialize as pressure, deception, trickery, or even bald lies.[263] As Justice Stevens said in *Shatzer*, the Court's new *Edwards* exception not only gives police an extra coercive grenade, but one that detonates the shrapnel of a lie. As he put it, when police tell suspects that they have the right to an attorney, that they do not have to speak without an attorney present, and that an attorney can be provided to them at no cost, all of that amounts to "a significant promise."[264] But, if the police start ques-

---

257. *See supra* notes 246–54. *See also* Minnick v. Mississippi, 498 U.S. at 153 (discussing how once a suspect requests counsel, subsequent requests for interrogation increase the risk of coercion, which adds to the pressure that starts when the individual is in custody, and is likely to "increase as custody is prolonged"). *See generally* Godsey, *supra* note 110, at 803–05 & n. 95 (discussing the right to counsel prong of the *Edwards* rule).

258. *See Minnick*, 498 U.S. at 151 (explaining how the *Edwards* presumption of involuntariness "conserves judicial resources which would otherwise be expended in making difficult determinations of voluntariness").

259. *Id.*

260. *See* Patterson v. Illinois, 487 U.S. 285, 291 (1988) (Edwards aims to "[p]reserve the integrity of an accused's choice to communicate with police only through counsel.").

261. *See* Roberson, 486 U.S. at 686. *See also* Shatzer, 130 S. Ct. at 1230 (Stevens, J. concurring) (citing *Miranda*, 485 U.S. at 686); Mosley, 423 U.S. at 110 (White, J. concurring) ("[T]he accused having expressed his own view that he is not competent to deal with the authorities without legal advice, a later decision at the authorities' insistence to make a statement without counsel's presence may properly be viewed with skepticism.").

262. *See supra* note 246–61 and accompanying text. *See also* Michigan v. Harvey, 494 U.S. 344, 350 (1990) (*Edwards* "prevents police from badgering a defendant into waiving his previously asserted *Miranda* rights."). *See also* Shatzer, 130 S. Ct. at 1220 (Justice Scalia, opining that a prophylactic rule applies "only where its benefits outweigh its costs," concludes that the "benefits of the [*Edwards* rule] are measured by the number of coerced confessions it suppresses that otherwise would have been admitted.").

263. *See generally Miranda*, 455 U.S. 477 (discussing the various tactics and deceptive methods the police use to extract confessions).

264. *Shatzer*, 130 S .Ct. at 1230 (Stevens, J. concurring).

tioning after a short hiatus (like only two weeks later), and do so without honoring the promise, suspects, still without counsel, are "likely to feel that the police lied to [them] and that they really do not have any right to a lawyer."[265] Such already pliant individuals, who tend to feel overpowered, will see their asserted choice as trumped, their invocation as "futile" and a "confession (true or not) as the only way to end [the] interrogation."[266]

Of course, if, after *Fields*, the police still bother to Mirandize their incarcerated suspect, it is also now permissible, after *Powell*, for police to obfuscate the message that the right to an attorney entails having one present during the interrogation.[267] Now, interrogators can lie, and ice that cake with a driblet of ambiguity. The *Shatzer* Court has thus given prisoner-interrogators a deceptive maneuver of the sort that *Edwards* deleted from inventory. In so doing, the Court has infused more pressure into what is already a virtual pressure cooker.

Second, Scalia distorts prison life, which, after incubating a while, re-emerges as the contradictory predicate for the *Fields* decision, the one that completely expels *Miranda* from prison. Scalia begins by finding a distinction between the *Edwards* cases' fact patterns and that of *Shatzer*.[268] He opines that, in cases in which the Court has applied *Edwards*, police "arrest suspects for a particular crime" and hold them in "uninterrupted custody" while they investigate.[269] Scalia then contrasts the "paradigm *Edwards* case[s]," with those arising in prison, where suspects "regain[] a sense of control or normalcy after they [are] initially taken into custody for the crime under investigation."[270] In Scalia's view, where suspects are released from custodial interrogation and returned to a "normal life" before the interrogators resume fourteen days later, there is little danger of *Edwards* coercion.[271]

From there, Scalia does his little exegesis on coercion-free normalcy, and it is here that we can easily lose sight of the fact that he is talking about *prison*.

---

265. *Id.*

266. *Id.* (quoting *Davis v. United States*, 512 U.S. at 472–73 (Souter, J. concurring in judgment). Justice Stevens also cites *Cooper v. Dupnik*, 963 F.2d 1220, 1225 (9th Cir. 1992 (en banc), in which the court "describe[d] an elaborate police task force plan to ignore a suspect's requests for counsel, on the theory that such would induce hopelessness and thereby elicit an admission." *Id.*

267. *Powell*, 130 S. Ct. 1995. *See supra* notes 154–56 and accompanying text (discussing the effect of *Powell*).

268. *Shatzer*, 130 S. Ct. at 1220–21.

269. *Id.* at 1220.

270. *Id.* at 1220–21.

271. *Id.* at 1221.

He states that, once released from interrogation, suspects "no longer" feel isolated and have "likely been able to seek advice from an attorney, family members, and friends[,] and … know[] from [their] earlier experience that [they] need only demand counsel to bring the interrogation to a halt."[272] In his mind, prisoners, shipped back to their cell, "regain[] a sense of control or normalcy," make choices, and shape their own destiny.[273] This culminates in Scalia's elaboration on Shatzer's supposedly cushy life in his medium-security state correctional facility:

> Inmates in these facilities generally can visit the library each week, … have regular exercise and recreation periods, … can participate in basic adult education and occupational training, … are able to send and receive mail, … and are allowed to receive visitors twice a week.[274]

What is, of course, surprising is that Scalia does not wax eloquent about the hot tub, massages, golf course, and chocolates on the pillows at night. For Scalia, the "inherently compelling pressures" of custodial interrogation end when Shatzer returns to a "normal life," one likened to (or rather "Scalia-sized" into) a near Ritz Carlton stay.[275] In an almost uncanny retort, Dostoevsky says that "[n]o convict feels *at home* in prison" and that "the convicts lived … not as if this were their home, but as in some wayside inn, *en route* somewhere."[276] Justice Stevens, reprising the gist of the Russian novelist's assessment, says that "a trip to one's prison cell is not the same [as a trip to one's home,]" and thus, cannot possibly "change the *Edwards* calculus."[277] The reality is that prisoners, whose whole life is at the mercy of government control, have little to no freedom. Because such facilities, like Dead House, typically limit communications, residents cannot readily (especially within a little two-week time frame) access advice from attorneys, family members, and friends.[278]

Justice Stevens also asserts that for prisoners, detentions are not necessarily "disconnected from their prior unwillingness to cooperate with an investi-

---

272. *Id.*
273. *Id.*
274. *Id.* at 1225.
275. *Id.*
276. DOSTOEVSKY, *supra* note 1, at 128, 133.
277. *Shatzer*, 130 S. Ct. at 1232 (Stevens, J. concurring).
278. *See id.* (citing *Montejo v. Louisiana*, 556 U.S. 778) ("Nor, in most cases, can [a prisoner] live comfortably knowing that he cannot be badgered by police; prison is not like a normal situation in which a suspect 'is in control, and need only shut his door or walk always to avoid police badgering.'").

gation."[279] Prisoners may reasonably sense that prison guards, the very ones who puppeteer every move in their lives, "may not look kindly upon" resistance.[280] Further, even if there is no real partnership between guards and interrogators, prisoners are not likely to see it that way. When a guard marches captives off to some chamber to speak to police, they are reasonably inclined to view guard and interrogator as yokemates and will likely fear that their insubordination, or their election of silence or request for counsel, will trigger retaliation.[281] On top of that, most inmates know that cooperation is often a factor in parole hearings.[282] As such, the "break," likened to going "home," which, according to Scalia, ruptures the causal chain of coercion, is more likely to have the diametrically opposite effect of intensifying the pressure.[283] Most individuals, like Shatzer, will feel that they have no choice and, wanting to get the damn thing over with, give a confession (true or not), even without what might have been promised in recited *Miranda* warnings—namely, without that lawyer at their side.[284]

As discussed, the *Edwards* rule is one of few somewhat hearty *Miranda* veterans, but since *Shatzer*, prisoners have essentially been blocked from its benefits.[285] Scalia's set time frame for the "break" converts *Edwards* into a "how to" manual, one conceivably entitled *Coercion For Dummies*. When prisoners say "lawyer," all the interrogators need do is escort them back to their cell, calendar fourteen days, and then begin anew in the absence of counsel.[286] Con-

---

279. *Shatzer*, 130 S. Ct. at 1233.

280. *Id.*

281. *See id.* (quoting Illinois v. Perkins, 496 U.S. at 297 (emphasis added by Justice Stevens) ("'Questioning by captors, who *appear* to control the suspect's fate, may create mutually reinforcing pressures that the Court has assumed will weaken the suspect's will.'")

282. *Shatzer*, 130 S. Ct. at 1233. *See also supra* note 244 and accompanying text (discussing factors in parole hearings).

283. *See supra* notes 270–75 and accompanying text (discussing Scalia's distorted portray of prison life).

284. *See infra* notes 322, 347–48 and accompanying text (discussing how suspects frequently confess, and even confess to things they didn't do). *See also supra* Chapter III (The Confessant Gene: *Crime and Punishment* and *The Brothers Karamazov*).

285. *See supra* notes 246–66 and accompanying text (discussing the Supreme Court's reluctance to engraft exceptions onto the *Edwards* rule).

286. *See* Shatzer, 130 S. Ct. at 1233 n. 10 (Stevens, J. concurring) ("With a time limit as short as 14 days, police who hope that they can eventually extract a confession may feel comfortable releasing a suspect for a short period of time" and "[t]he resulting delay will only increase the compelling pressures on the suspect."). *See generally* Leo, *supra* note 79 (discussing how police, using the *Miranda* decisions, are trained to violate or dodge *Miranda*).

trary to Scalia's hypothesis, the trip to prison cell "normalcy" does not "shake off any residual coercive effects of prior custody," but, likely weakening the suspects' resolve, will prompt the end result—a confession.[287] But for Scalia, that confession is "voluntary" and an "unmitigated good" because it lets law enforcement close the file.[288] Incidentally, for a time in Dostoevsky's Russia, rulers felt that way about corporal punishment, which was just the means to an end.

While *Shatzer* gives police leeway to circumvent *Edwards*, the *Fields* decision gives inmate interrogators license to ignore *Miranda* itself.[289] In so doing, the Court does not try to counter, but actually increases, the coercive forces already extant in prison. For the *Fields* Court, the inquiry boils down to deciding whether the case *sub judice* presents the same inherently coercive pressures as *Miranda*'s station-house questioning. Here the Court, recruiting *Shatzer*, distinguished Fields's "custody" from *Miranda* custody. The *Fields* Court opined that questioning an individual already serving time "does not generally involve the shock that very often accompanies arrest" and that, unlike the *Miranda* situation, such an individual is not whisked away from home to the unfamiliar "'police-dominated atmosphere.'"[290] The prisoner, in contrast to the presentenced accused, is unlikely to be "lured into speaking by a longing for prompt relief and knows that confinement will continue regardless of what transpires."[291] Also, the prisoner, unlike the station-house suspect, knows that interrogators lack power to abbreviate the sentence.[292] Consequently, the Court concluded that the factors present in *Fields* neither implicate *Miranda* policies nor necessitate its prophylactic safeguards.

See also Kyle C. Barry, *Protecting the Fifth Amendment:* Maryland v. Shatzer *and Prophylactic Rule-Making in the Supreme Court's* Miranda *Jurisprudence*, 36 Vt. B. J. 30, 32 (2010) (describing the pressure associated with the release and recapture procedure). Ryan T. Williams points out that, with respect to *Shatzer*, there is "potential for abuse," and that "[t]he FBI or some other government agency may attempt to use the *Shatzer* two-week window to exact undue pressure in an attempt to make them change their mind and waive *Miranda*." Ryan T. Williams, *Stop Taking the Bait: Diluting the* Miranda *Doctrine Does Not Make America Safer From Terrorism*, 56 Loy. L. Rev. 907, 940 (2010).

287. *Shatzer*, 130 S. Ct. at 1223. *See also id.* at 122–23 (Stevens, J. concurring) (refuting Scalia's reasoning).

288. *Id.* at 1222.

289. *Fields*, 132 S. Ct. 1181.

290. *Id.* at 1190 (citing *Miranda*, 384 U.S. at 456).

291. *Fields*, 132 S. Ct. at 1191.

292. *See id.* (citing *Shatzer*, 130 S. Ct. at 1224–25) ("And 'where the possibility of parole exists,' the interrogating officers probably lack the power to bring about an early release.").

By stressing that the extrication of a prisoner from the general population for interrogation is not enough to warrant *Miranda* protections, the Court ensured that the safeguards will rarely, if ever, apply to prisoners. The Court opined that the typical *Miranda* suspect feels coerced by the absence of family members, friends, lawyer, and others, who provide sympathy, advice, or support. For the *Fields* Court, separating an inmate from the others does not retract such a "supportive atmosphere."[293] For the Court, removal "is often in the best interest of the interviewee," who might want to keep the interrogation a secret.[294]

Here the Court, impugning its own reasoning in *Shatzer*, ignores the contradiction to create a new *per se* rule. In *Shatzer*, the Court portrayed the suspect's reunion with the general population as rejoining the family, where there is sympathy, advice, or support.[295] These were, in fact, the attributes that qualified the return "home" as *the* "break" in *Miranda* custody.[296] The *Fields* Court, in an implied retraction, indicted the general population as "hostile," as *non-familial*, and proclaimed that "[f]ellow inmates are by no means necessarily friends."[297] Thus, under *Shatzer-Fields*, *Miranda* is unavailable because other inmates are supportive, and *Miranda* is also unavailable because the others are not supportive. And although the Court conceded that inmates, pulled aside for questioning, may experience more curtailment of freedom, it found this to be immaterial because restrictive measures are "an ordinary and familiar attribute of life behind bars."[298] The reasoning here is not just disingenuous, but its effect is that an already restrictive place, as are all prison facilities, will probably never be deemed custodial.

Inmate interrogation inevitably comes in two flavors: it will address events allegedly occurring either outside of or within prison. The investigation could, of course, be hybrid and implicate both. The *Fields* Court indicated that none of these forms of interrogation are coercive, and thus they are exempt from

---

293. *Fields*, 132 S. Ct. at 1191.

294. *Id.* at 1192.

295. *See supra* notes 270–75 and accompanying text (discussing Scalia's distorted picture of prison life in *Shatzer*). *See also* James E. Robertson, *The "Turning-Out" of Boys in a Man's Prison: Why and How We Need to Amend the Prison Rape Elimination Act*, 44 IND. L. REV. 819 (2011) (describing how boys serving "adult time" are frequently sexually assaulted in county jails and state prisons, thus refuting the *Shatzer* Court's picture of prison life as warm, cordial, and familial).

296. *See supra* notes 270–75 and accompanying text (describing Scalia's distorted picture of prison life).

297. *Fields*, 132 S. Ct. at 1191.

298. *Id.* at 1192.

Miranda rules. The Court said that questioning about events on the outside is not more coercive than questioning about activity within the prison walls, because both can augur potential criminal liability and increased penalties. The Court also said that "an inmate who confesses to misconduct that occurred within the prison may also incur administrative penalties, but even this is not enough to tip the scale in the direction of custody."[299] Thus, interrogation that reasonably instills fear of penalties that can impair daily prison life cannot, and does not, coerce enough to summon *Miranda*. While the Court purports to adopt an approach that depends on whether the totality of the circumstances rises to the level of coercion, the Court systematically eliminates every conceivable circumstance that could figure into just about any inmate's interrogation-coercion argument.

In finding that the *Fields* record did not establish custody, the Court made it even more challenging, if not impossible, for inmates to ever lay claim to *Miranda* facts. The Court conceded that there were facts in the record bolstering Fields's position. Fields "did not invite the interview or consent to it in advance, and he was not advised that he was free to decline to speak with the deputies."[300] Fields endured a five to seven-hour ordeal in the evening, one which continued well past his usual bed time. The deputies were armed, and one even "[u]sed a very sharp tone" and profanity.[301] Although the Court said that such portions of the record "lend some support" to Fields's argument, it felt that other facts mitigated them, rendering the interview non-custodial: Fields was "not physically restrained or threatened" and officials initially told him, and reminded him later, that he could leave and return to his cell.[302] Moreover, officials kept Fields in a "well-lit, average-sized conference room, where he was 'not uncomfortable,'" sometimes left the door open, and offered him food and water.[303] For the Court, such things were not only "consistent with an interrogation environment in which a reasonable person would have felt free to terminate the interview and leave," but also suffice to excuse the other coercive, custodial attributes of Fields's five to seven-hour ordeal.[304]

The Court highlighted that the fact of life behind bars is what makes the situation non-custodial. It elaborated that Fields could not leave the room by

---

299. *Id.*
300. *Id.* at 1192–93.
301. *Id.* at 1193.
302. *Id.*
303. *Id.*
304. *Id.*

himself and "make his own way through the facility to his cell."[305] He had to be "escorted," and then had to wait for an officer to "escort" him back.[306] The Court said that such features were just part and parcel of prison life, and thus would have existed even if Fields had had to go to the conference room for any other reason. Consequently, after *Fields*, the deprivation of necessary medication plus an uninvited, prolonged, night-time interrogation in a chamber, apart from the general population, with armed deputies, and an officer speaking sharply and with profanity, will not amount to custodial coercion. The officers need only tell inmates that they can return to their cell, refrain from physical restraint or direct threats, offer food and water, ensure that the average-sized room is "well-lit," and intermittently swing open the door.[307] In short, interrogating inmates without the constraint of *Miranda* is now a piece of cake.

B. No Human Dignity

In *Dead House*, a paradoxical form of solitude, along with restraints and redundant torture, strips prisoners of human dignity.[308] Through its progressive anti-*Miranda* campaign, our Supreme Court has created an American gulag-analogue.

As discussed earlier, in the "forced communal existence" of Dead House, inmates suffer the relentless cognitive dissonance, loneliness with no alone-ness.[309] That is, while they rarely get solitude, escape bunkmates, or slip past ever-vigilant guards, the residents are famished for friendship, bonding, and conversation.[310] It is not surprising that throughout *Dead House*, we see men, exiled from families, friends, and communities, reaching out, spilling life stories, and even blurting out damning details of their crimes.[311] That is, there is endemic to prison life a force impelling residents to share and divulge.

Prison facilities in the United States are connate in their lonely non-aloneness. While limited space physically confines prisoners, who may spend hours by

---

305. *Id.*

306. *Id.*

307. *Id.*

308. *See supra* Part II. B (discussing how *Dead House* divests inmates of all vestiges of human dignity.)

309. DOSTOEVSKY, *supra* note 1, at 44.

310. *See supra* Part II. B (discussing how the inmates in *Dead House* are lonely, but nevertheless hungry for communion with others).

311. *See supra* note 59 and accompanying text (giving examples of Dead House inmates confessing, telling stories, and divulging secrets).

themselves, they are cognizant of the fact that they are never truly alone.[312] Under the Fourth Amendment, prisoners have reduced expectations of privacy, and know they can be, and are often, under the ever-vigilant government eye.[313] Guards, moreover, have virtually unbridled discretion to inspect and search.[314] Police can usually interview prisoners without formally placing them under arrest, and do so without probable cause.[315] Authorities can question at their pleasure, with no real evidence of guilt, undeterred by the prospect of liability for wrongful arrest.[316] Also, because the state need neither arraign nor initiate formal proceedings, the Sixth Amendment poses no obstacle to investigation.[317]

As in *Dead House*, due to such restraints and custodial pressures, inmates are prone to blabber, and this is no secret: police know and capitalize on it.[318] It is no coincidence that criminal procedure is chock full of cases in which prisoners deliver self-damaging goods to "friends," who turn out to be snitches or government ears.[319] The *Miranda* Court recognized that the "compulsion in-

---

312. *See* Brief of Amicus Curiae, *supra* note 239, at 25 ("Prisoners are physically confined in a limited space, often in the same place, and sometimes alone for several hours each day.")

313. *Id. See also supra* notes 239–44 and accompanying text (describing limitations on freedom in prison).

314. *See* Brief of Amicus Curiae, *supra* note 239. *See also supra* notes 239–44 and accompanying text (discussing the restraints typically associated with incarceration.).

315. *See Shatzer*, 130 S. Ct. 1233 n. 13 (Stevens, J. concurring).

316. *Id.*

317. *Id.* The Sixth Amendment right to counsel has no application prior to the time an individual is formally accused by the government. *See generally* Moran v. Burbine, 475 U.S.412 (1986) ("By its terms, [the Sixth Amendment] becomes applicable *only* when the government's role shifts from investigation to accusation" and does not "attach until after initiation of formal charges."); United States v. Gouveia, 467 U.S. 180 (1984) (concluding that the "right to counsel attaches at the initiation of adversary judicial criminal proceedings").

318. *See generally* note 59 and accompanying text (describing how various Dead House prisoners would try to share their stories and divulge secrets).

319. *See, e.g., Perkins*, 496 U.S. 292 (involving an incarcerated inmate, who makes incriminating statements to fellow inmate and undercover agent placed in cell block) and *supra* Part IV. A (discussing *Perkins*); United States v. Henry, 447 U.S. 264 (1980) (involving a prisoner who makes incriminating statements to another inmate, engaged as a paid informant for the FBI); Kuhlman v. Wilson, 477 U.S. 436 (1986) (involving an inmate who makes incriminating statement to another inmate, who agreed to act as a police informant and be the government's ear); Kansas v. Ventris, 556 U.S. 586 (2009) (Statements used to impeach Ventris, who testified at his trial, were obtained by a jailhouse snitch planted by

herent in custodial interrogation" and incarceration, the very epitome of inherent compulsion, can be the consummate catalyst for loose lips and the extraction of confessions.[320] Also, there is the reality, one that Professor Sharon
Dolovich addresses, that those "who end up under criminal justice control are
disproportionately likely to be suffering from drug addiction, severe mental
illness and/or learning disabilities," and often are "indigent, unskilled, under-
educated and/or illiterate."[321] Such individuals, tending to be especially in-
timidated by authority and susceptible to trickery and pressure, are the very ones
most likely to confess, and even falsely confess.[322]

As earlier described, *Dead House* guards administer floggings, which "hurt[]
like nothing on earth," and sharpen blows with psychological torture, comprised of anticipation, hiatus, and redundancy.[323] In recent anti-*Miranda* cases,
the Supreme Court has encouraged a mimicking *modus operandi* in our own
facilities. Because inmate suspects are already detained, police don't have to
worry about their flight or the ticking clock. Police can extract their sitting
ducks, interrogate, ship them back to their cell, let them stew awhile, and then
return them to the hot seat for re-interrogation. In connection with his *Edwards* analysis, commentator Kyle C. Barry has aptly called such a process a
"Kafkaesque game of catch and release," which causes a suspect to "feel even
more pressure to confess than one who is never released at all."[324] Dostoevsky,
who concurs, explains that one of the things that make Dead House lashings
most excruciating is the fact that they were methodically delivered in intervals,

---

police in Ventris's pretrial holding cell.) *See also* Dostoevsky, *supra* note 1, at 67 ("[In
prison], informing … is normally a flourishing business.").

320. *Miranda*, 384 U.S. at 458.

321. Dolovich, *supra* note 227, at 219–20

322. Daniel J. Seidman & Alex Stein, *The Right to Silence Helps the Innocent: A Game-
Theoretic Analysis of the Fifth Amendment Privilege*, 114 Harv. L. Rev. 430, 450 (2000) (discussing the "reality of police interrogation for neglected, alienated, weak, strained, subdued,
or feeble-minded suspects or for suspects who suffer from drug and alcohol problems, personality disorders, or physical diseases"). Seidmann & Stein also point out that "police intimidate many … suspects, some of whom are juveniles, and often these suspects would
say anything to please the interrogator." *Id.*

323. Dostoevsky, *supra* note 1, at 241. *See also supra* Part II. B (describing the corporal punishment in *Dead House*).

324. *See* Barry *supra* note 286 at 32 (discussing the pressure associated with such a redundant procedure). Barry quotes Franz Kafka, *The Trial* 197–199 (Willa & Edwin Muir trans.,
Random House 1956) (1937) ("'So then I am free,' said K. doubtfully. 'Yes,' said the painter,
'but only ostensibly free, or more exactly, provisionally free … it is … possible for the acquitted man to go straight home from the Court and find officers already waiting to arrest
him again.'"). Barry, *supra* note 286, at 32 n.38.

giving the victim a time-out vigil, in which they are forced to conterminously re-live and await misery.[325]

More and more, the Supreme Court is putting its imprimatur on prolonged, redundant intervals with putative breaks.[326] Not only do they evoke images of Dead House flagellation, but also revive the "privacy," "persistence," "isolation," "unfamiliarity," "show of hostility," and "trickery" in the techniques that the *Miranda* Court explicitly condemned.[327] Also, while the *Miranda* Court censured the police training that suggests that, "when normal procedures fail to produce the needed result, the police may resort to deceptive stratagems such as giving false legal advice," the *Shatzer* Court implicitly approved just such a "deceptive stratagem": police can falsely advise suspects of their legal right to an attorney, when they know full well that they can and will drag them back two weeks later to make them fend for themselves, in an isolated arena, without that promised lawyer.[328]

It is, moreover, ironic that both *Shatzer* and *Fields*, the cases ousting *Miranda* from the prison, involved inmates accused of child abuse. In *Dead House*, the most reviled residents are those who harm children: Goryanchikov, like his fellow inmates, is utterly repulsed by convicts like Gazin, who was reputed to be "fond of murdering little children, purely for pleasure," and those who "slit[] the throats of little children just for the hell of it, just in order to feel their warm blood on [the] hands, to savour their terror, their last dove-like quivering under [the] knife."[329] Our prison population, not unlike that of Siberia, also abhors child abusers and often bullies them to the point of distraction.

For prisoners suspected of child abuse, the fear that others will find out about it can be virtually paralyzing. In fact, the Supreme Court once acknowledged this in *Arizona v. Fulminante*, a case in which a government informer, questioning an inmate suspected of killing a child, promised him protection

---

325. *See supra* Part II. B (describing the way punishment is delivered in intervals in *Dead House*).

326. *See also* Oregon v. Elstad, 470 U.S. 298; Missouri v. Seibert, 542 U.S. 600; *supra* notes 139–46 and accompanying text (discussing the *Elstad-Seibert* loophole, which enables the police to get a confession by questioning without *Miranda*, and then duplicate the session with *Miranda* as long as it does not appear to be a deliberate evasion of *Miranda*).

327. *See supra* Chapter III (The Confessant Gene: *Crime and Punishment* and *The Brothers Karamazov*) (summarizing some of the methods that the *Miranda* Court condemned).

328. *Miranda*, 384 U.S. at 455. *See also supra* Chapter III (The Confessant Gene: *Crime and Punishment* and *The Brothers Karamazov*) (summarizing the methods that the *Miranda* Court condemned).

329. DOSTOEVSKY, *supra* note 1, at 72, 75–76. *See also id.* at 81 ("He was a villain of a kind that is rare, a man who carved up old men and children in cold blood.").

from fellow prisoners.[330] The Supreme Court, applying the due process test, deemed the confession coerced because the inmate's "will was overborne" by "a credible threat of physical violence."[331] Both Shatzer and Fields, likely dreading a "credible threat of physical violence" or, at least, ostracism, had to have been mortified that the child-abuse rumors would leak out to the general population and that their interrogators or guards might even precipitate just such a leak if they refused to cooperate.[332] Scalia, apparently, did not even factor this in when he insisted that Shatzer's trip home to supportive "normalcy" would "shake off residual coercive effects of prior custody."[333] In reality, it is likely that Shatzer's "release" had the opposite effect, and that he and Fields, as well, must have been shaking in their boots when guards lead him off to be badgered about alleged acts of pedophilia. Borrowing Dostoevsky's words about Dead House floggings, we can presume that Shatzer and Fields's "terror" must have been "involuntary and inexorable," the sort of thing that "overwhelms a man's entire mortal being."[334]

VI. Conclusion: Why Care?

In Part II, this chapter, initially focusing on Dostoevsky's *Dead House*, isolated the conditions that conspire to strip inmates of free will and human dignity. Dead House is hell, comprised of excessive regulation, coercion, and futility.[335] Its inhabitants endure the prolonged cognitive dissonance of lonely non-aloneness.[336] Compounding that, punishment is delivered in methodical, redundant intervals. Dostoevsky makes it plain that life in Dead House is torture and likens it to "being buried alive."[337]

---

330. Arizona v. Fulminante, 499 U.S. 279 (1991).

331. *Id.* at 287–88. *See id* at 288 ("[T]he Arizona Supreme Court ... noted that 'because [Fulminante] was an alleged child murderer, he was in danger of physical harm at the hands of other inmates.'")

332. *Id.* at 287–88 (tracking the language of the *Fulminante* Court). In *Shatzer*, Shatzer "became upset," and "started to cry." *Shatzer*, 130 S. Ct. at 1218. In *Fields*, Fields "became agitated and began to yell." *Fields*, 132 S. Ct. at 186.

333. *Shatzer*, 130 S. Ct. at 1221, 1223.

334. DOSTOEVSKY, *supra* note 1, at 239. *See also supra* Part II. B (discussing *Dead House* floggings).

335. *See supra* Part II. A (discussing the elements that destroy free will in *Dead House*).

336. *See supra* Part II. B (discussing the elements that destroy human dignity in *Dead House*).

337. *See supra* note 12 and accompanying text.

In Part III, exploring landmark Due Process Clause decisions, this chapter explained how the Supreme Court initially banned confessions extracted through physical torture.[338] While the Court later distended the concept of torture to include psychological coercion, the recent *Shatzer* and *Fields* decisions, discussed in Part IV, in cahoots with the plethora of *Miranda* exceptions, have inaugurated an era of advancing, or at least tolerating, interrogation methods that coerce and even torture.[339]

What makes this more troubling is that all of this sits on top of a bedrock of lies. While the Court has repeatedly indicated that clocks are turned back to the old totality-of-the circumstances approach, we have regressed further than that, landing in an ostensibly antediluvian era, one predating even the *Ashcraft* and *Spano* cases.[340] We have legalized methodology "so inherently coercive that its very existence is irreconcilable with the possession of mental freedom by a lone suspect against whom its full coercive force is brought to bear" and sentenced prisoners to Dead House, where officials are "possessed of an unrestrained power to seize persons suspected of crimes against the state, hold them in secret custody and wring from them confessions by [what amounts to] physical and mental torture."[341] In short, contrary to Supreme Court representations, we are not back to due process or voluntariness, but back *before* due process, back to a primitive acquiescence in the lashings of *in*voluntariness.

But why does this matter? Why should we give a damn about what happens in the prisons? Once again, Dostoevsky's ombudsman supplies answers, the first of which issues in the form of Goryanchikov's epiphany that there are innocent people locked up. For example, that nobleman convicted of parricide, who, "stripped of his nobility and government service rank, ... sentenced to ... deportation and penal servitude," is proclaimed innocent after serving ten of his twenty years, when "true perpetrators" came forth and confessed.[342]

---

338. *See supra* note 82 and accompanying text (discussing the physical torture cases).

339. *See supra* Parts III and IV (discussing the early Due Process Clause decisions, *Miranda*, the obliteration of *Miranda*, and the ouster of *Miranda* protections from the prison context).

340. *See supra* notes 157–61 and accompanying text (discussing how the Court has indicated that the only way to get a confession excluded is by showing actual coercion and involuntariness, which implicates the old Due Process Clause inquiry). *See also supra* Part III. A (discussing *Ashcraft* and *Spano*, along with the physical torture cases that preceded them and a discussion of the totality-of-the circumstances inquiry).

341. *Ashcraft*, 322 U.S. at 155. *See also supra* Part III. A (discussing the concerns that arose in *Ashcraft* and *Spano* and how the Court sought to preserve confidence in our criminal justice system and distinguish our process from those of less civilized nations).

342. DOSTOEVSKY, *supra* note 1, at 37, 302–303.

Goryanchikov opines on this "tragic profundity … [of] a young life ruined," and how it "adds a … glaring facet to the overall picture of the House of the Dead."[343] It is no secret that our facilities today also house the innocent.[344] Not only has DNA exonerated no small number, but here, as in *Dead House*, individuals have been acquitted after (and sometimes *long* after) the truly guilty party is found or *sua sponte* surrenders.[345] Deeming constitutional safeguards categorically inapplicable to those serving time overbroadly sweeps in the innocent "tragic profundit[ies],"and like whipping an unhealed, already lacerated back, is preordained to exact trauma.[346]

In contrast to Dostoyevsky's innocent convict, who never did confess to the crime, "scholars, legislators, courts, prosecutors, police departments, and the public [are increasingly aware] that innocent people [do] falsely confess, often due to psychological pressure placed upon them during police interrogations."[347]

---

343. *Id.* at 303.

344. *See generally* Barry Scheck & Peter Neufeld, *DNA and Innocence Scholarship*, in WRONGFULLY CONVICTED 241 (Saundra D. Westervelt & John A.Humphreys eds., 2001) and Innocent Project.com. http://www.innocenceproject.com (giving the ever rising number of DNA exonerations). *See also* Steven A. Drizin & Richard A. Leo, *The Problem of False Confessions in the Post-DNA World*, 82 N.C. L. REV. 891 (2004) (discussing how the innocent are wrongfully convicted); Brandon L. Garrett, *The Substance of False Confessions*, 62 STAN. L. REV. 1051 (2010) (analyzing wrongful convictions); Witmer-Rich, *supra* note 110, at 1237–29 (discussing the wrongful convictions and the exoneration of convicts).

345. *See generally supra* note 344. *See also* Witmer-Rich, *supra* note 110, at 1237 (discussing "the ongoing trend of DNA exonerations" by convicts); Alan Hirsch, *Threats, Promises and False Confessions: Lessons of Slavery*, 49 How. L. J. 31. 31 (2005) (discussing how "DNA tests are exonerating scores of persons wrongly accused and convicted of crimes").

346. DOSTOEVSKY, *supra* note 1, at 303.

347. Garrett, *supra* note 344, at 1052–53. *See generally supra* notes 342–45. *See also* Hirsh, *supra* note 345, at 31–32 (explaining how "pioneers in law and psychology have warned that false confessions occur surprisingly often," that "[r]oughly one-fourth of those exonerated … confessed," and that "[b]ased on statistics and other data, there is reason to believe that false confessions occur with staggering frequency"); Richard A. Leo & Richard J. Ofshe, *The Consequences of False Confessions: Deprivations of Liberty and Miscarriages of Justice in the Age of Psychological Interrogation*, 88 J. CRIM. L. & CRIMINOLOGY 429, 436 (1998) (In a study, sixty confessions had the common characteristic that "an individual was arrested primarily because police obtained an inculpatory statement that later turned out to be proven, or highly likely, a false confession."); Witmer-Rich, *supra* note 110, at 1237–38 ("[T]he ongoing trend of DNA exonerations by convicts, including a number who falsely confessed to their crimes, has proven that suspects in interrogation are more susceptible to false confession than had previously been thought possible."). A recent film, *The Central Park Five*, shows how black and Latino teenagers were wrongfully convicted of raping and beating a female jogger in New York's Central Park, and how, thirteen years later, these boys

While it is beyond the scope of this chapter to traverse the complex terrain of false confessions or analyze the many reasons why they are not uncommon, it suffices to say that there is consensus that police tactics, replete with *Miranda* loopholes, fuel the travesty.[348] Here, let us stop and imagine, if only for a moment, that Shatzer and Fields are innocent. They are imprisoned after falsely confessing, then delivered to an interrogation chamber to be bombarded with a new barrage of accusations. Rationally, we might conjecture that these inmates have learned a lesson and will now keep their mouths shut. It is also conceivable, however, that irrationality, mingled with sheer post-traumatic terror, kicks in to compel them to blurt out a new set of self-incriminating sound bites.[349] And, since we are doing the "what ifs," let us embrace the possibility

---

were found not guilty and had their convictions overturned. *See* Lasalle, *supra* note 163, at 13G (describing how the "cops rounded up a score of teenagers who were in the park that night and subjected them to harsh, relentless and repetitive questioning")

348. *See generally supra* notes 344–47. *See also* Hirsch, *supra* note 345, 33 (Using the analogy to slavery, he explains how interrogation tactics, especially threats and promises, play a role in the "unspeakable tragedy: punishment of the innocent."); Maoz, *supra* note 83, at 1338–39 ("[P]olice tactics leading to ... false confessions were lengthy interrogations, confessions induced by promises of leniency or threats of harsher punishment for remaining silent, and trickery designed to misrepresent evidence of a suspect's guilt."). With respect to the boys who falsely confessed to the rape and beating of the Central Park jogger, "the police told them that if they were to confess to a certain prepackaged set of facts, they could go home that night," and these "kids, ranging in age from 14 to 17, "were scared," and "they thought the cops were being helpful." Lasalle, *supra* note 163, at 13G. They "made false confessions on videotape, and the next morning New York City had five new faces to hate." *Id.* Other commentators believe that suspects confess because they believe that sticking with silence makes them look guilty. *See, e.g.,* Godsey, *supra* note 110, at 793 ("While many reasons certainly contribute to the willingness of Mirandized suspects to talk to the police, a major factor undoubtedly is that many suspects naturally believe, albeit incorrectly, that remaining silent will make them 'look guilty' and will be used against them as evidence of guilt."). *See also* Jeremy Bentham, The Works of Jeremy Bentham 39 (John Bowring ed., Russell & Russell, Inc. 1962) ("[S]ilence ... by common sense, at the report of universal experience, [is] certified to be tantamount to confession."); Seidman & Stein, *supra* note 322 (rebutting the Bentham cliché). Seidman & Stein argue that the "right to silence helps to distinguish the guilty from the innocent by inducing an anti-pooling effect that enhances the credibility of innocent suspects[,] ... [an] effect[, which] occurs because the right to silence affords a guilty suspect an attractive alternative to imitating an innocent suspect through lies." *Id.* at 433. They assert that "[s]uch lies obscure the differences between the guilty and the innocent and, consequently, reduce the trustworthiness of accounts given by innocent suspects." *Id. But see supra* Chapter III (The Confessant Gene: *Crime and Punishment* and *The Brothers Karamazov*) (discussing the compulsive self-incriminator).

349. *Cf.* Seidmann & Stein, *supra* note 322, at 450 (pointing out that "police interrogate virtually all suspects in a hostile environment, subjecting them to physical and psycholog-

that their second confessions are also false. As Goryanchikov would say, "if a case such as this is possible, this very possibility adds a new and glaring facet to the overall picture of the House of the Dead."[350]

There is a second reason why the Supreme Court's effectual recreation of Dead House should matter. Here, Dostoevsky, speaking of what we call recidivism, again lends his assistance. As earlier discussed, one of the *Dead House* motifs is the power of hope, which keeps men alive or sane. When exiles "lose hope, the resultant anguish will frequently turn [them] into ... monster[s]."[351] Dead House, with its regulation, coercion, and futility, tends to "suck[] the vital sap from a man, enervate[] his soul, weaken[] it, intimidate[] it and then present[] the withered mummy, the semi-lunatic as a model of reform and repentance."[352] Goryanchikov, making it plain that such an environment neither rehabilitates nor ignites a flicker of repentance, says that if the inmates "had not been depraved before they came to prison, they became so here."[353]

Proponents of the psychology of procedural justice, along with therapeutic jurisprudence scholars, have discovered through research what Dostoevsky learned from experience. They have found that when individuals participate in a process, what influences them most is not the result, but their assessment of its fairness.[354] Human beings tend to thrive when they feel that they are

---

ical pressures designed to make the suspects' choices irrational," and that, "[w]hen these choices become irrational, an abstract and cold-blooded game-theoretic framework cannot capture them").

350. DOSTOEVSKY, *supra* note 1, at 303. The possibility of getting a false confession out of a prisoner is even greater because of what Professor Dolovich points out: "In the United States, those who end up under criminal justice control are disproportionately likely to be suffering from drug addiction, severe mental illness, and/or learning disabilities; to be indigent, unskilled, under-educated and/or illiterate." Dolovich, *supra* note 227, at 219–20. *See also supra* note 318–22 and accompanying texts (explaining why individuals housed in prisons are the ones most likely to be coerced into confessing); *See also* Seidmann & Stein, *supra* note 322, at 450 (Although the approach is to treat the "typical suspect as ... rational," they concede that it "fails to capture the reality of police interrogation for neglected, alienated, weak, strained, subdued, or feeble-minded suspects or for suspects who suffer from drug and alcohol problems, personality disorders, or physical diseases."). Seidmann & Stein also point out that "police intimidate many ... suspects, some of whom are juveniles, and often these suspects would say anything to please the interrogator." *Id.*

351. DOSTOEVSKY, *supra* note 1, at 305.

352. *Id.* at 36.

353. *Id.* at 33.

354. *See generally* Keri A. Gould, *Turning Rat and Doing Time for Uncharged, Dismissed or Acquitted Crimes: Do the Federal Sentencing Guidelines Promote Respect for the Law?*, 10 N.Y. L. SCH. J. HUM. RTS. 835, 865 (1993) (concluding that those who "experienced a legal

being treated fairly, have choices, and believe that they are making, or at least participating in, their own decisions.[355] According to the research of the MacArthur Network on Mental Health and the Law, it is beneficial when people feel non-coerced, even in inherently coercive situations, and these are the ones more likely to reform or change destructive behaviors.[356] By the same token, criminologists have concluded that offenders who feel that they have

---

procedure that they judged to be unfair had less respect for the law and legal authorities and are less likely to accept judicial decisions"); Kristin Henning, *Defining the Lawyer-Self: Using Therapeutic Jurisprudence to Define the Lawyer's Role and Build Alliances that Aid the Child Client* in DAVID WEXLER, REHABILITATING LAWYERS: PRINCIPLES OF THERAPEUTIC JURISPRUDENCE FOR CRIMINAL LAW PRACTICE 327, 330 (David B. Wexler ed. 2008) ("Individual autonomy, self-determination, and choice are … important components..that promote the psychological well-being of those who are involved in legal proceedings."); Tom R. Tyler, *The Psychological Consequences of Judicial Procedures: Implications for Civil Commitment Hearings*, 46 SMU L. REV. 433, 437 (1992) ("Studies suggest that if the socializing influence of experience is the issue of concern (i.e., the impact of participating in a judicial hearing on a person's respect for the law and legal authorities), then the primary influence is the person's evaluations of the fairness of the judicial procedure itself, not their evaluations of the outcome" and "[s]uch respect is important because it has been found to influence everyday behavior toward the law."); Amy D. Ronner, *Punishment Meted Out For Acquittals: An Antitherapeutic Atrocity*, 41 ARIZ. L. REV. 459, 472–77 (1999) (discussing how unfairness creates disrespect for the law, disregard for human life, rage, and a sense of helplessness);

355. *See generally supra* note 354. *See also* RONNER, *supra* note 6, at 21–24 (discussing how an individual's perception of the fairness of those who control their destiny has an impact on their future behavior and rehabilitation).

356. *See generally* Bruce J. Winick, *Therapeutic Jurisprudence and the Civil Commitment Hearing*, 10 J. CONTEMP. LEGAL ISSUES 37, 47–50 (1999) (discussing the work by the MacArthur Network on Mental Health and the Law with respect to the salutary effect of patient perceptions of non-coercion even in coercive situations, like civil commitment); BRUCE J. WINICK, CIVIL COMMITMENT: A THERAPEUTIC JURISPRUDENCE MODEL 149–54 (2005) (discussing the "psychological effects of coercion and voluntary choice"); Nancy S. Bennett et al., *Inclusion, Motivation and Good Faith: The Morality of Coercion in Mental Hospital Admission*, 11 BEHAV. SCI. & L. 295 (1993) (giving patient accounts of coercion and morality in mental hospital admissions). *See also* RONNER, *supra* note 6, at 21–24 (discussing how a sense of choice promotes rehabilitation and can lead people to change destructive behavior patterns); Gould, *supra* note 354, at 865 (explaining that, when people feel that things are unfair, it can impede rehabilitation and promote disrespect for the law); Tyler, *supra* note 354, at 437 ("When people believe that legal authorities are less legitimate, they are less likely to be law-abiding citizens in their daily lives."); David B. Wexler, *Therapeutic Jurisprudence and Readiness for Rehabilitation* in WEXLER, *supra* note 354, at 171 ("Prior work in therapeutic jurisprudence has underscored the importance of procedural justice elements on an offender's judgment as to whether the process was fair and on his or her acceptance and compliance with adverse judgments.").

been poorly treated at times respond with "defiance" and can be prone to "commit new offenses—even ones more severe."[357] Once released, Goryanchikov, although not a recidivist, is left broken, "distrustful to the point of insanity," with a demeanor of "suffering and weary exhaustion."[358] Dead House drained him and spit out a dysfunctional husk.

In *Dead House*, Dostoevsky, with his astute insight into the human psyche, is depicting a form of desiccation, a process known to cause a condition that psychologist Martin Seligman labeled "learned helplessness," the elements of which are: "[f]irst, an environment in which some important outcome is beyond control; second, the response of giving up; and third, the accompanying cognition: the expectation that no voluntary action can control the outcome."[359] Seligman gives an account of experiments on animals who were subjected to pain that they could neither influence nor avoid. Unlike those in the control group, with a means of escaping, the helpless subjects eventually became limp and death-like.[360] Seligman, paralleling "learned helplessness" in animals and in Homo sapiens, concludes that, when human institutions or procedures re-

---

357. *See generally* Lawrence W. Sherman, *Defiance, Deterrence and Irrelevance: A Theory of the Criminal Sanction*, 30 J. Res. Crime & Delinq. 445 (1993). *See also* Wexler, *supra* note 356, at 171 (discussing how "criminologists have posited a 'defiance' effect of persistent, more frequent, or even more serious violations".) In contrast, when individuals see the legal system as fair, and feel non-coerced, or feel as if they made choices and participated in the process, they are more inclined to accept responsibility and change. *See generally* John Thibault & Laurens Walker, Procedural Justice: A Psychological Analysis 83–84, 94–95, 118 (1975). King points out that, when "[p]eople see social institutions and people in authority with whom they interact as important in valuing their identity and status in the community," and feel that they have been "treat[ed] ... with an ethic of care[, it] confirms their status as a valued member of society worthy of respect." Michael S. King, *Therapeutic Jurisprudence, Criminal Law Practice and the Plea of Guilty*, in Wexler, *supra* note 354, at 231. In such situations, "people respect the institution or the court—or other justice system instrumentality or professional—and obey its orders." *Id. See also* Ronner, *supra* note 6, at 22 (discussing the psychologists and criminologists whose studies show that, when individuals feel non-coerced and see the system as fair, they are "more inclined to accept responsibility for their own conduct, take charge, and change").

358. Dostoevsky, *supra* note 1, at 23–24.

359. Martin E.P. Seligman, Helplessness: On Depression, Development, and Death at xvii (W.H. Freeman & Co. 1992)

360. *Id.* at 42–44 (describing how uncontrollable shock produced more anxiety in rats and resulted in the "breakdown of a well-trained appetitive discrimination"). *See also id.* at 44 ("[H]elplessness is a disaster for organisms capable of learning that they are helpless. Three types of disruption are caused by uncontrollability in the laboratory: the motivation to respond is sapped, the ability to perceive success is undermined, and emotionality is heightened.").

semble the animal laboratory that induces learned helplessness, they too promote "the expectation that no voluntary action can control the outcome" and send the message that all efforts are futile.[361]

The Supreme Court's recent ouster of constitutional safeguards from our prisons fosters conditions that, as Dostoevsky and psychologist Seligman knew, cast humans into learned-helpless beings or "withered mummies."[362] Decisions like *Shatzer* and *Fields* tell inmates that all outcomes are "beyond [their] control" and that "voluntary actions," like silence or requests for a lawyer, are mere exercises in futility.[363] Like Seligman's lab specimens, or the Siberian prisoner before flogging, our inmates are crouched in the corner of futility, with no escape hatch.

The third reason why bad decisions, like *Shatzer* and *Fields*, should matter to all of us is because, literally and figuratively, they do not stay confined to prison. This is not just due to *stare decisis*, which enables such decisions to break out, start a new life on the outside, and become precedent for the progressive (and perhaps final) slaughter of *Miranda* and its *Edwards* offshoot. Nor is it just due to what Friedman so aptly reveals as the costs of "stealth overruling," which "obscures the path of constitutional law from public view, allowing the Court to alter constitutional meaning without public supervision," and thus, blocks the "ability for dialogic engagement with … constitutional decisions."[364]

More broadly, corrosive cases like *Shatzer* and *Fields* leak out of the prisons to fuel what Dolovich coins " 'society's carceral bargain,' by which the state commits to keeping separate from society those individuals singled out for banishment by the criminal justice system, thereby allowing society's remaining members to regard the incarcerated as people about whom they need never spare another thought."[365] For Dolovich, the end product of this "carceral bar-

---

361. *Id. at* xvii. *See also id.* at 31 (discussing how helplessness "is a general characteristic of several species, including man."); Gould, *supra* note 354, at 873 ("The amotivational system takes over when a person perceives 'that there is no relationship between behaviors and rewards or outcomes. Perceived competence, self determination and self esteem tend to be extremely low. People who are amotivational feel helpless, incompetent and out of control.'") (quoting Bruce J. Winick, *The Side Effects of Incompetency Labeling and the Implications of Mental Health Law* in 33 LAW IN A THERAPEUTIC KEY: DEVELOPMENTS IN THERAPEUTIC JURISPRUDENCE (David B. Wexler & Bruce J. Winick, eds. 1996)).

362. DOSTOEVSKY, *supra* note 1, at 36.

363. *Supra* notes 359–61 and accompanying text. *See also supra* note 359–60 and accompanying text (elaborating on the effect of "learned helplessness").

364. Friedman, *supra* note 106, at 4, 63.

365. Dolovich, *supra* note 227, at 229 (quoting Sharon Dolovich, *Cruelty, Prison Conditions, and the Eighth Amendment*, 84 N.Y.U. L. REV. 881, 892, 922 (2009).

gain" is that "people in prison or jail come to be collectively regarded as not just non-citizens but also nonhumans, who exist beyond the shared public space in both a physical and a moral sense."[366] In short, decisions like *Shatzer* and *Fields* reinforce that "us" versus "them" mentality.

Dolovich's thoughts resonate with Goryanchikov's most passionate revelations in *Dead House*. These, in turn, meld with those of Dostoevsky, who, also of an educated, elite class, lived cheek-by-jowl with peasant-convicts, met "positive characters of unimaginable beauty and strength" and "encountered signs of the most advanced spiritual development among the sufferers of this oppressed … *milieu*."[367] Goryanchikov elaborates:

> In prison, it sometimes happens that you might be familiar with a man for several years thinking he was a wild animal, and you would regard him with contempt. And then suddenly a moment would arrive when some uncontrollable impulse would lay his soul bare, and you would behold in it such riches, such sensitivity and warmth, such a vivid awareness of its own suffering and the suffering of others, that the scales would fall from your eyes and at first you would hardly be able to believe what you had seen and heard.[368]

Goryanchikov, debunking the "carceral bargain," tells us that "[e]veryone, whoever he is and however lowly the circumstances into which he has been pushed, demands, albeit instinctively and unconsciously, that respect be shown for his human dignity."[369] He proclaims that "no brands, no fetters will ever be able to make [a convict] forget that he is a human being [a]nd since he really is a

---

366. *Id. See also* Robertson, *supra* note 42, at 1005–06 (discussing how "inmates of warehouse prisons have few avenues of redress" and how "[t]heir powerless status invites indifference and neglect by the elected branches of constitutional government").

367. DOSTOEVSKY, *supra* note 1, at 306.

368. *Id. See also* RUTTENBURG, *supra* note 4, at 24 (discussing the "conversion hypothesis which has long dominated the critical understanding of Dostoevsky's transitional decade, particularly his experience in the hard-labor camp"). She explains that "[t]he conversion theory proposes that during the writer's incarceration he underwent a spiritual-ideological reversal of his former convictions, which alleviating his alienation from the peasant-convicts, revealed beneath their repellent appearance and behavior a Christian humility that he would later identity with Russianness itself." *Id.* She states, however, that "[i]n his book, conversion remains unconsummated, suspended, and rebirth deferred." *Id. See also* IVANITS, *supra* note 14, at 43 ("Dostoevsky's life alongside the people in the Dead House opened his eyes to their inner strength and cleverness.").

369. DOSTOEVSKY, *supra* note 1, at 145. *See also supra* notes 365–66 and accompanying text (defining what Dolovich calls "society's carceral bargain").

human being, it is necessary to treat him as one."[370] That was once the Supreme Court's perspective as well, and we, heeding Goryanchikov, should not lose all hope that it might be so again.

---

370. DOSTOEVSKY, *supra* note 1, at 145. *See also* Letter from Fyodor Dostoevsky to Mikhail Dostoevsky (January 30, 1854) in I LETTERS, *supra* note 12, at 190 ("People are people everywhere ... Even in prison among brigands, I, in four years, finally distinguished people. Believe it or not, there are profound, strong, marvelous personalities there, and how delightful it was to find gold under a coarse crust.").

Chapter Five

Conclusion: *Stushevatsia* and Other Expressed Ideas

This book opened with Ippolit's lamentation that the most important ideas are the inexpressible ones that refuse to emerge from "the skull."[1] Throughout his life, Dostoevsky was similarly consumed with what he felt was unrequited— a desire to express that "serious human idea"—along with a nagging suspicion that he might "die without perhaps ever having conveyed [it] to anyone."[2] Despite such angst, Dostoevsky makes a "full confession" in *A Writer's Diary* that, "in the course of [his] literary career, what [he has] liked *most* is the fact that [he] managed to [express and] introduce an entirely new word [*stushevatsia*] into the Russian language."[3] He explains:

> The word '*stushevatsia*' means to disappear, to perish, to be reduced *to naught*, so to say. But it means to perish not all at once, not by being wiped from the face of the earth with crashes of thunder, but delicately, so to say, gradually, sinking imperceptibly into nothingness. It's like a shadow on a pen-and-ink drawing that gradually shades from black ever more lightly until it's reduced completely to whiteness, to *naught*.[4]

While Dostoevsky takes credit for introducing the word into literature, he admits that he did not coin it, but traces its genesis to classmates at the Main School of Military Engineering. When Dostoevsky was studying there, students, required to draw various structures, fortifications, and military build-

---

1. Fyodor Dostoevsky, The Idiot 460 (David McDuff Trans., Penguin Books 2004) (1868). *See also supra* Chapter I (Inexpressible Ideas: A Multifaceted Life and Legal Lens) (begining with Ippolit's lamentation).
2. Dostoevsky, *supra* note 1, at 460.
3. Fyodor Dostoevsky, II A Writer's Diary 1186 (Kenneth Lantz, Trans., Northwestern University Press 1994) (1877–1881).
4. *Id.* at 1184.

ings, used "*stushevatsia*" to refer to "shading, … the gradual fading of a shade, the transition from dark to naught" and over time, imbuing the verb with figurative import, began to say, "now you'd better disappear ('*stushevatsia*')," or ask, "where did you manage to disappear ('*stushevatsia*')?"[5] *Stushevatsia* encapsulates a "serious human idea," one that Dostoevsky did express and, in fact, developed throughout his career.[6] It denotes a thanatotic self-annihilation into the void, or effacement, reminiscent of the ineluctable denouement of Golyadkin, the "hero" of Dostoevsky's *The Double*.[7]

Chapter II focuses mainly on *The Double*, one of Dostoevsky's early, but lesser known, works, in which civil servant Golyadkin suddenly meets his identical twin, who seemingly wreaks havoc on his life.[8] In this novel, which upset readers of his day and continues to do so, Dostoevsky explores the concept of a *doppelganger*, an individual splintered into two.[9] While some commentators have suggested that the novel is a depiction of a mental breakdown, Chapter II suggests that there is nothing definite with respect to Golyadkin's psychological condition.[10] The chapter, placing Golyadkin in the context of contemporary legal testamentary capacity and insane delusion doctrines, shows how Dostoevsky, through the technique of obfuscation and retraction, implicitly posits what today's law substantiates—namely that, in many instances, we mortals (in-

---

5. *Id.* at 1186.

6. Dostoevsky, *supra* note 1, at 460.

7. Fyodor Dostoevsky, The Double (George Bird, trans., 1958) (1846), *reprinted in* Great Short Works of Fyodor Dostoevsky, 1 (1st Perennial Classics ed., 2004). In *The Double*, Dostoevsky repeatedly calls Golyadkin "our hero." *Id.* at 30, 31, 57, 81, 90, 116, & 144. *See generally supra* Chapter II (The Impenetrable Mental Capacity Doctrine: *The Double*).

8. *See generally supra* Chapter II (The Impenetrable Mental Capacity Doctrine: *The Double*) (recounting the putative story of *The Double*).

9. *See generally supra* Chapter II (The Impenetrable Mental Capacity Doctrine: *The Double*) (discussing why the novel was not well-received, and even viewed as a set-back in Dostoevsky's early career). *See also* Leon Burnett, *Effacement and Enigma in the Making of* The Meek Girl, *in* Aspects of Dostoevskii: Art, Ethics and Faith 149, 154 (Robert Reid & Joe Andrew, eds. Rodopi B.V. 2012) (explaining that "one of … [the] 'idea-forces' that Dostoevskii sensed in the 1840s as part of the 'great dialogue' of the time was that of the double, or *Doppelganger*, the individual divided within himself" and that "Dostoevskii was not referring to the idea of the *Doppelganger* itself, but rather to the use that he put it in his fiction").

10. *See generally supra* Chapter II (The Impenetrable Mental Capacity Doctrine:*The Double*) (discussing many of critical theories about *The Double* and Golyadkin's mental condition).

cluding lawyers, judges, and jurors) are not adept at discerning a solid line between reality and hallucination. On a broader level, however *The Double* presents *stushevatsia* in slow motion.

Not surprisingly, Dostoevsky first used *stushevatsia* in connection with *The Double*. As he relates in *A Writer's Diary*, this happened when Vissarion Belinsky "insisted that [Dostoevsky] read at his house at least two or three chapters of [*The Double*]…, arranged an evening party for this[,] and invited his close friends."[11] Dostoevsky says, "it was right then, at this reading, that the word '*stushevatsia*,' which later was to become so popular, was used, by me, for the first time."[12] This account makes sense, because Golyadkin, whether he be sane or delusional, personifies effacement: he is the man who "disappear[s], … perish[es], … [is] reduced to *naught*" and, in the throes of doubling, his self "gradually sink[s] imperceptibly into nothingness."[13] Golyadkin, the "shadow on a pen-and-ink drawing that gradually shades from black ever more lightly until it's reduced to whiteness, to *naught*," emits that lethal shriek right before divestiture of freedom, without solid proof that his take on reality is bizarre or even implausible.[14]

While readers, lawyers, and mental health experts might never agree on whether the events in Golyadkin's anomic universe are real or imagined, they are likely to concede that this character's *modus vivendi*, comprised of the mundane—job, money changing, pseudo-shopping, visiting the doctor, posing in a café, crashing a party, and blushing in his sleep—is missing the essentials of heart and soul.[15] Golyadkinism equals solipsism, with its unswerving fixation on self that foredooms beings to *stushevatsia*: his is a vacuous non-life, devoid of the vital compassionate, spiritual, moral, and philosophical arteries that tie individuals to the whole human race.

---

11. Dostoevsky, *supra* note 3, at 1184.

12. *Id.*

13. *Id.*

14. *Id.* at 1186. *See generally supra* Chapter II (The Impenetrable Mental Capacity Doctrine: *The Double*) (recounting the putative story of *The Double*). *See also* Leon Burnett, *supra* note 9, at 150 (explaining that "Dostoevskii's preoccupation with the theme of effacement can be traced back to the composition of *The Double* in 1846").

15. *See generally supra* Chapter II (The Impenetrable Mental Capacity Doctrine: *The Double*) (recounting the putative story of *The Double*). *See also* John Jones, Dostoevsky 73 (Clarendon Press, 1983) ("Even in his sleep, Mr. Golyadkin blushes."); Deborah A. Martinsen, *Introduction* in Notes From Underground, The Double and Other Stories xlviii (Barnes & Noble Books, 2003) ("For [Dostoevsky], self-annihilation most clearly evidenced an individual's lack of belief in God.").

In true "pro and contra" format,[16] Dostoevsky expresses another "serious human idea," in the form of his proposed antidote to *stushevatsia*.[17] In later years, especially in *A Writer's Diary* and *The Brothers Karmazov*, the Russian "prophet" repeatedly told readers that "what is obligatory and important is merely *your determination to do all for the sake of active love,* all that you possibly can, all that you yourself sincerely believe is possible for you to do."[18] He stressed that the "sole reward is love," and that, when "you are working in the cause of love, ... you cannot help but encourage love."[19] Kindred gems radiate in Dostoevsky's commentary on Tolstoy's elucidation of "a great, everlasting, vital truth," which "at once illuminated everything," where "[h]atred and lies began to speak in words of forgiveness and love," and "[i]n place of vapid social conceptions there appeared only a love of humanity."[20] For Dostoevsky, suffering, an inevitable component of the spiritual regeneration, can foster empathy, bring forgiveness of self and others, and inspire the awareness that all beings are worthy of respect.[21]

Similarly, *stushevatsia*'s counteragent features in Dostoevsky's "The Dream of a Ridiculous Man: A Fantastic Story," which is also included in *A Writer's Diary*.[22] The narrator, a self-proclaimed "madman," at first resolves to end his own life, but has a chance encounter with a little girl, then a dream, and then an epiphany, which reverses *stushevatsia*: he realizes that "we can truly love only with suffering" and exclaims that "the main thing is that you must love others as you love yourself; that's the main thing, and that's everything, and absolutely nothing more than that is needed: you'll at once find a way to build paradise."[23] Also, in his celebrated Pushkin speech, Dostoevsky extolled "the panhuman

---

16. *See* Fyodor Dostoevsky, The Brothers Karamazov (Richard Pevear and Larissa Volokhonsky, trans. 1990) (1879–80) (entitling Book Five "Pro and Contra"); Dostoevsky, *supra* note 3, at 904 (entitling a section in *A Writer's Diary* "Pro and Contra").

17. Dostoevsky, *supra* notes 1 & 2 and accompanying text (referring to that "serious human idea"). *See also supra* Chapter I (Inexpressible Ideas: A Multifaceted Life and Legal Lens) (discussing Ippolit's lamentation in *The Idiot*).

18. Dostoevsky, *supra* note 3, at 882.

19. *Id.* at 883.

20. *Id.* at 870.

21. *See generally supra* Chapter I (Inexpressible Ideas: A Multifaceted Life and Legal Lens) (discussing Dostoevsky's views on suffering).

22. Dostoevsky, *supra* note 3, at 942–61.

23. *Id.* at 942, 952, & 960. *See* Martinsen, *supra* note 15, at xlvi ("*The Dream of a Ridiculous Man* illustrates a point Dostoevsky makes and argues repeatedly elsewhere—belief in God leads to love of life" and "[b]y unlocking his capacity to love, the dream restores him to the earth and human community.").

and all-unifying Russian soul" and urged his audience "to enfold all our brethren within it with brotherly love."[24]

Stushevatsia, along with its countermanding life-affirming axiom, threads its way through Chapter III, which focuses primarily on *Crime and Punishment* and *The Brothers Karamazov* with their timeless insights into confessions and criminal justice. While the United States Supreme Court, with its long-standing hate-love relationship with confessions, has concerned itself with outside factors that coerce confessions, and at least in the past, has made putative stabs at ensuring that such evidence is the product of a free and rational choice, Dostoevsky is worlds apart.[25] In his writings, confession, an elusive phenomenon of infinite variety, pertains solely to the individual soul and psyche. For him, the sincere confession, often detached from free will and rationality, is woefully misplaced in the mortal courtroom. That rarity, whether it ensues from a Raskolnikov-obsessive need to come clean, a Mitya-shame, or an Ivan-spiritual crisis, can minister to one process alone: it has the potential to serve as an incipient step in an individual's spiritual evolution.[26] Confession can begin to lift a suffering soul out of the ever-deepening abyss of *stushevatsia*, away from the nihilistic credo that "everything is permitted," toward the light of Zosima-ism, that "experience of active love," and the realization that "we are all responsible for everyone and everything."[27]

---

24. DOSTOEVSKY, *supra* note 3, at 1294. It is concededly difficult to reconcile Dostoevsky's spiritual views and praise of love and compassion with his anti-Semitism, which appeared to get worse in his later years. *See supra* note 98 and accompanying text in Chapter I (Inexpressible Ideas: A Multifaceted Life and Legal Lens) (discussing Dostoevsky's association of gambling with the Jews) and note 160 (giving examples of and scholarly theories about Dostoevsky's anti-Semitism. *See also* DOSTOEVSKY, *supra* note 3, at 901–925 (in which Dostoevsky elaborates on and defends his attitudes toward the Jews, which he repeatedly calls "the Yids").

25. *See generally supra* Chapter III (The Confessant Gene: *Crime and Punishment* and *The Brothers Karamazov*).

26. *See generally supra* Chapter III (The Confessant Gene: *Crime and Punishment* and *The Brothers Karamazov*) (discussing Raskolnikov as the compulsive self-incriminator, Mitya's confession as a purgation of shame, and Ivan's confession as borne out of a spiritual crisis).

27. DOSTOEVSKY, *supra* note 16, at 263 ("everything is permitted"); 56 ("experience of active love"); 289 (describing Zosima's brother's realization that "each of us is guilty before everyone, for everyone and everything"). *See also supra* Chapter III (The Confessant Gene: *Crime and Punishment* and *The Brothers Karamazov*) (discussing the opposing philosophies, the cannibalistic credo of "everything is permitted" pitted against the "experience of active love," and how both are reiterated throughout *The Brothers Karamazov*); Ralph E. Matlaw, *On Translating* The Brothers Karamazov, *in* FYODOR DOSTOEVSKY, THE BROTHERS KARA-

Chapter IV, shifting from investigatory and trial issues to post-conviction, focuses on *Notes From the House of the Dead*, Dostoevsky's fictionalized account of his four years of suffering and privation endured as a convict in Tsar Nicholas I's Siberian penal institution.[28] The chapter anatomizes the prison environment that conspires to strip Siberian inmates of their free will and human dignity.[29] Dead House is a hell, comprised of excessive regulation, coercion, and futility. Its inhabitants endure prolonged cognitive dissonance, in which they are lonely, but never alone. Compounding that, prisoners are fettered, sometimes chained to the wall, and redundantly lashed in a manner preordained to pulverize body and soul.

Chapter IV, moving forth in time, juxtaposes the nineteenth-century Russian Dead House with the rise and fall of free will and human dignity under seminal United States Supreme Court Due Process Clause and *Miranda* decisions.[30] It tracks not just the progressive dismemberment of *Miranda*, but dissects the reasoning in recent Supreme Court confession cases, which effectually detriment the lives of human beings imprisoned today.[31] It aims to disclose not only how contemporary legal decisions condone, and even encourage, tactics that resemble the dehumanization that once presided over Dostoevsky's notorious gulag of misery, but also the baneful message they transmit to all people, even those living outside prison walls.[32]

On a broad level, Dostoevsky's autobiographical novel suggests that it is not just individuals who are susceptible to *stushevatsia*, but collectively people can construct institutions that efface and lacerate captives until they "sink[] im-

---

MAZOV 671 (W.W. Norton & Co., Inc. 2011) (1979–80). Matlaw points out the "the leading idea in the novel is that we are all responsible for everyone and everything," but to "translate the word" "responsible" as "guilty" would not work, because it would "both limit the meaning and introduce an unwarranted legal note," along with a "more specifically psychiatric connotation [that] Dostoevsky may [not] have intended." *Id.* at 672.

    28. FYODOR DOSTOEVSKY, THE HOUSE OF THE DEAD (David McDuff, trans. 2003) (1862). *See generally supra* Chapter IV (Prisons of Coercion: *Notes from the House of the Dead*).

    29. *See generally supra* Chapter IV (Prisons of Coercion: *Notes from the House of the Dead*) (describing Dead House as a place where its inhabitants are stripped of free will and human dignity).

    30. *See generally supra* Chapter IV (Prisons of Coercion: *Notes from the House of the Dead*) (describing the rise and fall of free will and human dignity under the Due Process Clause and *Miranda*).

    31. *See generally supra* Chapter IV (Prisons of Coercion: *Notes from the House of the Dead*) (describing the "ouster of *Miranda* from the Prison").

    32. *See generally supra* Chapter IV (Prisons of Coercion: *Notes from the House of the Dead*) (describing how the Supreme Court has recreated Dead House and explaining why everyone should care about the ouster of Constitutional protections from the prisons).

perceptibly into nothingness."[33] Even before such themes have matured in *The Brothers Karamazov* and *A Writer's Diary*, in Dostoevsky's writings there is an embryonic belief that humanity can oppugn the forces of institutional *stushevatsia*. For example, in *Notes From the House of the Dead*, Goryanchikov, prefiguring "we are responsible for everyone and everything,"[34] implores all to respect "human dignity," and admonishes that "no brands, no fetters, will ever be able to make [a convict] forget that he is a human being [a]nd since he really is a human being, it is necessary to treat him as one."[35]

In *The Brothers Karamazov*, institutional *stushevatsia* manifests itself as a miscarriage of justice in a courtroom in which it seems that "everything is permitted"[36] and plenary forces "reduce [souls] to naught."[37] Justice derails for Mitya (and also for Ivan) partly because mortal constructs, such as the legal system, are simply not designed to, and cannot, accommodate genuine confessions. This is perspicuous when Ivan spews unadulterated truth, and the judge tells him point blank that "your words are incomprehensible and impossible in this place."[38]

But there are other quirks that make truth "incomprehensible," and the dispensation of justice "impossible," all of which fall neatly under the heading of excessive self-interest.[39] Both prosecutor and defense counsel finesse psychological theories and impressive narratives to elicit jury sympathies for or against Mitya, but none of these are motivated by concerns with truth, justice, or re-

---

33. DOSTOEVSKY, *supra* note 3, at 1184,

34. *See supra* note 27 (describing the significance of "we are responsible for everyone and everything" in *The Brothers Karamazov*); *supra* Chapter III (The Confessant Gene: *Crime and Punishment* and *The Brothers Karamazov*) (describing the combatant philosophies at work in *The Brothers Karamazov*).

35. DOSTOEVSKY, *supra* note 28, at 145. *See also supra* Chapter IV (Prisons of Coercion: *Notes from the House of the Dead*) (explaining why all people should care about the plight of those incarcerated in Dead House).

36. *See supra* note 27 (describing the significance of "everything is permitted" in *The Brothers Karamazov*); *supra* Chapter III (The Confessant Gene: *Crime and Punishment* and *The Brothers Karamazov*) (describing the competing philosophies at work in *The Brothers Karamazov*).

37. DOSTOEVSKY, *supra* note 3, at 1184.

38. DOSTOEVSKY, *supra* note 16, at 686. *See also supra* Chapter III (The Confessant Gene: *Crime and Punishment* and *The Brothers Karamazov* (analyzing the miscarriage of justice in *The Brothers Karamazov*).

39. DOSTOEVSKY, *supra* note 16, at 686. *See also supra* Chapter I (Inexpressible Ideas: A Multifaceted Life and Legal Lens (introducing the defects in the trial in *The Brothers Karamazov*); *supra* Chapter III (The Confessant Gene: *Crime and Punishment* and *The Brothers Karamazov*)(analyzing the miscarriage of justice in *The Brothers Karamazov*).

sponsibility toward the accused, the victim, or society.[40] These legal players manipulate empathy, rhetoric, and storytelling solely for self-aggrandizement and to persuade attentive attendees of their own deific talents.[41] Even the "educated and humane" judge is "rather vain" and chiefly concerned with his own image as the "progressive man."[42] The Karamazov courtroom was not what Dostoevsky wanted for the justice system.

What Dostoevsky wanted for the justice system was exactly what he wanted for humanity. For him, the New Testament image of Christ, along with the ideal of compassion and brotherly love, must be integral not only to our understanding of what it means to be a free moral agent, but also to our notions of innocence, guilt, and forgiveness.[43] There is an inkling of this in *A Writer's Diary*, when Dostoevsky elaborates on Tolstoy's revelation of "the truth of life," in which beings forgive and support one another, an ecstatic moment where "[n]o one [is] found guilty: each admitted his own guilt without reservation, and in so doing … [is] at once acquitted."[44] Dostoevsky envisioned legal players, like jurors and judges, humbly accepting their own mortal limitations, conceding that "we are all guilty before everyone"[45] and striving for that active, compassionate love for others:

40. *See supra* Chapter I (Inexpressible Ideas: A Multifaceted Life and Legal Lens) (discussing the trial in *The Brothers Karamazov*); *supra* Chapter III (The Confessant Gene: *Crime and Punishment* and *The Brothers Karamazov*) (analyzing the miscarriage of justice in *The Brothers Karamazov*). *See also* GARY ROSENSHIELD, WESTERN LAW, RUSSIAN JUSTICE: DOSTOEVSKY, THE JURY TRIAL, AND THE LAW 16–17 (University of Wisconsin Press, 2005) (elaborating on how "[t]he trial scene in *The Brothers Karamazov* directly addresses the abuse of empathy and narrative in the courtroom").

41. *See supra* note 40 (pinpointing places that focus on the miscarriage of justice in *The Brothers Karamazov*). *See also* ROSENSHIELD, *supra* note 40, at 17 (explaining how "the [lawyers'] use of narrative is done less in the interest of the state or the defendant than in the interest of the lawyers themselves, who wish to display their talents in the courtroom to a national audience" and how "[i]n the end, empathy, storytelling, orality, and emotion become tools for personal and professional self-aggrandizement").

42. DOSTOEVSKY, *supra* note 16, at 658. *See also supra* Chapter I (Inexpressible Ideas: A Multifaceted Life and Legal Lens) (introducing the defects in the trial in *The Brothers Karamazov*); *supra* Chapter III (The Confessant Gene: *Crime and Punishment* and *The Brothers Karamazov*) (analyzing the miscarriage of justice in *The Brothers Karamazov*).

43. *See generally supra* Chapter I (Inexpressible Ideas: A Multifaceted Life and Legal Lens) (discussing various critical perspectives applied to Dostoevsky's works, including the philosophical lens, which is virtually inextricable from theophany and Dostoevsky's homage to the New Testament's image of Christ).

44. DOSTOEVSKY, *supra* note 3, at 871.

45. DOSTOEVSKY, *supra* note 16, at 289 (describing the realization that Zosima's brother has—that "each of us is guilty before everyone and everything"). *See also supra* note 27

The human judge himself ought to know that he is not the final judge; that he himself is a sinner; that the measure and the scales in his hands will be an absurdity *if* he, holding that measure and scales, does not himself submit to the law of the yet unresolved mystery and turn to the only solution—to Mercy and Love.[46]

His vision of a legal system that imbibes a higher spiritual consciousness, with Christ as role model, also emerges in his "Imaginary Speech by the Presiding Judge," in which Dostoevsky pens what the judge should impart to guilty parents who were acquitted of child abuse: "you are acquitted; but remember that apart from this court there is another court—the court of your own conscience. You must act so that this court as well should acquit you, even if only in years to come."[47] This fictional adjudicator, "knowing that he is not the final judge," urges the exonerated defendants to "[s]eek out love and store it up in your hearts. Love is so all-powerful that it can regenerate even us."[48]

As discussed in Chapter I, Dostoevsky, role-playing as lawyer for pregnant Ekaterina Kornilova, who was initially convicted of pushing her small stepdaughter out of a window, actually helped secure her ultimate acquittal.[49] While the Karamazov trial, in which creatures of self-interest pontificate, posture, and perform in a scandalized sellout, becomes the *stushevatsia*-venue that can offer no justice, no forgiveness, and no salvation, the Kornilova re-trial depicts the consummate opposite:[50]

> But now, feeling that she is guilty and considering herself such, and suddenly having been forgiven by people, showered with mercy and blessings, how could she not feel restored and reborn into a new life,

---

(discussing the competing philosophies in *The Brothers Karamazov*); *supra* Chapter III (The Confessant Gene: *Crime and Punishment* and *The Brothers Karamazov*) (analyzing two contrasting credos at work throughout *The Brothers Karamazov*).

46. DOSTOEVSKY, *supra* note 3, at 1071. *See also id.* at 1074 ("[E]veryone on earth understands or can understand that we must *love our neighbor as ourselves.* That knowledge, in essence, contains the entire *law* of humanity, as was also declared to us by Christ Himself.").

47. *Id.* at 1054.

48. *Id.* at 1059.

49. *See generally supra* Chapter I (Inexpressible Ideas: A Multifaceted Life and Legal Lens) (discussing the Kornilova trial).

50. *See supra* notes 39–42 and accompanying text (discussing the miscarriage of justice and self-interest in the trial in *The Brothers Karamazov*). *See also supra* Chapter III (The Confessant Gene: *Crime and Punishment* and *The Brothers Karamazov*) (discussing the miscarriage of justice in the Karamazov courtroom).

higher than her old one? It was not just one person who forgave her; *everyone*—the court, the jurors, and therefore society as a whole— showed mercy to her. After that, how could she not take with her a sense of the enormous debt that would last all her life—a debt to all who had shown mercy to her, meaning all people on the earth.[51]

Here, Dostoevsky suggests that had Kornilova been exiled to the Siberian situs of *stushevatsia*, she would have "fallen and perished there," but her trial, transmitting the message, "[g]o thou and sin no more," promised salvation, "arouse[d] a higher consciousness," and instilled belief "in the goodness of people and their love for one another."[52] While the Kornilova acquittal was controversial in its day, and Dostoevsky himself felt compelled to defend it, it became his opportunity to share his vision of a more utopian justice system, which can bestow "an eternal, beneficent, impression of the boundless mercy of people"[53] and express his "serious human idea."[54]

---

51. Dostoevsky, *supra* note 3, at 1244. *See also id.* at 1243 ("There is no greater happiness ... than to be assured of people's mercy and love for one another. This is faith, a whole faith, for an entire life! And what happiness is superior to faith?").

52. *Id.* at 1243–44. *See also* Rosenshield, *supra* note 40, at 233 ("For Kornilova, the public trial was essential because her salvation depended on the confession of her guilt before the entire community and on experiencing the forgiveness of people of all classes.").

53. Dostoevsky, *supra* note 3, at 1244.

54. Dostoevsky, *supra* note 1, at 460. *See also supra* Chapter I (Inexpressible Ideas: A Multifaceted Life and Legal Lens) (introducing the concept of that inexpressible "serious human idea").

Index

Book titles and names of cases are in italic font.

Golyadkin, Yakov Petrovich (in *The Double*), 36. *See also* mental capacity doctrine
  critical reaction to, 92–93n. 263
  "Doppelganger complex" of, 94
  Double, authenticity/reality of, 59, 90, 112–17
  Double, meeting of, 57, 88–89, 103–6, 121
  meaning/origin of name, 100, 109n. 390
  mood swings of, 98–99
  post-Double, 106–12
  pre-Double, 97–103
  psychological condition of, 59n. 8, 59–60n. 9, 95–96, 103–6, 115n. 442, 278–81
  psychological perspective on, 96
  room of, as "objective correlative," 98
  scream by, 57–58, 121
  twins, separated and meeting in real life, 114n. 437
Goryanchikov, Aleksandr Petrovich (in *Notes from the House of the Dead*)
  child abuser and, 266–67
  community/friendship, lack of, 223–24
  on deflating hope, 219–20
  on hope, in prison, 218–19
  on human dignity, 275–76
  inspiration for, 211–12
  on penal labor, 217
  on prison community, 224n. 60
  on prison conditions, 215–17, 251–52
  on prison floggings, 225–26
  solitude, lack of, 222

Grand Inquisitor (in *The Brothers Karamazov*), 180–85, 197
Greenwood v. Greenwood (1790), 66n. 36
Grigorovich, Dmitry, 10, 31n. 103
Grigory (in *The Brothers Karamazov*), 166, 194
Grigoryev, Apollon, 24n. 77
Gulf Oil Corp. v. Walker (1956), 72, 74n. 92, 113

H
Haroun, Ansar, 65n. 31, 68–69n. 57, 69n. 59, 70n. 65
Harris v. New York (1971), 237
Harrison, Lonny Roy, 59–60n. 9, 95–96, 114–15
Harwood v. Baker (1840), 66n. 36
Havens, United States v. (1980), 237
Hegel, Georg Wilhelm Friedrich, 39n. 148
Heidegger, Martin, 40n. 151
Henning, Kristin, 272n. 354
Henry, United States v. (1980), 136, 264n. 319
Herzenstube, Dr. (in *The Brothers Karamazov*), 194
Hirsch, Alan, 269n. 347, 270n. 348
The History of the Russian State (Karamzin), 6
Hobbes, Thomas, 39n. 143
Hoffa v. United States (1966), 245n. 179
Holland v. Traylor (1969), 79n. 138
homeopathy, in *The Brothers Karamazov*, 189–90
Honigman's Will, In re (1960), 80–83
hope, in prison, 218–21, 271